HELL'S BENT ON ROCKIN'

Dedicated to I, P & F, from Daddio

HELL'S BENT ON ROCKIN'

A HISTORY OF PSYCHOBILLY

CRAIG BRACKENRIDGE

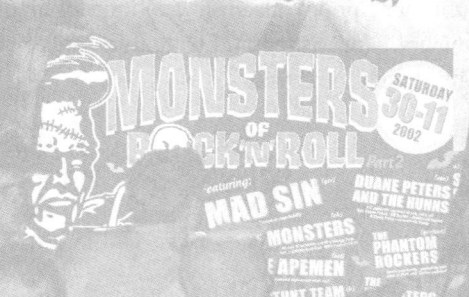

CHERRY RED BOOKS

First published in Great Britain in 2007 by Cherry Red Books (a division of Cherry Red Records Ltd.), 3a Long Island House, Warple Way, London W3 ORG.

Copyright © Craig Brackenridge, 2007

ISBN: 9781901447804

All rights reserved. No part of this book may be reproduced or transmitted in any form or by any means, electronic or mechanical, including photocopying, recording or any information storage and retrieval system, without permission in writing from the publisher.

This book is sold subject to the condition that it shall not, by way of trade or otherwise, be lent, resold, hired out or otherwise circulated without the publisher's prior consent in any form of binding or cover other than that in which it is published and without a similar condition being imposed on the subsequent purchaser.

Design: Dave Johnson
Printing: Biddles

FOREWORD	6
ACKNOWLEDGEMENTS	7
INTRODUCTION	8
Chapter One: PSYCHOBILLY BEGINNINGS	11
Chapter Two: THE PIONEERS	19
Chapter Three: TAKIN' IT TO THE STREETS	49
Chapter Four: SONIC BOOM - PSYCHOBILLY GOES BALLISTIC	57
Chapter Five: PSYCHO ATTACK OVER EUROPE	99
Chapter Six: PSYCHO STYLE	141
Chapter Seven: THE NEXT DEGENERATION - PSYCHOBILLY IN THE NINETIES AND BEYOND	149
Chapter Eight: YANKED INTO THE PIT - PSYCHOBILLY HITS AMERICA	185
Chapter Nine: WRECKIN' ALL OVER THE WORLD - THE GLOBAL PSYCHOBILLY SCENE	207
Chapter Ten: PSYCHOBILLY NOW	217
CONCLUSION	227
RECOMMENDED WEBSITES	228
STOP PRESS - RECENT NEWS FROM THE SCENE	230

FOREWORD

As Paul Roman of The Quakes said; "Nervous is the Sun Records of Psychobilly". I'm pleased (and honoured) to be known as that and I'm proud to be a part of it. Those of you who have been into it from the beginning have probably tripped up over me in the past either at The Klub Foot or some other such lowlife dive! For those of you who have got into Psychobilly in more recent years, this book will provide great insight into the origins of this music and for older fans of the scene, there are sure to be nuggets of information and pictures that will bring the memories flooding back.

KAPTAIN ZORCH Nervous Records 2007

ACKNOWLEDGEMENTS

Very special thanks to Alan Wilson who offered help before I even started this project and has continued to offer support ever since.

Big thanks also to Adam Velasco and his unstinting patience as this book rolled to its conclusion through the years.

Without them the Psychobilly scene would look a whole lot different and their continuous assistance helped shape this book, so a big hunk 'o' thanks to Roy Williams of Nervous Records, Howard Raucous of Raucous Records and Dell Richardson of Fury Records.

Much appreciation goes out to all those who helped me when compiling photographs, info and illustrations for the book but special thanks must go to: Jo Jackson, Bal Croce, Mark Pennington, Jo Shalton, Jane Williams, Patrick Rhrle, Jan Van Hal, Kenny Mitchell, Christophe @ Drunkabilly, Loz Dolan, Mark Pennington, Simon Ling, Pete Davis, Russ Ward, Guido Neumann and Bernd Malner.

Getting this book together required me to bend a few ears, call in a few favours and pester folks on the electronic superhighway so salutations to all those who heeded my plea: Titch, Strangy, Malc Pike, Kev Saunders, Lucky, Scott Milsom, Tatsuya, Paul Gonzalez, Broughton Hackett, Valle & Stoni, Paul Roman, Mark Carew, Joey Fangface, And Monkeyplums, Simon Wilding, John McVicker, Stan Brennan, Ant Thomas, Eddie the Daz, Jon (Son Of Youngblood), Mick Geary, Dave Razorback, Paul Wainwright, Mudman, The Mudmen, Viktor Kopytin, Duaine, Big Keith Smith, Slinger, Rockin' Carl, The Black Puma, Ash Ghoulmore, Steve Chapman, George Miller and Tobe. To everyone else who I forgot to mention, thanks first and apologies second.

Finally, endless thanks to The Meteors, Mad Sin and The Caravans whose songs 'Rockabilly Psychosis', 'Nothing's Alright' and 'Psychobilly Popstar' (respectively) kept me going every time I felt that completing the book was NEVER going to happen and needed inspiration.

AUTHOR'S INTRODUCTION

Through the years I have grown tired of the way Psychobilly has been consistently ignored by the mainstream music press. Working in record stores throughout the 1980s and 1990s, I had seen a flood of flash-in-the-pan sub-genres being heralded as the second coming by the UK music press…only to be unceremoniously dumped soon after as fad-chasing journos moved on to the next big thing. But where was Psychobilly? Why were bands I and many others liked, many of whom had prolific back catalogues of record releases, never mentioned? Why was Psychobilly blacklisted from the pages of music history despite being a thriving worldwide scene for over 20 years? At least in the 1980s you could count on occasional reviews of gigs and records, even though most of them lampooned Psychobilly and wrote off its followers as a posse of glue-sniffing lunkheads. After that there was nothing. Only a handful of dedicated fanzine writers wafted the oxygen of publicity over the scene.

As a naturally lazy bastard, I decided to sit and wait at the end of the century, secure in the knowledge that someone would eventually see Psychobilly as a subject ripe for a full-length publication. Nothing happened, so in 2002 I eventually decided to make my own attempt. I felt that if the genre was as important to many others as it was to me, then surely someone would want to read it.

As I began to write, I realised that the history of Psychobilly is a pretty large, lumbering beast of a subject and that, in my position as a father for the first time, there was no way that I could do an entire review of the Psychobilly genre in the near future. I kept writing anyway, and the result was 'Let's Wreck: Psychobilly Flashbacks From The Eighties & Beyond' (Stormscreen Productions, 2003). It was a slim tome that pretty much did what it said on the cover and featured my scattered ramblings documenting my personal discovery of Psychobilly and continued love of the music over the years. Although it did feature some brief informative notes on the basics of the genre (key bands, records, venues etc), I still felt that a longer, more detailed book was long overdue.

Luckily Cherry Red Records felt the same and, late in 2003, I started work on this very book you are now gripping between your fingers. At the time I stupidly vowed to the publishers that I could complete the book within a year. Thankfully they took that with a pinch of salt – when I began to write, I realised the Psychobilly beast could never be committed to paper with only

HELL'S BENT ON ROCKIN'

AUTHOR'S INTRODUCTION

365 days of frantic keyboard bashing. That did not even touch the tip of the Psychotic iceberg.

Despite being a fan of the music for almost a quarter of a century, I underestimated just how hugely Psychobilly has spread its disease across the world. Firstly, I had to look at how Psychobilly evolved from Britain's Rockabilly scene along with some of the other musical styles which have contributed to its sound. Once I moved beyond the UK, there was the genre's hardcore grip on Europe to investigate, closely followed by the rapidly booming US scene and Psychobilly's far-flung outposts in Japan, Australia and beyond. I also felt that the lifestyle reaches far beyond the bands themselves and fans of the music, promoters, determined fanzine writers and webmasters, along with specialist record labels, all deserved to be included in the book. And all the time I was writing, Psychobilly was experiencing its biggest boom in years, throwing up yet more bands and individuals dedicated to the scene.

It had to end somewhere and here it is, my attempt to capture some of the history behind the scene that dares not speak its name. I realise there may be queries regarding why some bands have been afforded more space than others, and perhaps why some bands have not been featured at all, but I have made as much of an effort to give a flavour of the 'Global' scene as possible. I have also had to piece the whole story together through a mist of album covers, flyers, dog-eared cuttings and hazy recollections of many of the bands themselves who often have a job remembering key details of their own careers. The history of Psychobilly is probably like the 1960s – if you were really there you probably do not remember it all! At least you can sleep safe in the knowledge that the brain cells you lost were probably whacked out of you in the wrecking pit or the result of drinking endless cans of out-of-date supermarket lager (probably).

Anyway, enough of these demented Caledonian ramblings. You haven't coughed up your hard-earned cash to read the wild waffling of a raving Scotsman who has been soaked to his underpants under a sea of Psychobilly over the past three years. Turn the page! TURN THE PAGE!

BRACKO
Nottinghamshire, August 2007

CHAPTER ONE

PSYCHOBILLY BEGINNINGS

What follows is a true story – only the details and identity of the culprits have been altered to protect the guilty. A school in the East Midlands, new term 1981-82. A new boy enters the class and is introduced by the teacher. He has spiky hair and wears a T-shirt, Doc Martens and tight denims with tiny turn-ups. He is instructed to sit next to the nearest empty seat. The boy beside him has a flat-top and wears a tartan shirt, crepe shoes and loose denims with big turn-ups. As the latest addition to the class takes his seat he mutters to his new neighbour "Rockabilly bastard!". "Fucking Punk" replies his schoolmate, and they glare at each other menacingly. One year later they are wrecking wildly together at a Meteors gig – best of mates.

There is no denying that Psychobilly has always drawn a huge variety of followers. Its genre-bending style, with its wide range of influences, has also united many elements of street culture since its birth in the 1980s. Since the teenager was born in the mid-1950s (before that you graduated from schoolkid to young adult when you started working), lines have always been sharply drawn particularly in membership to working-class street clans. Although Ray Winstone's character, greasy ton-up boy Kevin, claimed in the film 'Quadrophenia' that "I don't give a fuck about Mods and Rockers" it did not stop him getting a kicking from a gang of rowdy scooterists while his Mod mate Jimmy looked on.

Membership of specific street cults has always been contradictory in the same way that football thugs will happily battle with other teams supporters all season but unite behind their country when International rucking is required. Similarly, Psychobilly has often drawn together many types of street herberts such as Teds, Punks, Rockabillies, Skins, Mods, Scooterists, Heavy Rockers and Terrace Boot Boys, who would previously have been mortal enemies. More often than not, things were sorted out on the dancefloor as opposed to a punch-up outside the kebab shop.

Bands from a variety of music genres have regularly faced restrictions on the limits their sound "should" take. The Who were immersed in the Heavy Rock scene when they created their Mod-odyssey album 'Quadrophenia' in 1973, and the British Beat boom which followed The Beatles' success in the mid-1960s featured legions of bands containing tattooed Teds with their quiffs teased into mop-tops, often purely to stay in fashion and attract randy Beat birds. Many Glam bands were also often simply Rock'n'Rollers stripped of their sweaty denims and forced into spandex suits and hastily slapped on mascara to meet the demands of a teenybop audience.

However, no style of music has faced so many divisions, internally and externally, in the way Psychobilly has. Despite over twenty five years of bitching, sniping, rivalry, hostility and (even worse) being ignored from elements outside and within, the scene is still going. Psychobilly will never go away. Like the runt of the litter it has been pushed away, disregarded, written off and dismissed almost consistently but today it is as strong as ever and stubbornly sticking to the music business like a hairy wart. It seems that Psychobilly will never lose it.

Psychobilly itself is the bastard of all music genres, and a bastardisation of many. It is a form of music embraced by many but equally held at arm's length by a number of bands for fear of being tainted by its many connotations. It is a musical style which has blatantly pilfered from a variety of sources and also one which has exploded into a bizarre, and often pointless, selection of sub-genres. Punkabilly, Punk'n'Roll, Trashabilly, Horrorbilly, Swampabilly and a whole load of other terms have been employed

PSYCHOBILLY BEGINNINGS — HELL'S BENT ON ROCKIN'

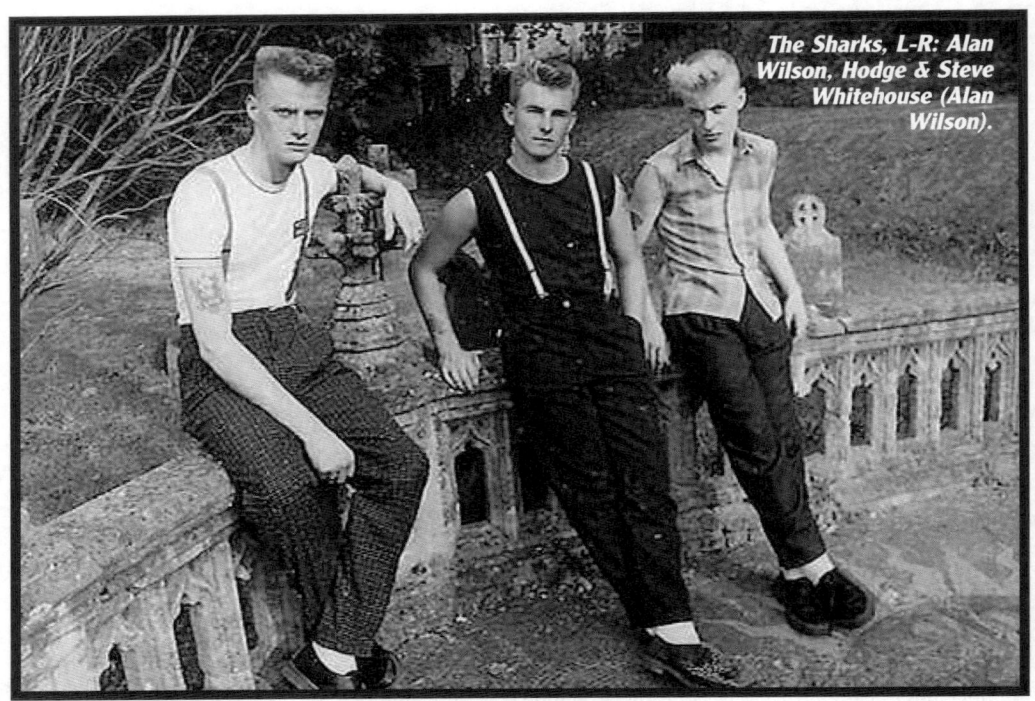

The Sharks, L-R: Alan Wilson, Hodge & Steve Whitehouse (Alan Wilson).

over the years either by bands treading some form of new ground or those who felt that the term Psychobilly was somehow limiting.

But no matter how diverse the ingredients of Psychobilly seem to be they all (eventually) reflect their true roots – Rockabilly. The Rockabilly universe is almost too dense in which to uncover every artist from that genre who has left their mark on Psychobilly but again and again whenever bands and fans discuss their influences the same names pop up again and again: Charlie Feathers, Johnny Burnette, Roy Orbison and Sun Records' 'Million Dollar Quartet' of Johnny Cash, Carl Perkins, Jerry Lee Lewis and a certain Mr E.A. Presley.

Alongside these legends, Rockabilly has also had a large number of darker, 'backwoods' artists whose twisted takes on Rockabilly were the perfect precursor to the Psychobilly genre. Many of these acts were resurrected in the 1980s on album series such as 'Wavy Gravy' and 'Desperate Rock'n'Roll' which offer up collections of tracks by what amounts to 'hillbilly punks' purging themselves of dark, twisted songs too controversial and sinister for many of the all-American 'mom and pop' type radio stations of the 1950s. Whoever bought these limited run releases at the time remains unknown but you certainly would not have wished to meet them whilst creeping through the woods (particularly if you were not keen on being made to "squeal like a pig").

Rockabilly itself is often buried beneath the general term of 1950s Rock'n'Roll but when 'fifties music' is referred to as a generic shorthand for Rock'n'Roll it obliterates the wide range of rockin' styles which that decade produced such as Doo-Wop, Rhythm & Blues, Country, Bluegrass, Hillbilly and Rockabilly itself. It is not only the Rockabilly sound that provides the backbone of the Psychobilly beat but also the template for the trio of double-bass, guitar and drums. This classic set-up was also resurrected in the Neo-Rockabilly boom, most notably by The Stray Cats, and has remained the form of many Psycho-related bands such as Frenzy, The Sharks, Torment, Long Tall Texans and Tiger Army and while it has also been a featured line-up through the years for others such as The Meteors, Mad Sin, The Coffin Nails and Demented Are Go.

Trying to define Neo-Rockabilly is a complex task which may arouse the righteous fury of revivalists,

HELL'S BENT ON ROCKIN'   PSYCHOBILLY BEGINNINGS

purists and musical snobs but it is safe to say that this movement went some way to re-establishing Rockabilly as the rough-house sound it had been at its roots after a period in the late 1970s when some Rockabilly groups drifted dangerously close to the mainstream and the fancifying effect of major record label neutering. It could also be argued that 'Neo' also dragged Rockabilly into a contemporary setting while acknowledging other influences, particularly Punk.

The blurring of the line between Neo-Rockabilly and Psychobilly is probably best illustrated not only by The Meteors but also by The Sharks and The Ricochets. The Meteors transition is documented on their first record appearance. Though recorded under the guise of Raw Deal, The Meteors first made their debut vinyl outing on the 1980 Alligator Records' compilation 'Home Grown Rockabilly'. Though, even then, featuring the distinctive input of P. Paul Fenech and Nigel Lewis the three tracks, 'Crazy Love', 'Go Away' and 'My Baby Loves Me', are pretty close to the modern Rockabilly of other acts on the album such as The Polecats, The Rhythm Cats and Johnny Key and The Kool Kats (almost a pussy overdose). However, none of

Above: Ricochets' and Guana Batz bassman Sam Sardi, 1986 (Jo Jackson).

Below: Nervous Records. Spotters of early Psychobilly talent (Roy Williams).

P. Paul Fenech... He don't worry about it! (Jan Van Hal).

these tracks really hinted at the seismic shock which was about to follow as their recording career progressed.

A similarly sharp change from Neo to Psycho appeared on The Sharks' live LP 'First & Last'. Although the album was released by Nervous Records in 1993 it features recordings from 1982 and 1983. The 1982 side featured a tight but fairly traditional set of Rockabilly tracks while the flip side from around a year later featured many of their harder-edged rockin' tracks, such as 'Death Row' and 'Moon Stomp', that were part of the band's debut album 'Phantom Rockers' which became one of the foundation albums of the Psychobilly genre.

The Ricochets were another act who made a relatively rapid evolution. Originally a 'strictly covers' Rockabilly combo called Pink & Black they adopted a name change, recorded a debut album and broke out of the pure Rockabilly mould into becoming a rockin' band with the added excitement and energy of Punk. Their first and only album for over two decades, 'Made In The Shade' (1982), was one of Nervous Records' early releases and hinted at a change in the Rockabilly scene to a more frenzied sound. While still Rockabilly, albeit with a darker side particularly on tracks such as 'Witchcraft', 'Migraine' and 'Hit Man', The Ricochets' place on the scene is never as widely credited as it should be

PSYCHOBILLY BEGINNINGS — HELL'S BENT ON ROCKIN'

and with members of the band moving on to join The Meteors, The Guana Batz and The Highliners, their influence on early Psychobilly was sizable.

Rockabilly and Rock'n'Roll are genres far too dense in which to pick specific artists who have influenced Psychobilly as most bands have illustrated their own preferences through their choice of covers; The Cramps and The Meteors chose Sun-era Roy Orbison in their early days, The Guana Batz favoured Chuck Berry and later Billy Fury, and King Kurt were never shy about their debt to Bo Diddley but there were certainly some artists more than others who have had moments in their career which have infected the Psychobilly genre forever.

Though it is obvious that everyone will have their own opinion as to what rockin' influences they hear running through Psychobilly, who could argue that the likes of Link Wray's 'powertwangs', Screaming Jay Hawkins swampy voodoo and Screaming Lord Sutch's lurid Rock'n'Roll and onstage theatrics have not in some way shaped Psychobilly? In fact Sutch's clod-hopping stomper 'Loonabilly' is virtually a blueprint for most of the Psychobilly bands who took a less than serious approach to the music.

What also has to be remembered is that many of the first generation of Psychobillies were often ignorant about the history of Rockabilly and gained their love of Rock'n'Roll not from lovingly collecting twenty-five year old 45's tracked down in dusty American record stores but by watching 'Grease' and 'Happy Days' alongside seeing Matchbox and The Stray Cats on 'Top Of The Pops'. This was a generation weaned on 'The Wanderers', 'Lemon Popsicle' and stacks of low-rent TV advertised Rock'n'Roll albums. These were the kids who would go on to form bands which would invariably play or record 'Brand New Cadillac' at least once in their career, even though they probably heard The Clash's version first. They may not have known who Narvel Felts and 'Groovey' Joe Poovey were but they sure as hell had heard of Darts and Showaddywaddy and they undoubtedly knew "who put the bomp in the bompshoobompshoobomp" never mind the fucking ramalamadingdong!

While Rockabilly was undoubtedly the backbone of Psychobilly, it influenced another diverse musical style which in turn was to leave its mark all over the Psychobilly genre. Garage Punk from the 1960s was yet another genre which to this day almost defies labelling and covers a wide range of bands who only truly share one element — primitive Rock'n'Roll fury! The whole garage scene was probably best summed up two decades later on the back cover of the 1983 Big Beat album 'These Cats Ain't Nuthin' But Trash': "They called it Rock'n'Roll. They called it Rockabilly. They called it Beat. They called it Punk. They call it TRASH."

Though eventually remembered mostly for their Psychedelic leanings many Garage bands also created demented, speed-freak versions of Rock'n'Roll and Rockabilly classics (something Psychobilly bands would continue to do) such as The Ready Men's 1964 pill-poppin' sprint through 'Shortnin' Bread' and Dean Carter's screeching demolition of 'Jailhouse Rock' from 1967. Also with frightening similarity to the Psychobilly scene, the Garage Punk boom set the standard for no-hit wonders and countless bands who hit the scene with a blast before disappearing, leaving only a single or meagre set of vinyl releases behind.

The link between the many genres of the 1950s and 1960s and Psychobilly is probably best illustrated by the 1984 Big Beat album 'Rockabilly Psychosis and the Garage Disease'. This compilation, compiled by Nick Garrard, was the perfect introduction to the many strands of musical dementia which contributed to the Psychobilly scene while also showcasing the new talent of the day such as The Guana Batz and The Sting-Rays alongside The Meteors and The Cramps.

The album features a collection of Rock'n'Roll dementia including early-1960s Rockabilly oddities from The Phantom, The Legendary Stardust Cowboy and Hazil Adkins along with Garage Punk from later that decade by The Sonics, The Trashmen and The Novas. The album also included some early-1980s US rockin' from The Gun Club and Tav Falco & The Panther Burns which, though far from Psychobilly, was definitely a Transatlantic taste of how some American bands were tapping into the same sources and doing their own thing.

Although the back-end of the 1970s would witness the first stirrings of the Psychobilly beat, another much maligned musical from earlier in the decade would leave its stack-heeled imprint on the wreckin' genre. Although Punk (arguably the music that pushed Psychobilly into being) was on its way, Glam Rock provided another legacy. Although Glam Rock itself was yet another bastardised version of Rock'n'Roll, this time from the decade that fashion forgot, it left behind some musical influences which would feature in the overall sound of many Psychobilly bands along with a back catalogue of classic, rebel-rousing songs ripe for cover versions.

Glam also became a convenient umbrella term for a wide variety of bands in a very similar way to Psychobilly. The Glam banner fluttered over diverse groups such as pretty boy popsters The Bay City Rollers, reformed hippies T-Rex and end-of-the-pier Rock'n'Roll revivalists Showaddywaddy. However, deep in their hearts (some deeper than others) was the Rockabilly beat. It was Rock'n'Roll to a boot-stomping bass line, backed by tub-thumping drums and terrace chants. An undeniable combination of teeth-rattling musical force when it was done well.

Like every mainstream pop phenomenon, Glam was simply a record company wheeze devoted to jamming together similar groups of pop bands in a bid to stimulate seven-inch single sales in an era of 'albums-only' rock gods, prog snobs and wheezy singer-songwriters. Many of what we now regard as 'Heroes of Glam' have no real connection: Sweet were heavy-rockers in waiting, Slade were as Glam as Les Dawson in drag and Mud were long-haired Teds with a camp guitarist. Glam's hottest solo star, Alvin Stardust, was simply early 1960s UK Rock'n'Roller Shane Fenton with darker hair, tighter trousers and one glove. In reality, the two most truly Glam artists of the 1970s were David Bowie and Roxy Music, even though both acts often avoided the Glam brand due to their prodigious album careers and arty backgrounds.

The acknowledgement of Glam as an influence on Psychobilly is almost as easy to trace as Rockabilly by simply perusing the many cover versions in the Psychobilly back catalogue. Ironically one of the earliest nods to Glam's legacy was an original composition, 'I Don't Worry About It' from The Meteors, groundbreaking second album 'Wreckin' Crew'. Featuring an undeniable 'glam stomp' from the rhythm section, this tune could have been worthy of a 'Top of the Pops' appearance in a previous decade had it not featured P. Paul Fenech's trademark guitar twang and the liberal use of 'fuck', 'cunt' and 'wank' in the lyrics. Nevertheless, it proved how similar Glam's boot-boy sound could be to the Psychobilly beat.

King Kurt proved themselves to be the bastard sons of the Bay City Rollers with their strangulation of the Jock teenyboppers' hit 'Bye Bye Baby'. Kurt's version, recorded as The Kurts, appeared on a single in 1989 and remained a live favourite of the band's especially amongst their hardcore scooterist following.

Batmobile, always a band unashamed to show their influences through their choice of cover versions, truly turned the heat up on the Glam tribute with their blistering take on The Sweet's yob-rock anthem 'Ballroom Blitz' from their 1986 LP ' Buried Alive', their version of Gary Glitter's 'Do You Wanna Touch' on 'Bambooland' (1986) and their take on Mud's 'Tiger Feet'. Mad Sin have probably acknowledged their debt to Glam Rock most openly with their album of unissued material '99 Psycho'n'Glamrock Demos' (2003) on Bad Bob Records and The Long Tall Texans have whipped many a crowd into a frenzy with their cover of Gary Glitter's 'Rock'n'Roll Part II'.

Quite clearly though, if it had not been for Punk it is unlikely that Psychobilly would have ever drawn breath. Everything about Punk has in some way influenced the genre from Punk's energy and anger to its DIY recording ethic and the basic creed that anyone can be in a band, promote gigs or start record labels regardless of their background. Certain elements of Punk fashion are also impossible to separate from Psychobilly style and for many the Rockabilly elements of The Clash and Sid Vicious' rowdy mauling of 'Something Else' still lay heavy in the memories of many early Psychobillies.

No observation on the many influences which have contributed to Psychobilly would be complete without mentioning The Cramps. Many would argue the The Cramps should be featured along with Psychobilly bands themselves but it is safe to suggest, and the band have emphasised the point in

PSYCHOBILLY BEGINNINGS

HELL'S BENT ON ROCKIN'

The Reverend King Kurt (Jo Jackson).

interviews, that The Cramps were 'not' a Psychobilly band. On paper the band's combination of Rockabilly, Punk attitude and lyrical themes of sleaze, horror and similar B-movie material looks like the very blueprint of Psychobilly but The Cramps belong in their own unique genre.

Formed in Akron, Ohio way back in 1976, The Cramps were literally and stylistically miles away from the birth of Psychobilly in the UK. They were already an established act long before even the first fist was thrown in a wrecking pit. As legend would have it, when Erick Purkhiser picked up teen hitchhiker Kristy Wallace they soon discovered a mutual love of authentic Rock'n'Roll and B-movie exploitation flicks. Seeking new kicks and with the intention of forming a band they both relocated to New York City. Erick then ditched his, almost unpronounceable, surname in favour of the stage name Lux Interior and Kristy was reborn as head temptress and luscious hellcat 'Poison' Ivy Rorschach.

At this time the early 'Noo Yawk' Punk scene was kicking off and the centre of this universe was the infamous CBGB's Club, an unassuming downtown venue next door to a dosshouse in the city's rundown Bowery neighbourhood. Originally opened by ex-Jazz club owner Hilly Kristal it was intended as a Country, Bluegrass and Blues club (Geddit!?) but soon became the spiritual home of Punk, populated by a host of soon-to-be massive bands such as The Ramones, Television, Blondie, Jayne County and Patti Smith. This piss-soaked dungeon soon became a regular stomping ground for The Cramps who, after two female drummers had passed through their ranks, settled on a line-up with Lux on vocals, Ivy on guitar, Bryan Gregory on (another) guitar and Nicholas 'Nick Knox' Stephanoff on drums.

What immediately marked this early line-up out from the legions of sweaty Punks and angst-ridden New Wave bands was their unique sound. With no bass, two guitars and the most basic of drum kits The Cramps were pure stripped-to-the-bone Rock'n'Roll. With Nick laying down a pounding – almost monotonous – beat, Ivy twanging furiously, Gregory generating a wall of fuzz and Mr Interior screaming out a barrage of vocal dementia, the music itself was a brew of 1960s Garage Punk, Surf and any other number of adrenaline driven vibes from the 1950s and beyond. But what always prevented this mass of influences descending into cacophony was the band's unique way of tying the whole thing to a stomping Rockabilly beat.

In a bizarre way The Cramps exist in almost a parallel universe to Psychobilly itself. Their roots, their sound and their lyrical content are similar but a huge gap between both elements is present. Their image, while perhaps more representative of the current Psychobilly scene was vastly at odds with early Psycho fashion which consisted of mainly boots, tartan shirts, T-shirts and denims. With their combination of black leather and black PVC adorned with chicken bones, boot-lace ties and mascara, The Cramps also instantly attracted large numbers of Europe's Goth population. This was something which few Psychobilly bands ever did as, although both cults were closely linked through shared 'alternative' venues across the land, fans of each genre often had a healthy disregard for each other's music.

With two Indie singles under their belt, on their own Vengeance Records, 'Human Fly'/'The Way I Walk' and 'Domino'/'Surfin' Bird', the band caught the attention of Miles Copeland, brother of drummer Stewart Copeland from The Police, and boss of a new record label IRS. Both singles, along with an extra track 'Lonesome Town', were re-released in a single mini-album by the label in the Autumn of 1979 under the title 'Gravest Hits'.

Six months later the band's first full-length album 'Songs the Lord Taught Us' (1980) was released and shortly after that, following a clash of opinion over The Cramps' direction, Bryan Gregory left – pinching the band's van and equipment in the process. Sometime after high-tailing with the band's gear Gregory formed the band Beast but soon drifted into obscurity and unfortunately his next appearance in the music press was his obituary, following a heart attack in 2001.

Gregory's replacement, after the band employed Julian Greinsnatch for a short period, was former Gun Club guitarist Kid Congo Powers who was to feature on their third album for IRS 'Psychedelic Jungle' (1981). Despite producing a fine album, which boasts many Cramps' classics such as 'Greenfuz', 'Goo Goo Muck' and their 'Cramped' covers of 'The Crusher' and 'Green Door', the band began to fall out with their major label masters. They then entered a period of contract wrangling which effectively held them back from further studio work and only able to earn a crust from touring while at the same time leaving them unable to showcase new material for fear of bootleggers poaching their set.

After almost two years, the band were freed from the clutches of IRS and immediately delivered a six track live album 'Smell Of Female' to their new label Enigma (released in the UK by Big Beat Records). Fans had been waiting for new material and 'Smell Of Female' did not disappoint. Far more than the usual live fodder taped at the back of a sweaty dancehall, this was a well-recorded Cramps revue from no less than New York's Peppermint Lounge – ground zero of the Big Apple's beat boom of the 1960s. The Cramps' strode from the shadows and were, more than ever, sexy burlesque with a Rockabilly beat from the tuppence-licking anthem 'You Got Good Taste' to their bombastic version of the busting-bosom theme to Russ Meyer's girl-power cult flick 'Faster Pussycat! Kill! Kill!'.

It was a long time coming but their next album was at last a stroke of luck for the band as they delivered an excellent album at a time when their combined audience of Psychobillies and Goths were at a peak across Europe. Continuing with the UK label Big Beat (home of The Vibes, The Sting-Rays etc.) they delivered their classic album 'A Date With Elvis' in 1986. The album was recorded in Hollywood late in 1985 with Lux, Nick and Ivy. Miss Rorschach played bass and guitar during the sessions but they were to be joined onstage by the mysterious 'Fur'. To support the album they toured Europe, with The Sting-Rays in support for the UK dates, and packed large halls across the land stuffed with so many hairspray-soaked punters that each gig was surely a fire risk of huge proportions.

Singles lifted from the album, such as 'Can Your Pussy Do The Dog', 'Kizmiaz' and 'What's Inside A Girl', also contributed to the album's success and The Cramps were once again enjoying high times, particularly after the protracted and bitter wranglings with IRS. That label did however deliver a 'kiss off' final compilation album 'Bad Music For Bad People' either as a contractual obligation or a last-ditch attempt to milk the band's continuing success – you decide!

PSYCHOBILLY BEGINNINGS

The Cramps' deal with Big Beat in the UK continued and while the band never crossed over to anything approaching mainstream success there are more than enough loyal Cramps' fans in the world to ensure that every album was a solid seller. 'Stay Sick' (1990) was rather slow in arriving but was followed rather more sharply by 'Look Mom, No Head' in 1991, showcasing on both the outside and inside covers the increasingly bizarre Mr Interior clad in high heels and a black PVC posing pouch.

The band's line-up fluctuated wildly from 'A Date With Elvis' onward, with a parade of bassists/rhythm guitarists backing up Ivy, then a stack of sticksmen following the loss of long-time drummer, and icon of cool, Nick Knox in 1991 after eye surgery led to his retirement.

After their poor experience with IRS, the band were not keen on getting back into bed with another major label and this resulted in some multi-label releases of their albums across the world. While the band stayed with Big Beat in the UK from 1983 to 1991 their albums were often released by other labels outside Britain. 'A Date With Elvis' was released by a whopping six labels in 1986 alone (with more to follow). This label-hopping got even more confusing when the band eventually left Big Beat and first landed in the Creation Records stable, then booming under the almighty success of Manc hooligans Oasis. Not that the label made much difference as The Cramps managed to pursue their own direction on the album 'Flamejob' (1994) with no (apparent) meddling from millionaire Creation head-honcho Alan McGee.

Having jumped to Epitaph Records for their 1997 album 'Big Beat From Badsville' the band's next move was to reactivate their own label Vengeance which had lain dormant since 1978, when their first two singles were released. The label had been dragged back to life only once before with the release of their 1987 live album 'Rockinnreelininauklandnewzealandxxx'. Their first project was a series of coloured vinyl releases in 2001 of all their post-IRS albums to celebrate the band's 25th anniversary. This was followed by their first album of new material for Vengeance, 'Fiends Of Dope Island'. This album was to mark the departure of the band's second-longest serving drummer Harry Drumdini who, despite a few periods AWOL, served the band handsomely for over nine years.

In 2004, The Cramps dug deep into their past archive tapes and released a bootleg-busting collection of early rarities running to almost two and a half hours long. Many of these demos and live tracks were from the 1976/77 period of their career and showed a band, rather unusually, lovingly exhuming material from their earliest days. However, as The Cramps now pass the mark of thirty years in the biz it's not all about looking back. With Bill Bateman on drums and Chopper Franklin from sleazy rockers Charley Horse on bass the band still tour continuously. Never resorting to a nostalgia trip, The Cramps are as sick, depraved and exciting as they ever were. Just don't mention Psychobilly!

While the origins of Psychobilly are as wild and varied as the genre itself, there can be no real doubt that The Meteors have always been at the eye of the Psychobilly hurricane. Though folklore about the term itself reaches back through The Cramps' early days to the use of the word in the lyrics to the classic Johnny Cash song 'One Piece At A Time', the Man in Black's lyric has little to do with a gang of 'crazies' punching fuck out of each other to the sound of Rockabilly from hell on a wet London night. When P. Paul Fenech explained to a journalist early in their career that The Meteors' music was based around "…werewolves, psycho-killers and Rockabilly" it's not hard to discover where the scene got its name.

For most Psychobilly fans from the early 1980s and beyond, it was seeing or hearing The Meteors for the first time that brought Psychobilly to their attention and even members of some other pioneering Psychobilly bands, such as Pip Hancox of The Guana Batz, have openly admitted that it was The Meteors that drove them to form a group and create their own rockin' racket. However, regardless of its origins – Psychobilly was about to become an unstoppable dark force on the music scene.

CHAPTER TWO

HELL'S BENT ON ROCKIN'

THE PIONEERS

Though occasionally a contested issue, there can be no real argument against the presence of The Meteors at ground zero of the Psychobilly boom. The Cramps were, and will probably always be, revered by legions of Psychobillies but they were from a different scene, a different culture and a band almost beyond categorisation. As The Meteors' Mark Robertson claimed in the hallowed pages of UK rock mag 'Sounds', "We've shared the same influences as The Cramps but we're not influenced by The Cramps".

The Meteors rose from the ashes of a number of Rockabilly bands such as The Southern Boys, Rock Therapy and Raw Deal, all featuring P. Paul Fenech on guitar and Nigel Lewis on double-bass. In Raw Deal, Fenech and Lewis first recorded together on three tracks which would eventually appear on the compilation album 'Home Grown Rockabilly' (then credited as The Meteors). After this the band began dabbling in a harder-edged sound but this almost immediately led to their drummer and second guitarist jumping ship for fear of drifting too far from a strict Rockabilly template. In the Spring of 1980 they drafted in Mark Robertson, an experienced sticksman from Punk band The Models, who proved to be the spur they required to single-mindedly pursue their own direction. However, having the audacity to include a Punk drummer instantly infuriated strait-laced Rockabilly revivalists and occasionally garnered a frosty reception at their earliest gigs in London's Rock'n'Roll circuit.

The Meteors storm 'Sounds' Rockabilly chart in April 1981 (Mason Storm Archive).

Having been largely isolated from the Capital's Rockabilly scene, The Meteors made their own way playing venues such as Dingwalls, The 100 Club, The Marquee and The Hope & Anchor. Soon they gathered their own following 'The Crazies', a motley collection of ex-Punks and Rockabillies all looking for something more rowdy. A weird hybrid of 'Psycho Rockabilly' was born.

The regulars at performances by The Meteors indulged in some rambunctious, dancefloor movements which, to the untrained eye, resembled a Wild West saloon brawl. They called it 'going

19

THE PIONEERS

mental' but it became known as the fine art of 'wrecking', 'stomping' and a host of other names. To punters unfamiliar with The Meteors in concert, this wild dancing soon gained the band an unfairly bad reputation for attracting 'bovver' at their gigs leading to some venues refusing to book them for return visits even though the 'wrecking' was essentially good-natured. Nonetheless, with their growing army of new fans and an increasing Punk following, The Meteors were rarely short of gigs.

Although for a while The Meteors were the Capital's best-kept secret, they soon caught the collective eye of the nation's youth, not on radio as many bands did but in the cinema. 'Dance Craze' was a feature-length flick released to cash in on the Ska revival phenomenon, which was ironically on its way out by the time Chrysalis Pictures attempted to exploit the nation's youth at the box office in 1981. The film, while capturing the excellent live excitement of the Two-Tone Records roster, was really no more than a compilation of concert footage featuring most of the bands associated with the label such as The Specials, The Beat, Madness and The Bodysnatchers.

However, jammed before it, for those early and attentive enough to catch the first feature (this was back in 'ye olden days' when cinema attendees often got a supporting flick instead of reams of shite ads and 'turn off your mobile' warnings) was 'Meteor Madness'. This seventeen-minute short featured performances from The Meteors squeezed into a whacko B-movie plot about the Devil (played by Brit actor Keith Allen) and his fiendish plot to destroy the world through a dastardly keep-fit regime(!?). After what seems like endless bouts of Allen's goofing The Meteors appear (literally) in a puff of smoke, run around the streets of London for a bit then burst into a live performance in a tiny club.

This celluloid oddity paved the way for The Meteors' debut single, the four-track 'Meteor Madness EP' released in 1980 on Chiswick, the label which eventually evolved into Ace Records – legendary home of soul, R&B and a variety of other influential roots music. This single presented two future Meteors' classics, 'Voodoo Rhythm' and 'Maniac Rockers From Hell', along with two more leisurely-paced offerings, 'My Daddy Is A Vampire' and 'You Can't Keep A Good Man Down'. The EP was an excellent introduction to the band but was not really able to capture The Meteors' blistering live energy. Although released as a seven-inch single a small quantity of ten-inch vinyl versions of the EP were also produced. Despite bearing only a white label and poorly photocopied cover these rarities are highly sought after by Psychobilly connoisseurs and regularly change hands for over £100.

As the band's reputation grew, in 1981 The Meteors secured their first 'John Peel Session' for the UK's national station Radio 1. On a single day that Summer the band recorded five tracks for the Indie music Godfather: 'Voodoo Rhythm', 'Love You To Death', 'Rockabilly Psychosis', 'My Daddy Is A Vampire' and 'Rockhouse'. The Meteors' following single 'Radioactive Kid'/'Graveyard Stomp', again on Chiswick, really captured the band's wild style and was a further indication for those who had yet to witness the band in concert that The Meteors were busy creating a new monster sound from the body parts of Rock'n'Roll's corpse. Next up, their debut album was to take The Meteors, and Psychobilly itself, to a far wider audience. Despite two excellent singles, Chiswick/Ace were not really offering The Meteors the back-up they deserved to push them forward nationally. After some Radio One sessions, a TV appearance on the pop programme 'White Light' and the front cover of 'Sounds' the band soon attracted the attention of Island Records A&R man Andrew Lauder.

The Meteors onstage in Cologne in the 1980s (Jan Van Hal).

HELL'S BENT ON ROCKIN'   THE PIONEERS

The Meteors' 'In Heaven', ground zero of the Psychobilly explosion (Cherry Red Records).

After an amicable split from Chiswick, The Meteors signed with Island to produce their debut album and in the process a sizable wad of cold, hard cash (in the form of an advance) changed hands. At the time this was a major label deal for The Meteors and a radical departure for Island, a label more closely associated with 1970s rock and folk along with a selection of hard-hitting Reggae acts such as Bob Marley and Steel Pulse. With this in mind the imprint label 'Lost Soul Records' was created to benefit both label and band by disassociating The Meteors with the rest of Island's roster.

Recorded in just a week and produced by the band themselves with engineer Rob Keyloch, 'In Heaven' was an accomplished long-player. Kicking off with a live recording of 'The Crazies' chanting the whacko ballad from the movie 'Eraserhead' which gave the album its title, the crowd are then offered the opportunity to 'Go Mental!' by a screaming Nigel Lewis. What follows are fourteen tracks of groundbreaking Psychobilly. 'In Heaven' featured Fenech and Lewis alternating vocals on each track to accompany their own compositions. To further illustrate their existing stockpile of excellent songs only one cover version appears and even that track, a version of The Rolling Stones 'Get Off Of My Cloud', included a lyrical reworking by Nigel Lewis. In the same way that The Damned produced the first LP of the Punk era, The Meteors launched Psychobilly onto the long-playing platter and, despite retrospective bickering over Psychobilly's roots (ie. The Cramps, Neo-Rockabilly…), they obviously set the ball rolling for a new generation of rowdy, rockin' bands who were about to elbow their way into the recording studio.

After their debut album release, Island followed up with a single 'The Crazed'/'Attack Of The Zorchmen' (1981) but then Andrew Lauder, the man who signed the band, left the company. This left The Meteors alone at a major label receiving no assistance or back-up to promote them any further. To add to the situation, relations between Paul Fenech and Mark Robertson were deteriorating which then led to Robertson's departure from the band. One final single, featuring the original line-up, was released around this time under the moniker of The Clapham South Escalators. This three-track seven-inch was released by Upright Records and featured some trashy, Garage-Punk classics recorded during leftover studio time at the 'In Heaven' sessions.

Long-time Meteors fan, and Punk guitarist, Woodie was quickly drafted in to perch on the drum stool and after a period of regular gigging in London the band hit the road nationally in 1982, on a tour supporting Theatre of Hate. This tour revitalised the band and started to bring them the national exposure they deserved. On returning home they were back in the studio recording the first new songs of the mark II line-up. These ten tracks of demos would later appear in a variety of guises and also collected together on the Big Beat album 'Teenagers From Outer Space' but at the time they progressed no further as a week after the recordings Nigel Lewis and manager Nick Garrard jumped ship leaving P. Paul Fenech with no label, no bass player and no management.

Undeterred, Fenech pressed on with a new line-up and a single 'Mutant Rock' was released in the Autumn of 1982. Featuring 'The Hills Have Eyes' on the B-side, this seven-inch appeared on the WXYZ label and consisted of tracks from the final Meteors mark II line-up with Nigel Lewis' slapping overdubbed by new Meteor Mick White on electric bass. The band then signed to new label ID Records which provided them with their first album release 'Wreckin' Crew' in early 1983, yet again another Meteors album that would become a genuine classic of the genre.

Though the band had changed drastically since their own debut album, this second Meteors album was also a groundbreaking release which featured a host of tunes, the title track in particular, that would become Psychobilly classics. Without joint-frontman Nigel Lewis, P. Paul took control and firmly pursued his vision of 'pure' Psychobilly. 'Wreckin Crew' brought the band to an even wider audience and they capitalised on this with a rampant touring schedule, establishing hardcore crews of Meteors fanatics across the country. For anyone unlucky enough not to catch the band during their frequent live performances, or those too fucking lazy to get to gigs, The Meteors' first concert album 'Live' appeared on Wreckin' Records in 1983. It captured the band's energy perfectly at gig in Glasgow's infamous Rooftops venue and also featured firm favourites such as 'Mutant Rock' and 'Wreckin Crew' along with covers of 'Wipeout' and 'Lonesome Train' which at the time were unavailable elsewhere. As the year drew to a close another 'Peel Session' was secured featuring the new Meteors line-up with Rick Ross on bass and Matthew Fraser on drums. Late night listeners were treated to another single day of recordings which produced 'Ain't Gonna Bring Me Down', 'You Crack Me Up', 'Lonesome Train' and 'Long Blonde Hair'.

A single 'Johnny Remember Me', a cover of John Leyton's teenage death ballad, was also released by ID but then ties with that label were severed. Despite constant touring, Paul Fenech established his first label 'Mad Pig' and The Meteors' third album 'Stampede' appeared in 1984. The Mad Pig label stretched to six singles releases and another album including the classic 'I'm Just A Dog' single in 7" and 12", two 7" EP's 'Fire Fire' and 'Bad Moon Rising' and the 12" only 'Stampede EP' and 'Hogs & Cuties EP'.

As 1985 came around The Meteors were setting a pattern of constant hard work on the road and regular record releases that few, if any, bands on the Psycho-scene could match. In that same year Mad Pig's final release was The Meteors' 'Monkey's Breath' album. This was similar in style to 'Stampede' but with standout tracks such 'Rhythm Of The Bell', 'Ain't Gonna Bring Me Down' and 'Meat Is Meat' which proved that despite an almost insane touring schedule P. Paul was still creating new Meteors' tracks at a rapid rate, a factor which would eventually lead The Meteors' frontman to create further outlets for his compositions.

Throughout the 1980s, the band line-up fluctuated regularly with a procession of drummers and bass-men passing through the ranks as Fenech doggedly pursued his vision of The Meteors. Serving their time on The Meteors' juggernaut were characters such as Toby 'Jug' Griffin, Ian 'Spider' Cubitt, Austin Stones and Nev 'The Spectre' Hunt. A few stood the pace but generally each album generated a new line-up in some form.

With Mad Pig Records no longer in operation, The Meteors saw out the decade with top UK Punk and New Wave label Anagram Records, a division of Cherry Red Records. The first fruits of this unholy union was the 'Surf City EP' on 7" and 12" in 1986 followed by the album 'Don't Touch The Bang Bang Fruit' in 1987 and a single of the same name. Around this period many other labels were attempting to get on board The Meteors bandwagon releasing whatever they could get their hands on. Dojo Records were particular culprits with their motley selection of live tracks and other bits and pieces

THE PIONEERS

King Kurt join Polydor Records (Jo Jackson).

King Kurt dressed to thrill! (Jo Jackson).

stretched over three albums; 'The Curse of the Mutants' (1984), 'Live II: Horrible Music For Horrible People By This Horrible Band' (1986) and 'Night Of The Werewolf' (1987). Dojo's close associates Link also delivered a Meteors concert recording as part of their 'Live and Loud' series in 1987. From that period probably the most interesting item was the Castle Records rarity 'Archive 4 EP' (a 12" limited to 5000 copies).

In a bid to rein in this flurry of material which The Meteors no longer had any control over, the band's next album for Anagram was a collection of re-recordings of previous issued material. 'Only The Meteors Are Pure Psychobilly' was released in 1988 and if the title was not subtle enough the cover artwork, featuring the band's Mad Monkey character riding roughshod over the gravestones of Frenzy, King Kurt and The Guana Batz, hammered the point home – Paul Fenech had no intention of relinquishing The Meteors' title as the 'Undisputed Kings Of Psychobilly'.

1988 was a particularly strong year for The Meteors/Anagram partnership three further EPs and another album 'The Mutant Monkey And The Surfers From Zorch'. The pace continued with the band delivering another new album to Anagram in 1989, 'Undead, Unfriendly & Unstoppable', before the relationship grew to a close at the end of the decade. Though both band and label would work together in the future the honeymoon was over and Anagram's parting gift was the third volume in The Meteors 'Live' series, 'Live Styles Of The Sick And Shameless' (1990), a suitable landmark for the band's first decade.

As Psychobilly established itself in the early 1980s, another band were to become a focus of attention and provide a light-hearted 'ying' to The Meteors' dark 'yang'. As any follower of the genre will tell you, mentioning Psychobilly music to most members of the public will only result in a blank expression and, if pushed, any vaguely sussed punter on the street may throw up The Meteors' name but for the majority of Joe Soaps the answer will usually be along the lines of 'Eh… like King Kurt?'

Although the band left behind relatively few record releases, at least compared to The Meteors prodigious output, they remain the most mainstream face of early Psychobilly mainly due to a handful of TV appearances and some headline-grabbing tabloid coverage of their outrageous live antics. Much of what became King Kurt legend (rats, dressing as Zulus, dead animals, flour and egg throwing, wearing dresses etc.) actually occurred on or around the period of the band's formation in late 1982. The story begins in the early 1980s with a band called The Uglies featuring guitarists 'Handsome' John Reddington and Paul 'Thwack' Laventhol. The group evolved into The Rocking Zulus and then to Rocking Kurt and the Sour Krauts. Joining John and Paul in this live line-up were future King Kurt

23

regulars Robert 'Bert' Boustead and youthful sax player Alan Power, soon to be known only as Maggot.

Rocking Kurt's frontman was Geoff Harvey, a wild-haired but reasonably out-of-tune singer and writer of a number of the band's songs including the future Psychobilly anthem 'Rockin' Kurt'. Geoff's off-key warblings have been acknowledged as one element which led to many of King Kurt's future backing-vocal led compositions. Often Rocking Kurt backing vox were designed to drown out Geoff's bum notes and the blinding gaps which he often left in songs when he forgot the words. Nevertheless, Geoff was an essential member of the group and the band were gutted to find out he was leaving.

The band felt Geoff would be hard to replace not only as a unique frontman but also as a key member of a close group of friends. However, they kept it together as a band and placed an advert for a new singer: "WANTED: EX-RAMPTON PATIENT. Must have full control of mouth and silly haircut. OAPs considered."

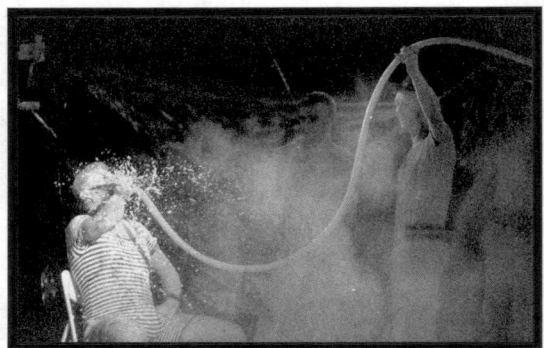

Top: King Kurt shoot their load into yet another punter's mouth (Jan Van Hal).
Above: King Kurt parading their 'Big Cock' onstage (Jan Van Hal).

As Rampton is one of the UK's top hospitals for the criminally insane only one patient actually applied along with two other no-hopers. Despite this demented attempt at recruitment, the band eventually secured the vocal talents of Gary 'Smeg' Cayton from low-rent Brighton band Smeggy and the Cheesy Bits. After a quick name change, dropping out 'Roc' and 'and the Sour Krauts', the six-piece King Kurt was born.

Though forever linked with The Meteors as the two-pronged spear of British Psychobilly, both bands were radically different. King Kurt were twice the size for a start with their twin guitar attack and sax. This line-up itself created a completely unique sound but still one which presented a fast-paced and deranged version of Rock'n'Roll that instantly appealed to many fledgling Psychobillies.

The band's outrageous live performances rapidly gained them notoriety and some music press. Lurid headlines in daily newspapers even warned of alcohol poisoning, dead animals launched into (and out of) the crowd and a variety of sex acts performed in the audience. How accurate the reporting was remains to be seen but anyone who witnessed these early gigs would probably testify that they were not far from the truth. One gig refused entry to any blokes not wearing dresses and most live shows became a foodfight of 'Animal House' proportions.

While The Meteors would often offer the front row a mouthful of chicken's blood (courtesy of P. Paul Fenech), King Kurt gigs resulted in widespread attacks of flour bombs, eggs, shaving foam, fire extinguishers and anything else which came to hand – along with a few unmentionables. Drinking games were also part of the gig experience including a live favourite which would follow later in the band's career, the infamous 'Wheel of Misfortune' a huge wheel to which punters were strapped to and spun after being fed a bucket of booze through a hose. This often resulted in the victim being left in an unconscious stupor or forced them to let go a multi-coloured fountain of puke. Snakebite was the supposed content of the bucket but many would shudder to think what foul potions were also added to the receptacle.

HELL'S BENT ON ROCKIN'   THE PIONEERS

In 1982, King Kurt took themselves into the studio to produce their debut single. Having worked extensively on their set live they slapped down recordings of 'Zulu Beat' and the B-side 'Rockin' Kurt'. The seven-inch appeared on the independent label Thin Sliced Records, financed by a character known only as 'Catweazle' who had witnessed the band live and coughed up the cash for their debut. Each single was wrapped in a luridly coloured printed sleeve featuring the first appearance of King Kurt, the alcoholic rat himself. Far rarer, hand-drawn sleeves were also created featuring the cartoon King Kurt in a variety of guises. As a further mark of good taste the seven-inch was released in a selection of coloured vinyl. A twelve-inch single also appeared from Thin Sliced with the addition of the band's earliest recordings of 'Ghost Riders' and 'Oedipus Rex'.

With the single's release, and the band's increasingly high profile live, they soon attracted further record company attention in the shape of Stiff Records – the home of Pub Rock, Punk Rock, Two-Tone and New Wave. Stiff signed the band in 1983 and bunged them in the studio with Dave Edmunds, a well respected Rock'n'Roller who had already produced The Stray Cats and had many hits of his own over three decades. Edmunds managed to capture the band's rowdy live energy while still producing a high-quality, groundbreaking Psychobilly album. That is to say, he did not fuck about and attempt to smooth down their rough edges and the debut LP 'Ooh Wallah Wallah' still sounds great over two decades later.

The album was also backed up with some major promotion in the form of nationwide gigs, press publicity and even some entertaining promo videos. The first single to be lifted from the album was 'Destination Zululand' and it was supported with a video of Kurt antics mostly filmed in a quarry, an obvious stand-in for the real 'Zululand'. It was an immediate success and gained King Kurt the holy grail of 1980s UK pop stardom, a Top 40 chart position sneaking in at number 38. This also led to a 'live' appearance on 'Top of the Pops', Britain's premier music show on TV. Although this was to be the peak of King Kurt's mainstream success, the follow-up single 'Mack the Knife' fared less well. Failing to dent the mainstream charts with their following singles they were to remain superstars of the Psychobilly underground.

Nonetheless, the band later had another poke at chart success with what, even by King Kurt standards, was a bit of a novelty. 'Banana Banana' (1984) was a glorious, whacked-out number with its riff ruthlessly pinched from a 1970s peanut advert ('...they're jungle fresh!') although the original tune was 1950s standard 'The Peanut Vendor'. Regardless of the song's roots, Kurt bashed it into submission and took their fetish for jungle rhythms to their absolute peak with this singalong anthem. Although it was released on seven-inch, twelve-inch and banana-shaped picture disc it never set the charts alight, which is a great pity as if it had maybe today whole families would gather on the dancefloor at weddings and anniversary parties and shake it to 'Banana Banana' instead of the fucking 'Birdy Song'.

In 1985, things began to get a little rocky within the band and bass-player Bert departed along with guitarist Handsome John. Both band members dropped off the radar for many years and retired from the music biz with Bert eventually moving into publishing and John Reddington becoming a lawyer (though he would return to the band for a short period). Their replacements were

Stiff Records' promo photo of Smeg and the boys (Jo Jackson).

THE PIONEERS HELL'S BENT ON ROCKIN'

youthful guitarist 'Whistling' Jim Piper and bass player Richard 'Dick Crippen' Coppen. Crippin came from a solid background of Rock and Punk and had previously been a member of Tenpole Tudor, themselves a unique model of demented Rock'n'Roll.

Around the time of Bert and John's departure, Stiff had initially tired of the band's wild reputation and fearing they would be held liable for the band's shocking financial state, at a time when bills for hotel damages often outweighed the cash generated by touring and merchandise sales, they parted company. However, when King Kurt returned from their first successful US tour both label and band were reunited and the new line-up returned to the studio for Stiff with producers Pat Collier, who worked on most of the album, and David Batchelor, who lent his talents for four tracks. Crippen immediately made a contribution to the proceedings, mixing the album along with Mick Glossop, and writing the song 'Momma Kurt'. The whole process was a fairly democratic venture with songs by Thwack, Maggot, Smeg and Rory all making their way onto vinyl.

Then in 1986 it happened! King Kurt thrust their 'Big Cock' at the unsuspecting record-buying public, with initial copies appearing in 'throbbing red vinyl'. Though this 'Carry On...' style wit was the perfect example of the saucy seaside humour which Brits are famous for, King Kurt's amusingly titled second album genuinely disturbed many easily-offended squares as if Punk Rock had never happened. Fearing quiffed-up hooligans would terrorise shop staff by demanding 'Have you got King Kurt's Big Cock?' some retailers, particularly WH Smith, refused to stock the album. For less sensitive record stores, the standard album release simply featured a small group photo nestling under the band's name and a picture of a huge rooster but the coloured vinyl edition delivered the title starkly with King Kurt/Big Cock filling the twelve-inch pink sleeve (ooer!) with bold black lettering.

Despite the predictable backlash, which only stimulated further interest in the band, 'Big Cock' was another collection of excellent material along with their stomping cover of Eddie Cochran's 'Nervous Breakdown'. Future classics littered both sides such as 'Pumpin' Pistons', 'Horatio', 'Kneebone Knock', 'Alcoholic Rat' and the previously released singles 'Road To Rack'n'Ruin' and 'Billy'. One track missing from the line-up was 'Slammers' which was also a single prior to the album's release. Though 'Big Cock' was another King Kurt classic for Stiff, their relationship with the band was soon over as the band signed to major label Polydor later that year.

King Kurt's deal with Polydor got off to a good start with a 7" and 12" release featuring the band's mauling of the 'West Side Story' anthem 'America (...What A State)'. Though the band played fast and loose with the original lyrics it featured a powerful production job and, though difficult to reproduce live, it certainly was unlike any Psychobilly-influenced record of the time.

Their following release for Polydor was again a unique tune for King Kurt, the booming spaghetti-western themed 'The Land Of Ring Dang Do' (1987), a stomping ballad soaked in mariachi trumpet. 'Handsome' John Reddington brought his guitar back to the fold and, despite reasonable promotion from the label, including a limited edition double single in a gatefold sleeve, the band's career with Polydor was effectively over. If Polydor did not appear to appreciate the band, King Kurt remained massive on the Psychobilly and Scootering scenes and took their raucous live shows regularly across the UK, Europe and Japan. It therefore came as a great surprise to many that late in 1987 the band's ever reliable 'Rat and Rodent Club' issued a newsletter announcing King Kurt's demise.

Although the band were no more that did not stop the records coming and their new label GWR gathered together many of the singles tracks and B-sides which had not featured on the band's first two long-players and compiled the album 'The Last Will & Testicle' in 1988. Smeg, Maggot and Thwack continued for some time as The Kurts but their only recording was the 7" and 12" single on GWR featuring their live favourite, a rowdy mauling of the Bay City Rollers teen anthem 'Bye, Bye Baby'. As The Kurts themselves faded and the decade neared its end, their concert recording of a gig in Japan was released by Link Records as part of their 'Live and Rockin' series and it provided a suitable epitaph to the first chapter of the King Kurt story. Quite why King Kurt went from their high position in the Psychobilly foodchain to nothing in eight years was a mystery to many but there was

HELL'S BENT ON ROCKIN'   THE PIONEERS

CLARENDON HOTEL Hammersmith W6

EVERY FRIDAY
ALAN GOFF'S
Heavy Metal Roadshow

EVERY SUNDAY
NEAL KAY'S
Heavy Metal Soundhouse

The shocking truth! Before the Klub Foot The Clarendon hosted hairy rockers of another kind (Mason Storm Archive).

still life in the old rat and the road to rack and ruin would continue in the 1990s and beyond.

Alongside The Meteors and King Kurt in the early 1980s, another band would go on to enjoy something approaching mainstream success during their career and book themselves a lasting place in the Psychobilly hall of fame. Bursting out of Feltham, West London in 1983 and inspired by some of The Meteors' earliest gigs, Guana Batz quickly established themselves as leading lights of the early UK Psychobilly scene and excellent live performers. Their first gig was in January 1983, offering home support to King Kurt at Feltham Football Club. They were an immediate success and before the number of gigs they had played were in double digits they were supporting the mighty Bo Diddley at London's Lyceum.

The original line-up featured singer/guitarist Pip Hancox, guitarist Stuart Osborne, drummer Dave 'Diddle' Turner and double-bass player Mick Wigfall. Like most Psychobilly bands their early days were a transitional period and this line-up did not release any material until Wigfall was ditched in favour of ex-Meteors electric bassist Mick White. The band had attracted the attention of Big Beat Records which led to their first seven-inch vinyl 'Your So Fine', a four track EP released in 1983. This featured the Batz 'electric bass' line-up and showcased a band still forming what would become the Guana Batz' trademark style and it contains the punkiest recordings among the band's back catalogue.

The following year saw Guana Batz appear on another Big Beat single, 'The Cave c/w 'Werewolf Blues'. Like its predecessor, the single gained sizable UK radio airplay, particularly on John Peel's Radio One show which at the time was the benchmark of all UK independent music. Despite the relative success of both these singles, or perhaps because of it, what followed next was a long journey towards the Batz' debut LP – a trip that excited but also infuriated many fans who could not get enough of the band and desperately hankered for an album full of stomping tunes. The band had made further appearances on vinyl with their own composition 'Just Love Me' on the legendary compilation 'Rockabilly Psychosis & The Garage Disease' in 1984 and the track 'Cannibal Run' on Anagram Records early Psychobilly/Indie compilation LP 'Blood on the Cats', but their long-player was nowhere to be seen.

While the band were enjoying this reasonable success on vinyl they were garnering a far greater reputation for their blistering live performances. With their live sound, or 'Modern Rockabilly' as they once referred to it, they were distinctly different to The Meteors and King Kurt and set the template for

THE PIONEERS — HELL'S BENT ON ROCKIN'

the hard slappin', hard rockin' four-piece that many Psychobilly bands subsequently followed. They also went some way to forming other key trends of the Psychobilly movement such as excessive tattooing, wearing short trousers at gigs and near-nakedness in public.

Pip and Dave Diddle rarely wore their tops beyond playing the first few tracks of their live set and the flamboyant singer in particular disrobed almost entirely throughout the band's career onstage. Rather than being a fashion statement, or a chance to display tattoos, near nudity was often a necessity as Guana Batz performances were often so frantic that sweat dripped out of every gig – from the band and from the punters. The Guana Batz put everything into their gigs and the fans could (literally) feel it.

Around 1984 the band experienced two key events which would push their career much further. Mick White moved on and the band reverted to the use of double-bass when they recruited former Ricochets slapper Sam Sardi. Sam was a well-respected bass man and The Ricochets had been one of the main influences on many Psychobilly bands since their emergence from the UK Rockabilly scene of the late 1970s. This was the first real classic line-up of The Guana Batz and one which cemented the 'Guana Beat' and led to far greater success.

The first recording from this incarnation of the Batz was to be a live recording, and where better to capture the band than at their spiritual home – The Klub Foot. 'Stomping At The Klub Foot' was the first in a series of big-selling live albums recorded in the 1980s at the Clarendon Hotel Ballroom, or 'Klub Foot' as it was known at weekends. The first LP captured a live gig featuring The Guana Batz alongside Restless, Thee Milkshakes and The Sting-Rays. With Restless waving the flag for pure Rockabilly and Thee Milkshakes and The Sting-Rays representing the emerging Trash scene, The Guana Batz were obviously a firm favourite amongst that evening's sizable Psychobilly population. It was during this recording that Pip confirmed that there would be a Guana Batz album, but as 1984 drew to a close the long awaited album had yet to appear.

In June of 1985 The Guana Batz' debut album finally materialised as the suitably titled 'Held Down To Vinyl... At Last'. It appeared on the ID label and was only the company's fourth release after LPs by The Meteors, Richard Hell and The Anti Nowhere League. If creating demand by the LP's belated appearance in record stores was the goal, then it succeeded as 'Held Down...' leapt to the top of the UK independent charts. This was a sizable achievement back in the days when truly independent labels and distributors had an important place in the music, unlike much of today's music-biz output in which the notion of an 'Indie' label often appears to be simply an imprint or sub-division of one of the major players.

Though expectation alone may have driven the album to the number one spot it was the LP's quality and broad appeal which maintained its position in the Indie charts. At a time when most Psychobilly albums operated mostly at one pace (mental!) with the odd slow tune jammed in to give listeners a breather, the Guana Batz' debut started slow with 'Down On The Line' and 'Got No Money' and never really broke sweat until the end of Side One. Though the Batz did not deliver the flat-out stompfest many expected, tracks such as 'Can't Take The Pressure', 'King Rat' and 'Bust Out' kept the pace up admirably.

This combination of styles showed a certain confidence from a band who were delivering a measured album and not just a blast through their live set captured one day in the studio. Though many bands have benefited from this technique, The Guana Batz appeared to maintain the quality control on all their releases, including their debut. With this determination they also delivered an album of equal interest to many Rockabillies, Indie fans and nosy music lovers who wanted an introduction to this 'thing called Psychobilly'. It also placed the band in the trio of Psychobilly bands, along with The Meteors and King Kurt, who non-believers had actually heard of and they remain to this day one of the names many people drop when trying to explain the roots of the wreckin' genre.

Before and after the album's release, The Guana Batz cemented their reputation as an ear-flattening, high-quality rockin' combo by constant touring across the UK and Europe. They regularly visited many

HELL'S BENT ON ROCKIN' THE PIONEERS

Pip from The Guana Batz, live in Portsmouth in 1986 (Jo Jackson)

toilets, dives and backroom boozers up and down the country before quickly graduating to headline gigs at many respected rock venues, festivals and student unions. For the uninitiated, or the faithful, the last half of the 1980s offered punters the very real opportunity to catch the band live somewhere close to home – even in the more isolated areas of the country.

Thankfully a visual record of this period remains in availability on some form other than the booze-soaked memories of old Psychobillies. A DVD, released in the UK by Cherry Red, features two archive films of Guana Batz – 'Live Over London' from around the 'Held Down...' period and 'Still Sweating After All These Years' dating from a later gig with the same line-up. Both concert films capture the band at their peak and illustrate the band's live mania in contrast to their more measured studio recordings.

Despite all this touring, the band did not let too much time pass before delivering their second long-player for ID Records 'Loan Sharks' (1986). If you accept that under two years is pretty speedy on the Guana Batz time scale then in 1986 Batz fans were to witness a mighty flow of vinyl releases in comparison to the band's previous release schedule. 'Loan Sharks' was to be another big success for the band worldwide, even though it had the audacity to peak at number two in the UK Independent charts. Nonetheless, this fact was small potatoes as chart positions were never of any great worth to any Psychobilly act within a record industry that rarely gave a fuck for the genre.

Their second long-player was a far more polished album than 'Held Down', from its well photographed cover artwork to the sound of a band who were water-tight after extensive touring and more at home in the studio than before. Again the band delivered some speaker-rattling rockers such as 'Piledriver Boogie', 'Slippin' In' and 'I'm Weird', alongside three choice covers and a surprisingly radio-friendly track. The covers were 'Shake Your Money Maker', The Swingin' Blue Jeans 'Hippy Hippy Shake' and Chuck Berry's teenage make-out anthem 'No Particular Place To Go' (accompanied by a few lyrical tweaks by the Batz).

Between them, these originals had elements of Blues, Beat and Rock'n'Roll – styles which illustrated the band's own unique sound and perhaps explains the Guana Batz appeal inside and outside of the Psychobilly scene. Though these influences, and a variety of others, were present in many bands who stalked the Psycho-scene of the time one track from 'Loan Sharks' really broke the mould.

'Radio Sweetheart' was a chirpy, shuffling, good-time Rockabilly love song with a crystal clear production which could easily have seen the Batz following The Stray Cats, The Polecats and The Jets onto 'Top of the Pops' and the British charts had it been released as a single. No seven-inch ever appeared, which is probably just as well as it would undoubtedly have left the Batz open to cries of 'sellout' from the hard-core Psychobilly fraternity. Restless had already had their fingers burnt with a similarly pop style makeover on their album 'After Midnight'. Regardless of the commercial potential of 'Radio Sweetheart' the song was, like the evenly paced opening tracks on 'Held Down...', yet another

THE PIONEERS   HELL'S BENT ON ROCKIN'

Guana Batz on the road (Mason Storm Archive).

firm signal from the Guana Batz that they would refuse to be strait-jacketed by many of their fans' desire for tracks of high-speed dementia with no real variety.

For The Guana Batz' fanbase there were other vinyl treats on offer, especially after the long wait for 'Held Down…'. 1986 also saw the release of the twelve-inch single 'Seethrough', a three track offering which also featured the Batz version of 'Batman' (another fine TV tribute which perfectly matched their legendary live rendition of 'Joe 90'). Two of the band's extra live tracks from their original 'Stomping At The Klub Foot' recording, 'You're So Fine' and 'No Particular Place To Go', also made an appearance on the double LP 'Stomping At The Klub Foot: Vol. 3&4'. This was an unusual release designed to capitalise on the growing popularity of this series of live recordings and it featured one album worth of new material and a collection of unused cuts from bands who had appeared on the previous two Klub Foot albums.

The band finally released a cut from an album with the title track 'Loan Sharks' getting a single release but before this they released another single which again highlighted either the band's refusal to be typecast or was another stab at mainstream success. 'I'm On Fire' was a Bruce Springsteen cover that was distinctly rocked by the Batz but not in the same way that Demented Are Go would mutate The Osmonds 'Crazy Horses' into a Psychobilly masterpiece.

The Guana Batz version of 'I'm On Fire' was undoubtedly a stomping overhaul of the original but one which even 'The Boss' may have approved of. This was a brave move as many Psychobillies who had emerged from the early Punk scene would surely have regarded Springsteen as an overblown Rock superstar worthy only of contempt. However, once again The Guana Batz had almost crossed over into the mainstream without isolating the Psychobilly faithful – a remarkable feat.

After the success of both albums and yet more consistent touring, including trips to South America and Japan, a recording of the band live in concert was the obvious choice for the next album and 'Live Over London' appeared in 1987, on ID. Captured in all their sweaty glory at the 'Klub Foot' (where else?) this album served as a welcome memento to anyone who had worked up a sweat in the wreckin' pit at a Batz gig. It also offered fans an opportunity to hear the band live without the usual background noise of grunting, fists pounding flesh and the occasional snap of broken bones.

Guana Batz guitarist Stuart Osborne (Jo Jackson).

Despite being a classic Guana Batz performance this line-up featured former Meteors drummer Steve 'Ginger' Meadham, who had been drafted in to cover for an injured Dave Diddle. Ginger had already played with Sam Sardi in The Ricochets and easily fitted into the Batz' live show. The album also served as a quick fix for a record label desperate for more Guana Batz product and a chance for the handful of Psychobillies who had yet to catch the band in concert to experience the band's unique live sound.

Guana Batz setlist from 1986 (Jo Jackson).

HELL'S BENT ON ROCKIN'   THE PIONEERS

1988 saw the Guana Batz release their third studio album 'Rough Edges', which was to be their final offering on ID Records along with their final ID seven-inch 'Rock This Town'. Though probably not as successful an album as their previous offerings, 'Rough Edges' did include many tracks that would remain Batz favourites including 'Streetwise' and 'Love Generator'. Yet again there were some choice cover versions in the form of Buddy Holly's 'Rock Around With Ollie Vee, Baker Knight's 'Bring My Cadillac Back' and an excellent Guana Batz rendition of Elvis' 'One Night'. 'Rough Edges' was something of a progression for the band, showcasing their developing songwriting and recording skills and combining new elements to their sound while still sounding like a resolutely rockin' Batz release.

This album not only drew to a close a very successful period of the band's career with ID Records but also saw the end of another era as drummer, and founding member of the group, Dave 'Diddle' Turner decided to leave the band and focus on his building job and his girlfriend. The band's constant, and often hectic, touring schedule was cited as the reason for his departure. Unfortunately, Dave would never return to the band as he died in the Summer of 2001 from a stroke, leaving his family, friends, former bandmates and loyal Batz fans shocked and saddened. However, at the time despite Dave's departure and the move from ID, the Guana Batz were about to move on regardless into the 1990s.

The Krewmen are unique amongst the early pioneers of Psychobilly as their influence on the scene remains huge but they are a band who have operated almost independently of the scene, sticking with the same record label for almost twenty years and pursuing their own, constantly evolving, sound regardless of musical changes in the genre.

Perhaps their fierce independence comes from the fact that the band were seasoned performers long before their 1986 debut album 'The Adventures Of The Krewmen' which is another cornerstone of early Psychobilly. Originally formed in 1982, the Surrey-based outfit were initially a Rockabilly covers band called The Starlites but even then they stood out amongst the huge number of bands peddling the same thing at the time. So much so that they caught the attention of the producers of 'Elvis – The Musical', a stage show which hired them to play as The King's band and they entered a period of professional touring across the UK, USA and Canada.

After their spell of musical theatre the original drummer and bass player split from the band leaving Tony on his own. He recruited drummer Jimmy Fahy along with guitarist/vocalist Carl Sonny Leland and moved onto bass himself. With this line-up reshuffle the band continued their career as a Rockabilly act but now began writing their own material far more and developing their sound in a Bluesier direction. During this period they released two singles, the 'What You Are Today' 7" and the 12" 'Ramblin''. These records sounded far different to the band's now legendary Psychobilly style and recording sessions from this time appeared many years later on the CD 'Klassic Tracks From 1985' (2000) on Lost Moment Records.

Although an accomplished Rockabilly act, group leader Tony McMillan could not see a way forward for their rockin' blues and began to look to the blossoming Psychobilly scene for inspiration. Carl and Jimmy did not share Tony's enthusiasm and McMillan once again found himself with fistful of songs, the band's name and not much else. Seeking to pursue a wilder direction and focus on his own writing and producing skills, McMillan recruited a new singer – Mark Cole, Dominic Parr on drums and double-bass player Jason Thornton (leaving Tony free to return to guitar). The surviving original member then prepared Lost Moment for a new direction, far beyond the sound which had secured them a record deal in the first place.

With this new line-up and direction everything clicked and The Krewmen went on to create a trio of Psychobilly albums which remain legendary. 'The Adventures Of The Krewmen' (1986) was an assured debut from its striking comic book cover to its collection of fine tracks (all penned by McMillan and Cole) and it featured a drastically different sound to their previous two incarnations. The Krewmen toured furiously to promote the album and the creative partnership continued on their second album 'Sweet Dreams' (1987) which contained mostly McMillan and Cole compositions and both the guitarist and

The Sharks; crossing over in 1982 (Alan Wilson).

vocalist produced the album. 'Sweet Dreams' fitted seamlessly alongside 'Adventures…' and was a frantic and powerful collection of songs.

With two albums available, the band headed off on their first major European tour taking in over eighty gigs to some very enthusiastic audiences. Amidst this lengthy bout of road fever, The Krewmen's third album 'Into The Tomb' was released. Again this LP was warmly received and had its own individual style but the McMillan/Cole writing partnership had withered to only one track and three cover versions were employed to bolster up the album. This trio of covers ('Should I Stay Or Should I Go', 'Solid Gold Easy Action' and the Jewish wedding anthem 'Hava Nagila') were well done and not an unusually large amount for a standard Psychobilly album but were noticeable as The Krewmen were noted up to that point for their mainly original compositions. The cracks were beginning to show not only in the studio but also on tour.

Early in the European tour the band had agreed that Cole's attitude did no favours for The Krewmen or their fans and by the end of the tour the band were once again a trio with Tony as vocalist/guitarist.

The band continued for over a year as a three-piece then drummer Dominic and bass player Jason began to feel the strain of The Krewmen's constant touring and recording and they left together in 1988. McMillan had no intention of letting The Krewmen story end there and brought in drummer Steve Piper and double-bassist Mark Burke (now better known as The Phantom Rockers mainman).

The Krewmen's fourth album, 'Plague Of The Dead', was released in 1988 and preceded by two four-track 12" singles, 'My Generation' and 'Do You Wanna Touch Me'. Both titles were covers, of The Who and Gary Glitter, and they also featured on the album. Although Mark was credited on the album, the studio recording featured Tony McMillan on bass and it was not long before Burke was replaced by Graham Grant (Demented Are Go). This line-up toured to promote 'Plague Of The Dead' including gigs in America in 1989.

Around this time, U.S. record label Skyclad licensed a dozen tracks from Lost Moment's Krewmen back catalogue and created the album 'Curse Of The Graveyard Demon'. Had the band relied on purely American Psychobilly support they would probably have starved but The Krewmen (as they have throughout their career) always drew fans from many musical genres and once gig-goers realised that a double-bass does not always signify another bunch of Stray Cats copyists the band's reputation began to grow in the States.

Things changed again when the band returned from America and Graham Grant was replaced on bass by Paul Oxley (ex-Radiacs). As the band stabilised they began moving in a heavier direction which resulted in the 1990 album 'Power'. This was indeed a powerful album with elements of Punk, Hardcore and Metal which (with some foresight) suited the fracturing Psychobilly scene of the 1990s and The Krewmen's fans outside of the genre.

By now the band had played across America, Japan and Europe and were still looking for new countries to conquer. Just when everyone thought they were getting to grips with the band's direction The Krewmen delivered their ominously titled album 'The Final Adventures Of The Krewmen' (1991). The album title left many wondering if this was the beginning of the end for The Krewmen and the following years did little to confirm or deny this.

In 1992, Steve Piper strode to the front of the stage as rhythm guitarist and Tony Gallagher became the band's drummer. Despite many fans regarding the McMillan/Cole/Thornton/Parr line-up as the definitive one, from 1992 to the present the later four-piece have played a lot longer, and arguably with greater harmony, than before. The Krewmen have slowed down considerably since then and though the band have toured sporadically all over the world new material has not been forthcoming.

1994 saw the release of the Lost Moment collection 'The Krewmen Singled Out', bringing many of their non-album tracks together in one handy package. A new deal with Lost Moment, for four albums, was announced in 1998 and a new album was promised which never materialised. Around this time the band referred to their own schedule as: "one Psychobilly festival each year in Europe".

Surprisingly, given their loyal fanbase, The Krewmen have failed to capitalise both on the recent resurgence of Psychobilly and the power of the internet as a promotional tool. Nonetheless, as they have never officially 'thrown in the towel' a whole host of old fans and curious newcomers may yet have the opportunity to witness a Krewmen revival. When Mark 'Mad Dog' Cole reappeared on the scene, late in 2006, rumours were rife that the McMillan/Cole partnership was to be reunited but these murmurings were quickly squashed by McMillan's management. However, Cole returned to the live scene in 2007 with a spot at Germany's 'Kings Of Psychobilly' event.

While many of the classic UK Psychobilly groups of the early 1980s were from London or its surrounding area (even Demented Are Go made the move to the big smoke as their fame grew), the wild, wild, West of England produced two major acts who left an indelible mark on the Psychobilly scene – The Sharks and Frenzy, another hard-slappin' trio who would become mainstays of the musical style that dare not say its name.

In August 1983, Steve Whitehouse, now no longer a member of The Sharks, got together with his old friend guitarist Simon Brand and formed Frenzy. With drummer Merv Pepler on board the band were

THE PIONEERS

soon up and running. Their first release was the 'Robot Riot' single on 7" and 12", which included two songs which rapidly became early Psychobilly anthems; the title track and 'Cry or Die'. The extended version of this release also included the song 'Torment', a title which would have important significance for guitarist Simon Brand some years later.

Although a new name on the scene, many had witnessed Steve Whitehouse's powerful slapping with The Sharks and his earlier group The Shakin' Quiffs so it was no surprise that Frenzy rapidly gained a large and enthusiastic following which soon saw them bypass support slots to become regular headliners at a growing number of Psychobilly hoe-downs. Frenzy also enjoyed a certain live infamy by being one of the first bands out of the 'Neo' scene who were quickly growing too 'Psycho' for many Rockabilly clubs, an early sign that Psychobilly was really establishing itself as a completely new musical genre.

An album deal with Nervous followed soon after and led to the 'Hall of Mirrors' album in 1984 but before the record's release Simon Brand was on the move, to make plans for his seminal Psychobilly group Torment, and he was quickly replaced by Cavan 'Kev' Saunders. Brand had left after a gig in Holland in the Spring of 1984 and Saunders was initially approached purely to stand in for one concert that June at a major Dutch music festival. During rehearsals for the date Saunders' guitar style, honed during his previous ten year residences in a variety of bar and club bands, fitted the band well and it was agreed that he would become a full-time member of the band.

Frenzy's debut featured Brand on tracks such as 'Frenzy' but for the album cover and the majority of the recordings, Saunders was in the picture. Along with Brand's contributions the album also included re-recordings of the tracks 'Skeleton Rock' and 'Ghost Train' which had both appeared on The Shark's debut album. With further vinyl appearances on a host of compilations including the groundbreaking 'Zorch Factor One', and almost a residency at the Klub Foot, Frenzy soon became known as one of the top, unashamedly, Psychobilly bands of the early 1980s.

Midway through the decade, things really got moving within the band and alongside their popular Klub Foot shows they played many of the Capital's other major rockin' venues such as The 100 Club, Dingwalls and the lesser known Psychobilly haunt The Headstone in Harrow. Home gigs in the West Country were relatively rare but they were a hard-working unit and never afraid to take their live performance up and down the country, including many towns often ignored by many touring bands.

Though their reception from UK audiences was warm, in Europe it was almost ecstatic. While the band were largely ignored by the British press, even when their single 'I See Red' was a top five UK Indie hit, in countries such as Holland, Germany and Finland they were front page news. Unfortunately, this was to prove to be the same story for many other British Psychobilly bands – almost barren press coverage at home compared to acres of newsprint devoted to them in Europe. Frenzy even appeared on a Dutch television show, miming frantically to 'Nobody's Business', at a time when a UK TV appearance would have been out of the question in Britain due to the dual music television stranglehold of 'Top of The Pops' and 'The Tube'.

Although 'I See Red' also gained favourable airplay on a variety of radio stations, including many of the evening shows on Radio 1, ID Records would not consider the release of a red-vinyl 12" version of the single which the band believed would have promotional potential. This decision may have prevented the record from pushing that little bit further and crossing Frenzy over from Indie to mainstream chart success. Nonetheless, the band were too busy to ponder over what might have been and instead focused their energy into continued touring and their second album. 'Clockwork Toy' was released in 1986 on ID Records and saw Frenzy at an early creative peak. After countless gigs their sound was tight, each member of the band was writing new material and they were occasionally employing session players to strengthen their line-up.

After the release of the album the band were getting so many offers to tour across Europe that a major decision was made. Kev Saunders remembers: "We decided to turn fully professional in Summer '86, we were starting to get bigger tours. Instead of two or three gigs in Holland or Germany we were now starting to get offers of tours in Scandinavia." Unfortunately, this increased workload meant that

HELL'S BENT ON ROCKIN' — THE PIONEERS

drummer Merv Pepler could no longer continue with the band as he was still serving an apprenticeship and would be unable to take more time off to tour. Merv's replacement was Adam Seviour, a drummer connected to the band from the studio where they recorded the demo which had led to their debut album deal with Nervous.

With Adam on board they blazed a trail across Europe, adding Belgium, Switzerland, France and Italy to their touring schedule. Back in Finland they even found themselves alongside the unlikely company of Maxi Priest and Katrina & the Waves at an open-air festival in front of a crowd of around 20,000 people. In Holland they were besieged by autograph hunters and mobbed by fans – a far cry from their early days in the UK bundling their gear out the back door of some sweaty pub past a few pissed-up Psychobilly well wishers. To accompany this wealth of touring throughout 1987 was the Nervous album 'Live At The 100 Club', featuring a recording from the London hotspot made the previous year.

What happened next in the Frenzy story became a matter of some controversy. While Frenzy's position as a premiere live attraction never diminished, their third album 'Sally's Pink Bedroom' was received with mixed emotions by critics and fans. Kev Saunders explains the background to this troubled release: "We wanted to get out of our contract with ID Records, and one of the plans was to record an album of cover versions. We didn't want to give them any more new material but were contractually obliged to record another album for them. In the end a compromise was reached, we would record an album of half originals, half covers. This was the 'Sally's Pink Bedroom' album and there still seems to be some differences of opinion amongst people, regarding the content of this album. As well as reasons of contract fulfilment, we also wanted to branch out in different musical directions. Steve was using bass guitar on some of the tracks and we were using session players in the studio as well as live."

In 1987, with Psychobilly still in its formative stages, the album was a relatively bold (and risky) step. Many fans could just about handle a boot-stomping cover version of the likes of Sweet, Mud or Motorhead but Frenzy's choice to cover tracks from the likes of Roxy Music and Wall of Voodoo raised a few eyebrows. This was a time when many music fans stuck rigidly to music of similar genres and even the use of keyboards, beyond the beat-driven rumble of a Hammond organ, was viewed

Frenzy's Steve Whitehouse... slappin' legend (Jan Van Hal).

THE PIONEERS

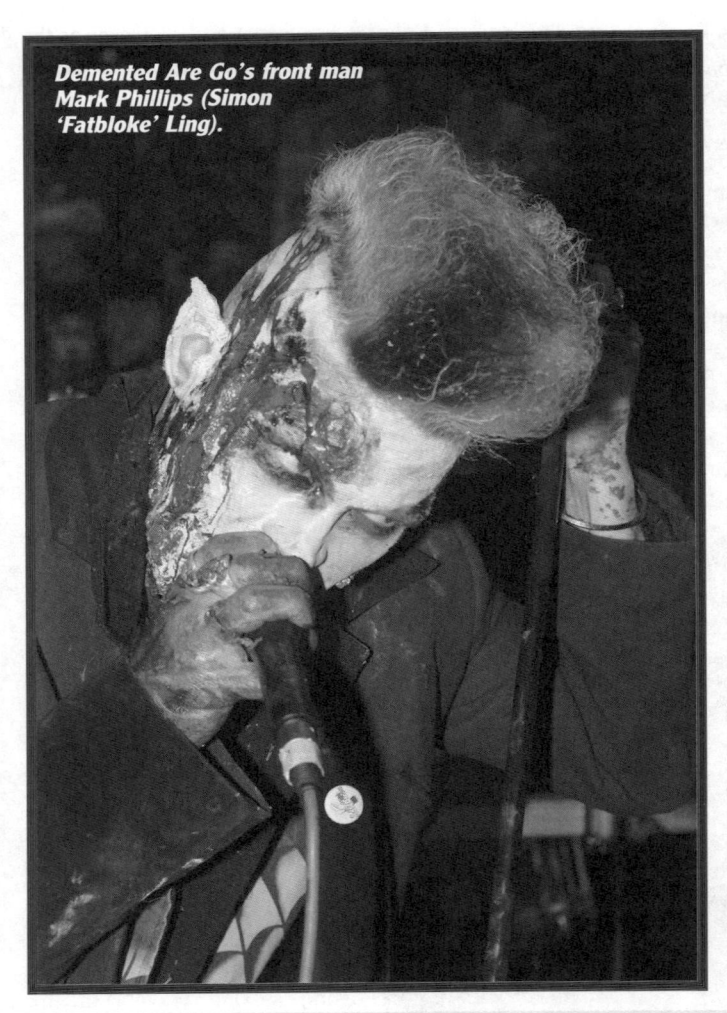

HELL'S BENT ON ROCKIN'

Demented Are Go's front man Mark Phillips (Simon 'Fatbloke' Ling).

with suspicion so the band's synth-driven version of 'Love Is The Drug' left many pondering over Frenzy's future direction.

In retrospect, 'Sally's Pink Bedroom' was never intended to be seen as their third studio album proper but despite being the release which simply brought their contract to an end with ID it also hinted that the band were finding the Psychobilly genre too restricting. Steve and Kev especially had years of experience between them in writing, playing and recording and there is no doubt that 'Sally's Pink Bedroom' showcased a far more polished, and commercial, Frenzy sound. Things were changing but by the end of 1987 the unfortunate loss of a booking agency deal saw a sizable number of gigs disappear — after a tour of Germany, Kev Saunders left the band and Frenzy were effectively in retirement.

The following year, Steve Whitehouse got the Frenzy story in motion once again. The release of the Jettisoundz video 'Just Passin' Through' in 1988, featuring a live recording from the Barrel Organ in Birmingham and a promo for 'Clockwork Toy', got Steve, Adam and Kev back together for a viewing after six months in the wilderness. The video encouraged the band to resume proceedings but with Kev unwilling to return to the Psychobilly scene, Steve and Adam began a search for a new guitarist. After some unsuccessful auditions, including one with former member Simon Brand, Frenzy settled on ex-Rapids guitarist Spike.

After a few gigs, work began on the fourth Frenzy studio album 'This Is The Fire'. Though this album would see both Frenzy's songwriting and recording mature it was to be a fractured creation comprising of a variety of sessions and personnel mainly due to Steve's involvement as Restless' replacement bass-player. For some time, Steve would divide his touring and recording work between both bands. The earliest recording of the album took place in Adam Seviour's absence using electronic drums accompanying Steve and Spike. Further recordings involved Shaun Kirkpatrick, owner of Kirk Studios in Somerset where the album was recorded, joining Spike on guitar then replacing him completely when Spike moved on before the album's completion. As well as the digital percussion used on these sessions, ex-Sharks' drummer Hodge contributed to two tracks as well as replacing Adam at further Frenzy gigs.

Despite the 'Frankenstein' nature of the album's recording over a relatively long period of time, Steve Whitehouse's vision shone through and upon its release by Rage Records in early 1990 Frenzy found

HELL'S BENT ON ROCKIN'   THE PIONEERS

themselves at the receiving end of a number of good reviews and further offers of gigs. However, as the band had evolved during the creation of 'This Is The Fire' a stabilised line-up was a priority before Frenzy could move into the 1990s with any confidence.

Although arriving a little later than most of the pioneering acts, one band have left an indelible mark on the Psychobilly scene. The Demented Are Go story is a hard beast to pin down. It started around 1982 and continues to this day but along the way lies a chequered history of revolving band members, special guests, booze-soaked memories, hazy recollections of gigs, fights, nights in jail, drugs, slugs, mugs, jugs and an infamous Osmonds song. At the centre of this maelstrom is lead singer and songwriter Mark Phillips (aka Spark), a character who can often be responsible for so much chaos offstage yet still deliver 100% pure showmanship at almost every gig. Demented Are Go have offered a blueprint for a depraved Psychobilly lifestyle yet have rarely left their fans short-changed with disappointing no-shows or sub-standard performances.

This tortured tale begins back in the early 1980s when young Punk Ant Thomas and his cousin Mark Phillips first got together in Cardiff and started a band influenced by the music they enjoyed, mainly Punk, Rock'n'Roll and 1960s Garage. Initially Mark was the drummer and Ant was up front but this soon changed into what was to become the partnership that forged the legendary Demented Are Go sound. This original line-up seems hard to imagine as Ant's machine-gun drumbeat and Mark Phillips' unique, and often imitated, vocal style are such an outstanding feature of the band's recording output.

A move to London was required and with guitarist Dick 'no relation' Thomas on board things slowly got rolling, especially as Dick was a more accomplished band member and one who knew how to get things moving on the rockin' scene. The band's first vinyl appearance was on the 1985 Nervous compilation LP 'Hell's Bent On Rockin''. Alongside good company from the likes of The Sharks, The Meteors and Frenzy, Demented showcased two tracks: 'One Sharp Knife' and 'Rubber Rock'. While most bands on the brink of an album deal would probably be tempted to keep all their best tunes for their debut long-player, Demented had such a growing catalogue of future Psychobilly anthems that they let these two quality tunes make their appearance on this compilation. This was probably just as

Demented Are Go join the Fury roster (Dell Richardson).

well as their next offering would not see the light of day till almost eighteen months after 'Hell's Bent...' hit the streets.

With ID Records growing roster of top-class talent, such as The Meteors, Guana Batz and Restless, it was no surprise when Demented Are Go inked a deal with the label. This resulted in their groundbreaking debut album 'In Sickness and In Health', which was released in 1986. Groundbreaking is not a word to be used lightly but the album was exceptional in a number of ways. At a time when many new bands were emerging, a lot of Psychobilly debut recordings were often bashed out on a limited schedule and a tight budget. The majority of these records maintained the band's energy and excitement but many often lost a little of the band's live power even when played through the finest stereo systems. Demented's debut was a bit more assured, produced by esteemed Psychobilly and Trash knob twiddler Mickey Mutant, it featured a combination of instruments including the use of both electric and acoustic guitars, electric bass, double-bass and even fiddle.

The album also created a whole new aspect of lyrical perversion in Psychobilly which has remained a huge influence on many bands to this day. Though The Meteors were, once again, at the forefront of this movement with the deliciously dark 'Sick Things' from their 'Wreckin' Crew' album, Demented took smut, sleaze and dirty doings to new heights and almost every track on their first album details some form of sexual depravity. Tracks like 'Pervy In The Park', ' (I Was Born On A) Busted Hymen' and 'Rubber Buccaneer' tell their own story but on closer inspection the likes of 'PVC Chair' and 'Pickled And Preserved' also unveil high-levels of top-grade grindhouse sleaze. Even the folks down at the record plant got under the influence and scratched lewd statements into the album's vinyl run-out groove with the inscriptions 'I lost my virginity to a rubber giraffe' on Side One and 'I lost my virginity to a vacuum cleaner' on Side Two.

The album cover, and inside artwork, also hinted that this new form of Psychobilly perversion was not to be a passing phase for Demented. With Mark Phillips in full drag and make-up as a blushing bride alongside 'Vicar' Ant Thomas and Dick as the groom, many Psychobillies were wondering what the fuck this band were all about, especially at a time when most bands on the scene boasted little more than a splash of hairspray and a new tattoo in the form of stagewear. The inside cover also hinted that Phillips' 'slap' was not just an isolated incident for the album cover, with more photos of the man in make-up and an even more bizarre peek at the band onstage with an array of dildoes, rubber dolls and fetish wear. On top of all that Side Two kicks off with 'Transvestite Blues', a track that surely resulted in a number of straitlaced rockers initially sticking this LP to the back of their collection.

In retrospect, this all seems to be a case of the band fucking with their early fans' expectations of what a Psychobilly band 'should' look like. However, no one could argue with the consistent quality of every track and the clear, well-rounded production that left Psychobilly stereos across Europe vibrating in rockin' ecstasy. This steamrolling sound was not just the creation of a trio and the album also featured the short-lived input of Ray Thompson on double-bass and the fiddle of Simon Cohen, a gent who would return to the studio with Demented and also produce occasional artwork for the band. Guesting on double-bass for one track, 'Rubber Love', was Torment's Simon Crowfoot, a short-lived member of an early Demented line-up and friend of the band from the old 'West Country Showcase' gigs which had featured both Demented and Torment alongside Frenzy.

Their debut album obviously brought the band to a far wider audience, even though before its release a huge buzz was already building for Demented Are Go on the Psychobilly grapevine. Their unique sound also attracted followers outside the Psychobilly fraternity particularly amongst many Punks, a scene that would later keep the band going when Psychobilly faced near extinction in the late 1990s. This all resulted in a healthy touring schedule for the band throughout the UK and Europe – so healthy that their follow-up album would take almost two years to appear.

'Kicked Out Of Hell' was Demented Are Go's second full-length release and it, once again, appeared on ID Records. Within two years much had changed in the group – Dick Thomas and Ray Thompson were long gone and Simon Crowfoot's time was now monopolised by the success of Torment. Ant

Thomas and Mark Phillips were all that remained from the 'In Sickness & In Health' period apart from a recurring special guest appearance from Simon Cohen on fiddle. Filling in the gaps on double-bass and guitar were Graeme Grant and Lex Luther respectively. Though future line-up changes were on the cards, 'Get Off My Land' Grant and 'Lightning' Lex would both play a major part in the Demented saga which was about to unfold.

Once again, 'Kicked Out Of Hell' was a well produced, full-bodied creation dripping in sleaze and perversion. Tracks such as 'Human Slug', 'Cripple In The Woods' and 'Sick Spasmoid' probably tweaked the bad-taste-ometer more than any other Psychobilly tunes (apart from The Coffin Nails' 'Myra Hindley') and 'Rubber Plimsoles' popped up at the end of Side One, just to show that the band's healthy preoccupation with all things kinky was still evident. Allegedly most of the tracks on the album, aside from the covers of 'Jet Tone Boogie' and 'Old Black Joe', were penned by candlelight in one of the squats which some of the band shared in 1987. Whatever the circumstances, it was a productive session which produced an album's worth of high-quality compositions. Many of the tracks became Demented signature tunes and the success of the album fired the band into more gigs across Europe and beyond.

Not that he needed much persuasion but years of living on the road as Psychobilly royalty had turned lead singer Sparky into a booze'n'drug soaked party animal. While many members of the band, past and present, have been able to hold their own, Sparky often took things to extremes. Though many of his antics have now been passed into legend it would be impossible, and probably slanderous, to list them all.

Some tales have often been wildly exaggerated by Chinese whispers and half-truths but it would be safe to suggest that many are either true or derived from actual events. Amongst them – stories of shit throwing, ass-pinching, vacuum cleaner blow-jobs, bust-ups, bust-outs, fucking, fighting, fire-starting and puking have all helped to create a legendary portrait of Demented Are Go's frontman. This kind of recklessness is not to everyone's taste and some time after the release of 'Kicked Out Of Hell', Graeme Grant and Lex Luther both left the band leaving things all quiet on the Demented front for a few months.

After this brief gap in the Demented saga, Mark Phillips appeared on Ant Thomas' doorstep with guitarist Mike 'Lord Adonis Claypole Montcrief VII' and bass player Bill 'Doody Mindwrencher'. A three-day stretch had been booked in the studio and in that time Demented Are Go's third album was created from scratch and recorded. Simon Cohen again made a fiddle contribution on his 'Splattervarius' and a mysterious character, known only as Fink, provided backing vocals. The result of this studio-based drug'n'booze fest was the mini LP 'The Day The Earth Spat Blood'. It was released in 1989 by Link Records under the imprint 'Chuck Flintstone Presents…', a series of albums overseen by the Frantic Flintstones frontman.

While by no means classic Demented Are Go, it was still an accomplished effort, albeit one that looked and sounded like pure chaos. The cover especially caused most confusion with its almost illegible writing and listings of bizarre stage names for the band such as Sparky Retard DeVille for Phillips and Anton the Impaler for Thomas. The front of the album also credited the band under the alternative banner of 'Demented Are Go Present The Demon Teds'. To add to the dementia, eight tracks are listed on the cover while seven appear on the record label – although one of the tracks is a three part 'Warp Mix' of 'Now She's Dead' (!!?).

With a re-recording of one of the band's earliest tracks, 'One Sharp Knife', thrown in to encourage flashbacks, this album left many fans reeling and wondering who was in the band and what direction they were heading in. What was on the cards was the ditching of guitarist Mike 'Lord Adonis' in favour of the return of Demented's classic stringbender Lex Luther. Though this album shot the band out of the 1980s in a confused state the Demented Are Go story was just beginning and as the 1980s drifted into the 1990s a revitalised, and relatively stable, Demented would be back on the road.

While The Meteors, King Kurt, Guana Batz, Frenzy and The Krewmen offered a variety of different mutated hybrids of Rockabilly, the Rockabilly scene itself also gave birth to a host of new bands in the late 1970s/early 1980s who would become closely associated with the Psychobilly scene. While many

THE PIONEERS

HELL'S BENT ON ROCKIN'

would argue pointlessly over the dividing line between Neo-Rockabilly and Psychobilly there were a number of 'Neo' bands who remained true to their own rockin' scene whilst attracting a sizable following of Psychobillies. Though many early Psycho bands and their followers emerged from the Rockabilly scene, there were also a first generation of Psychobillies who had appeared from Punk, Mod or Skin backgrounds and had no real appreciation of true Rockabilly beyond knowing who The Stray Cats were.

Nonetheless, there remain a number of Rockabilly acts who are so closely associated with the scene that no record of the genre could possibly ignore them. Bands such as Restless, The Sharks, The Caravans, The Wigsville Spliffs, The Rapids, The Pharaohs and The Ricochets all possessed a hard-edge Rockabilly sound which attracted large numbers of the growing Psychobilly population, especially from 1981-83 when the notion of

Restless front man, Mark Harman (Jan Van Hal).

'pure' Psychobilly was still in its infancy. These bands also possessed their own home-grown Psychobilly following which included original Rockabillies who had been 'mutated' by the Psycho-sound.

Of all these bands, Restless were perhaps the most warmly welcomed by the Psycho-nation. The band were initially centred around the Ipswich-based Harman brothers, Mark and Paul. With Mark on guitar, Paul on slap-bass and drummer Ben Cooper they formed a red-hot rockin' trio and began knocking out a powerful selection of original tunes, courtesy of the Harmans' songwriting skills and some choice cover versions. After establishing themselves on the live scene pretty rapidly from their debut performance in the Spring of 1980 they found that their sound was also attracting an appreciable audience in Europe where they enjoyed their first record release, a self-titled seven-inch single for Sunrock Records in Sweden. This relatively minuscule pressing of four hundred copies is now much in demand by collectors but eventually brought to a larger audience when it was licensed by Nervous Records and re-released in 1983. Prior to this, it was to be Roy Williams who signed the band for their debut album 'Why Don't You Just... Rock!' which was released in 1982.

While clearly popular on the modern Rockabilly scene, and rightful successors to previous leading acts such as The Polecats and The Blue Cats, Restless were something of an enigma to the world of Psychobilly. With their fresh-faced, almost pop idol looks and flamboyant collection of Rockabilly

Neo-Rockabilly double-header. The Caravans & The Deltas tour Holland (Mark Pennington).

clobber their image was immediately at odds with the stripped-down style of much of their Psychobilly following. But Restless could win over any audience, no matter what their preconceptions, with the sheer power of their live performance. Their debut album may have displayed their quality songwriting skills and musicianship but in concert they delivered set after set of pure, hard Rockabilly that even the most po-faced wrecker could not resist. This was just the start of a fruitful recording career for Restless but they undeniably stamped their unique brand of rockin' all over the early Psychobilly scene.

The band particularly found a rabid audience for their high-energy Neo-Rockabilly at The Klub Foot and in some way played their own part in this iconic club's formation. Regular gigs downstairs at The Clarendon, with bands such as Restless and The Guana Batz, were simply getting too cramped as a growing number of eager punters flooded in so the hotel's ballroom, which was able to handle a capacity in excess of 1000 people, was utilised for gigs and The Klub Foot was born. Both bands' contribution was rewarded when they appeared, along with Thee Milkshakes and The Sting-Rays, on the now legendary 'Stomping At The Klub Foot'.

After recording their second album for Nervous, 'Do You Feel Restless' (1984), the brothers Harman had a bitter bust-up and Paul left the band to be replaced by Jeff Bayley. As the band's touring schedule increased, helped along by the independent chart success of their Big Beat single 'Mr Blues' (1984), they also drafted in an additional guitarist Mick Malone. It was with this line-up that the band would enjoy their greatest success with extensive gigging, TV and radio appearances and a new record deal with ABC Records.

The deal with ABC got off to a good start with the release of the 'Vanish Without A Trace' single (on 7" and 12") and the label was rumoured to have invested a five figure sum in recording the band's first ABC album but the record in question, 'After Midnight' (1986), remains Restless' most controversial album... for all the wrong reasons. 'After Midnight' was an unashamedly blatant move by the label to push Restless towards a more mainstream pop audience, from the glam cover image of the boys to the mult-instrumental (synthesiser, brass and piano) production job. For many Psychobillies and Rockabillies, though, the album was seen as something of a sell-out and it would be many years before they would reconnect with the band.

THE PIONEERS

In retrospect it was all a storm in a teacup and aside from the dodgy cover the album was far from the mainstream pop offering which it has been painted as. Two singles from the album. 'Just A Friend' (1986) and 'Somebody Told Me' (1986), were big successes but it is undeniable that the band's hard-slappin' Rockabilly sound from their previous albums was muted on 'After Midnight' but in concert they were as raw and exciting as ever.

In 1987 ABC squeezed a live album from the band, 'Live and Kickin'!' (recorded at the Klub Foot), and a final four-track twelve-inch 'Ice Cold' which was a re-recording of their 1982 track which appeared on their debut album for Nervous. When their deal with ABC ended some further personnel changes followed when Mick Malone left, citing the band's constant touring as his reason for his departure. With the band back to a trio once again they signed with Madhouse Records in what was to become a productive deal resulting in four albums within three years. Their first release for the label was 'Beat My Drum' (1988) an album generally remembered as a terrific return to rockin' form after the disappointment that was 'After Midnight'.

The following year, Jeff Bayley surprisingly handed in his notice to quit and for some time it looked like Restless were soon to be no more. Intending to tour Japan with a stand-in bassist then disband, the band secured the services of Frenzy's Steve Whitehouse. The threesome enjoyed the tour so much that on returning they decided to continue as Restless but with Steve still maintaining his commitment to Frenzy.

Restless recorded a further two albums for Madhouse, 'Kickin' Into Midnight' (1989) and 'Movin' On' (1990), before original member Ben Cooper walked out after repeated disagreements with the band's manager (and producer of the 'Klub Foot' albums) Pete Gage. Ben was replaced by Rob Tyler (from Dave Philips and The Hot Rod Gang) and after the first album from the Harman/ Whitehouse/ Tyler line-up, 'Number 7' (1991), Gage also moved on after almost seven years guiding the band's career.

The movement within the band continued as their deal with Madhouse ended and they went back to Nervous for one album, 'Figure It Out', in 1993. By this time Frenzy's career was once more on the rise and it was not long before Steve Whitehouse returned to focus purely on his own band once more. Fortunately the decade-long rift between the Harman brothers had eased and Paul Harman was back on bass. Restless continued for four years gigging and recording but a statement from the band issued late in 1998 announced that after a final gig at London's Tennessee Club in November of that year, Restless would be no more. The gig went ahead but as is the way of things on the rockin' scene the lure of Rock'n'Roll was too strong to resist and Restless were back in action in 2002 with the original line-up of Mark, Paul and Ben Cooper.

Mark had not been idle during the break though and was also a member of The Space Cadets, an outer-space themed combo consisting of Mouse (Red, Hot & Blue), Ricky Lee Brawn and Anders Jane (both from The Big 6 and The Stargazers). He also played and recorded with Paul Harman as The Harmany Brothers as well as enjoying a brief solo career.

With the original trio back gigging, another album was always on the cards and 'Do Your Thing' was released in 2002, on CD through Roadblock Records and on vinyl from Vinyl Japan. This was to be the band's final recording although a number of collections, such as 'The Lost Sessions' (1996), 'Rock'n'Roll Beginners' (1998) and 'Rarities' (2003), all featuring the band's earlier recordings, have surfaced over the years.

The band continued to gig after 'Do Your Thing' including tours across Europe, Japan and the USA and an appearance at the first Speedfreaks Ball in 2005 but in 2006 the word was out that, once again, Restless were to split. Their last UK gig was in December 2006 at The Scala in London's Kings Cross. After a quarter of a century on the rockin' scene it looks as though this split may be permanent but with so much talent squeezed into this trio it is hard to believe that any of the band will ever completely desert the music business.

Along with Restless, The Sharks were another Neo-Rockabilly band who made an important contribution to the early Psychobilly scene. Originally formed in the late 1970s by guitarist Alan

Wilson, they were initially a straightforward Rockabilly combo featuring Wilson on guitar with brothers Kevin and Paul Hancock on bass and drums respectively. After a radical line-up change in 1982, Wilson was joined by teenage slap-bass fanatic Steve Whitehouse and drummer Paul 'Hodge' Hodges. Steve and Hodge had previously been in the band The Shakin' Quiffs and two of their tracks, 'Shake Your Quiff' and 'Cherie, Cherie', had featured on the Nervous Records' compilation 'Stack-A-Records' (1983).

It was during this line-up that The Shark's sound gradually changed to a harder rockin' beat which, in retrospect, hinted at yet another direction for future Psychobilly sounds. While essentially another Rockabilly three-piece with a bad-ass attitude, The Sharks possessed their own unique sound brewed outside of the nation's capital in the hillbilly confines of the South West.

What The Sharks did share with other pioneers of demented Rockabilly was super-tight musicianship and an unexploited catalogue of stomping tunes. Nervous Records signed the band in 1982 and within two weeks their debut LP 'Phantom Rockers' was complete. Capturing the band's unique Neo/Psycho sound, this album boasted lyrical content of a far darker nature than most trad Rockabilly albums of the time, with songs such as 'Skeleton Rock', 'Death Row', 'Ghost Train' and 'Take a Razor to Your Head'. Despite releasing such an established debut album, within months The Sharks were no more, offering only the old chestnut of 'musical differences' as the reason behind the split. One can only imagine their reasons but bassist Steve Whitehouse's future direction may have held some clues.

Probably one of the most successful Neo-Rockabilly combos of the Klub Foot era, alongside Restless, are The Caravans. Coming together in 1984 they opted for a fairly unique combination of vocals/double-bass, drums, lead guitar and two rhythm guitars. This not only gave the band a powerful sound but also created an impressive line-up onstage. All five original members – Mark Pennington (vocals/bass), Rich Caso (guitar), Lee Barnett (drums), Darren Frances and Brian Gillman (rhythm guitars) – took the stage over when they played and, with no members skulking in the background, The Caravans were rarely less than a full-on live experience.

In a similar fashion to the Guana Batz, the road to their debut album was long but built on their

Mark Pennington of The Caravans (Mark Pennington).

well-received live reputation. After four years together their back catalogue consisted of the single 'On The Rocks' (1988) on Raucous Records and appearances on a number of compilations including Northwood Records 'James Deans Of The Dole Queue', 'Zorch Factor II' (Nervous) and 'Stomping At The Klub Foot: Vol. 3'. Their first long-player 'Easy Money' finally appeared on Nervous Records in 1988, and was a well-produced slab of solid Rockabilly with strong bass-slapping and a jolting triple guitar wall of twang. Though a bit slick for many Psychobilly hardliners it proved that while The Caravans were capable of shaking up large gatherings of stompers, they remained true to their Rockabilly roots.

Although the decade saw many Psychobilly bands enter the 1990s with a bang and leave it with a splutter many of the Neo-Rockabilly bands close to the scene experienced the opposite, none more so than The Caravans. The band, for whatever reason, were initially not as prolific as many bands on the 1980s scene. The follow-up to their 1988 Nervous Records debut LP, 'No Excuses' took two years to appear eventually surfacing on Chuck Flintstone's Chuckeedee Records in 1990. This was followed by three years' gaps between their next full-length release 'Straightside' (1994) on Gary Day's label Rock-Out and the mini-album 'Action or Slander' (1997) which featured Day on bass.

Paradoxically in the late 1990s when many rockin' bands saw their profile dip, The Caravans powered ahead with an album each year between 1998-2000: 'Glamorous Heart' (Fury), 'Saturday Night's Alright' (Crazy Love) and 'Return To Zero' respectively. Their 2003 album 'Treasures & Trash' on Black Sky Records consisted of demos and rarities spanning 1985-2002 but in 2004, after two decades on the scene, they delivered the double whammy of an excellent studio album 'Less Smoke, More Powder' (Tombstone Records) and their very own 'Best of...' collection on Cherry Red, 'Living With Dinosaurs'.

Throughout their twenty year career The Caravans line-up has changed often with only Mark Pennington remaining as an original member and even he has switched from bass to lead guitar. In 2005 the band also toured with, and supported, Rockabilly legend Levi Dexter – a challenging set of dates which saw the band perform their own blistering set then returning to the stage for another full show with Dexter. Arguably as strong now as they ever were in Spring 2006, the band grew even closer to their Psychobilly following with their harder-edged album 'No Mercy' on Drunkabilly Records.

Other veterans of the 1980s Rockabilly scene equally at home on the Psychobilly dark side were The Pharaohs. Klub Foot regulars and regular rockers of the flat-topped faithful, the band were formed earlier in the decade by vocalist/guitarist Glenn Daeche. Their first album was another Nervous Records creation, 'Blue Egypt' released in 1986. Despite its quite traditional-looking Rockabilly cover, which may have dulled the attention of Psychobilly hardliners, the platter was a devil of a stomping album in disguise.

Its success saw them tour further afield to ever-growing audiences and to back it up came their second vinyl platter 'Hammer & Sickle Blues' (1988). The band entered hibernation in the 1990s before returning in the new millennium with their album 'London 1888' (2000) on Crazy Love Records, featuring The Caravans' Mark Pennington guesting on slap bass. Throughout the band's career they played at many of the major UK Psychobilly events but they always maintained a solid standing on the Rockabilly scene.

While The Caravans and The Pharaohs remain two of the missing links between Neo-Rockabilly and Psychobilly, there was no place where both these forms of rockin' collided so spectacularly than The Klub Foot. During its short history Neo and Psycho bands rubbed shoulders with frightening regularity and were mostly enjoyed by all.

If The Beatles changed the perception of The Cavern from a dingy, below-stairs nightspot to that of the holy temple of the Beat boom, then the wreckin' nation of a few decades later spread enough enthusiastic word of mouth to ensure that the Klub Foot will forever be remembered as the legendary first mecca of Psychobilly. It began in 1982 in what was no more than a creaky upstairs function room at the Clarendon Hotel in London's Hammersmith Broadway. However, when the Klub Foot crew were promoting their evenings of musical delight the venue was transformed into a sweat-soaked palace of pummelling. 'Downstairs' at The Clarendon had been active for some time, promoting Psychobilly,

HELL'S BENT ON ROCKIN'

THE PIONEERS

The Pharaohs (Roy Williams).

Rockabilly and Trash and many bands made their first appearance there before graduating to the main hall. Some even preferred the claustrophobic clamminess of the back room.

The venue first came to national, and international, attention in 1984 with the release of the first 'Stomping at the Klub Foot' album on ABC Records which was a unique compilation of live tracks from four Klub Foot regulars, captured on the 22nd of September of that year. The album featured a quartet of tracks each from Restless, The Sting-Rays, Thee Milkshakes and The Guana Batz. The recordings, by producer Pete Gage and engineer David Jacob, perfectly captured the band's live sound along with the atmosphere of the club itself. It also illustrated the venue's eclectic booking policy which would always extend beyond the solely Psychobilly tag which it carries to this day.

From this point on, however, The Klub Foot was 'thee' venue for any aspiring Psycho bands and the list of Klub Foot regulars began to grow, with the likes of Frenzy, The Coffin Nails, Demented Are Go, The Long Tall Texans and Torment all treading the Clarendon Hotel stage with frightening regularity. After the success of the first Klub Foot album, Volume Two was available less than a year later. This album, again on ABC Records, opted for more bands on one disc showcasing each group with two live tracks. Recorded on the 24th of August 1985, with Pete Gage once again at the controls, the gig featured a range of rockers and again illustrated the variety of bands who appeared on the hallowed Klub Foot stage.

In the same way that Restless had appeared on the first album, The Rapids and The Pharaohs held up the Neo-Rockabilly, but Psychobilly-friendly, end of the bill with powerful, slap-driven sets. The Styng Rites made a blazing, twang-driven racket that still defies categorisation and The Tall Boys proved that their Trash-seeped brand of Rock'n'Roll existed beyond the recording studio. Confusingly, The Primevals – Glasgow's gloomy garage merchants – kick the album off. This appears a rather unusual choice for a classic Klub Foot recording as the band had a very small Psychobilly following, even North of the border, but it showed the venue's inclusive booking policy and possibly found the band treading similar ground to The Tall Boys.

The highlight of Volume 2 has to be the appearance of Demented Are Go and Frenzy. For anyone who failed to own a copy of the Nervous compilation 'Hell's Bent on Rockin'' this was Demented's first appearance on vinyl to many and a fantastic introduction to the (soon to be) Psycho legends who, from

47

this point, continued to produce the goods live and in the studio. Although still promoting their recently released 'Hall of Mirrors' album, Frenzy's tracks were also an introduction to any folks who had yet to witness the band's excellent live performance. Frenzy were always a powerful band in concert mostly due to frontman Steve Whitehouse's speed-crazed, slap-bass and vocal combination and any members of the audience who remained un-rocked were either dead or deaf. Frenzy, in particular, would become a headline favourite at the venue, regularly drawing in punters from all over the UK and Europe.

The Klub Foot recordings were a perfect showcase for many bands as their razor-sharp recordings were often far superior to many live Psychobilly albums which were to follow, although to achieve this occasional overdubs were recorded after the event. The albums also brought the power and excitement which many bands possessed live to a wider audience as some groups lost a little of their 'buzz' during the often hurried studio sessions which contributed to their vinyl output.

While many nights at The Klub Foot were crammed with hairspray-soaked, boots'n'denim-clad mutant rockers, the venue was not exclusively a Psychobilly haunt. Obviously it was closely linked to the Trash scene and alongside The Sting-Rays, The Tall Boys and Thee Milkshakes bands like The Cannibals, The Vibes and the Prisoners regularly trod the boards. Another underground youth movement also made their pilgrimages to The Klub Foot. Although The Bat Cave in London was the Valhalla of the UK Gothic scene many Goth, and Goth-related bands, passed through the Clarendon's stage door. Alien Sex Fiend were a semi-regular attraction often joined by the likes of Play Dead, Ghostdance and Turkey Bones & the Wild Dogs.

The live albums series continued to be popular with the next release taking the form of a double album 'Stomping At The Klub Foot: Volumes 3&4'. This collection was created from a single concert in the summer of 1986 featuring Torment, Rochee & The Sarnos, The Wigsville Spliffs, The Coffin Nails, Batmobile and The Caravans. The second album of this set contained further songs from both of the sessions which featured on Volume 1&2 of the series, featuring Restless, The Guana Batz and The Milkshakes from 1984 and Frenzy, The Pharaohs, The Primevals, The Styng Rites, Tall Boys and Demented Are Go from the following year. Drawing the whole saga to a conclusion was the final 'Stomping...' album 'Volume 5' which, while not the most memorable of the series, showed that the 'Klub Foot' promoters were constantly encouraging new talent such as The Long Tall Texans, Skitzo, The Highliners, Shark Bait and Fractured.

Although the albums were a success and the venue continued to build on its status as the premier venue of UK Psychobilly, attracting legions of Psychos from Europe and beyond, property developers in London (who probably regarded the club as no more than a creaky hotel occasionally populated by sweat-soaked numbskulls) began planning the buildings demise. In 1988, the entire building was levelled to make way for a new Post Office – and the souls of a thousand Psychobillies wailed in torment (probably). Before the demolition ball powered its way through the hotel's faded facade, wrecking of another kind took place on the ballroom floor as part of The Klub Foot's final run of gigs. During this time many Psychobillies, amongst others, took the opportunity to release their impotent fury at the big business slaughter of their favourite venue by kicking fuck out of the Clarendon's fixtures and fittings (paying particular attention to the gents' bogs).

In the years since its demise The Klub Foot has passed into legend and memories of the venue can still push many old-school Psychobillies to misty-eyed acts of reminiscing but to anyone who ever strode the stage or slid across its beer-soaked floorboards it was the first place where the Psychobilly scene found its spiritual home. Nonetheless, when the venue disappeared there was still rockin' to be done and everyone simply moved on.

CHAPTER THREE

HELL'S BENT ON ROCKIN'

TAKIN' IT TO THE STREETS

As the 1980s' newest branch of street culture, Psychobilly drew converts from a wide range of musical faiths and rarely asked new disciples to cast out records from other genres which they had previously gained much pleasure from. The soundtrack to the Psycho scene always strongly featured other styles of music both in terms of tracks spun at Psychobilly venues and gatherings and the influences which many bands drew on for their own creations. Undoubtedly, fans of Rockabilly, Rock'n'Roll, Oi, Punk and Ska provided many conscripts to the growing Psychobilly army but also many ex-Mods and Heavy Metal freaks joined up. Any others who were turned on by the Psychobilly beat were in the minority, for example the numbers of disgruntled Jazz fans who threw down their Jazz mags in disgust yelling "Fuck this be-bop bullshit, I'm going Psycho!" remain unrecorded.

For legions of UK and European Rockabillies in the early 1980s the transition to the Psychobilly lifestyle was fairly straightforward. Many London venues, such as Dingwalls and The Hope & Anchor, could book a Rockabilly and Psychobilly band on consecutive nights and still attract much the same audience and Europe has consistently been able to attract fans of both kinds of 'billy on a regular basis. Generally though the rockin' scene comprised of Rockabillies with no taste for Psycho, Psychobillies for whom anything less than non-stop wreckin' was purgatory and a good measure of interested parties on both sides who could appreciate the scenes history and progression. However, not all these elements existed in sweet harmony, as Jo 'Psychodame' Shalton remembers from her earliest days on the scene:

I got into Psychobilly when I was 17 years old and was most definitely a Punk, covered in zips and safety pins with the obligatory spiky hair! In my innocence I got friendly with two of the slightly more broadminded local Teds (who were really Rockabillies), who started to take me along to some of the Teddy Boy Clubs. My presence at these clubs went down like the proverbial cup of cold sick, but I was hooked and by the time I came across the likes of Ray Campi and Charlie Feathers, the love affair with Rockabilly was in full bloom!

To cut a long story short, I eventually moved to London in order to follow the Rocking scene better and settled quickly into life as a Rockabilly although I never stopped listening to and liking other types of music; ie Punk, Ska, Indie etc. In those days the Rockabilly scene was tremendously cliquey and it was heavily frowned on if you weren't wearing the "right" clothes or had your hair in the "right" style, needless to say, being a rebel to the last, I still had cropped bleached hair and generally wore whatever I felt like wearing.

After a while I got totally pissed off with the narrow-minded attitudes of most of the Rockabillies, and I drifted away from and finally dropped out of the Rockin' scene for a while and then lost touch with what clubs there were and what the cool places were to hang out at. (No Internet then!)

It wasn't until I began work at the Post Office (with my big blonde quiff), that I had a strange encounter in a lift. This bloke got in the lift with a flat top, but it had no back or sides, and it sloped at a strange angle (Unknown to me, I'd just had my first encounter with Psychobilly). We kind of stared

Jo Shalton (Jo Shalton).

TAKIN' IT TO THE STREETS   HELL'S BENT ON ROCKIN'

at each other in amazement and got out of the lift talking excitedly to each other – much to the amusement of the other Posties who witnessed this encounter of freak meeting freak!

Needless to say, I started to go to the Klub Foot with him and was completely blown away by my first outing there, I think I saw Demented Are Go, and as I stood and watched and listened to the band I had a strange sense of "coming home" as I realised that at long long last, here was a type of music that covered my two main musical loves; Punk and Rockabilly. It also filled in the missing link for me, as I'd always felt that there MUST be something more musically than what I'd been used to hearing. I also saw many more bands at the Klub Foot that I still follow to this day, the two other most memorable ones being Skitzo and The Guana Batz.

I've made many loyal friends on the Psycho scene, some more unexpected than others and have always been grateful for the continuing lack of prejudice that the Psycho scene has always shown to its followers.

Though it would be unfair to claim that the Rockabilly scene was totally unimpressed by the Psychobilly phenomenon, young Punks often made a smoother transition into the movement. Punk (in all its forms), like Rockabilly is almost impossible to refer to as anything but an integral part of the Psychobilly movement. Psychobilly not only drew on the speed and fury of Punk for its sound but also on the DIY ethics of the scene with regards to promoting gigs, releasing records and publicising bands.

If Psychobilly bands had waited vainly to attract major music biz interest at any time the whole movement would have been no more than a memory by 1984. Punk also gave the early Psychobilly scene its immediacy as bands sprung up all over the UK and Europe and began playing and recording. Though many were rough and ready, and their recordings often rudimentary, they got out there, gave the scene its buzz and (more importantly) had a good time in the process. Many of these bands imploded within a few years but just as many went on to craft some true Psychobilly classics having gained their experience 'on the job'.

Jo Jackson (Jo Jackson).

HELL'S BENT ON ROCKIN'   TAKIN' IT TO THE STREETS

Another cult which embraced the Psychobilly lifestyle was the renaissance of Scootering in the UK during the early to mid-1980s. Commonly regarded as the key form of transport for original 1960s Mods and their post-Punk revivalists of the late 1970s, Scootering entered a new phase in the 1980s which comprised of a motley collection of ex-Mods, Skins, Punks, Northern Soul fanatics and (of course) Psychobillies. As probably the truest form of collective youth cults, Scootering became a major part of the Psychobilly lifestyle for many but equally did nothing for legions of other maniac rockers.

For those who arrived at Psychobilly after being Punks, Mods or Skins, Scootering was a natural progression but for Psychobillies with Rockabilly, Rock'n'Roll or biker roots it often held little excitement and occasionally led to disgruntled ton-up boys attending rallies purely to accompany their mates and catch many of the major Psychobilly bands who played at these events.

Webmistress of the 'alcoholic rats' website Jo Jackson has a story similar to many with a scootering background:

Well I wish I could say there was one significant moment that turned me to Psychobilly but I think it was a combination of events, though the order in which it all happened is a bit hazy. Some of the purists amongst us, and indeed the bands themselves, might argue that King Kurt and The Cramps aren't Psychobilly but they were the ones who probably let me on the road to rack'n'ruin.

I'd always gone to gigs as a young teenager and went along the school girl mod bit, to getting my first scooter and going on a couple of mod rallies and coming back a scooter girl, as many people did back in the early 80s.

The first "Psychobilly" song I heard that really sticks in my head was a track by The Cramps played in a nightclub in Benidorm whilst I was on a family holiday. I came back and told one of my mates about it and he did me up a compilation tape of The Meteors, Guana Batz and some Cramps stuff. That was it, I was hooked. Psychobilly music and fashion was starting to rear its head at many of the national scooter events too.

I was also into the Medway/garage/trash sound as well and used to go and see The Prisoners a lot, especially downstairs at The Clarendon (think it was called Broadway), so it was here that I found the legendary Psychobilly Mecca, The Klub Foot, which was held upstairs. From then on I was attending gigs there on a regular basis. People still ask what was so special about that venue and it's hard to pinpoint anything cos it was a real dive if we're honest and just like many venues today it took forever to get served at the bar, but the atmosphere there was electric, there was always a huge wrecking pit and mostly great bands on. That was the one venue "everyone" from all over the country went to. Getting tanked up on the London Link on the way to Hammersmith was all part of the enjoyment for many as well.

We were lucky living half way between the South coast and London as it meant we could get to gigs fairly easily in either direction, Grannies/Basins in Portsmouth was a favourite and Dingwalls, Town and Country Club, Hammersmith Palais and the Electric Ballroom in London were often hosting Psychobilly gigs. The scene was getting massive which meant almost every weekend we were either at a gig or a scooter rally. Reading too was fairly local and we did some great gigs at The Majestic. I can't actually remember who the first Psychobilly band was that I saw but I presume it was one of the Klub Foot gigs. The place still holds fond memories, not only for the bands and friends, but it was where I later got together with my husband and where we went on our wedding night. We kicked everyone out the reception early cos we wanted to see The Guana Batz and The Coffin Nails.

I can, however, still recall my first King Kurt gig as if it was yesterday. Friends and family of Emmet, a local scooterist, had arranged a surprise 18th birthday party for him at Guildford with King Kurt to play live. All the local scooterists were invited so it would have been one hell of a night anyway, but with KK playing and then staying on to party with us all afterwards it remains one of the most memorable nights I have had. They instantly become one of my favourite bands, and I travelled all over the country to see them. I loved all the mess, the mayhem, the drinking games and they were a top bunch of blokes too.

TAKIN' IT TO THE STREETS

HELL'S BENT ON ROCKIN'

Us girlies decided it was time to form our own scooter club and there was really only one name for it "The Alcoholic Rats Scooter Club". Three of us were big KK fans and all six of us liked a little tipple now and then! I came up with an idea for a T-shirt design and Maggot kindly drew it up for us in typical KK stylee. To this day that remains one of my most treasured possessions and the original drawing is still framed and hanging up on my wall.

The demise of the Klub Foot in the late 1980s did put a bit of a dampener on the scene, but we still had the Rumbles at Hemsby and went to a lot of Frantic Flintstones gigs right up until 1993 when our first born arrived. Thankfully the new millennium gave us a social life back again and we are back out attending gigs again. It's great to see most of my old favourites are still going and some great new bands too. Only difference now is I don't go wrecking and the old man takes longer to heal when he does.

Jane Williams, globetrotting gig-goer and regular contributor to Deathrow Database, was another devotee of the scooter scene who received her life-changing introduction to Psychobilly:

My obsession with Psychobilly started totally by accident. It was 1986, and I got a job in a nightclub in Cardiff. At that time, I was very involved in the scooter scene and mostly interested in going to as many rallies as possible. I've been going to gigs since I was a teenager, so I was interested when someone at the club recommended a band as being really good, and they told me they were playing the following weekend. As it was my night off, I went along. It was at a regular weekly alternative night, which drew a very mixed crowd including psychos and they sometimes had bands playing, so this was where I went.

It was packed and I hardly knew anyone, so it was a case of hanging around until the band came on. They weren't just good, they were brilliant – it was The Guana Batz. I was fascinated by the music, the slap bass and Pip's tattoos which I actually thought was a T-shirt until I made my way nearer the front to get a better view! Little did I know at the time that this particular night would totally change my life.

However, this didn't immediately lead to a complete change of lifestyle. I had no idea about Psychobilly and although there were plenty of quiffs about, I found a lot of people pretty scary and didn't want to approach them. This wasn't helped a few weeks later when Demented played at the club. I'd never heard anything like it, the noise was incredible. I was working the cloakroom opposite the doors to the hall, so I could hear the gig, and see the guys coming out covered in blood. The wrecking was incredibly rough in those days. In fact, at one point an unconscious psycho with blood on his face was carried out. They dumped him on

Jane Williams with Ant of Demented Are Go (Jane Williams).

52

HELL'S BENT ON ROCKIN'

TAKIN' IT TO THE STREETS

Loz Dolan (Simon 'Fatbloke' Ling).

the counter in front of me and I was asked to look after him! Luckily he soon came round and staggered off. To an outsider, it was all really scary and I wasn't even brave enough to go and look through the doors so unfortunately, I can't say that I actually saw Demented that far back!

So where did that leave me? Well a bit stuck really. I went round all the record shops but couldn't find anything by the Batz or much else either. Someone helpfully suggested that I should buy some Cramps stuff as they were Psychobilly, I bought an LP but hated it so it was back to square one. However the psycho bug had bitten and there was no getting away from it. Eventually, I made friends with a couple of psycho scooterists, and asked one of them if he would tape some stuff for me. Now I was getting somewhere! The tape included lots of bands like King Kurt (that's where I first heard 'Horatio' and it's still one of my favourite tracks) and I loved it.

That led gradually to a change of hairstyle and clothes. The Batz came back to Cardiff on several occasions and I still loved them! I got to see more bands like The Pharaohs, The Meteors, Long Tall Texans and by 1989, had made my first trip to London for an alldayer. That was at the Robey, I knew absolutely no-one but got talking to a few people, had a great time and really felt like I belonged there. I've been travelling to gigs all over Europe ever since!

Those in the far North East of England also found it hard to evade the Psycho-disease and Loz Dolan of The Hangmen had a similar baptism:

When I was a kid I'd present myself as a Rockabilly rebel, listening to the wild 50s rockers whilst secretly enjoying punk releases as well as the first wave of new Rockabilly bands on Nervous etc. I first heard the P word in association with The Cramps in the music press, I'd already been introduced to their records and have been a lifelong fan, shortly after that I heard about The Meteors. I remember seeing a leather clad black quiffed punk/rocker in town one Saturday afternoon where we'd gang up, he had Psycho-Billy stencilled onto his leather below an emblem I later discovered represented Adam & The Ants(!).

My first schooldays garage band would play Rockabilly covers via The Cramps interpretations and without a bass, as it suited our capabilities at the time. I began attending a regular Rockabilly night

53

TAKIN' IT TO THE STREETS
HELL'S BENT ON ROCKIN'

when they'd let me in as I was well underage, I heard 'Voodoo Rhythm' and instantly deduced who it was. The older rockabillies there seemed to like the band at that time. I caught The Meteors live with Nigel Lewis (Woody on drums by now) at our local college (support act was Southern Death Cult) and saw Psychobillies in action for the first time. Wrecking as it stands wasn't really the order of the day, it was more just general freaking out and colliding.

At the time I was disappointed in the gig, expecting a similar atmosphere to that experienced at my first gig (The Polecats), but on reflection it was a milestone and I soon adopted the look of those early 'crazies' (bleached jeans, short bleached flat-tops, wraparounds, studded belts, cropped T-shirts etc.) and stocked up on the band's releases. My punk genes were allowed out on display at last! Eventually I was in 'the scene' which shouldn't need any describing.

I ditched playing in bands whilst I enjoyed all the scene had to offer, when things started to wane in the early 90s I'd amassed a lot of ideas and joined a couple of local (low on originality shall we politely say) 'Psycho' bands which eventually led to me splitting and forming The Hangmen with drummer Pumpkinhead – who would later part company on amicable terms due to domestic commitments hampering the band's increasing activities.

With the spread of Psychobilly so close to the border it was only a matter of time before the Scots received their taste of the genre that dare not speak its name. Kenny Mitchell of The Termites was one such victim:

The first Psychobilly song I ever heard was 'Wreckin' Crew' and it changed my life forever. In Kilmarnock, every housing scheme, school, etc had its own wreckin' crew. We were the 'Tap Shoaps' (Ed's Translation: shops at the top of the street) wreckin' crew, hard and always fighting. We stood outside the chippy every night and hassled everyone that walked by. We all wore Meteors T-shirts, bleached jeans, day-glo socks, creepers, and crombies. Every one of us dressed exactly the same, it looked awesome... and intimidating. My dad said we were just like punk teddy boys. Times were good. 'Wreckin' Crew' got me into 'In Heaven' which remains one of my fave albums to this day. I never get sick of it and i've been listening to it for 22 years.

Kenny Mitchell (Kenny Mitchell).

HELL'S BENT ON ROCKIN'   TAKIN' IT TO THE STREETS

I got into psychobilly at 14 or 15, so there was not much time to get into anything else. I was always into the teddy boy thing because of my dad, combing my hair up and stuff. Even the movie 'Grease' was cool because of the T-birds (ha-ha). I was too young to be a Punk although I was buying Sex Pistols singles as they came out and I was a primary school Sid Vicious. So Punk was my first interest but my main music was the whole new 2 Tone explosion which I was totally caught up in. Then I heard 'Wreckin' Crew'!

The first live band I saw was The Meteors in Ayr, and because I was in the scene right from the start I saw all the bands. This was back in the day when Guana Batz and King Kurt would play in a local hotel party room. It was awesome, there were gigs everywhere and they would be packed out with flat tops. No huge quiffs back then, just greasers and flat tops. The Killie (Kilmarnock) scene was awesome with The Termites and The Longhorns gigs always selling out. I had never played to anything less than a packed out hall right from the start. I was 16 and living it up. The whole town was full of psychos (the new craze), punks, skins and goths. It was amazing because they would all come to the gigs.

We were going to gigs at Rooftops (Glasgow) right away, around 1986/87. It seemed like there was a band on every week. All the big names were playing there and there was loads of trouble at the Glasgow gigs. It was the only scene where we fought each other instead of teaming up and fighting Mods or something... weird? Later on, much later on, all the crews seemed to join forces as the scene was dying out but I still don't like a lot of folk from back then though!

I actually moved to London in 1988/89, met up with The Klingonz and that was that. I went to all the gigs and met all the people that I had been sitting in my room listening to, crazy times! I still count them among my friends today! All through 1986 to 1991 The Termites were rising, getting record deals and playing with bands that I considered myself a fan of. It was amazing playing next to them and the best times of my life. After 1991 we were all the unfashionable lot and sniggered at for the way we looked but now it's all back and big in the USA, spawning a hole new breed of Psychobilly – morphing Metal, Ska, and Punk.

A lot of it I hate, a lot of it I like but my fave bands are still the ones that have come from the original period. I wonder if the "billy" has been lost. The only "billy" thing about a lot of the new stuff is the hair and double bass. All the bands I originally got into had electric basses, the double came later in the second phase of bands (apart from Mr Lewis of course). However, 'In Heaven' will never be beaten!!!!

Although separated by the English Channel many European Psychobillies

Guido Neumann (Crazy Love Records).

had very similar experiences to their cousins in the UK. Guido Neumann of Crazy Love Records remembers his early days in Germany:

I was born in 1964 and for my age, I think, I got into it very late. I heard The Sex Pistols in 1978, then a bit later on The Clash, Stiff Little Fingers, Sham 69 and that kinda stuff. In the middle of 1983 I bought my first Gene Vincent LP, an Eddie Cochran compilation and the first Stray Cats album. I also saw The Sharks' 'Phantom Rockers' LP and had not seen them before.

In October 1983 I was at a Stray Cats gig in Dusseldorf and me and my friends tried to find more stuff on LP. In December we drove to London and there I bought the Sharks LP and the first Colbert Hamilton album. Back here I found a shop and bought The Meteors 'In Heaven', The Polecats 'Polecats Are Go' and The Ricochets 'Made In The Shade' beside some Toy Dolls stuff. Well, the virus was born and I saw some gigs in a club called Aratta with the likes of Frenzy, Guana Batz and The Sting-Rays. The Frenzy gig in October 1985 was about the best live gig I have ever seen.

The spread of Psychobilly was rapid, particularly throughout the mid 1980s, and its growth was even more remarkable as it was a street level movement. The scene was fuelled by word-of-mouth, recommendation and the general enthusiasm of converts to this exciting, new form of music. People were distributing flyers, making compilation tapes for their friends, creating fanzines, bullying Indie DJs to "play some Psycho" and promoting their own local gigs and events. Ok, so this may sound like a repetition of the Punk boom less than a decade earlier but this movement had far less mainstream press coverage and had it not been for the enthusiasm which Psychobilly generated amongst its followers, few outside of London would have ever known it existed. Being a Psychobilly has never been an easy option but for the faithful the rewards are too damn great to ignore.

CHAPTER FOUR

SONIC BOOM
PSYCHOBILLY GOES BALLISTIC

Alongside the general exclusion of Psychobilly from the mainstream music press and TV, major record companies have often been notoriously wary of any band associated with the genre. Things started badly with The Meteors' experience at Island Records when a label shake-up left the band adrift within the company and no one sure what to do with this furiously rowdy three-piece. Stiff Records gave King Kurt some considerable back-up but for whatever reason were unwilling to continue supporting the band far beyond their 'Big Cock'. Mad Sin would also have their brush with a major which resulted in their excellent 1998 album '…Sweet & Innocent? …Loud & Dirty!' for Polydor but despite the quality package neither band nor label seemed too bothered when their brief flirtation came to an end.

Quite simply the only labels that can deal effectively with Psychobilly groups are those that really know the scene and understand the bands, the followers and the importance of a solid live reputation. Psychobilly bands are rarely created through studio trickery and fancy press releases but instead they develop on stage, dragging their gear round as many dives, roadhouses and grotty boozers as possible while working flat-topped crowds into a sweaty frenzy.

At the forefront of the whole movement is one, undeniably important, label, Nervous Records. The Nervous roster is a who's who of Psychobilly, boasting the likes of Restless, Frenzy, Skitzo, Batmobile, The Coffin Nails, Torment and The Frantic Flintstones alongside an even greater selection of Rockabilly, Neo-Rockabilly and straight-up Rock'n'Roll bands. The powerhouse behind Nervous is the one man who has attempted to keep the world rockin' – Roy Williams. Williams was a teenage Ted in Aberystwyth who never lost the fever.

After moving to London in search of a Rock'n'Roll scene, Roy soon began DJ'ing and promoting at a variety of rockin' concerts and gatherings including his appearance as MC at the Rock'n'Roll weekender at Hemsby in 1979, a gig which was filmed and eventually released on the big screen as the movie 'Blue Suede Shoes' (1980). He also stuck his finger in a number of other Rock'n'Roll pies including promoting the scene on TV, radio and the press, working and advising record companies and even early record mogul work bringing Hank Mizell's 'Jungle Rock' into the UK charts at Number 3, not bad for a record then nineteen years old.

Rather than simply trading on the revivalist scene, Roy has always determinedly attempted to move the scene forward or as he puts it, 'drag it kicking and screaming'. His vision would appear to focus on bringing a sense of professionalism and a business-like attitude to the scene. If the early Psychobilly scene seemed unique in its sense of the shambolic – missed gigs, forgotten deadlines, poor-quality promotion – the truth was that much of the 1970s' rockin' scene from Rock'n'Roll through to Rockabilly revival were often similarly shoddy. Throughout the decade, Roy carved his name on the scene

Nervous' back catalogue grew rapidly throughout the 1980s (Roy Williams)

SONIC BOOM   HELL'S BENT ON ROCKIN'

Roy Williams and friends (Roy Williams).

before deciding to earn his living in the 'business' side of the music industry.

Band management was his first role, bringing The Jets to national attention and securing them their first record deal. This led to a need for the band to publish their own songs and, in what was to become a legendary vault of rockin' tunes, Nervous (Music) Publishing began. Nervous Records itself began in 1979 when, after The Jets had moved on, Roy signed The Polecats and the label's first 7" 'Rockabilly Guy' was released. This was followed by the band's second single 'Marie Celeste' before The Polecats also capitalised on Roy's sterling promotion work and jumped ship to major label Polygram.

Realising that releasing singles was never going to put food on the table, Roy eventually looked to establish Nervous as an albums label. The album which did it was The Deltas 'Boogie Disease' (1981), an important release which not only convinced Roy that album sales would help Nervous expand its empire but also, musically, a release which illustrated the way the Rockabilly scene was developing into 'Neo' and beyond.

Roy continued to seek acts amongst the wealth of new talent on the Neo-Rockabilly scene and groundbreaking debuts from Restless, The Sharks and The Ricochets followed hot on the heels of The Deltas. Unsurprisingly, Roy was well aware of the emerging Psychobilly scene and Nervous acts such as The Sharks and The Ricochets were particularly influencing this new movement. What followed from Nervous were two compilation albums from the label which remain foundation stones of the Psychobilly scene.

'Hell's Bent On Rockin'' (1985) showcased all of the Neo bands already mentioned along with other roughhouse Rockabilly bands who were regularly entertaining Psycho audiences such as The Rapids, The Outer Limits and Rochee and The Sarnos. The album also featured full-on Psychobilly from The Meteors and Frenzy while introducing an unknown Welsh group called Demented Are Go to an unsuspecting public.

HELL'S BENT ON ROCKIN'   SONIC BOOM

'Zorch Factor I' (1986) appeared the following year and alongside a variety of Rockabilly bands the album included some fresh Psychobilly talent in the form of Torment, The Long Tall Texans and The Coffin Nails. 'Zorch Factor' then became something of a mini-series of compilations with two other volumes following in 1987 and 1990. Alongside these two important compilations, Nervous quickly became home to the cream of Psychobilly talent releasing debut albums from Torment, The Frantic Flintstones, The Coffin Nails, Skitzo and Frenzy in rapid succession. As the 1980s drew to a close many Psychobillies would happily cough-up the cash for any new Nervous album as the label's brand, and the pedigree of releases behind it, was a safe bet for those seeking hard-rockin' kicks in exchange for their hard-earned greenbacks.

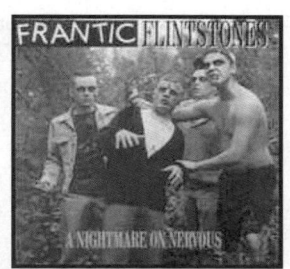

The Frantic Flintstones make their debut (Nervous Records).

Roy Williams appears to have always harboured a desire to move forward and the 1990s was another period of transition for the label. While many of Nervous' early Psychobilly successes such as Frenzy and The Frantic Flintstones had moved on, other acts recorded again for the label (The Coffin' Nails, Restless...) and Torment and Skitzo remained with Nervous for all their album releases. Roy captured Batmobile for a single album, 'Bail Was Set At $6,000,000' in 1988 along with other imported talent of the 1980s with The Quakes and The Nekromantix. It was abroad that the label also looked to in the 1990s for fresh talent and International acts including The Elektraws, Three Blue Teardrops, Hayride To Hell and The Screaming Kids were all to appear on Nervous, many slipping album recordings in during trips to the UK for gigs such as The Big Rumbles.

The compact disc boom was another area where Roy refused to be excluded, despite offending many wax-headed rockers who worshipped vinyl and saw the CD as a shiny sliver of pure evil which would reduce music as we know it to sterile digital beeps and beats. In the mid 1990s Nervous boldly ceased pressing vinyl and devoted their efforts to releasing, and re-releasing, their catalogue on compact disc. Skitzo's 'Terminal Damage' was the first album to receive the five-inch treatment and since then the label has continued to keep CD as the sole format for all its releases.

Alongside all this, Nervous was about to take an even larger step forward. As usual, for a man constantly pushing the scene forward and dragging the rest on, Roy Williams was the first to establish Psychobilly on the net. Roy spotted the early potential of the web and nervous.co.uk was up and running in 1995. This huge site now offers a wide range of goods, from the Nervous label and many other companies, along with reviews, product info, track listings and many other rockin' related features. The Nervous website was also at the forefront again relatively recently when it launched a massive back catalogue of MP3 downloads for sale. These tracks, with each sold separately, not only allow buyers to pick

Early Psychobilly fanzine, The Crazed (Paul Wainwright).

59

their favourites from the back catalogues of Nervous and many other labels but also have made available many tracks from albums that have been deleted for many years.

Quite simply, Roy Williams' contribution to the Psychobilly scene alone has been massive. Behind the scenes Roy, more often than not, has shared his expertise with other labels rather than jealously guarding his experience. Nervous continues to this day releasing new albums and signing fresh talent but focusing mainly on the current Rockabilly and Rock'n'Roll scene along with exhuming lost classics from the vaults. Nervous is also making a number of tracks from other, often defunct, labels available once again for download ensuring modern MP3 players can be stuffed with raw, hard rockin' tracks instead of the bland mainstream bilge which pollutes many of the world's dominant download sites.

One British label which has worked closely with Nervous Records for many years has been Fury Records. The label celebrated their twentieth anniversary in 2006, not bad for a company initially driven purely by the desire to get exposure for a roster of new talent on the rockin' scene in the early 1980s. The man behind Fury is a character well respected on the rockin' scene for over a quarter of a century and one who has helped countless bands take their first steps in the music business, Derek 'Dell' Richardson.

The road to the initial Psychobilly boom in the 1980s was a long and twisted route through Rockabilly, Rock'n'Roll, 1970s Ted Revival and Neo-Rockabilly and Dell is the one man who has kept the flame burning almost as long as Roy Williams. Fury remains an integral part of the Neo-Rockabilly and Psychobilly and since the late 1960s Dell has built his reputation as a DJ, promoter, stage manager, festival organiser and label boss. Throughout the 1980s Dell ran a Rock'n'Roll club in Eastcote, Middlesex called The Clay Pigeon and this regular Sunday night fixture often offered new rockin' bands a chance to play. He soon built up contacts with a number of acts and made a decision to create a compilation album featuring some of these acts.

Dell Richardson of Fury Records (Dell Richardson).

HELL'S BENT ON ROCKIN' — SONIC BOOM

Along with his partner Steve Chapman, they established Fury Records in 1986. The label's debut was 'She's Just Rockin'' (1987) a compilation of Rock'n'Roll and Neo-Rockabilly featuring the likes of The Wigsville Spliffs, The Niteshift Trio, The Deltas and The Playboys. A thousand copies were pressed and Dell completed the artwork himself. A local printer provided the finished album sleeves but Dell and Steve had to glue them together by hand... every one of them. The album's title was taken from The Sticks Trio's song of the same name which appeared on the compilation and this method of naming the collections would continue with the next few releases.

Having secured some essential distribution deals, courtesy of the sage-like Roy Williams, album sales soon turned a profit and work began on a second album. This was to be a similarly themed collection of rockin' called 'I Love My Car' (1987) featuring new bands including The Midnighters, Niteshift Trio (again), Rockin' Rocket 88 and The Bootleggers. Once again the album proved how much talent was bursting through on the scene but, as yet, there was little sign of the Psychobilly sound which was to eventually become a large part of Fury's back catalogue.

It was the label's third collection which introduced many Psychobillies to Fury. 'Gypsy Girl' was released in 1988 and this time the album promised 'Rockabilly and Rock'n'Roll and Psycho' and nestling between the more traditional rockin' bands were tracks from fledgling Psychobilly acts The Griswalds, The Termites and The Go-Katz. This theme was continued in Fury's fourth collection, 'I Ain't Lonely No More', featuring Spook & The Ghouls and The Surfin' Wombatz amongst others but it was Fury's seventh album which would prove a Psychobilly landmark.

Having spotted The Klingonz' at the LMS in Hendon, Dell persuaded the band to enter the studio for a frantic eight-hour recording session. Having left behind an emotionally shattered studio engineer, 'Uuuurnchk!! Psychos From Beyond' was created and marked a new dawn for Psychobilly as it approached the end of the decade. The Klingonz' deal with Fury continued throughout the 1990s resulting in some of the most memorable Psychobilly albums of the UK scene. Demented Are Go and Mad Sin also joined the label with DAG already well established and the Sin near the beginning of their career.

In 1995 Steve Chapman moved on and focused instead on establishing his, now booming, rockin' retail business Spindrift Records. With a base in both the UK and US, Spindrift operates a worldwide mail order service offering all forms of Rock'n'Roll and Steve himself can be found at a huge range of events with a wide selection of music and merchandise. Spindrift has also released a number of records and CDs on their own label with an eclectic line-up including Psychobilly groups The Photon Torpedoes, The Alphabet Bombers and Los Gatos Locos.

Fury continued, solely with Dell at the helm, and Psychobilly continued to play a part within the label. Something Shocking and Os Catalepticos joined the Fury roster along with a number of other rockin' acts such as Red, Hot'n'Blue, Hot Boogie Chillun, The Caravans, The Blue Devils and The Razorbacks who were all well known to Psychobilly audiences. Fury has also continued to issue many compilations over the years, including many of a heavier persuasion such a 'Rumble Party Vol. 3', their 'Best Of Fury Psychobilly' series and three volumes of the label's 'Psychobilly Sampler'. Though the label ceased production of vinyl in 1996 much of their back catalogue has found its way onto CD.

Beyond managing the label, Dell has also continued to work on the rockin' scene. As well as organising and promoting gigs, most notably as the kingpin behind the Big Rumbles in Gt. Yarmouth throughout the 1990s, he has also found time since 1998 to helm Radio Caroline's flagship Rock'n'Roll show 'Good Rockin' Tonight'. The show, which is now available on a variety of platforms worldwide, delivers a weekly three-hour dose of modern and traditional Rock'n'Roll and Rockabilly along with occasional live bands and special guests from the scene such as Sonny Burgess, Alan Wilson, Restless, Matchbox and the late Screaming Lord Sutch. Accompanying Dell regularly on the show are his wife Karen Richardson and 'Professor' Roy Williams.

Dell initially got his break in radio back in 1997 when the country music station CMR were looking for a replacement Rock'n'Roll DJ. It was there that he learned his trade and when the station eventually folded he managed to continue his radio career elsewhere until the position at Radio Caroline appeared. Rapidly approaching a decade in broadcasting and with over twenty years as a label boss, Dell is truly one of the most recognisable characters on the UK rockin' scene and Fury Records remains one of Britain's top Rock'n'Roll specialist labels.

Alongside Nervous records, and its stablemate Fury, there is another rockin' empire which has done more than most to keep the Psychobilly flame flickering. Selling vinyl and CDs, releasing records, promoting concerts – Raucous Records has done it all over the past two decades and continues to this day with a website containing hundreds of rockin' releases consisting of classic reissues and all manner of material from new and established bands from across the globe.

Raucous has been, and remains, the domain of one man – Howard 'Raucous' Piperides. Initially started as a mail-order company back in 1986, Raucous first dipped its toe into the record label business with the release of Howard's band The Go Katz' self-titled EP in 1987. This record was an important release, not only as four tracks of late 1980s underground Rockabilly but also as the forerunner to a tremendous amount of Raucous Records releases which would include many early singles, from the likes of The Frantic Flintstones, Spellbound, The Griswalds, The Caravans and The Termites, that now document the growth of Psychobilly. Indeed many of the bands who made their first appearance on Raucous have become household names on the Psychobilly scene or at least have left behind some great debut albums.

The first album release from Raucous was the 1989 LP 'Psycho Tendencies', a legendary showcase for a new wave of UK Psycho bands, and from then on the label continued to grow with long-players from Empress Of Fur, The Sabrejets, The Hicksville Bombers and compilations including 'Live From The Charlotte' and the seminal collection of American Psychobilly 'Only Freeways To Skinner Kat'. Vinyl production more or less ceased in 1994 when Howard began concentrating on CD releases after the label's debut CD, the Deuces Wild album 'Johnny Rider'.

Raucous embraced the CD boom heartily, transferring many of their early releases onto this format. Within five years the label had a strong back catalogue of titles on CD featuring new acts (Thee Waltons, Empress Of Fur, The Sabrejets, Drugstore Cowboys), reissues of major players such as The Meteors, Demented Are Go and The Frantic Flintstones and a heap of Rock'n'Rollers, swingers and wild cats from other rockin' genres that perfectly illustrate the label's already eclectic range of artists.

When Raucous' business premises moved from Leicester to the English seaside town of Lytham St. Annes, Howard continued to promote his alldayers and weekenders at the legendary Princess Charlotte in Leicester but also began promoting gigs in the North West. As a label renowned for years for their regularly dispatched, densely-packed mail order catalogues, like Nervous, Raucous also embraced the potential of the internet and their website has increasingly provided a huge range of titles covering Rock'n'Roll in all its forms.

Many of these are Raucous titles as the label has grown successfully alongside the mail order business and is still releasing new material (Union Avenue, The Vincent Razorbacks, The Astro Zombies, The Hyperjax...) as well as boasting an impressive reissue programme bringing delights from the back catalogues of Crazy Cavan, The Deltas, Frenzy, Matchbox, The Polecats and The Meteors to the CD generation. In 2006, Raucous celebrated their 20th Anniversary in style with a line-up of seven rockin' bands live at the label's 'other' headquarters, The Charlotte in Leicester. However, with the current healthy state of Psychobilly and Neo-Rockabilly worldwide, and Raucous position firmly at the heart of the scene, this is simply the end of one chapter in the label's history.

Two other important UK record labels who helped drive the 1980s Psychobilly scene were ABC and ID Records. These labels were two faces of the same company, an organisation led by John Curd, the man behind the Klub Foot phenomenon who promoted gigs under the Camouflage Concerts banner. Both labels left behind a back catalogue which went on to form a sizeable chunk of most Psychobilly record collections but the label also had a wide range of acts from different genres.

The ID story began back in 1982 from the ashes of WXYZ Records. WXYZ was a Punk label of John

HELL'S BENT ON ROCKIN'

SONIC BOOM

Howard Raucous with The Go Katz (Howard Raucous).

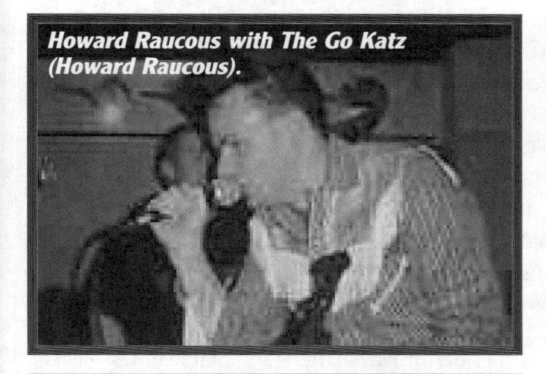

Raucous Records' 'Psycho Tendencies', showcasing a new wave of Psychobilly bands (Howard Raucous).

Curd's which at the time was mostly famous as the organisation who released The Anti-Nowhere League's infamous 'Streets Of London'/'So What' single, back in the days when the Police still kicked down record company doors brandishing copies of The Obscene Publications Act. The label also signed a N. Ireland Punk four-piece called The Defects, a band who toured with The League and a rowdy new rockin' outfit known as The Meteors. Unsurprisingly, WXYZ's first step into the Psychobilly genre was The Meteors' 'Mutant Rock' EP in 1982. That same year when WXYZ morphed into ID Records, their debut was another single from The Meteors, the very successful 'Johnny Remember Me'.

ABC Records got under way in 1984 with its first album, a live offering 'The Birth, The Death, The Ghost' from The Gun Club, closely followed by another live album from drugged-up rocker Johnny Thunders. However, it was the label's third release, the seminal 'Stomping At The Klub Foot', that put them on the map with Psycho and Trash audiences. While ABC continued to release their 'Klub Foot' series of live albums their roster of other acts were mostly bands influenced by Punk and 1960s Garage and Psychedelia, such as The Sting-Rays, The Fuzztones and The Playn Jayne.

ABC did have a couple of other rockin' success stories in the form of Restless, who recorded four singles with the label and two albums (including the infamous 'After Midnight'), and also The Highliners with their catchy single 'Henry The Wasp'. Both bands during their time at ABC drifted as close to commercial success as any rockin' band had since King Kurt and they also made a joint attack on the British independent charts.

ID was the label which dealt more memorably in Psychobilly and issued many cornerstones of the genre such as The Meteors' 'Wreckin' Crew' album (the label's first LP) and classic debut albums from The Guana Batz and Demented Are Go. They also offered bands such as Frenzy and The Deltas the opportunity to switch labels and create some of their biggest records. Frenzy's 'I See Red' single and their 'Clockwork Toy' album heavily dented the UK Independent charts as did other ID releases such as The Meteors' 'Johnny Remember Me' and Guana Batz' 'I'm On Fire'.

ID also signed rockin' bands such as The Sureshots and Fractured who rubbed shoulders with unlikely new labelmates Dr. Feelgood, The Damned and Anti-Nowhere League. The ABC/ID story may have been relatively short-lived, 39 albums and 28 singles over 6 years, but the quality of their Psychobilly acts and the memorable releases which they left behind will forever mark the label as a major player on the early Psychobilly scene.

63

SONIC BOOM

HELL'S BENT ON ROCKIN'

Rockabilly labels had been quick to spot the early potential of Psychobilly so it was no surprise when Punk labels witnessed the rapid growth of this new underground genre and wanted to get involved. One of the true bastions of Streetpunk was Link Records a label set up in 1986 by Lol Pryor, previously behind the Punk label Syndicate Records and one time manager of The Business, along with that band's ex-bassist Mark Brennan.

Link could see that Psychobilly and Punk crossed over easily, particularly on the resurgent British scootering scene where Punks, Skins, Northern Soul boys and Psychos mingled freely. The label made their first venture onto the Psychobilly scene in 1987 when they released a live album from The Meteors as part of their 'Live and Loud' series which had already featured Stiff Little Fingers, Sham 69, Vice Squad and The Polecats. Further Psychobilly 'Live and Loud' (or 'Live and Rockin'') albums would eventually follow, including concert recordings of Demented Are Go, The Tailgators, King Kurt, The Radiacs and many more.

The Tailgators (Simon 'Elv' Wilding).

Link's next Psychobilly album was important in a number of ways. The Frantic Flintstones 'Rockin' Out' was a strong seller and convinced Mark and Lol that further Psychobilly releases were worthwhile. Around this time Link also enlisted the talents of Flintstones' main man Chuck Harvey as an A&R type who was given the task of tracking down new and established talent from the Psychobilly scene. This resulted in new releases from established Psychobilly bands such as Demented Are Go and a flood of debuts from new bands like The Termites, The Tailgators, Rantanplan, The Batfinks, Sugar Puff Demons, The Radiacs and Spellbound.

Despite becoming a breeding ground for new Psychobilly talent, and a continuing source for Street Punk, the dawning of the 1990s saw Mark and Lol go their separate ways. Lol initially set up Dojo Records, a label that continued to release a number of 'Live' Psychobilly LP's alongside a collection of 'Best Of…' compact discs from artists such as King Kurt, The Guana Batz and Demented Are Go. These were obviously aimed at the growing market of aging Psychobillies from the early days, eager to update their collections after their original albums had been lost, sold or jammed in the loft.

Dojo eventually joined forces with Castle, a major label in the world of reissues and compilations drawing from a variety of genres who possessed a huge back catalogue of tracks. Castle itself then became part of the Sanctuary Records Group, an even bigger organisation whose current catalogue boasts extensive reissues from The Damned, Sham 69, The Toy Dolls and the excellent reissue of The Meteors' 'Wreckin' Crew'.

Mark Brennan took some time out before forming the Captain Oi! label in 1992. Captain Oi! focuses on quality reissues on CD but leaves Psychobilly behind and concentrates purely on Punk, New Wave, Ska and Mod revival. The licensing for the Link back catalogue was then acquired by Cherry Red Records and once again the results of Chuck Harvey's tireless campaign to get new Psychobilly bands on vinyl around two decades ago, are gradually appearing on the label's 'Psychobilly Collectors Series'. These obscure rarities are once again available to old diehards looking for a flashback or new converts to Psychobilly who want to discover the scene's early roots.

Anagram's success within the UK Punk scene also made it an ideal home for the then emerging Psychobilly scene. Like Link, it was one of the few labels who embraced Psychobilly from a Punk background rather than most of the other companies who brought Psycho on board to compliment their existing Rockabilly acts. Anagram is a division of long-running Indie label Cherry Red Records, a

HELL'S BENT ON ROCKIN'

company founded by Iain McNay in 1971. Though initially concert promoters, Cherry Red were driven by the Punk movement and released their first single in 1978. As a label they soon became major players on the UK independent scene and their roster of talent grew. Anagram was created in the early 1980s to deal with the punkier acts on their books such as Vice Squad, One Way System, The Vibrators and The Angelic Upstarts.

Anagram's first venture into Psychobilly was in 1983 with the compilation album 'Blood On The Cats'. Though somewhat of a mixed bag it contained tracks from The Meteors, The Guana Batz, The Escalators, The Ricochets and The Sting-Rays alongside some decidedly un-Psycho fare such as Alien Sex Fiend, Bone Orchard, Shockabilly and The Jazz Butcher. In retrospect these bands appear to have little to do with Psychobilly but at the time many of them would often appear on the same bill as many Psychobilly bands as they were all part of the same 'alternative' underground scene of the 1980s. Alien Sex Fiend played far more regularly at The Klub Foot than most rockin' bands and 'upstairs' at The Clarendon had a fairly large Goth population on most nights.

Regardless of its pedigree, 'Blood On The Cats' spawned the successful 'pussies' compilation series which included 'Revenge Of The Killer Pussies' (1984) featuring amongst others The Vibes, The

The Meteors join Anagram (Cherry Red Records).

Meteors, The Tall Boys, The Guana Batz and The Blubbery Hellbellies. This was followed by 'For A Few Pussies More' in 1987 (Restless, Demented Are Go, Frenzy) and 1988's final chapter 'A Fistful Of Pussies' (Batmobile, Thee Milkshakes, Ug & The Cavemen).

The label's first full Psychobilly LP was The Meteors' 'Sewertime Blues' (1986) which commenced a partnership that was to last for six albums and six singles in a period that would cement The Meteors' position as 'Kings of Psychobilly'. Anagram were no 'one-trick pony' however and also enjoyed success with The Long Tall Texans, The Sharks, The Frantic Flintstones and Thee Waltons.

In recent years Anagram's programme of CD reissues has left virtually no stone unturned in chronicling British Punk and the label's focus on the history of Psychobilly has also been extensive. The 'Psychobilly Collectors Series' began in 1999 with the CD reissue of The Meteors 'Undead, Unfriendly and Unstoppable' and has since grown to over fifty releases. With assistance from guru of the scene Alan Wilson, Anagram has trawled the labels of Nervous, Raucous, Link, ABC/ID, Rage, Razor and its own vaults to release definitive collections, long-deleted rarities and unreleased tracks from the cream of the Psychobilly scene, all accompanied by quality packaging and informative liner notes.

Big Beat was another important label which played its part at the heart of the Psychobilly and Trash scene of the early 1980s. The label itself was a sub-division of Ace Records which had evolved from within the walls of Camden Town's legendary record store 'Rock On'. The shop and label were established by Ted Carroll who had built his reputation on the rockin' scene throughout the 1970s with his 'Rock On' stall in London's Soho Market. Ace itself evolved from Ted's first label Chiswick, home of a young metal band called Motörhead, Joe Strummer's pre-Clash outfit The 101'ers, The Damned, Rocky Sharpe and a motley selection of young Punks and pub rockers. The label was also the home of The Meteors' debut 7" 'Meteor Madness'.

As the 1980s progressed, Chiswick could no longer see a future for themselves breaking new acts in the video age and a decision was made to focus on reissuing classic Rock'n'Roll, Blues, R&B and Soul from the 1950s and 60s. Chiswick had already had some success in this area with reissues of previously released material from Link Wray and Vince Taylor & His Playboys.

Despite the success of Ace as a reissue specialist, the rockin' renaissance of the 1980s encouraged the label once again to sign up new talent and Big Beat was established with Roger Armstrong at the helm. On the Psychobilly front, The Meteors, The Cramps, Restless and The Guana Batz all spent some part of their early career at the label but it was the emerging 'Trash' scene that attracted the label most. The Tall Boys (and their previous incarnation The Escalators), The Sting-Rays, The Vibes, Thee Milkshakes and The Prisoners all released vinyl through Big Beat and the pioneering album 'Rockabilly Psychosis & The Garage Disease' was the label's snapshot of the emerging scene accompanied by some of the original acts who influenced it.

Only The Tall Boys and The Sting-Rays stayed with the label for any period of time but Big Beat remains memorable as one of the labels that helped kickstart the genres of Psychobilly and Trash. These days it is renowned far more for its lovingly researched and well presented Beat, Psychedelia and 1960s Garage-Punk reissues, many of which are compiled and researched by ex Sting-Ray Alec Palao.

Alongside Big Beat, Media Burn was a label which showcased much of the cream of the Trash scene. Media Burn was established in 1984 by Stan Brennan from within the 'Rocks Off' record shop. Stan had previously found employment at Ted Carroll's 'Rock On' shop. He was active on the underground scene long before Trash reared its ugly head and had worked with early 'Rocks Off' employee Shane McGowan when he produced the debut single of Shane's first band The Nipple Erectors (later to be known as The Nips). The connection would continue with Stan's involvement in The Pogues' early career.

Media Burn's first album was The Sting-Rays' 'Live Retaliation' album, a recording from one of Stan's regular club nights at The Pindar of Wakefield in London's Kings Cross area. The Media Burn roster went on to boast a number of acts who were popular on both the Trash and Psychobilly scene such as The Purple Things, The Sting-Rays, Thee Milkshakes, Ug & The Cavemen and Nigel Lewis (on a solo outing with his album 'What I Feel Now'). They also released vinyl from other artists with a far

The Sting-Rays... pure trash (Bal Croce).

deeper Garage/Surf/Psychedelic sound such as The Golden Horde, The Surfadelics, Bad Karma Beckons, The X-Men and The Locomotives.

Many of the releases featured some contribution from The Sting-Rays' Bal Croce, either in the form of production or cover artwork, and he was effectively the label's A&R man seeking out talent and also playing a part in influencing the general look and feel of the label. Bal was also heavily involved in the Media Burn 'showcase' gigs which were held at The Sir George Robey.

Despite the consistent quality of their releases the label were out of business before the end of the 1980s. In a brutal stroke of bad luck Media Burn moved their record distribution from Rough Trade to a relatively new organisation, Red Rhino. When Red Rhino went bust their receivers flogged off their stock rather than returning it to the labels. As a record retailer, Stan found himself being offered his own albums for sale at a pittance from deletion specialist companies who had snapped up Red Rhino's stock for peanuts.

The label never recovered from this financial blow despite strong advance sales for the later albums including Thee Milkshakes' double-LP 'The 107 Tapes' and The Sting-Rays' vinyl epitaph 'Goodbye To All That'. This back catalogue of classics has been chronically under-served by the CD reissue boom and most of these releases remain the most sought after collectables of the Trash scene but some light has appeared on the horizon with a selection of titles scheduled for release in 2007.

Another popular UK label of the 1980s was the Hertfordshire-based Lost Moment Records. Though the label will forever be associated with The Krewmen, who remained with the label for the majority of their career, their remaining roster of talent was far more Rockabilly-influenced with bands such as The Rattlers and The Cruisers on their books. Many of their earliest releases were compilations with a distinctly Rockabilly flavour such as 'Dance To It' (1984) and 'The Rockin' Won't Stop' (1985). These compilations featured many names who were well known to audiences of the Klub Foot era such as The Wigsville Spliffs, The Long Tall Texans, Ant Hill Mob and The Rapids. The label also released two volumes of their 'Rockin' It Up' compilations between 1987 and 1988.

Lost Moment's biggest success was The Krewmen who initially signed to Lost Moment as a Rockabilly/Blues outfit, appearing in this guise on 'The Rockin' Won't Stop'. The band then sufficiently persuaded the label that their new Psychobilly direction was the way forward. The gamble paid off, The Krewmen were a huge success and they remained with the label throughout their career. Although their early releases were determinedly Neo-Rockabilly, Lost Moment did venture further into Psychobilly following The Krewmen's early success and probably their strongest act alongside them were The Surf Rats who released two excellent albums for the label, 'Trouble' (1988) and 'Straight Between The Eyes' (1989), before disappearing from the face of the earth.

SONIC BOOM   HELL'S BENT ON ROCKIN'

The Sting-Rays rock Dingwalls, 1982 (Mike Tighe).

Lost Moment has also acquired a lower profile and since the mid/late 1990s the label has mostly concentrated on re-releases of their classic titles on CD. Though no longer one of the UK's larger labels, Lost Moment has enjoyed some huge success and quietly carved their niche in the Neo-Rockabilly and Psychobilly scene.

By 1985 the British Psychobilly scene was well established, with many of the genre's classic debut LPs lodged firmly in the record collections of flat-tops and mutant rockers across the country. One album which perfectly captures the development of the scene up to that moment is 'Hell's Bent on Rockin'', appropriately released by Nervous Records the very label that had supported a host of bands as they made their way into the dark, uncharted regions of Psychobilly. Although bands such as King Kurt and Guana Batz are not included, tied as they were to labels intent on protecting their investment, 'Hell's Bent...' showcases the cream of devout Psycho-artistes like The Meteors, Frenzy and Demented Are Go along with the harder-edged Rockabilly acts who were so important to the scene such as Restless, The Ricochets, The Sharks, The Deltas and The Rapids.

When viewed in retrospect this album, along with the Klub Foot live recordings, offers a clear picture of the UK Psychobilly scene halfway through the 1980s. The scene started relatively slowly as it shook off the chains of Rockabilly to stand on its own as a new and distinct musical style. Its followers took a little longer to get their act together as well. It is understandable, given the minimal publicity Psycho bands received in the media at the time, that the scene took some time to spread across Britain from its nexus in London. Ironically, from the mid 1980s as the minimal publicity declined the genre grew stronger. More bands formed, and waiting in the wings were future Psychobilly legends such as Torment, The Coffin Nails, The Frantic Flintstones, Skitzo and The Long Tall Texans. Many of these bands had already made their mark by the middle of the decade but would enjoy greater success as the 1980s progressed, while the established Psychobilly pioneers would find their popularity growing.

Not many bands in the mainstream music business have a longevity even approaching the careers of many Psychobilly groups. As most Psycho bands face tightly budgeted record deals and refuse to fleece fans with inflated prices for concert tickets and merchandise, they are often forced to seek a living elsewhere while keeping their band on the move. The downside of this can often be a high turnover of band members but, on a positive note, many bands get the chance to move between labels, develop their sound and maintain a healthy shelf life. This longevity often builds a stronger, loyal following, allowing bands to drift off the radar for periods (often years) but return to the scene when they have something new for the faithful.

It is a very different matter for many major label bands and Indie flavour-of-the-month favourites

HELL'S BENT ON ROCKIN'

SONIC BOOM

who find that during any break in their career their fad-chasing fans have disappeared like shit off a hot shovel to follow the latest trend. All over the world Psychobilly bands have signed up for lengthy tours of duty such as The Hellbillys' and The Quakes long-standing commitment to rockin' the US, Mad Sin and Nekromantix' refusal to stay buried in Europe and many British bands have also refused to play dead.

One band who will always be remembered fondly, from the period now referred to as old school, are Torment. The Bristol trio were one of the most original bands on the scene but their career ended in tragedy with the suicide of lead singer and guitarist Simon Brand.

As a regular on the Bristol rockin' scene with his band The Joint Jumpers, drummer Kev Haynes was aware of the growing Psychobilly movement and was also a friend of Frenzy's Steve Whitehouse. When he decided to form his own rowdy combo in 1985 he approached Steve's friend, and former Frenzy guitarist, Simon Brand. Brand had left Frenzy in 1984 when a personality clash with Whitehouse resulted in Brand being shown the door with only two tracks of the band's debut album completed. Initially the duo were joined by double-bassist Sean Holder, another member of The Joint Jumpers.

The trio began rehearsing and some of Torment's earliest tracks began to take shape. With new manager 'Nutty' Dave behind them they were ready to perform and played their first two gigs, one with the Long Tall Texans in Brighton and another supporting The Coffin Nails in Bristol. These were to be Sean Holder's only appearances with the band and he was briefly replaced by Tony Biggs, who had played with Brand in his pre-Frenzy outfit The Firebirds, who also moved on. A more permanent solution was found when Simon Crowfoot joined up and the legendary Torment line-up was formed.

Roy Williams got a hold of the band's earliest demo and offered Torment their first album deal with Nervous. Prior to this the band had also appeared on the label's classic 'Zorch Factor 1' (1986) album contributing two tracks, 'The Source' and 'My Dream', both Simon Brand compositions. That same year their debut 'Psyclops Carnival' appeared along with their four-track twelve-inch 'Mystery Men' and an appearance on 'Stomping At The Klub Foot Vol. III & IV'.

Throughout all these releases ran a similar theme: intelligent lyrics, an avoidance of many traditional Psychobilly themes (horror, lurid sex, mental illness etc.) and super-tight musicianship. None of Torment's songs gave the impression of being rough, album-filling material and most tracks seemed carefully crafted and contained a depth that many Psychobilly tunes lacked. They still rocked furiously but something more lay between the grooves. Apart from two covers ('The Last Time, 'Slow

Early Torment promo material (Roy Williams).

Down') every song on the album was a Brand composition with Kev Haynes and departed bassist Sean Holder receiving co-writing credits on a song each. The album was released in the summer of 1986 at a time when the band were already live favourites across the UK and Europe and Torment saw the year out on the road.

Torment's follow-up album was their second for Nervous, 'Three's A Crowd' (1987). This was again an impressive creation with the added bonus of Steve Whitehouse in the producer's chair. Lyrically the band again avoided standard Psychobilly themes and Brand took a hand in penning all of the tracks on the album but with equal writing credits shared with Simon Crowfoot on five tracks. Having settled into the line-up, Crowfoot appeared to contribute more than ever to the band's set and the only cover version on the album is the band's own interpretation of The Ricochets' 'I'm A Loser'.

For a band of such originality, Torment's third album moved their sound forward in another direction. Nervous' faith in the band was still strong and 'Round The World' (1989) was distinctly different to their previous two albums, both in image and sound. The initial impact of the album was the front sleeve. Gone were the band's trademark shaved heads, towering quiffs and sunglasses in favour of a more moody, rocker look of greased-back pomps, immaculate denims and biker jackets. The two Simons were captured moodily staring into the distance with Kev Haynes posing manfully astride a classic British bike.

This image change immediately hinted at the sounds within as Torment kept their unique rockin' edge but with a more polished production, which the sleeve notes described as "the Blending of Twentieth Century technology with 50s frenetics". Regardless of the band's new direction, 'Around The World' was still classic Torment and almost expected as, even after two albums, it was obvious that Torment were too original to be contained by any strict parameters of the Psychobilly genre.

As the 1990s dawned things were slowing down and the classic trio were about to disintegrate. Torment's fourth album, 'Hypnosis' (1990) was far closer in tone and style to their first two albums. Once again many of the tracks were memorable such as the title track and the storming opener 'Worse And Worse'. The two cover versions featured on the album were bold choices. 'Who Do You Love?' had already been battered by countless bands but Torment still gave it an original spin and their version of the weepy soul ballad 'I Can't Stand The Rain' was inspired.

Not long after the release of the album, while touring in Holland, Simon Crowfoot fell in love with a Dutch girl and never came home. Though he was still keen to tour Europe with the band, realistically his time was over. His replacement was Vince Mildren and between Torment gigs the trio also began playing under the name The Nervous Brothers and pursuing a more Rockabilly direction. As Torment, there were to be no more recordings released and things were about to take a more tragic turn.

Simon Brand, 'Tormented Genius' (Frank John).

Throughout his musical career, Simon Brand was often regarded as 'challenging' to work with but in the music business this can often be seen as simply a side-effect of a talented musician striving to present his work in the best way possible. As the Torment story progressed, Simon began to suffer some real psychological problems which some have attributed to his erratic relationship with his wife and family. With the band possibly acting as his only outlet for these pressures, as Torment's activities decreased the strain on Simon apparently grew. Though Brand and Haynes were still talking about Torment's future in 1994,

HELL'S BENT ON ROCKIN'   SONIC BOOM

Torment tour Europe in the late 1980's (Frank John).

having been admitted to hospital whilst suffering depression, Simon took his own life and hung himself from a tree in the hospital grounds. The Torment story was over in one of the saddest endings in Psychobilly history.

The Coffin Nails started over two decades ago in Reading, a town along the Thames valley only a kick in the arse away from London. Formed by the unforgettable Humungus (or Steve 'Klunky' Clarke to his friends) in 1985, the original line-up was Humungus on guitar, Tony Szjaer on vocals, Toby Griffin on drums and laconic bass player Gra (Graham Farr). Their first two gigs got them off to a fine start. Both were at The Paradise Club, their hometown hotspot in Reading, supporting first The Sting-Rays and then The Guana Batz. After less than a year the band were already established on the Psychobilly scene and eventually found themselves onstage at the hallowed Klub Foot.

With an appearance on Nervous' 'Zorch Factor One' compilation, with their song 'Plymouth Fury', and two tracks on 'Stomping At The Klub Foot: Vol. 3' (including the first vinyl appearance of the band's anthem 'Let's Wreck') The Coffin Nails career was moving quickly, too quickly. The band's increasingly high profile brought Toby to the attention of P. Paul Fenech and after a period 'on loan' to the Godfathers of Psychobilly, and a spell in The Frantic Flintstones, he subsequently joined The Meteors full-time. Toby's friend, and follower of the Nails, Dave Ward took over the empty drum stool then soon moved upfront to replace departing vocalist Tony as he left the band for a move to Coventry.

Before Tony left, The Coffin Nails also featured on the album 'Sick, Sick, Sick'. Slightly more than the usual compilation, this early effort from ID Records teamed The Coffin Nails with Demented Are Go and Skitzo with each band bashing out live tracks recorded at the Klub Foot in April 1987. Though it was a hastily cobbled-together project, even sticking a picture on the cover of the wrong Coffin Nails line-up, it was a perfect snapshot of three of the hottest new Psychobilly acts of the time.

It was third time lucky for the band as drummer 'Smurf' settled into the line-up, after a false start with another drummer who lasted only a few gigs, and the revitalised four-piece were ready for their next challenge – the debut album. Obviously impressed by the band's 'Zorch Factor One' appearance and growing live reputation, Roy Williams offered the band a deal and recording began on what was to become 'Ein Bier Bitte'. Though relatively rapidly recorded the album featured a dozen quality tracks and was released in 1987.

As is often the case with debut albums, the songs were mostly tried and tested after two years of gigging and The Coffin Nails resorted to only two covers, 'Natural Born Lover' and 'Greased Lightning' (with added smut). If any of the tracks were 'fillers' cooked up in the studio it did not show and two tracks in particular, 'Let's Wreck' and 'Uncle Willy', have continued to remain live favourites across the decades.

With a successful album behind them, The Coffin Nails got the chance to do what many Psychobilly acts before (and after) them did and tour extensively through Europe. For Psycho bands this is often the only way to promote albums, due to mainstream media disinterest, and also a handy way to generate beer money and enjoy the sweaty stench of several geezers in a transit van belching fumes down the autobahn. A Psycho band's reputation is earned on tour and The Coffin Nails soon became renowned for solid sets of blistering Psychobilly and also for putting on an entertaining show. The band, Humungus in particular, worked the crowds into a frenzy with good-nature abuse, banter and their obvious sense of humour – never afraid to take the piss out of the audience or themselves.

Despite good sales of the album and constant gigging, Dave Ward left the band midway through 1988, choosing to make his departure just before going onstage leaving Humungus to complete the gig by stepping up to the mike. In what now seems like an obvious move, Klunky was a natural frontman and the classic three-piece Coffin Nails line-up was born. After working as a three-piece on the road, the band made a move to top Punk'n'Indie label Link Records and Humungus, Gra and Smurf recorded their second album 'A Fistful Of Burgers', which was released late in 1988.

A familiar cycle of album sales and touring across Europe followed and, as is Coffin Nails tradition, somebody else left the band. Disillusioned by the dwindling Psychobilly venues in the UK, Gra took his electric bass and moved on to a metal band, resulting in youthful upright bass slapper Scott 'Mad Man' Milsom joining. With a change in bass styles, as well as personnel, The Coffin Nails sound changed dramatically and this was almost a rebirth of the band as the Humungus/Mad Man partnership has continued to this day.

This line-up was not to remain stable for long, though, as Smurf jumped ship to play in a Ska band and his replacement Alex 'Fraddy' Dalimore lasted just long enough to feature in the band's first live album, their contribution to Link Records 'Live and Rockin'' series. Recorded during a gig at Sheffield, the album was released in 1989 and two other tracks from the night made it onto the live compilation 'Rockin' At The Take-Two: Vol. 2' (1990). Fraddy's departure, like Dave Ward's, was also poorly timed as he phoned his notice in a day before the band were due to appear at a major German festival.

Thankfully, Scott was a long time friend of drummer Nasser Bouzida from Ska band The Loafers and he was

The Coffin Nails; L-R: Humungus, Fraddy & Madman (Coffin Nails).

HELL'S BENT ON ROCKIN'

SONIC BOOM

> MIDHURST DETOURS
> PRESENT
> A
> CHRISTMAS EXTRAVAGANZA
> WITH
> LIVE MUSIC FROM
>
> # THE COFFIN NAILS
>
> AND
> THE BOOZE BOYS
> ON
> SATURDAY 21ST DECEMBER
> AT
> THE CROWN MIDHURST
>
> Admission = £3 on door
> for more info contact DIZZY on 0730 815422

The Coffin Nails, regular favourites on the scooter scene (Mason Storm Archive).

hastily roped in. Ever the professional, Nasser learnt the band's set while listening to it on his personal stereo en route to the gig. The date went well and after the festival Nasser stayed with the band for a short while as a temporary drummer but, upon the demise of The Loafers, became a full-time 'Nail. With Humungus as the sole remaining member of the original line-up the band returned to Nervous Records and in 1991 released 'Who's He?', their fourth and most accomplished album at that time. The band were now, more than ever, a headline act particularly across Europe and two years of solid gigging followed. Though they entered the decade in a strong position the 1990s were to be a time of mixed fortunes for the band.

Another band who enjoyed similar success to The Coffin Nails were a band who initially shared the same drummer. The Frantic Flintstones, previously simply The Flintstones until their live reputation was established, formed in 1986 with Chuck Harvey on vocals, Toby Griffin on drums, Rick on guitar and Clive Howling on slap-bass. Chuck had previously played in Punk bands Mute and What's This Fish? before getting involved in the Psycho scene and deciding that that was the way forward. After a chance meeting at a gig with Coffin Nails drummer Toby 'Jug' Griffin who was also interested in forming a 'Psycho' band with the emphasis on 'Billy', the earliest incarnation of The Frantic Flintstones began.

In what was to become a regularly-evolving line-up, after just four months Toby left to join The Meteors full-time (leaving both The Flintstones and The Coffin Nails) and guitarist Rick simply could not take the pace. Chuck enlisted drummer Andy 'Monkey' Gunning from his previous band and guitarist Neil 'Nodger' Smith then this line-up ventured on the road for some serious gigging, taking in some legendary venues such as The Klub Foot, Dingwalls, many regional Psycho venues and a fair share of sleazy pits and shit holes. The Frantic Flintstones were also a popular support act but soon began to headline their own gigs as their reputation grew.

Along the way, bass player Clive Howling got lost in the haze of booze and drugs and a stand-in, Ginger Jones, held on until an ad in a music paper attracted now legendary bass-slapper Gary Day. With this line-up in place, the band entered the studio to lay down five tracks which would eventually launch their recording career with the release of their 'Bedrock' EP on Raucous Records in 1987. However, before the single was released Chuck Harvey, then only 23, found his years of drug ingestion and boozing catch up with him rapidly when he found himself in intensive care following a heart attack.

Thankfully Chuck pulled through and after a month in hospital he was back with the band. Things were moving rapidly for the Flintstones and following the success of the EP they secured a deal with Nervous Records. Returning to the studio with Mark 'Swordfish' Hunt, a producer Chuck would continue to work closely with over the years, they began creating what would emerge as the appropriately named 'Nightmare On Nervous' album in early 1988. 'Nightmare…' was a mammoth affair which proved that The Frantic Flintstones had no shortage of quality material and kicked off what was to be a prolific series of record releases. It showcased the Flintstone style which, considering Chuck's previous experience was on the Punk scene, was decidedly more 'Billy' than 'Psycho' and unafraid to raid other genres such as country and blues.

In retrospect this was a grass-roots Psychobilly release that rocked its way through all its tracks with relentless energy. Despite the success of the album and the steady flow of gigs which followed, Chuck and Gary Day decided a new guitarist was needed and just before some gigs in Germany Nodger was replaced by the youthful Jonny 'Pug' Peet. Pug had previously played in the short-lived combo The Mysterons alongside Day and his initiation of booze, smoke and diesel fumes on the road with The Frantic Flintstones began.

This new line-up made a label switch to Link Records as Chuck's craving for more recording grew and 1988 saw the release of 'Rockin' Out', an eight-track mini album which sold as rapidly as their debut. Despite its success this album would also have a casualty as Gary Day left (for the first time) soon after its recording to join Neo-Rockabilly outfit The Nitros. His replacement was Gasty, formerly of The Blue Ridge Rockets, and this new bass-player did some recruiting himself soon after joining dragging Martin 'Griz' Smith into the fold to cover for Flintstones' drummer Monkey who had broken his arm in a car accident.

As 1988 drew to a close the band remained busy recording another EP for Raucous, 'Frantic Flintstones', and a full LP for Link, the 'Not Christmas Album', a 12-track affair which featured four Christmas-themed stompers along with the addition of a touch of sax and banjo to their sound. Link also recorded the band at a gig in Bracknell in November of that year for release as part of their 'Live & Rockin'' series. Both albums would appear in 1989 and during this time Chuck had secured a lucrative side-project with the label with his 'Chuck Flintstone Presents…' imprint for Link Records.

The albums for Link continued with 'A Nightmare Continues' in 1989. It was a furious album of darker, heavier floorfillers that was snapped up by the punters whose appetite for Flintstones' records, seven in just two years, matched Chuck's desire to keep pumping out new releases. No Flintstones album would be complete without a line-up reshuffle and drummer 'Bim Bam' and bass player 'Sloth' joined up, only to be replaced early the following year with the return of Gary Day and new drummer Rich Taylor. Regardless of any dip in the fortunes of the rockin' scene, The Frantic Flintstones left the decade when Psychobilly dawned in a stronger position than many.

Among other early pioneers of Psychobilly, Skitzo were a band whose huge influence on the scene was unbalanced by their relatively short career. In only five years they established themselves as one of British Psychobilly's top bands, live and on vinyl. Though they were to reform in the mid 1990s, they initially ceased to be late in 1990 after five years together.

Skitzo were an enigma, as a band heavily influenced by Rockabilly they were among the earliest bands to push Psychobilly far closer to Punk. Formed in 1985, the London based band initially featured Phil Connor on vocals, Anthony 'Mac' McVey on guitar, double-bassist Tony 'Moses' Bromham and drummer Rod Connor. By the time of their first demo, an injury to Rod had resulted in the recruitment of new drummer Steve Tomlinson. At this time the band were known as The Electros, and gigged regularly until bass-player Tony was detained at Her Majesty's Pleasure for six months. When Tony again tasted sweet freedom the band were back on the road sporting a new monicker – Skitzo.

Having learnt Skitzo's set from tapes he received in jail, Tony found himself slapping a bass at a gig on the same day he was released from the clink. This was followed the next evening by a support slot

HELL'S BENT ON ROCKIN'   SONIC BOOM

with The Meteors in London. Pretkty soon the band were playing at Hammersmith's hallowed booze-hole and music venue The Clarendon Hotel before making a move upstairs to The Klub Foot. With relative ease the band became Klub Foot regulars and soon attracted the attention of Roy Williams. With a deal for their debut album in the bag, the band made their way to XXX Studios in London with Roy Williams and Paul 'Doc' Stewart behind the mixing desk.

The result was 'Skitzo Mania', released in 1987, and it proved to be yet another landmark debut in Psychobilly history. Their own compositions on the album not only featured some furious stompers, such as the title track and 'Witching Hour', but also a change of tone on less frantic tracks like 'Under Pressure' which showed that the band were far from standard Psychobilly fare. The band were actually approached by Elvis Costello on the strength of that track, but nothing came of it. Although a third of the tracks were covers they were all good-natured stomps through a handful of Rockabilly and Country classics including one in particular which was a standout reworking of an already well-worn tune.

New buyers of the album may have initially heaved a sigh when noticing 'Lonesome Train' on the tracklisting, as King Kurt and The Meteors had already provided pretty definitive versions of the song for a Psychobilly audience and many others had employed it mindlessly to stretch out their live performances. However, Skitzo's version was totally original, employing jagged beats and guitar riffs with deadpan vocals and some studio trickery. All in all, 'Skitzo Mania' was an album of genuine variety that made a real impression on the scene, rather than simply offering a quick run through of their live show in the studio.

With the album selling consistently in the UK and Europe the band made their first visit to Germany where 'Skitzo Mania' was particularly popular. The growing success of Nervous Records was also helpful as many record buyers were aware of the label's back catalogue and trusted that their Psychobilly releases would often guarantee a high-standard of rockin' with teeth-rattling potential. Despite the band's growing popularity, Steve Tomlinson moved on and new drummer Strut brought a harder, heavier sound to the band's songs – something which hinted at Skitzo's future direction. Another line-up change was also on the horizon.

The band were asked to appear on a live recording for 'Stomping At The Klub Foot Vol. 5' and on the night of the concert the performance of overly-drunk guitarist Mac was questionable and led to a back-stage bust-up which eventually saw to the guitarist leaving the band. The tracks 'Your Cheating Heart' and 'Folsom Prison Blues' were salvaged from the session and appeared on the album, despite protests from the band. An earlier Skitzo performance at the Klub Foot also appeared on the ID Records live compilation album and video 'Sick, Sick, Sick' with The Coffin Nails and Demented Are Go.

A replacement for Mac was a matter of urgency, with many gigs already booked, and luckily long-time friend and follower of the band Pete Davis stepped up. Pete already knew the band's repertoire and just as well, as within days of joining Skitzo he was playing live. After the new line-up had worked together on the road, preparation for their second album began. This follow-up was never destined to be 'more-of-the-same' as the band were about to take their sound in a far heavier direction. Although the influence of Hardcore Punk, Thrash and a whole host of heavy styles are commonplace in Psychobilly now, Skitzo made a pioneering move in pushing their sound in a more extreme direction. Pete and Phil worked long and hard on new songs which, along with Tony and Strut's input, saw Skitzo enter the studio with a radically altered sound.

Though they never turned their backs on Psychobilly's roots in Rockabilly (all the album's cover versions were solid rockers) their own material was much tougher than before. Phil roared on every track while the rest of the band beat their instruments senseless. The result was 'Terminal Damage', released by Nervous in 1988 and certainly the label's heaviest album up to that point. This change of direction was not to everyone's taste as many saw the album as a step further from Psychobilly's roots but equally many recognised it as a new way forward.

Ironically, as this new sound sparked further interest in the band it was also having an effect on Phil Connor's wellbeing. Years of delivering his trademark screams in Skitzo songs, combined with increased

Skitzo at The Klub Foot (Pete Davis).

demands to perform powerhouse vocals for the 'Terminal Damage' material were putting a strain on the singer's voice. Diagnosed with nodes on his throat, Connor had no choice but to step down as the band's frontman or face further medical difficulties. This set in motion a general slide in the band's fortunes. Tony took over on vocals with his role replaced by electric bass player Justin Kielty but by the end of 1989 he too left the band. Six months later Strut left to emigrate to Sweden, and by the time of the band's final gig at the first Big Rumble in 1990, their line-up was virtually unrecognisable from their Klub Foot days. The gig was booked several months in advance, but the remaining band members chose to fulfill the booking rather than disappoint by cancelling so late in the day.

As time moved on, new listeners continued to discover the band's small, but perfectly formed, back catalogue and rumours about their reformation began to circulate. Pete Davis was instrumental in bringing the group back together, first approaching Phil late in 1993. With Phil back on board, original drummer Rod returned along with Tony Bromham. Their debut gig was at the 7th Big Rumble in Autumn 1994, four years after they had splintered at the first stompfest in Norfolk. Their reunion was a success amongst old fans and many new ones who had never witnessed the band live but had appreciated their albums.

With Phil's condition in mind, their gigging was more select but their songwriting was as strong as ever. Two new tracks, 'Misery' and 'Deep River', were recorded live for Fury Records' 'Rumble Party' series of albums and four new studio tracks appeared on the Fury Records 7" EP 'The Glove' (1995). Far from trading on past glories, Skitzo continued to create an album's worth of new material and recorded demo versions of them all. Nervous again picked up the album and work on what was to become 'Vertigo' began. Their third long-player was released in 1996 but the band were generally unimpressed with the finished article, both in its recording and cover artwork, and another downward slide began which eventually led to their final performance at High Wycombe's Flint Cottage venue in 1997.

In the current climate of a resurgent Psychobilly movement, Skitzo remain a memorable old-school Psychobilly band whose influence on the scene is now more apparent. They took Psychobilly harder and faster than any before them but still left behind many moments of pure Rockabilly in their recordings,

HELL'S BENT ON ROCKIN'

and as many of their line-up shuffles were relatively good natured, a 'third wave' of Skitzo does not seem impossible.

Despite their varied roots, influences and past histories many of the first wave of UK Psychobilly bands shared similar sounds and themes. More distinctly, many bands had an air of adrenalin-fuelled menace about them. Songs such as 'Wreckin' Crew', 'King Rat' and 'Let's Wreck' stirred the blood and demanded a vigorous workout in the wrecking pit or at least aroused the desire to kick some shit about the bedroom for listeners at home. Aside from the relatively short-lived jollity of King Kurt, one band brought a real sense of fun to the scene and created a fine collection of tunes which soaked the Psychobilly community in a sweaty party atmosphere – all driven by a maniacally grinning, double-bass slapping frontman.

Long Tall Texans formed in Brighton in 1984, seemingly driven by more of a desire to party and sup free booze than to feed any ego. Almost immediately their enthusiasm was infectious and their early gigs not only began to attract the first legions of their soon-to-be loyal army of followers but also those rockin' record company types. The original line-up consisted of Mark Carew on vocals and double-bass, Mark Denman on guitar and drummer Bill Clifford. After securing major support slots with The Meteors and King Kurt, their live reputation continued to build but after eighteen months Clifford left. His replacement was Anthony Theodotu and 'Theo' quickly became part of a trio who remain to this day one of the finest rockin' bands on the Psychobilly scene.

Their first vinyl appearance was on 'Sounds of the Southern Scene', a compilation album featuring a variety of bands from England's South coast. This was followed by two tracks on Lost Moment Records compilation 'The Rockin' Won't Stop', while another two of their early recordings 'One More Time' and 'Non Stop Loving' also appeared on the first of Nervous Records' groundbreaking 'Zorch Factor' LPs. They then signed a deal with the Punk label Razor Records, home to the likes of The Adicts, Newtown Neurotics and The Angelic Upstarts, which led to the release of their debut album 'Sodbusters' in 1986. After a European tour to support the album, demand was high for more Texans' material and they returned to the studio for Razor Records and produced a number of tracks which would surface in 1987 on the mini-LP 'Los Me Boleros' and a 12" EP 'Saints & Sinners'.

Skitzo rockin' downstairs at The Clarendon (Pete Davis).

With constant gigging and a growing following the band had conquered much of the Psychobilly scene by 1988 including headline tours of the UK and Europe alongside top billing at the Klub Foot and a number of rockin' festivals. Seeking to move things forward they looked to the singles charts for inspiration, a brave move with Psychobilly as such a strong underground movement and single releases a relative rarity in a scene so focused on album sales. First off the mark was a Razor Records 7" featuring the band's trademark cover of The Clash's 'Should I Stay Or Should I Go', an absolute riot-starter at Texans' gigs and obviously a good choice in attempting to draw a wider audience. The second single was 'Get Back Wet Back', a Long Tall Texans original, and again a trademark of the band which enjoyed a 7" and 12" release.

While neither single hit the UK Top 40 they both gained airplay on Radio 1, the British station which held a stranglehold on the UK music scene, and they made impressive dents on the Independent charts at a time when Indie music sales were an important part of the British music industry. The band also recorded a Radio 1 session which was again a prestigious achievement (shared with The Meteors, Guana Batz, Frenzy and of late, Tiger Army) as most bands with a Psychobilly connection where often sneered upon by the sniffy establishment-types at the BBC.

For the curious who had not yet witnessed the band's mastery of live venues a video also appeared in 1988, which captured the Long Tall Texans' spirit and energy in concert. 'Blood, Sweat & Beers' was recorded at the 'Night of the Long Knives' event at Birmingham's Hummingbird and perfectly illustrated the good-natured riot that was a Texans gig. The following year saw the band back in the studio creating their third album for Razor, 'Saturnalia' (1989).

'Saturnalia' caught the band at their peak, showcasing their unique blend of Psychobilly, Rockabilly, Ska, Reggae and anything else that took their fancy. It was another eclectic album demonstrating the band's 'Texas Beat', a style impossible to pin down and one which avoided many traditional Psychobilly themes yet still attracted a massive Psycho audience. Featuring a revamped version of 'Get Back Wet Back', future favourites such as 'Cairo', 'Don't I Know It' and a song which was to be a continuing feature of the band's career. 'Bloody' was a cover version of a relatively obscure Golinski Brothers tune from 1980 and the Texans' version should have been a great British pop hit.

Though never released as a single, it certainly could have enjoyed similar success to the likes of The Housemartins' hit 'Happy Hour' had the Rockabilly/Psychobilly music biz not been regarded by the mainstream music industry as a genre relatively widely known but rarely mentioned in polite company. The album was a perfect example of the Texans' natural appeal to a far larger fanbase that still never betrayed their Rockabilly roots. In a relatively short period of time The Long Tall Texans had established themselves as a trio with a loyal following, gathering members of the Psychobilly, Rockabilly and Scootering fraternity, while also opening their sound to a wider audience. With a strong live reputation, three albums and a handful of popular singles behind them things were looking bright for the Brighton combo.

For many who failed to see beyond the inclusion of a saxophonist, a wacky sense of humour and the occasional synchronised dance movement, The Highliners were far more than the band who picked up where King Kurt left off. Rather than freezing their arses off touring the skankiest venues which Britain had to offer for up and coming Psychobilly bands, The Highliners spent the early part of their career busking and gigging all summer long in the South of France. Even then the band had a truly individual style and did their travelling in a bright pink VW camper van with the band's logo splashed across it.

On returning to the UK, and experiencing a constantly revolving drum stool, the band fell in with Steve 'Ginger' Meadham who by the mid 1980s was one of the Psycho' world's most noted drummers having already been behind the tubs for The Ricochets and The Meteors. With Ginger on board things moved rapidly and rather than fight their way up the greasy pole of support band status by 1987 the band were already headlining at the Klub Foot and had signed a deal with ABC Records. The ABC deal resulted in two top selling singles, 'Double Shot Of My Baby's Love' and 'Henry The Wasp', both of

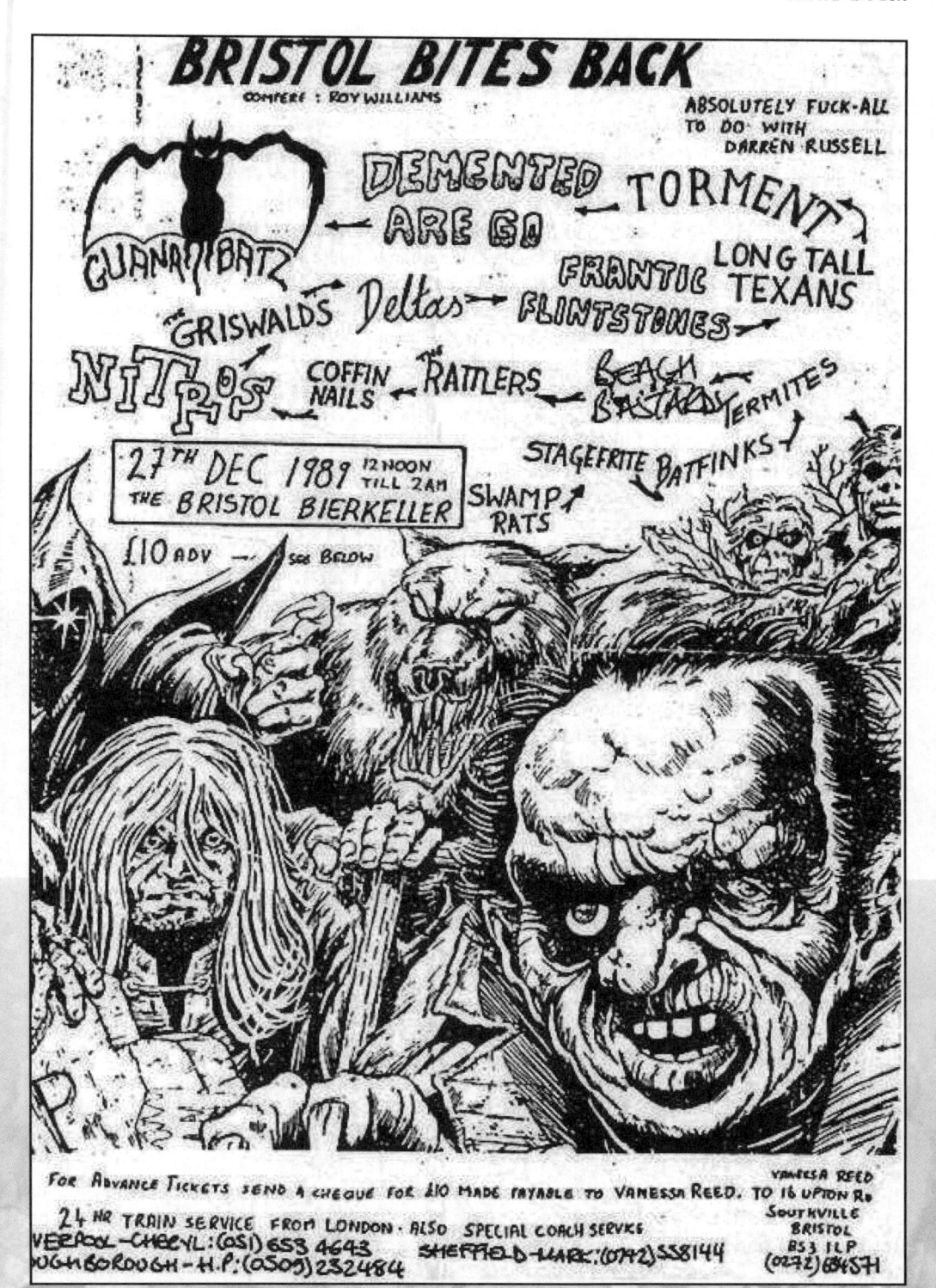

Psychobilly heaven! A fistful of top rockin' talent in a West Country Bierkeller (Mason Storm Archive).

which outlined the blueprint of The Highliners success which was a serious approach to having a good time. Though the band delivered a humorous, fun-filled show they were well rehearsed, well prepared and highly professional.

As well as The Highliners' popularity on the Psychobilly scene, their lively performance also went down well with more general 'alternative' types of the late 1980s such as Goths, students and dole scroungers tanked up on snakebite. Their lively performances also saw them secure a spot on mainstream television in 1987 when they were enlisted as the house band on a Channel 4 series called 'Comedy Wavelength'. This weekly half-hour show featuring new comedy talent ran for ten episodes and was hosted by Paul Merton. Any Psychobillies sitting through late Tuesday nights hoping for a sniff of porn on this (then radical) new channel got the opportunity to catch The Highliners opening and closing the show which was recorded live onstage at London's Town & Country Club each week.

Work began on their debut 'Bound For Glory' but the break-up of ABC resulted in the album sitting for almost two years before gaining a release from Razor Records in 1989. When 'Bound For Glory' made a long-awaited move onto CD (Dojo Records, 1996) it featured additional 'B Sides' and Klub Foot recordings which made it a far more complete picture of The Highliners at their very peak. Going out on a high, the band moved into hibernation early in the 1990s but were set for a return later that decade.

Around the time of the demise of the Klub Foot, shrewd promoter Darren Russell appeared to have noticed a gap in the market and expanded on the three and four band line-ups which were common at the Klub Foot and other venues to create the UK's first major Psychobilly all-dayer 'The Night Of The Long Knives'. The first incarnation of this early Psycho fest took place at Birmingham's Hummingbird venue in July 1988. This was a sustained twelve-hour session of wrecking featuring The Meteors as headliners along with the Long Tall Texans, The Caravans, The Quakes, Skitzo, Frantic Flintstones, The Klingonz, Turnpike Cruisers, Boz & The Bozmen, The Tailgators and The Griswalds. The entire performance was filmed and a visual record of the event still exists on the Cherry Red DVD 'Psycho Attack'.

A follow-up event, featuring many of the same bands, was held later that year at Chapeltown in Leeds. In 1989 the event moved down to the capital and the suitably named 'Uppercut Club' in London's Forest Gate. As a dancehall well used to the spilling of blood, it was a suitable venue for another lengthy day of boozing and wrecking which took place with Demented Are Go and Skitzo headlining. London was again the place for the next 'Night Of The Long Knives' and the gig was stretched over two days and held in Bromley's Downham Tavern. By 1990 it was all over with a final gig at the UMIST in Manchester.

Though relatively short-lived, these were major events and each gathered a wide contingent of Psychobillies from all over the UK and Europe. Each one of them provided a major line-up of Psychobilly, Trash and Neo-Rockabilly bands in the true spirit of the Klub Foot and they proved to be a warm-up for the forthcoming Big Rumbles by encouraging an appetite for all-day boozing and wrecking amongst the Psychobilly community.

Alongside the Psychobilly boom of the 1980s was another genre which would forever be closely associated with the scene, a fact that occasionally disgruntled some of the bands under the same banner. The beginning of the UK Trash boom can probably be traced back to a series of gigs around London in 1982 which offered curious punters a 'Night of Trash'. The dark heart of the scene revolved around three bands who each offered their own bastard hybrid of Rock'n'Roll, Punk and 1960s Garage: The Cannibals, Thee Milkshakes and The Sting-Rays.

The Cannibals, at the time, were probably the most established band, playing regularly at clubs such as Dingwalls and their own Monday night residency at Stoke Newington pub The Pegasus. The Cannibals lead singer Mike Spencer tentatively offered the youthful Sting-Rays a gig at The Pegasus despite holding reservations that they were a little 'more Psychobilly' than The Cannibals' garage-loving audience. However, after their first appearance The Sting-Rays endeared themselves to the Trash guru.

Around this time, Spencer also brought Thee Milkshakes on board and the first Trash triple bill was set up for The Starlight Room in West Hampstead. The Cannibals headlined, Thee Milkshakes made it out of the Medway for their first London gig and The Sting-Rays raised such a ruckus at the bottom of the bill that they were moved up a billing for subsequent gigs. The final 'Night of Trash' took place later in 1982 on Friday 29th October at Oxford Street's legendary 100 Club – suitably a venue steeped in Rock'n'Roll, Beat and Punk history. All three bands played with the added attraction of The Black Velvet Underground, a band who would soon enjoy a little success as Pogue Mahone and a lot of success as The Pogues. As an added attraction free records were given away and many punters who stumped up the measly £2.50 entrance fee walked home with either a Sting-Rays white label, Thee Milkshakes' debut 7" or a copy of The Cannibals' 'Led Astray' single.

The story of Thee Milkshakes and Billy Childish's other bands before and after them is an epic tale which deserves a book of its own and Childish's occasional disdain for many 'billies saw them move steadily away from the Psycho scene into their own universe. Nonetheless, Childish's various outfits (Thee Mighty Caesars, The Headcoats, The Buff Medways...), each boasting their own variation of raw Rock'n'Roll, have continued to have a loyal following amongst the Psychobilly community.

Undoubtedly the band from those early trash nights with the largest Psychobilly following would have to be The Sting-Rays. Though they would forever disassociate themselves from the tag of Psychobilly their early quiffed-up image, their range of musical influences and the onstage dementia they created was always bound to attract the attention of hard-core 'billies particularly during their storming performances at the Klub Foot. Regardless of this, The Sting-Rays really were a very different band to the majority of unashamedly Psychobilly groups around at the time. Though they had a double-bass, a stripped down drum kit and they often screamed their way through some Rockabilly classics their sound was also steeped in Psychedelia and Garage Punk. Lyrically the band also had a bit more going on beyond the usual sex and horror themes and many of their songs had studied (and occasionally political) themes.

The road to The Sting-Rays formation was a relatively long one with all four members as Rock'n'Roll obsessed schoolfriends forming their first band late in 1976 in leafy Letchworth, a 'garden city' north of London. What followed was a series of practice sessions, new bands and line-up shuffles resulting eventually in what would become the first true Sting-Rays line-up of Bal Croce on vocals, Alec Palao on drums, Mark Hosking on guitar and Keith 'MK' Cockburn on double-bass.

After an abortive first gig, thrashing through some Rockabilly classics to bemused toffs at a rich girl's marquee party, their true debut was late in 1981 at Kentish Town's Bull & Gate pub. This was Bal's first full gig as frontman as previously he had only crashed the stage for the closing numbers of their set. Mark Hosking was originally vocalist/guitarist but Bal was a real force of nature onstage and instantly proved himself worthy of fronting the band.

With their first London gig behind them the band were soon on the line-up of the 'Night Of Trash' gigs which brought them some music press coverage in 'Sounds' who described them as; "Utterly awash in a glorious quiff rinse of 50s and 60s two and three chord classics", while the paper also garnered their front page in April 1983 with a cover shot of Bal in full flow onstage.

Ace Records supremo Ted Carroll caught the band at their early gigs and soon offered The Sting-Rays their first deal, despite having poo-pooed them earlier that year when they presented him with their first four-track demo. After a single evening in the studio, The Sting-Rays' first EP was completed. 'The Sting-Rays on Self-Destruct' (1983) was released on the Ace Records imprint Big Beat and boasted a stunning cover, featuring the band lurking beneath a huge roof painting of The Thirteenth Floor Elevators' debut album cover. Though somewhat rushed in the studio the band's furious energy shone through on the three self-penned tracks and a cover of The Thirteenth Floor Elevators' 'You're Gonna Miss Me'.

The prominence of Bal on the cover of 'Sounds' would prove to be a double-edged sword as although it drastically increased the band's profile, with only a single and four tracks on the 'These Cat's Aint Nothin' But Trash' compilation, an album was needed... and quick. Ace Records rushed the band into the studio with Robin Wills from The Barracudas as producer. The whole thing was recorded over a few evening sessions and coupled with a hurried production and The Sting-Rays eclectic compositions the result, 'Dinosaurs' (1983), was generally unrepresentative of the band's wild onstage performance. Nonetheless, for probably all the reasons which hindered its creation, it remains one of the most original debuts of the era.

In a fit of mischief during the album's recording the band, already tiring of the Psychobilly tag, laid down three frantic cover versions made famous to 1980s audiences by The Cramps: 'The Crusher', 'Love Me' and 'Surfin' Bird'. Sick of constantly being referred to in the same breath as The Cramps and The Meteors they decided to give the punters what they really wanted, albeit with a hint of irony. It certainly delivered and the single, released on Big Beat under the pseudonym The Bananamen, was the band's biggest seller and an Indie chart hit in the UK. Even more ironically the single, which was an undoubted favourite on the Psychobilly scene, marked a point when the band fell badly out of favour with many Psycho audiences who often could not see beyond the band's quiffs and double-bass and occasionally acted badly when confronted with the band's more progressive material.

1984 was a very busy and eventful year for the band, commencing with the recording of their second single, 'Escalator', on Big Beat. When 'Escalator' was released in March 1984, bass player Keith disappeared to concentrate on his final exams for medical school. This left the band entering the busiest period of their career with rotating bass-players including Jeff Mead of The Cannibals (who appeared on the band's 'Four On Four – Trash On The Tube' appearance), The Milkshakes' Michael 'Banana Bertie' Gilbert, The Vibes' Lloyd Tripp and even Alec himself on occasion leaving Tom Cullinan from The X-Men to deputise as Sting-Ray's drummer.

A more permanent solution to the band's parade of bass men appeared in the form of Jonny Bridgewood, a Norfolk string-slapper unceremoniously hi-jacked from East Anglian Rockabillies Fireball XL5 and pressed into service on a German tour. Jonny never returned to Fireball XL5 and finally early in 1985, with a stable line-up once again, the band moved forward.

Johnny's first recording with the band was to be The Sting-Rays' last for Big Beat. The single 'Don't Break Down' appeared in 1985 and marked the band's sound maturing in style and studio experimentation. The move away from Big Beat was prompted by a single deal from ABC Records which included the main support slot on The Cramps' 1986 'A Date With Elvis' tour, courtesy of label boss and promoter John Curd. Despite an excellent tour of major venues around the UK resulting in a growing following, and the band being tighter than ever, Alec was determined to push the band in a far more Psychedelic direction.

As sole songwriter and bandleader, Alec enlisted drummer Joe Whitney into the line-up and moved himself onto rhythm guitar. During the recording of what would become their second, and final, studio album Alec's proposed new direction lacked the primitive Rock'n'Roll which drove Bal through their earlier recordings and bouts of in-studio argy-bargy followed.

The album, 'Cryptic & Coffee Time' was eventually completed but effectively it finished the band off. The LP appeared on Kaleidoscope Sound in 1987 and followed the band's late 1986 12" for the label, 'Behind The Beyond'. All that was left was a final gig at the Sir George Robey in July 1987 and suitably the band ended their career with an explosive combination of Rockabilly and Garage Punk in a grotty London boozer, the same way they had exploded onto the scene a mere six years before. The gig was captured in all its gory glory and released by Media Burn Records as 'Goodbye To All That' and it became a suitable companion to that label's other live Sting-Rays album 'Live Retaliation' (1985) and the very rare 'Live' (1984) 10" album from Raucous Records. The concert recordings and studio performances, in retrospect, show the true schism of the band; wild and furious onstage but always trying to experiment and move beyond any expectations their following had when recording.

Time has also proven that the part of the audience which the band often attempted to distance themselves from, the Psychobilly nation, have mostly held The Sting-Rays in high regard and never let their legacy slide into oblivion. It is true that many audiences in the mid 1980s, desperate for a good stomp to Klub Foot era Sting-Rays material, occasionally gave the band a hard time when they were airing new songs. However, if the band believed their Psychobilly audience were too thick to appreciate studio experimentation and lyrics beyond graveyards, ghouls and crypt-kicking they were seriously underestimating many of their true fans.

With the band on the rocks they went their own ways but all continued to be active in the music biz. The break up of the band (and their equipment) left Bal with a chunk of cash which he invested in his own video shop, 'Psychotronic', in Camden Town. Trading in cult and exploitation titles, Bal's partner was Sam Burrell and later Gallon Drunk's bass man Mike Delainian following the unfortunate death of Sam. During this time Bal featured on the legendary self-titled Ug & The Cavemen album for Media Burn in 1987 then became a member of The Earls of Suave in 1991 alongside Mark and Joe. The Earls were a loose collective of Camden Town boozehounds almost designed to please themselves playing small pub venues to groups of friends.

Though with no great pretensions to please anyone other than themselves they released the singles 'The Cheat' on Camden Town Records and 'In My Dreams' for Vinyl Japan followed by a debut album, 'Basement Bar at the Heartbreak Hotel' (1994), again for Vinyl Japan before splitting. Bal moved on to work in television but from the remnants of the band Mark, Joe and former Gallon Drunk drummer Max Decharne formed The Flaming Stars in 1994. To this day The Flaming Stars have maintained a steady flow of single and album releases, alongside some critical mainstream acclaim, but have kept moving at their own pace and refuse to be pigeonholed and stranded in any specific genre.

Alec Paolo decamped to the USA and eventually settled in San Francisco where he put his record company experience and love of Garage Punk and Psychedelia to work. As an acknowledged authority on the genres, Alec has worked on the re-release of a huge number of reissues contributing liner notes and sourcing rare recordings, info and promotional material. Mainly working for the folks at Big Beat/Ace Records, Alec has also kept active musically and taken his place in recent line-ups of 1960s beat merchants The Chocolate Watchband and The Beau Brummels while Jonny Bridgewood has worked with Boz Boorer on a number of his solo projects and followed the former Polecat into Morrissey's band for a while.

The Sting-Rays remain a fondly remembered act from the 1980s and their stature is as major as ever. Strangely the CD reissue boom of the last ten years has not been as kind to them as other acts and, apart from their appearance on a handful of compilations, only one CD has appeared featuring solely their material – 'From The Kitchen Sink' (2002), on Big Beat Records. This compilation gathers together some of their best material from their Big Beat recordings but none of the original albums exist on CD and 'Cryptic & Coffee Time' has achieved the almost mythic status of a 'lost' album.

One band who firmly connected both scenes were The Tall Boys, a group whose sound was as individual as the Trash scene itself but as they featured one of the founding members of The Meteors they were always bound to attract a strong Psychobilly following. Nigel Lewis has remained a towering presence on the scene but his musical career has been somewhat enigmatic. When Lewis left The Meteors he soon joined up with another ex-member, Mark Robertson, and formed The Escalators. The name derived from the one-off single on Big Beat from The Clapham South Escalators, which featured three garage-themed tracks recorded during the end of The Meteors' studio recordings for 'In Heaven'. Having switched to guitar, Lewis brought in Bart Coles on bass then within months they were joined by drummer Woodie who had also recently left The Meteors. Woodie joined Robertson at the back, giving the band the powerful thump of two drummers in concert but he also alternated between thumping the skins and playing rhythm guitar.

The band's debut LP 'Moving Staircases' (1983) appeared on the Big Beat label and immediately established that The Escalators were far from Psychobilly and approaching something between an Indie sound and that of the then current Trash scene. Ironically, the band's single 'Monday' had the theme from the TV series The Munsters as its B-side and the track became such a massive success on the

Psychobilly scene that the 7" was re-released with 'The Munsters Theme' as a A-side, somewhat overshadowing the band's own song with what was essentially a throwaway cover version.

During this period, Nigel Lewis had suffered from recurring back pain and after an operation and a spell of recovery he decided that he had no further interest in the direction The Escalators were heading and set about forming a new band with a "harder, darker sound". The Tall Boys had already surfaced prior to The Escalators when two tracks from the Lewis/Fenech/Woodie partnership emerged in 1982. This debut Tall Boys' single on Big Beat, 'Island Of Lost Souls'/'Another Half Hour Till Sunrise', featured Lewis compositions salvaged from The Meteors mark II line-up's final recording session. Post break-up, Lewis took those tracks and Fenech left with The Meteors moniker, drummer Woodie and two tracks, 'Mutant Rock' and 'The Hills Have Eyes', for his next single. The two Lewis tracks were re-mixed by Nigel and one other song from that session, 'Dog Eat Robot', was to appear on The Escalators' debut album.

The Tall Boys were effectively The Escalators minus Bart Coles but with Nigel back on (electric) bass, Woodie full-time on guitar and Mark Robertson, once again, the sole drummer. Woodie was never to feature on any future recordings and after a series of live performances he was replaced by guitarist James Alan. This line-up then produced six tracks for Big Beat which were released as the mini-album 'Wednesday Addams' Boyfriend' in 1984 and also appeared on the UK TV music show 'The Tube' and its spin-off single 'Four on 4 – Trash On The Tube'.

The line-up was expanded in 1985 with the inclusion of Kevin Green (previously with The Deadbeats) who took over on bass leaving Nigel free again to concentrate on lead vocals and guitar. With their most powerful sound yet the band appeared on the compilation album 'Stomping At The Klub Foot: Vol. 2' and in the Spring of 1985 they recorded a further four tracks for Big Beat which were released as the 12" EP 'Final Kick'. This release showcased the band at their peak with the powerful thudding title track, a blistering instrumental 'Interceptor' and two choice covers in 'Dragster' and The Litter's freakbeat anthem 'Action Woman'. The Tall Boys also appeared on the movie soundtrack of the Hollywood gorefest 'Return Of The Living Dead'.

Despite this flurry of activity and some regular touring, including the support slot on two tours of duty with The Pogues, the band folded on the departure of Kevin and Mark. A final 12", 'Brand New Gun', appeared in 1986 but a full length debut album was not to be. As some form of consolation in 1996 Big Beat gathered together all the band's releases on that label along with many unreleased demos on the CD 'Funtime'.

Alongside The Tall Boys, Lewis created what was to be one of the first solo albums of the Psychobilly/Trash genre with 'What I Feel Now' (1987) for Media Burn Records. With Nigel singing and playing all the instruments on the recording himself this was an oddly reflective album featuring little of The Tall Boys' dominant swagger. Though his solo career more or less ended with that album, Nigel was once more in a group again when he formed The Johnson Family along with Woodie, Rockabilly queen Helen Shadow (sharing guitar and vocal duties) and a mysterious bass player known only as Dr Scully.

Their debut single was '(I Don't Want A Boyfriend, I Just Wanna) Motorcycle' (1990) for Nick Garrard's Camden Town Records. This was followed by a few personnel changes in which Woodie and Dr Scully moved on and Lewis was once again reunited with former Meteor Mark Robertson. The Johnson Family continued throughout the 1990s releasing one further single on Camden Town, 'Be My Rose', but, while never splitting up, they gradually faded from the scene.

Late in the 1990s, Helen and Mark formed The Queen B's with ex-Bea Pickles double-bassist Angie Boothroyd and Nigel continued working on a number of tracks at ex-Tall Boy Kev Green's studio, tracks destined to be either Johnson Family or Tall Boys songs. Lewis also occasionally appeared live on his own but his greatest solo performances were yet to come.

One of the most enigmatic bands of the Trash scene was The Vibes. The band's line-up consisted of Gaz Voola (aka Gary Boniface) on vocals, Johnny 'Tubbs' Johnson on lead guitar, Fuzz Fury on guitar,

HELL'S BENT ON ROCKIN'   SONIC BOOM

Nigel Lewis makes a welcome return to the live scene in 2006 (Simon 'Fatbloke' Ling).

Lloyd Tripp on bass and drummer Johnny L. Beat. Their first release was a four-track EP for Big Beat Records, 'Can You Feel…' (1984) and it was an impressive debut featuring two original tracks (Stranger In The House, The Underestimated Man) and two covers (Double Decker Bus, Mini Skirt Blues) along with sleeve artwork and some production input from The Sting-Rays' frontman Bal. Quite unlike any debut up to that point, it had a cavernous sound and was a perfect combination of early Rockabilly and 1960s Garage Punk that was still strikingly original.

Their second release, after a move to Chainsaw Records, was the legendary 'Inner Wardrobes Of Your Mind' 12", a deliriously Psychedelic blend of booming Trash and magic mushroom-induced weirdness. One track from the release, 'I'm In Pittsburgh And Its Raining', even made it into Indie Guru John Peel's 'Festive Fifty', as one of the legendary DJ's top selection of tracks from 1984 which, at the time, was the independent music event of the UK.

The band had also appeared on the compilation album 'Don't Let The Hope Close Down', a charitable collection of tracks designed to raise money for The Hope & Anchor music pub in North London. The Vibes' contribution, 'The Underestimated Man' was in good company alongside tracks from The Boothill Foot Tappers, The Sting-Rays and The Deadbeats.

Despite their growing popularity, The Vibes initially split later in 1984. For double-bassist Lloyd 'Captain' Tripp there was little time to ponder the group's demise as he was hastily recruited into a recently bass-free line up of The Sting-Rays and joined the band on a tour of France mere days after The Vibes' demise. Lloyd never appeared on any Sting-Rays recordings, beyond an unreleased demo, but he can be seen on the video recording 'Nothin' But Trash' filmed at Nottingham's 1984 Trash all-dayer.

Lloyd's time with The Sting-Rays was to be short-lived as The Vibes eventually reformed. The Rays' connection was to remain strong however as Bal continued to work with the band occasionally. Their debut album eventually saw the light of day and 'What's Inside' was released by Chainsaw Records in 1986. Despite most of the tracks on the album living up to the brilliance of their early singles their reformation never lasted so Gary and Johnny Tubbs went on to form The Purple Things and Lloyd

The Frantic Flintstones, always popular in the reissue market (Cherry Red Records).

formed The Bugs a Garage/Psyche outfit who released the album 'Darkside' on Big Beat in 1987. The whereabouts of Fuzz and Johnny Beat remains a mystery.

While the 1980s were a fertile period for the growth of Psychobilly in the UK, featuring many bands still active today, there were far more groups whose careers were much shorter. Some burned brightly then faded away, some lost interest and some could have been major acts had the dice rolled a different way for them. Nonetheless, all of them were important and helped in their own way to keep the Psycho boom booming even if it was just in their own town or city.

One such band were the North East of England's pioneering Psychobilly band The Sugar Puff Demons. The Sugar Puff Demons' story is unusual in that it has a very long beginning and a short, sharp end. They were probably the British 'one-album wonders' with the most potential and in retrospect they genuinely had a sound ahead of their time, so pardon the cliche.

Formed in the North East of England in 1985 the band comprised of Andy Summers on guitar and vocals, Mark Coppin on drums, rhythm guitarist 'Ditcha' and Ritchie on bass. Andy and Mark had been early pioneers of the Northern Psycho scene with their first band The Deadrocks, a band who had been preaching the Psychobilly gospel since 1982. Despite playing regularly, within a year the Sugar Puff Demons were no more but they were back together in 1987 with a new line-up featuring Andy and Mark alongside a new double-bass slapper, Drew Shanohan.

Drew soon dropped his stand-up bass and went electric, then the band really started to establish themselves across the UK and achieved their first vinyl appearance on the Raucous Records compilation 'Psycho Tendencies'. Having got wind of the number of new bands which Link Records were signing as

HELL'S BENT ON ROCKIN'

part of their 'Chuck Flintstone presents' series (including their local rivals The Batfinks) the band approached The Frantic Flintstones' frontman with a demo. They soon signed a management deal with Link which included a contract to record their debut album.

At this point bass-player Drew quit the band. Though his excellent timing almost fucked the band's deal up, Andy drafted in new bass player Steve Hindmarch who learnt their entire set within a month. With Steve up to speed they made their way south to Berkshire for a two-day recording session. With Steve fresh to the the band and Andy and Mark having played together for almost seven years they were tight, many of the songs were well-established and they made the most of their studio time.

They laid down fifteen tracks, consisting of only two covers (The Cramps' 'What's Behind The Mask' and Eddie Cochran's 'Nervous Breakdown') with the remainder being original compositions. The result of those sessions was their debut LP 'Falling From Grace' released by Link Records in 1989. This album outshone many of the others from the 'Chuck Flintstone' stable with each song well-written and healthily produced despite the short period it was recorded in. The years up to the release had seen the band work hard on many of these songs and any throwaway studio recordings were very hard to spot.

The songs themselves were also highly original despite dealing in some traditional themes such as

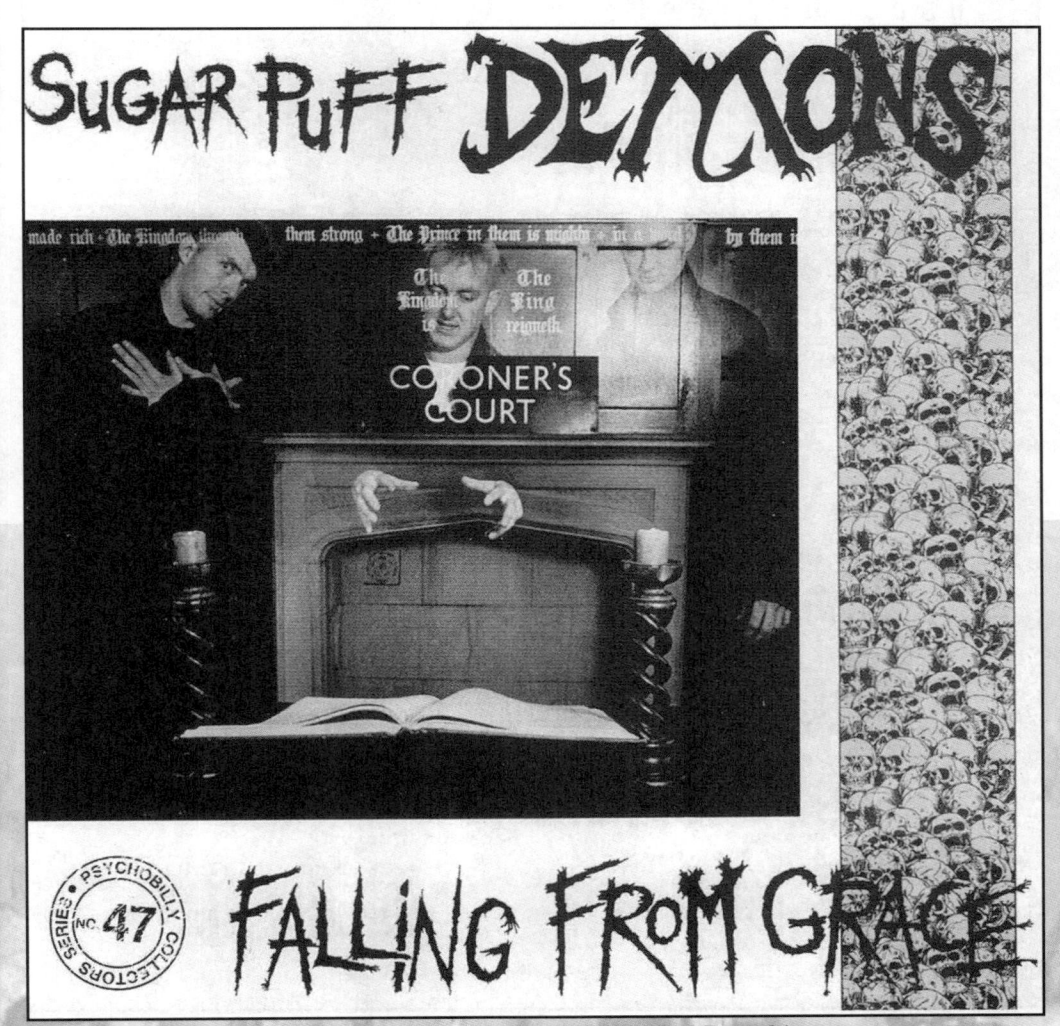

The Sugar Puff Demons' debut, resurrected in 2006 (Cherry Red Records).

Zorch News

The Coffin-nails have arrived!

At last the Coffin-nails have recorded an album. For some time now secret negotiations have taken place in the snug bar of the Skull and Coffin, that well-known drinking place frequented by Psychobilly bands. Of course the Coffin-nails first appeared on Nervous, and after a short flirtation with another company, they have chosen Nervous Records to issue their debut album.

So, what's this masterpiece called? After much scratching of various strange hairstyles, we came up with a brilliant idea. Our German freinds are great fans of Psychobilly, so we've given it a German title:-

Ein Bier Bitte

Translated into English this means - 'A beer please'. There's also an Old English meaning for the word 'bier' which gives a totally different meaning to the title. We'll leave you to work that one out...

A word of warning here. The Coffin-nails are not known for their subtlety, and some of the lyrics may disturb the local vicar so don't play it too loud on Sundays!

Also this is no slap-bass rockabilly going on. Psychobilly. This is the real mean stuff! However, there are references to a bygone musical era with a wild version of 'Greased Lightning' as well as a crazy hillbilly song called Uncle Willy, who has an unfortunate accident while brewing up his moonshine. These things happen according to the band! There's even a little something on this album for fans of the A-Team!

The Coffin-nails have built up a good following in England with several appearances at London's Klub Foot and other records and stand poised ready to make their entrance into Europe.

This is a slightly changed line up from the band that appeared on 'Zorch Factor One'. The drummer left to join the Meteors and the singer left to go and live somewhere in the Midlands. This leaves the original bassist and yes, the amazing Numungus is on lead guitar. He's even got an instrumental named after him on the album. With a new drummer and a dynamic new vocalist, the Coffin-nails are ready to roll! The Catalogue number of the album is NERD031, and UK distribution is via The Cartel.

Contact

The Coffin-nails via:

Dave Ward
58 Eastcourt Ave.
Earley, Reading RG6 1HH
Tel. (0734) 669348

Nervous Records at:

4/36 Dabbs Hill Lane
Northolt, Middx. UB5 4AF
Tel. (01) 422 3462
Telex 265871 MONREF G
Ref. 72:MAG 10814

Nervous Records' 'Zorch News'; keeping rockers informed long before the internet (Roy Williams).

killers, cannibals, necrophilliacs and dirty underpants. Though it was well-trodden ground, The Sugar Puff Demons had a knack of delivering disturbing lyrics in a light-hearted manner. No one could ever describe them as doom-mongers as even their song 'Burn The Church' took the theme of religious arson and turned it into a goodtime hoedown.

With a promising debut album behind them The Sugar Puff Demons touring increased and there was talk of a follow-up album but after some wranglings with Link, a low key tour of England and cancelled European dates main man Andy Summers walked away from the band and suddenly they were no more. Having taken so long to make their mark, then delivering one of the finest Psychobilly albums of the late 1980s, theirs is a story of a classic band that could have been so much more. In fact with their heavier sound and occasionally gore-filled lyrics (which the band referred to as 'Deathabilly') they would be much more at home amongst many of todays horror-obsessed Psychobilly bands.

With many tracks boasting a guitar sound far closer to metal (particularly on the track 'Burke & Hare') they could yet find an audience today as the Anagram release of the album on CD in 2006 has liberated this lost classic. However, with main man Andy Summers now AWOL (believed to have emigrated), Mark drumming in various rockin' bands and bass-player Steve appearing with The Hangmen and The Lunkheads, the group's reformation looks unlikely.

Though The Sugar Puff Demons' classic debut has mostly been appreciated in retrospect, The Griswalds' first album was a major release and a popular addition to many Psychobilly collections. The Griswalds were once referred to by Roy Williams in 'Zorch News' as a 'Neo-Rockabilly/Psychobilly answer to the Travelling Wilburys', that is they were comprised of members mostly from other established rockin' bands and each member took the family name Griswald in the same way that The Ramones posed as 'bruddas'. Their vocalist Gary Griswald was previously in The Nitros, drummer Keith Griswald was a former member of The Niteshift Trio, guitarist Jason Griswald came from The Furys and double-bassist Martin Griswald was the brother of The Rattlers' guitarist Robert Clark.

With this solid background, The Griswalds soon made their mark on the Psychobilly scene with a four-track EP for Raucous Records, 'Do The Hucklebuck' (1989), their track on the Fury Records compilation 'Gypsy Girl' and their memorable song 'Psycho Tendencies' which appeared on the Raucous compilation of the same name in 1989. It was a busy year for the band as they also signed an album deal with Nervous and produced their debut 'Who Framed The Griswalds?'. With its colourful album cover, aping Disney's cartoon/live action romp 'Who Framed Roger Rabbit?', and a couple of unexpected cover versions in the form of 'Who's Cryin' Now' and The Housemartins' 'Happy Hour', they set out their stall as a good time Psychobilly band with a pop edge and a quartet not attempting to take themselves too seriously.

Though probably one of the late-1980s' acts with strong potential for a bit of crossover to other indie types, they burned brightly and faded quickly. One of their onstage performances was captured on the 'Night Of The Long Knives' video but today Martin 'Griswald' Clark is probably the only member still making his mark on the Psychobilly scene, quite literally, as a tattooist with a fine reputation (particularly in styles of a Rock'n'Roll nature) at Lal Hardy's famous New Wave Tattoo studio in London.

Fellow labelmates of The Krewmen were English band The Surf Rats. Signed to Lost Moment Records they released only two albums then, much like The Vibes, they disappeared leaving behind a small but high-quality back catalogue which is still fondly remembered by Psychobillies of a certain age. Formed in 1987, their first long-player 'Trouble' appeared in 1988 and was a collection of well-written songs with a sound that was far nearer diamond hard Rockabilly than the Punkier end of the Psychobilly spectrum.

A year later the band produced a further album for Lost Moment, 'Straight Between The Eyes...' (1989). This remains an album like no other, showcasing a confident trio of musicians resisting the urge to simply belt through their set as many bands at the time were. 'Straight Between The Eyes...' was a well-produced with elements of blues and rock smoothly fitted into their Rockabilly/Punk hybrid. This was also reflected in their choice of cover versions, particularly the Blues chestnut 'Baby Please Don't Go' and AC/DC's 'Rocker'.

Their own songs were of a similar high standard and all their cover versions were given a distinct Surf Rats makeover rather than the simple 'rawer/faster' standard which was also prevalent on the scene. Despite obviously having a wealth of talent in the band and gaining such great recording reputation in such a short time, The Surf Rats' career was to be remarkably short-lived and they definitely remain one the UK's Psychobilly acts who dramatically failed to capitalise on their tremendous potential.

Despite the success of Raucous Records, Howard Raucous still found time to spend on the very band who launched the label. The Go-Katz were formed in Loughborough in 1987 and featured Howard on vocals, Mark 'Moff' Moffatt on double-bass, drummer John 'Wolf' Basford and guitarists Andy Young and Giles 'Beaker' Brett. This was the line-up who recorded the debut EP but the following year a shake-up left Howard, Moff and Andy as the remaining members being joined by new drummer Dave.

Alongside the release of the EP the band gigged regularly, including some prestigious slots at Belgium's first 'Psychofest' and the first ever UK Psychobilly alldayers in London and Manchester. However, a debut album never materialised and the band folded, leaving Howard free to concentrate on his growing business interests.

That may have been the end of The Go-Katz but after a short-lived new line-up which Howard initiated in the mid 1990s, there was a further incarnation of the band when globetrotting Howard teamed up in St. Petersburg with The Russian Bombers and played some border-hopping European dates. Though the official Go-Katz debut never appeared, Raucous did release 'Real Gone Katz' in 2002 which was a compilation of the band's recordings spanning fifteen years. Howard also recorded tracks under the name of Whip Me Houston and also Howard Raucous and the Bombers for the Meteors tribute album 'Sympathy For The Devil'. The final chapter of The Go-Katz has yet to be written but in 2005 a further new line-up was created featuring Howard, guitarist Graham Bateman, Jez Jordan on double-bass and Steve Clark on drums. Often found haunting the stage of The Charlotte in Leicester, new tracks are rumoured to be in the pipeline.

Much in the same way that Lenny Kaye exhumed long-lost Garage Punk rarities from the late 1960s for his 1972 compilation album 'Nuggets' the current Psychobilly scene has its own culture of long-deleted albums from bands who hold fond memories for many aging rockers and a certain bygone mystique for new converts to the cause. By way of addressing this, Anagram Records began reissuing out of print titles in 2006, as part of their Psychobilly collectors series. Amongst these were the Sugar Puff Demons' debut and albums from The Radiacs and The Tailgators, two bands who carved their own niche on the UK Psychobilly scene in the 1980s.

It may be 'grim up't North', but a healthy rockin scene has always been present above the Midlands. Often leaning a little more to the Rockabilly side there was still space for some harder material and Psychobilly quartet The Radiacs were a popular combo back in the late 1980s. The band grew from the scene around Sheffield's Take Two club, a regular venue for visiting Psychobilly and Trash acts, as well as aspiring Indie bands, and the location where many of Link Records 'Live and Rockin' albums were recorded alongside both 'Rockin' At The Take Two' compilations which were recorded at two of the club's Psycho/Neo alldayers.

The Radiacs' original line-up was pretty unique as it consisted of two sets of brothers, Dale and Shaun Williams on vocals and drums respectively along with Billy and Paul Oxley on guitar and double-bass. Their debut 'Hellraiser' came from Link Records in 1989 and showcased the band's Psychobilly (with an emphasis on 'billy) sound which was original but with the obvious influence of early Guana Batz and The Meteors. Though hastily recorded and featuring a good few cover versions, the album had some rattling good tracks which captured their brash live energy. The Radiacs attacked their gigs and were bold and cocky onstage. Thankfully 'Hellraiser' captured much of that spirit.

As was often the case for Link artists, their first album was closely shadowed the following year by a 'Live and Rockin'' LP recorded at their hometown venue. This album featured bassist Nev Preston, who replaced Paul Oxley when he became one of The Krewmen. After another brief line-up change in the early 1990s, the band signed to the German label Tombstone Records and created another great lost Psychobilly album, 'Going Strong' (1993). This was a more accomplished effort studio-wise and featured new bass player Charlie Fallensfeller from The Scum Rats.

Charlie was not available when the band began touring to promote the album and Dave 'Razorback' Bradbury joined the group as they headed across Europe for a number of gigs. Dave was well known on the Sheffield rockin' scene and had played in another of Sheffield's top rockin' bands Haywire, who peddled their own form of 'Desperate' Rock'n'Roll. Around this time, Shawn Williams also moved on so The Radiacs became a three-piece with Dale Williams handling drums and vocals and giving the band a more authentic Rockabilly sound in the process.

When The Radiacs story grew to a close in the late 1990s Dave 'Razorback' went on to join The Blue Devils with Billy Oxley and Dale gradually moved away from the rockin' scene. As well as The Blue Devils, Dave enjoyed a brief stint as a guest with Thee Waltons and also produced the rockin' fanzine 'Rocket' before focusing firmly on his merchandising and clothing business which can now be found at most of the major Psychobilly and Punk gatherings across Europe. Nev Preston never gave up either and in 2003 he joined the Yorkshire Punk band Grinn. A reformation was once mooted for The Radiacs, with some gigs in Germany on offer, but with Dale unable to commit the deal fell through and any further get together looks unlikely.

The recent resurgence in Psychobilly across the world has led to many cases of fans of the genre looking to the early days of Psycho and the bands which were part of the scene. Folks are also now investigating many of the bands who shared a stage with the major names way back then and The Tailgators are one such band.

Based in, and around, Shrewsbury in the West Midlands the band formed in 1987 and featured Dave 'Chopper' Kelsall on drums, Martin Wakeley on bass and a short-lived singer called Mickey who was a member for so little time none of the band can remember his second name. Obviously not having a guitarist was a bit of a handicap so when Simon 'Elv' Wilding came on board they began to take the band more seriously which eventually led to the departure of the mysterious Mickey and his replacement, Tigger, took over on the mike.

After some serious practise and a spate of local gigs the band accrued a following among many scooterists in their area which led to their first major gig supporting Frenzy at a scootering all-dayer in Oswestry. This pushed the band further into the national Psycho-scene and they began to gig more widely, particularly across the Midlands and South Yorkshire.

The Tailgators were one of the bands who attracted the attention of The Frantic Flintstones' Chuck Harvey for his 'Chuck Flintstone Presents' series of albums. Their deal with Link Records led to their self-titled studio album in 1990, as well as a live recording of the band recorded during a Psychobilly all-dayer at Sheffield's Take Two club which was released (unusually) before their debut, as part of Link's 'Live and Rockin'' series.

Despite this double bill of albums and their appearance at many major Psychobilly events, including the infamous Santa Pod Weekender and the first 'Night Of The Long Knives' extravaganza at Birmingham's Hummingbird, The Tailgators career was never fated to progress much further. As guitarist Elv summarises, "... we had never made any money, slept in loads of vans and never even got a whiff of a groupie!"

Around the time of the album's release the scene was slowing down for them and Martin Wakeley moved on to join The Frantic Flintstones. The band continued with Kev Massey on bass but as each member began to follow careers outside music their final gig was soon upon them. When it came it was to be an evening of mixed emotions. Bringing The Guana Batz to Shrewsbury's alternative night-club The Fridge in February 1991 The Tailgators played alongside one of Psychobilly's finest in a triumphant final show. The sting in the tale was that a freak snowstorm resulted in a greatly reduced audience leaving the band to foot the bill for the venue, the lighting and the Batz themselves.

Like many bands of the period The Tailgators were a band caught up in the Psychobilly boom, dragged through it in a haze of intoxication but never really possessed the determination to progress through the decreasing popularity of Psychobilly in the 1990s. However, along the way, despite the setbacks, they rode the torpedo of Psychobilly in its heyday and, as Simon Wilding notes, "we loved every minute of it!", which is essentially the key factor of the whole scene. Very few bands have ever made a fortune from the Psychobilly genre (or even a living) so unless they enjoy it there really is no point.

However, The Tailgators' relatively short history has had a posthumous note as their debut studio album was exhumed from the dusty archives of Link Records in 2006 and re-released on CD by Anagram/Cherry Red Records for the benefit of curious new fans and old-timey West Midland's boot-stompers.

Stage Frite were another Psychobilly act who released their debut album 'Island Of Lost Souls' (1989) as part of Link Records 'Chuck Flintstone Presents' series. This Norfolk based band folded not long after the album's release but most of the band, particularly bass player Clive Perchard and drummer Dave Rounce, have continued to be involved in the East Anglian rockin' scene with bands such as Dawg House and The Roswell Invaders. Their fortunes were also recently revived in 2006 when Anagram re-released their long-deleted debut accompanied by a variety of original demo tracks and unreleased material.

Fractured were also an act from the early UK Psycho scene who were a popular band but seemed to lose their way when the initial Psychobilly boom dipped towards the late 1980s. Fractured's sound was far closer to Neo-Rockabilly but their furious slap-driven beat had more than enough fury to appeal to the wreckers. The band's first appearance on vinyl was 'No Peace For The Wicked' an eight-track debut album on ID Records in 1987. The following year they appeared on 'Stomping At The Klub Foot, Vol. 5', but the Fractured story was to prove to be less than epic and despite their impressive debut and lively performances the band ended with the decade.

While it would be hard to deny that early Psychobilly was as English as bulldogs and jellied eels, the rest of the union and Ireland have all made sizable contributions to the era. England, and particularly London, is undeniably the spiritual centre of Psychobilly. Mainly because the country has been home to many of the pioneering bands and more importantly it has provided a wealth of venues, such as the Klub Foot, Billy's, The Sir George Robey, Hope & Anchor, Hemsby/Caister etc., which are all landmarks in Psychobilly history. Many of these haunts were visited regularly by 'Billies from North of the border but Scotland did have some Psycho action a little closer to home.

One of Scotland's earliest exports to the Psychobilly scene were The Styng Rites, a band named by Eugene of The Rezillos upon discovering The Sting-Rays monicker had already been grabbed down South. Ironically for a band who played such a key part in the live Psychobilly music scene North of the border they unashamedly resisted the label of Psycho and had a more inclusive attitude to the audience they attracted. Regardless of this, their rockin' sound could work up as frenzied a wrecking pit as any of the major Psychobilly bands who ventured into the cold wastes of Northern Britain and their furious Rock'n'Roll style endeared them to the flat-topped masses.

The band formed in 1980 in Greenock, and what followed was the usual young band merry-go-round of Church Hall rehearsals, tatty gigs in community centres and local boozers along with occasional line-up changes. The band eventually settled with George Miller on vox and guitar, Stephen Church (guitar), Ian Mathie (bass) and Jim Gallacher (drums). After hooking up with a booking agent they finally secured more suitable gigs and support slots including opening for The Revillos at London's Electric Ballroom and their gig at The Klub Foot which resulted in the recording of their two tracks for 'Stomping At The Klub Foot: Vol. 2'.

The band were then asked to release a record with Edinburgh Indie label and distributor Fast Forward. 'Baby's Got A Brand New Brain/Shake It UP ' was a three track, double A side, 7" which appeared on the band's own label Snaffle and featuring excellent cover artwork from George himself (something he would continue to do professionally as his career progressed). After a brief line-up change, The Styng Rites released the 12" 'Night Cruising' but by then they had moved even further from the Psychobilly scene in terms of musical style and they soon ended their career with a final gig at

HELL'S BENT ON ROCKIN'   SONIC BOOM

The Styng-Rites (George Miller).

Glasgow's legendary Psychobilly nitespot Strutz.

George went on to form the immaculate beat-combo The Kaisers and has recently been featuring in shows and recordings (as Kaiser George) with the Mexican-wrestling masked instrumental titans Los Straitjackets. The Styng Rites are still fondly remembered by many old school jockabillies but in reality, Psychobilly in Scotland really took the form of a three-pronged attack from a trio of very different bands: The Numbskulls, The Termites and The Radium Cats.

The story of The Numbskulls is so closely linked with that of their bass player Strangy that their tale belongs alongside that of The Klingonz, so the roots of Jockabilly must first be traced a little further south. The Termites from Kilmarnock in Ayrshire were an integral part of the Scottish Psychobilly scene and packed so much into their initially short career that their recent reformation has caused a buzz of mythical proportions. Much of this stems from their few but well respected recordings.

The Termites formed in 1986 with Kenny Mitchell on vocals, Scott 'Bally' Ballantyne on guitar and Ewin Murray on drums. All three were mates and teenage Psychobillies in a town where the Psycho scene was relatively large. When the joy of fighting the local squares outside the chippy began to wane they formed a band and within a few months they were ready for their first gig. With a stand-in bassist from the headline act, their debut performance was a local one in Kilmarnock supporting another band of Jockabilly hopefuls, The Longhorns. The gig would prove to be an omen for the band as it was similar to The Termites themselves — explosive!

For them there was to be no early career of paying their dues for years, trotting around endless venues to disinterested punters as their first crowd was rabid (charged up on cheap lager, Buckfast and glue), the wrecking was fierce and the venue was packed. After unleashing their set, Bally was ejected from the premises for being underage and a riot broke out. Encouraged by the rowdy reception of their first gigs the band recruited a full-time bass player Gerry Doyle and began to play more often. Relatively soon the band were getting noticed on the UK Psychobilly scene and appearing on the bill at many Psychobilly gatherings up and down the country.

Having recorded their first demo tracks in the Autumn of 1987 they began targeting labels and

The Termites, back together in 2006 (Kenny Mitchell).

some of their earliest tracks appeared on Fury's 'Gypsy Girl' (1988) compilation and Raucous Records' collection 'Psycho Tendencies' (1989). The Termites' self-titled debut 7" featured four tracks taken from their second studio recording in September 1988 and it was released by Raucous as part of their now classic series of EP's featuring bands such as The Frantic Flintstones, The Deltas and The Griswalds.

It was one-time Raucous labelmate Chuck Flintstone who secured the band a debut LP deal with Link Records in his position as the label's Psychobilly A&R man. As the band entered the studio it has to be noted that being in The Termites was often a dangerous occupation with punches, kicks and more forms of aggro regularly shared between band members. Their time in the studio was no different and Chuck Flintstone witnessed knuckles, bottles and ashtrays flying between the group as he sat on his producer's chair. Even before the recording was complete, the band's break-up was on the cards.

The album 'Overload' was released by Link in 1989 but by that time the line-up had changed. Despite creating an excellent album together, Bally then Ewin moved out to be replaced by Glasgow guitarist Colin Campbell and drummer Raymie McCabe (who would later join The Meteors). Gerry left soon after and his spot was filled by Stuart Muirhead who brought the double-bass sound to the band for the first time. With Kenny left as the sole original member, the enthusiasm was no longer there and this line-up drifted apart. Stuart and Raymie would eventually form a rockin' blues band together but Stuart is probably best known these days as the owner of Chelmsford's premier tattoo studio – Hepcat Tattoos.

Kenny tried to get the band back on track once more but, in a haze of booze'n'drugs, most of their gigs were when they busked outside of Marks and Spencers in Glasgow's Sauchiehall Street. This line-up featured Kenny and Colin along with stand-up drummer 'Yoker' Iain Campbell (Cottonfield Boys/Salem Dragsters) and saw the return of Gerry Doyle, this time on tea-chest bass. Even the addition of harmonica player Doogie 'Hannabis' Hannah could do nothing to salvage the band and again The Termites drifted apart.

In 1991 Kenny made another heroic attempt to return the band to their former glory and managed to bring Ewin back to the fold alongside Colin and Gerry making the band a closer approximation of their original line-up. The album had ticked over nicely despite the band's lack of major live work and they once again found themselves in demand. Their gigs were bigger than ever and they even recorded two new tracks for compilations on the German label Jungle Noise. Their version of 'Blue Christmas' appeared on 'Wreckin' Around The Christmas Tree' (1991) and a Termites' cover of 'Can't Find My Mind' featured on 'Songs The Cramps Taught Us' (1993). However, once again the band erupted in a burst of internal conflicts which seemed to call an end to The Termites completely.

And there the story may have ended but the band's potential still remained too strong to ignore. A chance meeting between Kenny and Howard Raucous brought The Termites together again in 2000 when Howard asked the band to play an alldayer at The Charlotte in Leicester. This line-up featured Kenny on vocals, Bally back on guitar, Raymie McCabe on drums and bass player Gordon from Kenny's

HELL'S BENT ON ROCKIN'   SONIC BOOM

Punk band of the time, Hateville Heroes. The Charlotte gig was preceded by a spot in the basement of Glasgow's 13th Note pub, a night which reunited many of Glasgow's Psychobilly old-timers for the first time in many years in the city that Psychobilly forgot. Things looked promising once again but in a stroke of irony, Kenny (the man who fought the hardest to keep the band alive) called time on any further action and moved to America to establish his career as a tattoo artist.

Still the beast refused to die and when Cherry Red Records approached the band in 2005 for input towards the re-release of 'Overload', The Termites found that their album had attained a 'lost classic' status and interest in the band around the world was still high. Many shared the belief that the band's recording career, which had shown so much promise, had ended too abruptly. The passage of time had also eased relations between the band and Kenny brought together Bally and Ewin to reunite the original line-up.

Gerry was unable to return so Matt Black from Hateville Heroes took on both electric and upright bass and a fiddler, Johnny Fiddles, also joined the ranks. 2006 brought on gigs in London, Glasgow and Amsterdam along with some lively new demo tracks and an album deal with Crazy Love Records. Almost two decades on, The Termites second full-length creation in 2007 looks set to be one of the most long-awaited follow-up albums in Psychobilly history. As long as they do not beat each other to a pulp before then.

Not far along the motorway in Scotland's capital city another altogether different band were making their move on the rockin' scene. Back in the early days of Scottish Psychobilly both cities had a distinctly different scene. Glasgow had a more straightforward taste for pure Psychobilly, booze, sweat and blood and was less reliant on style but intensely into the music. Edinburgh, while it still had its fair share of wrecking lunatics, had a cooler, more stylish appreciation of Psychobilly and its Rock'n'Roll roots. This difference was evident in spades with Edinburgh's finest export – The Radium Cats.

The Radium Cats were formed in 1987 from the ashes of a variety of Rockabilly groups by the Paterson brothers Lee (double-bass/vocals) and Paul (guitar/vocals) who rattled through a number of drummers as they began work on a Frankenstein-like sound carved from the offcuts of Rock'n'Roll. The band eventually settled with drummer Johnny Maben. While they steadfastly refused to accept the Psychobilly label, their unique sound and outrageous image found them far more at home with that audience than one which was strictly Rockabilly.

Too radical for the Rockabillies, The Radium Cats found a suitable audience amongst the Psychobilly scene and this had some effect on their debut release, the mini-album 'Munster Madness' (1989) on Mental Records. Although it fitted into the Psychobilly scene well the band somehow felt that they were playing what people expected them to play rather than what they wanted to. As Paul claimed in an early issue of UK rockin' fanzine 'Short Cuts': "We got caught in a trap, everyone kept saying "You're a Psychobilly band and gradually we became a Psychobilly band. So we had to record a Psychobilly album."

In 1989 the band enlisted a new drummer, Mark Carr, who quickly became an integral part of the band and they continued moving away from the Psychobilly label which they had been saddled with since the release of 'Munster Madness'. After 'Pink Hearse', the bands twelve-inch for Raucous Records, The Radium Cats released their first full-length album, 'Other Worlds' (1992), for Nervous Records.

This album captured their hybrid form of Rock'n'Horror and Voodoobilly far more faithfully than the more straightforward Psychobilly of their debut vinyl and with songs like 'Martian Hop', 'My Girl Is Like Uranium' and 'Surfin' D.O.A.', their Sci-Fi/B-movie influences were still evident. The critics at the time likened the band far more to The Stray Cats and The Cramps but the truth was that the band absorbed many of the same influences of those bands, and more before them, but still managed to maintain their own strong streak of originality.

In a way The Radium Cats were victims of their own success as their bold image and sound left them in a void between Neo-Rockabilly and Psycho. While they reached the same heights as many of the other rockin' bands of that period their recording career drew to a close and the band split in 1994.

Though these days The Radium Cats would be welcomed more than ever a reformation seems unlikely as Lee and Mark are no longer active on the music scene, and Paul has continued to tear it up to this day with his powerful twanging for Johnny Cash devotees Union Avenue and the very popular UK Rockabilly band Hi-Voltage.

Some low-key Scottish bands also briefly blipped on the Psychobilly radar such as the Full Moon Freaks who made an appearance in 1989 on the Raucous Records compilation 'Psycho Tendencies', then vanished, and the Glasgow four-piece The Rednecks who released one EP for Fury Records, 'For A Few Rednecks More' (1991), before imploding not long after an appearance at the 4th Big Rumble in Hemsby. In 1995 they popped up again with a single demo track, 'Wildman', on the CD compilation 'Fury Psychobilly Sampler: Vol. 1'. By that time three-quarters of the original Rednecks line-up were pursuing a trashier direction as The Salem Dragsters. In 2007 The Redneck's Macc Lads/Psychobilly crossover sound could also be found on the third of Fury's 'Psychobilly Sampler' series.

There were also a number of other underground Psychobilly groups lurking in the heather such as Four Walls Shakin', The Talismen, The Longhorns, The Batfinx (an Edinburgh combo who were on the scene before Newcastle's Batfinks but never released any tracks) and The Tombstones. All of these acts occasionally supported touring headline Psycho bands but left little recordings behind for posterity.

It was not all simply happening in Scotland and England however and elsewhere in the British Isles there was wreckin' afoot. Wales' most famous exports may remain Demented Are Go but despite their grand legacy to Psychobilly not many of their fellow countrymen have continued the good work. Swansea-based Psycho combos The Mad Hatters and The Rockin Retards did gig for some while but neither band left behind any vinyl releases. Across the Irish Sea things were a bit healthier. Though The Klingonz remain Ireland's biggest export in the field of Psychobilly there were other rockin' bands in the Emerald Isle, particularly in Dublin in the mid 1980s, but the unholy trinity of Sharkbait, Scared Stiff and Spellbound made the largest impact on the Psychobilly scene.

Sharkbait (not to be confused with the Japanese outfit of the same name) formed in Dublin in the early 1980s but despite a few of their recordings sneaking out on compilations, such as 'Stomping At The Klub Foot: Vol. 5', they never reached the debut album stage. This was due to a variety of reasons including an early bitter bust up combined with the new career of lead singer Dave Finnegan who was about to become a cinematic legend playing the head-butting, short-fused drummer Mickah Wallace in the film 'The Commitments'.

With Sharkbait in pieces, Finnegan formed Scared Stiff in the period between making the film and its eventual release. He hastily gathered a quartet of Dublin rockers and recorded a set of mostly Sharkbait material in a friend's home studio. The results were decidedly rough and ready but not without their charm. Finnegan penned most of the tracks himself and although their subject matter was mostly horror-themed tracks from the Psychobilly school of lyric writing their sound was far closer to Rockabilly and one track, 'One More Bite' was an accordion driven Zydeco song.

The album 'Dark Streets' was picked up by Link Records and released in 1989. Scared Stiff did play live after the album's release but never outside of Ireland and when Dave went Hollywood bound after 'The Commitments' massive success the band folded. These days Dave can be found fronting the successful touring soul band 'Dave Finnegan's Commitments' and rubbing shoulders with James Brown, B.B. King and Dan Aykroyd.

Spellbound were also from the Dublin rockin' scene but their legacy has reached far beyond that of Sharkbait and Scared Stiff. Formed in 1986 by brothers Frankie and Adrian Hayes they came from County Wicklow, South of Dublin. Determined to break away from the Irish scene they pursued gigs across the UK and Europe and eventually signed to the Dutch label KIX 4 U. Their debut LP 'Mystical Madness' appeared in 1988 and sold well, particularly in Europe where the band toured regularly. The band eventually returned to Ireland as a new decade approached but their follow-up album failed to materialise.

Things went quiet for over a decade until Doyley (from The Klingonz), an old friend of the band, got in touch with the brothers Hayes to inform them that 'Mystical Madness' had become something of a cult favourite amongst collectors. In 2003, Adrian (drums) and Frankie (vocals/backing guitar) got together with Doyley on guitar and ex-Sharkbait bass-player Simon Farrell. They began gigging again, including a spot at the 'Kings of Psychobilly 3' concert in Speyer, Germany but soon after Doyley moved on to one of his many other projects and Adrian also moved on leaving Frankie as the only original member.

Frankie persisted and along with Simon they recruited a new guitarist, Dave McDonald, and drummer Brian O' Higgins – both players with a solid pedigree on the Irish rockin' scene. Things became busy once more for the band as they continued gigging while Tombstone Records repackaged their debut album, along with the addition of bonus tracks, and released the CD as 'Legends Of The Past' in 2004.

The band's first new material appeared in 2005 on their second studio album 'A Fistful Of Spells', Although it took seventeen years to appear, the album proved that the band had lost none of their appeal and alongside newly written originals, the album also featured previously unrecorded tracks from their earliest days updated and finally captured on CD. Still touring, Spellbound are arguably enjoying as much success today as when their career initially peaked in the late 1980s.

Perhaps one final element of the first Psychobilly boom which highlights how close the genre came to the mainstream was the small number of 'celebrity Psychobillies' who graced the scene. Though all of them moved on to the worlds of film, TV and sport, lurking in their illustrious CVs are some dark, Psychobilly secrets. While Psychobilly has resolutely remained an underground music genre which bemuses most folks it has had its share of followers amongst some well-known faces in the entertainment biz. Most prolific is actor Shaun Pertwee, star of 'Dog Soldiers', 'I.D.' and many more, and also the son of well-respected thespian and former 'Doctor Who', Jon Pertwee.

Pertwee was a close friend of the boys from King Kurt and an occasional roadie for the band. He was also responsible for the 'booze, drugs'n'wasted jungle creatures' illustration which appeared on the Kurt's debut album 'Ooh Wallah Wallah'. Pertwee's infamy was further secured in 1983 when the police stopped a King Kurt concert and it was claimed he "jumped up and down covered in flour and thrust chicken claws at people". This resulted in a conditional discharge for insulting behaviour for Pertwee and a quick mention for King Kurt in The Mail on Sunday newspaper.

Not confining himself to King Kurt gigs, Sean was also part of the 'invite-only' audience who attended the recording of the legendary 'Trash on the Tube' special. Around this period, 1983-84, teenage Sean had yet to establish his acting career which did not truly kick off until his 1987 appearance alongside Gary Oldman, in the movie 'Prick Up Your Ears'. Pertwee, however, was not the only young Brit actor to beat a path to Hollywood.

'Reservoir Dogs' star Tim Roth almost has Psychobilly to thank for kick-starting his career. While waiting for a second interview for the part of Trevor the Skinhead in Alan Clarke's excellent TV drama 'Made in Britain', Tim met a young upstart who happened to be a member of King Kurt, and as they both chatted outside the offices in London's Soho Square some police approached them and told them to 'move along' or some other constabulary-based threat. Guessing that the film's producers may be watching him, Roth gave the old bill some attitude. The director admitted later that it had been at that point that they decided to cast him. After his groundbreaking performance in the film as an unhinged but intelligent racist, Roth never looked back and eventually established himself as a major British star before hopping over the Atlantic to Hollywood.

Probably the least well-known, but ominously most memorable, celebrity Psychobilly was UK actor David Scarboro. David appeared regularly on the BBC's flagship soap opera 'EastEnders' as the original Mark Fowler character, a moody teen with a sky-high quiff. Scarboro was briefly a major TV star between 1985-87 while being regularly spotted at a number of London Psychobilly gigs, including the Klub Foot. Depending on your outlook, the producers of the show obviously believed that his image as a demented wrecker fitted well with his character, that of a booze'n'drug quaffing teenage tearaway.

Tragically, in real life, David suffered bouts of depression and in 1988 he committed suicide by jumping to his death from a clifftop. His character in the soap was taken by Todd Carty, the former child star of 'Grange Hill', who neglected to assume the Psychobilly demeanour and proceeded to make the role his own for many years.

On a lighter note, yet another soap star appears to have been revealed as a fan of the rowdiest music genre. Chris Gascoyne, who plays the role of Peter Barlow in the UK soap opera 'Coronation Street' has passed into Psychobilly folklore as having attended many concerts by The Meteors. Whether this is actually Chris or a wreckin' crew devotee 'looky-likey' may forever remain the stuff of legend.

Probably the most aptly named star with a taste for Psychobilly is Stuart 'Psycho' Pearce. The England football International and ex-Manchester City manager is a known fan of Punk and admits to once blasting his team-bus tour mates with a taste of The Meteors during his days at Nottingham Forest FC (no doubt offending his soft-rock and Spandau Ballet-loving associates with his choice).

For followers of the scene, Psychobilly was growing at an alarming rate across Europe and its sickness was already spreading across the world. With more heads being shaved and tartan shirts flying off the shelves in greater numbers it was time to forget the fad-chasing cynics of the major music labels and the mainstream music press as the cult of Psychobilly was to be built on the streets and in the musical underground.

CHAPTER FIVE

HELL'S BENT ON ROCKIN'

PSYCHO ATTACK OVER EUROPE

While the UK, and London in particular, is acknowledged as the spiritual home of Psychobilly, in mainland Europe the acceptance of the genre spread rapidly. From Psychobilly's earliest days the London scene was always only a skip over the channel away and as the earliest word spread to Europe of this vibrant new rockin' style many made the trip to England's capital to find out for themselves what the fuss was all about. Psychobilly began attracting a massive audience across the nations of Europe but even taking into account the much larger size and population of the region, the music was also held in much higher regard by promoters, journalists and within broadcasting.

While major British Psycho-gatherings were conducted in old halls and skanky racecourses, European Psychobilly festivals were often massive open-air events. Psychobilly bands appeared on European radio and TV shows regularly, including UK bands who would find it difficult to even secure a spot on 'Crimewatch' back home. Even the music press across the channel gave Psychobilly serious consideration in the form of news, interviews and record reviews of all things rockin' – refreshingly avoiding the snide references or total disregard afforded to the scene by UK hacks.

The, at times almost mainstream, acceptance of Psychobilly in Europe has paid dividends as the scene started strong and has remained resilient even during the late 1990s when UK Psychobilly almost drew its last breath. It is also evident in the number of European bands who lead the way in the continued progression of Psychobilly, particularly in relation to the success stories of Mad Sin and Nekromantix. Even up against the relentless growth of American Psychobilly, Europe still maintains its grip on the genre and boasts some of the most influential labels, promoters and bands on the global Psychobilly scene.

Looking right back to the early days, few could argue that the Euro scene really began to take shape with the release of the compilation album 'Psycho Attack Over Europe' (1986). This collection from KIX 4 U Records gathered together established UK bands; The Meteors, Restless, Dave Phillips and Rochee & The Sarnos along with Euro newcomers such as Batmobile, POX and Voodoo Dolls. For many folks this was clear confirmation that something was happening in Europe although soon it would be evident that the region would become a Psychobilly stronghold.

As one of Europe's earliest Psychobilly labels, KIX 4 U was actually created as a subsidiary of the long-running Dutch Rock'n'Roll specialist Rockhouse Records and intended to showcase the emerging Psycho and Neo scene. Rockhouse had been in business since 1973, emerging from a record store, 'De Platenboer BV' (The Record Farmer), which offered one of Europe's largest selections of all forms of Rock'n'Roll – from original 1950's acts right up to the Ted revival artists and beyond. Shop owner Bert Rockhuisen had previously worked for EMI (Holland) as a producer and used this experience to create his own label.

Rockhouse debuted in 1974 with a single from the black leather playboy himself, Vince Taylor. Closely following the chain-wielding rocker was the label's first long-player, the legendary 'Crazy Rhythm' from Crazy Cavan and The Rhythm Rockers. As the 1970s progressed, Rockhouse not only signed the cream of the Rock'n'Roll scene, including Matchbox, Dave Phillips and Freddie 'Fingers' Lee, but also invested in the blossoming Neo-Rockabilly scene and signed a frightening number of 'cat' bands (Blue Cats, Square Cats, Stacy Cats… you get the picture!).

PSYCHO ATTACK OVER EUROPE

HELL'S BENT ON ROCKIN'

When the label noticed a rise in the number of new underground bands on the rockin' scene of the 1980s, Rockhouse used KIX 4 U as a showcase for these groups. The imprint came to the major notice of the Psychobilly nation when they released the seminal 'Psycho Attack Over Europe' album in 1986. Prior to this they had released albums from a number of bands on the scene such as Batmobile, Archie and The POX. (Psychobilly Orchestra Experiment) since their creation in 1983. The 'Psycho Attack Over Europe' series continued, eventually running to 5 volumes, and the label moved into the 1990s with some classic albums from the likes of The Numbskulls, The Tigermen, The Hillbilly Headhunters, Captain Coma and The Rockin' Bones.

Batmobile (Bennyzin).

However, the parent company Rockhouse was a rapidly growing business in the mid 1990s when, ironically, Psychobilly was treading water in many cases. CDs were still available from the KIX 4 U vaults but as a label they ceased releasing new material from the Psycho scene. Rockhouse were already a worldwide mail order music specialist but from 1996 onwards their business went ballistic when their early adoption of the internet as a way of generating sales was a huge success. Rockhouse began to serve not only rockin' enthusiasts but those from the Punk scene and any other genres that rocked (and rolled).

The KIX 4 U saga is far from over though as Rockhouse, now trading as CD Express, has entered into a joint ownership deal with a company known as E-Sound Productions, whose publishing wing has made the back catalogue of Rockhouse and KIX 4 U available for licensing – re-opening the vaults on some dusty but much loved stomping anthems from Europe's earliest Psychobilly scene.

While Europe has excelled in breeding a diverse collection of Neo-Rockabilly bands, in the early 1980s it still had some way to go to match the UK Psychobilly scene. Certainly one of the first groups to show that European bands were developing the Psychobilly sound in their own unique way was Holland's Batmobile from Breda. After a variety of false starts in a selection of other bands, singer/guitarist Jeroen Haamers and drumming schoolfriend Johnny Zuidhof got together with Rockabilly in mind. The hunt for a similarly-minded double-bass player was a long quest but they eventually enlisted ace slapper Eric Haamers (Jeroen's brother). Though older-brother Eric may have been an obvious choice, he was a more established player who took a little time to be convinced that Jeroen and Johnny meant business. When he was finally persuaded, Batmobile were born.

At first the band took a more traditional Rock'n'Roll route based around their early influences such as Elvis, Johnny Burnette and UK revival-Rockabilly such as The Blue Cats. However, the Batmobile threesome always had other influences, including Glam Rock, The Ramones and Motörhead, which would play an important part in their unique sound. Witnessing Frenzy live at a 1983 gig in Eindhoven would also prove to have an influence on the Dutch trio. After schlepping around local bars and clubs in the early days, performing mostly covers, Batmobile eventually took exception to some po-faced Rock'n'Roll purists yelling requests for the same old standards. The band turned the pace up on a few rockin' regulars and found this high-speed assault silenced the grumps and the new-found adrenalin rush instantly gave the band a new direction.

Batmobile signed to Rockhouse Records and their debut mini-album 'Batmobile' appeared in 1985 on KIX 4 U. In 1987 the band found an outlet for their recordings far closer to home when drummer Johnny Zuidhof formed his own record label and publishing company, along with band associate 'Eddie', called Count Orlok Records. Batmobile's first full-length album 'Bambooland' (1987) was released on the label and by this time the band were red-hot as a result of regular touring across Europe combined with a variety of radio and TV appearances. 'Bambooland' simply pushed their career further and led to their first major tour of Germany.

With one more release under their belts, the double vinyl collection of demos and live tracks 'Buried Alive' (1987), the band took up the offer of a deal with Nervous Records, at a time when the label was releasing many major Psychobilly albums, and the result was 'Bail Was Set At $6,000,000' (1988) an

STOMPIN' IN BELGIUM
Sat 23 OKT 1999

CAFE AU GAND
OVERPOORTSTRAAT
Gent - BELGIUM

BATMOBILE
Europe's best continental psychobilly band

GORILLA
One of the newest & hottest psychobilly band today (H)

THE ANDREWS SURFERS
On the mainstage between the breaks, one of Europe's surf top acts with members from 50 FOOT COMBO

AFTERPARTY WITH DJ ROCKIN' DEVIL
SKA, SURF, ROCK'N ROLL, ROCKABILLY, PSYCHOBILLY

+ DRUNKABILLY RECORD STALL

INFO + TICKETS: Tel/Fax - 32 (0)9 233 74

MISTERCOPY
Overpoortstraat 52
9000 Gent
TEL: 09/222.88.62
GB: 210-0458808-50
BTW BE 433.310.876

13

Batmobile kept rockin' throughout the 1990s (Christophe @ Drunkabilly Records).

album which confirmed that Batmobile were as big a force on the UK Psychobilly scene as they were in Europe. Despite the success of 'Bail...', Batmobile returned to Count Orlok and would remain with the label for a further six albums. Of these recordings only 'Amazons From Outer Space' (1989), 'Sex Starved' (1991), 'Hard Hammer Hits' (1992) and their final offering 'Welcome To Planet Cheese' (1997) were full studio albums. 'Blast From The Past' (1993) was a tenth anniversary 'worst and best' collection of re-recorded tracks and 'Batmobile Is Dynamite' (1990) was a mini-album with the novel theme of cover versions with some form of explosive connection in the title.

Throughout their career it is obvious that Batmobile refused to be restricted by Psychobilly and across all their releases they delved into a variety of musical styles (including Rockabilly, Rock'n'Roll, Glam Rock and Metal) particularly on 'Welcome To Planet Cheese' where they ditched their upright bass and went electric for that heavier sound. At the turn of the decade, Batmobile (like many others) felt that the time was right to disband and they bowed out of active service in August 2000 at a bizarrely remote venue in Oude Wetering, Holland.

Unsurprisingly, this was not to be the end of the line for the Dutch trio. During their absence, Japanese label On The Hill released their 'Tribute To Batmobile' compilation in 2001 which highlighted the band's global influence and featured covers of their songs from a huge range of artists including Mad Heads, Gorilla, Os Catalepticos and The Photon Torpedoes. This collection was followed by a second volume and both albums featured a new track on each by Batmobile themselves, their first new recordings since their split in 2000.

All three Batmobile members have also worked on a number of side projects both during, and after, their split. Eric Haamers worked on his own as The Penguin, releasing an EP 'Orang Utan Boogie' and a self-titled album in 1996, while he was also a member of The Gecko Brothers. Johnny Zuidhof maintained the Count Orlok label while drumming both for The Penguin and Sin Alley and Jeroen kept himself busy with a variety of side-projects including Taking Care Of Elvis, The Hammer Brothers and his other Elvis-fixated trio Triple Dynamite whose album 'Elvis In Wonderland' was released by Count Orlok early in 2007.

After an almost three year break the band were coaxed back for a one-off Psychobilly festival appearance at the Satanic Stomp in Speyer, Germany in the Spring of 2003. As the gig proved a great success, and the band enjoyed themselves so much, they began gigging again though not on such a huge scale as they had at their peak. Still maintaining their original line-up, they appeared in Antwerp and Amsterdam in 2004 and made a return to the Satanic Stomp in that same year. In 2005 they made it to the States for Hollywood's Rockabilly Showdown and returned to their patient, and ecstatic, UK fans at the second Speedfreaks Ball in 2006.

Though plans for an eleventh album have still to surface it seems unfeasible that Batmobile will disappoint. Always innovative, and always complete showmen, Batmobile are not only one of Europe's most influential rockin' bands but also one of the world's favourite Psychobilly groups.

While Batmobile were early pioneers, undeniably two other leading lights of European Psychobilly are Mad Sin and Nekromantix. Both bands

Batmobile go primitive onstage (Bennyzin).

HELL'S BENT ON ROCKIN'   PSYCHO ATTACK OVER EUROPE

The memorable Nekromantix logo (Die In Style).

formed in the 1980s and have weathered misfortunes, line-up changes, record label shifts and gaps of time between album releases. Fortunately for both bands their unswerving persistence and relentless gigging have paid off in the form of a hardcore Psychobilly following, warm acceptance beyond the scene and even the odd whiff of major-label cash, a luxury rarely afforded to UK Psychobilly acts.

Germany has always been a hot-bed of Psychobilly, a nation which took the genre to its heart and never let it go, and nowhere else could breed a more glorious, sweaty, debauched home for the Psycho-sound better than Berlin. A city seeped in sex and Rock'n'Roll needs a soundtrack – a speed-fuelled, balls-out, screaming, rockin' riot of a sound... and Mad Sin were the band to do it.

Conceived in 1987 as a three-piece featuring lead singer/drummer Koefte De Ville, Punk'n'Rockabilly guitarist Stein and Holly, a recent convert to the art of double-bass slapping, the band fine-tuned their early set schlepping around shady bars and clubs in Berlin and busking in the streets for beer money. During this time they often delved into the roots of Psychobilly playing covers of Rockabilly, Country and Punk tunes for the benefit of slack-jawed tourists. This rich back catalogue of songs, and the band's obvious love for those genres, would remain a large part of the Mad Sin sound and more immediately the cash helped pay for booze and rehearsal studios.

Koefte, with his hulking frame and always outrageous dress sense, was a hard figure to miss and already well known in the city's rockin' scene so gigs were secured regularly for the band and found them supporting visiting bands such as The Meteors, Guana Batz and Demented Are Go. Demented in particular became close friends with the band, as did The Klingonz, so Mad Sin backstage antics and aftershow parties soon became legendary for their debauchery and ability to reduce fine furnishings to firewood.

The buzz surrounding the band spread widely and quickly, eventually leading to their first record deal with Maybe Crazy Records and the debut album 'Chills and Thrills in a Drama of Mad Sin And Mystery' (1988). As with the majority of Psycho bands of that period, the album was a relatively low-rent affair which slightly muted the band's raucous live power but captured enough of their energy to interest promoters and many of the new attendees at the growing number of Mad Sin gigs across Europe. They soon became one of the key bands of European Psychobilly and quickly shed their support band status. For Koefte, Stein and Holly, Mad Sin was becoming a full-time occupation and their hard-rockin' work rate gathered a large following and a hardcore inner circle – The Sindicate.

1990 saw the band release their second album 'Distorted Dimensions' again on Maybe Crazy records. A hardcore spiral of gigs, parties and recordings continued throughout the first half of the Nineties leaving behind a fistful of appearances on Psychobilly and Punk themed compilations and a host of concert promoters and hotel managers with shredded nerves. The album recording also continued with 'Amphigory' on Fury Records hitting the streets in 1991 followed by the band's return to Maybe Crazy the following year with 'Break The Rules' which then led to their fifth album 'A Ticket Into The Underworld' in 1993. Following this album's release, Strangy (Klingonz/Numbskulls) took over on double-bass and played live with the band for over a year.

As the twenty four hour party that was Mad Sin continued, Koefte could no longer be contained behind the drum kit and a variety of sticksmen took over on tubs, leaving the towering Mr De Ville to lead from the front. Released from the strait-jacket of percussion, Koefte tore up the stage – screaming, shouting, megaphone wielding and inflicting grievous damage on fixtures, sound equipment, microphone stands and (occasionally) members of the audience.

As the band's following grew, stoked by their increasingly wild stage show, their reputation for erratic behaviour and criminal damage became a concern for many promoters and bookers of bands. Half way through the decade Mad Sin reached a precipice and faced up to the future. They could either hurtle towards self-destruction, pushing themselves to a point where no one would book them and the band would effectively implode 'or' take the whole business a bit more seriously and learn from their past fuck-ups. Thankfully, they took the latter option and from then on the band began to build on their career, ironically at a time when many bands on the Psycho scene were falling apart or, at the very least, entering a period of hibernation.

A youthful Mad Sin (Bennyzin).

While gigging in Holland, Mad Sin got in touch with the folks at Count Orlok Records, home of Bang Bang Bazooka and Batmobile. The meeting led to an album deal which the band took seriously from the start. Drawing on their past studio experience and their wide musical influences the album 'God Save The Sin' was released in 1996. While resolutely Psychobilly, the album also featured a far greater Punk influence than previous Sin albums alongside a taste of Rockabilly, Hard Rock, Ska and Country. The whole album was not only a breath of fresh air for many Psychobilly fans but also the perfect introduction to Mad Sin for many other Rock'n'Roll freaks outside the scene.

The variety which the album offered alongside the band's now more professional approach to touring, secured far more bookings including support slots with The Misfits, Gwar and Faith No More. While still prone to rampant partying, the band now arrived at gigs well prepared and always gave the punters a 100% sweating, screaming, rocking-fucking-rolling show. 'God Save The Sin' pushed the band forward in many ways; it unleashed them upon audiences beyond the Psychobilly scene more than ever before, it proved how much their sound could develop in the studio and it sent out the scent of blood to the major label sharks. So much so that they then embarked on a deal with the devil – well a honcho from Polydor Records with a suitcase full of cash.

After years on the breadline, living from gig to gig, the band happily accepted the deal, filled their pockets with greenbacks and fucked off to Malta to record an album. The biggest fear many fans have when their favourite bands are sucked into the mainstream music biz is that they will be neutered, watered down and reduced to chart fodder for the pimply-faced masses. With Mad Sin that was certainly not the case and the resultant album 'Sweet & Innocent?... Loud & Dirty!' (1998) only benefited from the filthy stench of big business bucks.

Recorded at Temple Studios in Malta, the album was produced and engineered by Uwe Sabirowsky who, along with Koefte and Holly as co-producers, squeezed the very best out of the sixteen tracks on the album. After overdubs and mixing back in Berlin 'Sweet & Innocent...' was a beast of an album waiting to be unleashed on Punks, Psychobillies and any other punters with a taste for loud and sleazy Rock'n'Roll. With the major deal came the usual benefits of the biz such as quality photo shoots, excellent album artwork and even a few bucks splashed out on promo videos and single releases for two album tracks 'All This And More' and 'Take A Ride'.

The album was a strong seller and with the extra backing Mad Sin toured around Europe and Japan and made many rock festival appearances alongside Rancid, Bad Religion, Turbo Negro, Die Toten Hosen and many other Punk and hard rock heavy hitters. Nonetheless, the relationship between band and label was never settled and despite releasing the album on the imprint 'Bonanza' (a common ploy when record companies attempt to disguise their involvement with previously independent bands) it was obvious that Mad Sin could never be persuaded to adopt a more mainstream approach to their music.

With the band refusing to play the game Polydor, a label more used to more gentler artist/label relations with the likes of The Style Council and Fairport Convention, simply offered Mad Sin a sack of cash to move on. In the same way that The Sex Pistols plied wads of readies from EMI and A&M Records who each then bottled out and paid them off, Mad Sin retired to the pub with healthy wallets, another fine album to their name and a still growing reputation as a shit-hot live act.

With a heavy schedule of gigs generated by the success of 'Sweet & Innocent?...' Mad Sin were temporarily without a record deal but they beefed-up their live sound with the addition of another guitarist. Tex Morton, a previous member of early Eurobilly legends Sunny Domestoz, joined up and as a five-piece band Mad Sin were a more powerful act than ever before. Often joined by backing vocalist and band mascot Hellvis, Mad Sin now filled the stage and made their growing number of shows even more memorable – especially to gig-going virgins of the cult of Mad Sin.

Despite this revitalised line-up, things certainly went quieter on the Mad Sin front. As the new millennium appeared the band were no nearer to an album deal and each member was involved in a variety of side projects – taking some time out after over thirteen years of Mad Sin madness. Koefte was first to experiment as a member of Psychobilly supergroup The Dead Kings. The band consisted of Koefte on vocals, Peter Sandorff of The Nekromantix on guitar, Batmobile's drummer Johnny Zuidhof and two veterans of The Klingonz and Demented Are Go, Doyley on guitar and Strangy on slap-bass.

This meeting between members of four of Psychobilly's biggest bands spawned an album, 'King By Death, Fool For A Lifetime' (2001) on Crazy Love Records. Surprisingly, alongside creating the supreme raucous racket you would expect from a band of this pedigree, 'King By Death...' also featured a number of accomplished acoustic tracks amid the filth and the fury.

While Koefte was swingin' with the 'Kings' Holly, Tex and Stein had their own things going on. Stein teamed up with members of The Frantic Flintstones and The Ripmen to form United Swindlers while Holly and Tex went back to their Rockabilly roots, twangin' and slappin' hard in their new combo Dusty Gray and His Rough Riding Ramblers. Despite all this moonlighting in other groups the Mad Sin saga was far from over, any fears that the band had drifted apart were groundless and a new deal was clinched with the charmingly named German label 'I Used To Fuck People Like You In Prison Records'. Also known as 'People Like You Records', it was a hard-edged Punk'n'Rock'n'Roll label with a reputation for excellent production values, both in recording and album packaging, and a roster of shit-hot acts such as The Hunns, The Bones and Adam West.

Crazy Love Records (Guido Neumann).

With quality support from their new label Mad Sin were back in Berlin recording, this time with Koefte fully in the producers chair. Tex had now settled firmly into the line-up and two guest drummers, Tommy Gun and Micha, were sharing the skin-bashing. Also guesting, with vocals on the track 'Communication Breakdown' was Tiger Army frontman Nick 13. The result was one of their finest albums up to that point, 'Survival Of The Sickest', and it hit the streets in 2002.

Musically and lyrically it was a strong album. The Sin had now been between studio walls many times and Koefte seemed reluctant to let any track avoid his high standards. With Tex on board the sound was already more powerful and the quality lyrics also included some social comment alongside the violence, sex and horror. This was a well crafted collection of songs that proved Mad Sin were progressing even fourteen years after their debut album, a period when many bands would be happy to regurgitate their back catalogue. The album had appeal for both die-hard Psychobillies and the Sin's

PSYCHO ATTACK OVER EUROPE · HELL'S BENT ON ROCKIN'

PSYCHOBILLY PARTY
in Münster
SUNNY DOMESTOS
& the Kaklsquellkids
THE P.O.X
THE TRANQUILIZERS
9.2. Aladin Walbeckerstr.

A triple bill of the finest early European talent (Jan Van Hal).

growing legions of Punks, heavy rockers and other Rock'n'Roll misfits, with a sound that continued to include their influences from a variety of music genres. With their finest album yet behind them they hit the road with a punishing schedule of over 300 gigs in the following two years. Japan and Europe were hit once again but this time shows all across the US were included.

In 2005, Mad Sin's collaboration with 'People Like You' continued. The label had extended their grip on the Psycho scene with new albums by The Meteors, Demented Are Go and The Heartbreak Engines while also re-releasing Mad Sin's major label debut 'Sweet & Innocent?... Loud & Dirty!' with bonus tracks and the promo video of 'All This and More'. They also released 'Young, Dumb & Snotty: The Psychotic Years 1988-1993', a collection featuring the highlights of Mad Sin's first four albums. Next up was to be a masterpiece – 'Dead Moon's Calling'.

Taking almost a year to record, 'Dead Moon's Calling' again featured Koefte in the producers seat while also contributing on guitar and keyboards alongside vocal duties. The line-up had also evolved with one dramatic change, Holly after eighteen years service moved on to be replaced by youthful bass-slapper Valle. On drums, a more regularly changing role within the band, was now Andy Laff. Tex and Stein were still providing a twin guitar attack and Hellvis provided backing vox while also taking a lead role on the track 'TCS' (Taking Care of Sin). If ever an album had the ability to kick the Psychobilly sound over the edge into mainstream rock then this was it, a strong blend of Punk, Ska, Rockabilly Swing, movie soundtracks, metal and more that never turned its back on its Psycho roots. Alongside all this was an excellent production job and some deep lyrics addressing love, death, politics and Koefte's venomous reflections on the fucked-up society of the 2000s.

'Dead Moon's Calling' showed Mad Sin at their peak as a band ready to unleash their strongest album yet and apparently with a settled line-up ready to tour once again. Unfortunately, for Tex it was time to move on and he left the band early in 2006. His replacement was Mad Pete 1 aka former Nekromantix and Dead Kings guitarist Peter Sandorff. While many bands peak early then spend the rest of their days trading on their early success, Mad Sin have grown stronger with every album release. It has been a rocky road, almost ending in self-destruction, but perseverance and the ability to learn from their fuck-ups has left Mad Sin heading through the second half of the 2000s with the possibility of even greater worldwide success.

While Mad Sin's dogged persistence through some lean times has paid off another European Psychobilly act has also soldiered on in a similar manner, never losing faith and dragging Psychobilly to a worldwide audience against all odds. Nekromantix were formed in 1989 by Dan Gaarde, now better known as Kim Nekroman, who obviously fancied a career change after eight years below the waves in the submarines of the Royal Danish Navy. The band consisted of the classic three-piece line-up with songwriter Kim on double-bass and vocals, Peter Sandorff on guitar and drummer Peek. After playing their first two shows in Denmark the band appeared at a major festival in Hamburg, a mere six months after their first rehearsal. Such a rapid ascent on the scene gained many people's attention and soon led to their first record deal with the rockin' German label Tombstone Records. Up to that point, Tombstone was releasing mostly Neo-Rockabilly material but had some bands, such as The Phantom Rockers and The Stringbeans, who had already crossed over onto the Psychobilly circuit. However, Nekromantix' debut represented the label's first, unashamed, Psychobilly album.

'Hellbound' was recorded in 1989 and released in 1990 in a handsome gatefold sleeve bearing the (soon-to-be-famous) Nekromantix 'coffin' logo. Nekroman was also responsible for the very stylish sleeve design and this appeared to mark an early indication that Kim had a very clear idea of the direction in which he wanted to take the band. Though simply a question of artwork, up to this point many Psycho bands had knocked out appalling album covers in a rough'n'ready manner. Though only a low-budget production, 'Hellbound' looked like a major release. Like P. Paul Fenech before him, and Nick 13 since, the band would remain mostly driven by his vision and belief in building a group with a longstanding reputation.

'Hellbound' was something of a success particularly amongst a British audience who, in the wake of storming European Psycho bands such as Batmobile and Mad Sin, were beginning to realise that Psychobilly had successfully crossed the channel and Europe was rapidly becoming the creative heart of the scene. Even more impressively, guitarist Peter was really the only member of the group with any studio experience. Sandorff had already played in several bands but Kim and Peek, having been together around six months, still had only a rudimentary grip on their instruments. In addition most of the tracks had lyrics in English and some, particularly 'Ride Danny Ride', 'Hellbound' and 'Spiders Attacking Manhattan', have stood the test of time and still appear in Nekromantix' live shows to this day.

After almost a year of constant gigging to promote 'Hellbound', the band attracted the attention of Nervous Records which led to the release of 'Curse of the Coffin' in 1991. Yet again the album was created on a low budget, with many lyrics created in the studio and a final mix which the band paid little attention to. Nonetheless, the quality of the songs shone through, especially the title track which was a well-crafted rock-out of epic proportions. A video for 'Curse of the Coffin' was also created and despite its low budget it appeared several times on MTV's underground band slot 'Alternative Nation'. The cover was yet again a quality production with a similar theme to 'Hellbound' giving both Nekromantix albums some continuity.

Now the band had two fine albums behind them and a finely tuned live set trademarked by Kim's frantic slapping on his coffin shaped double-bass. However, despite the band's growing fanbase as word spread on their powerful live act there was some restlessness in the ranks and Peter and Peek eventually left. Their replacements were Ian Dawn on guitar and 'Grim' Tim Handsome on drums, and with this line-up the band moved forward onto their third album 'Brought Back To Life' which was recorded in 1993 and released that same year on Inter Music Records. Ian was not to become one of Nekromantix' long-serving players and in the same year he made way for guitarist Emil Oelund.

The new line-up brought a different element to studio work and Kim's recording experience, following the work on the previous two albums, had improved resulting in a fuller sound than their earlier recordings. Obviously many people agreed and the album was a strong seller which was well received by grass roots fans who had followed the band since 'Hellbound' while attracting new devotees perhaps unaware of the band's far more powerful live presence than earlier albums had indicated. The touring continued and as well as hauling themselves around Europe with frightening regularity Nekromantix received a warm welcome in Japan, becoming yet another band drawn to the Far East by the nation's rapidly growing thirst for Psychobilly.

'Brought Back To Life' did highlight one downside in the band's career – the growing trend for gaps between album releases. 'Curse Of The Coffin' followed 'Hellbound' within a year but it was twice as long before 'Brought Back To Life' made an appearance. The gap would continue to widen and their fourth album 'Demons Are A Girl's Best Friend' took three years to follow. It was to be their last album of the 1990s and its follow up took another half a decade to emerge.

'Demons Are A Girl's Best Friend' appeared on Record Music Denmark in 1996 and featured another new guitarist, Soeren Monk. Many found this album the most distinctive sounding of the band's output, including future releases, but it was not to everyone's taste. The Nekromantix studio sound had reached its peak with a clarity and sound quality far beyond previous releases. Occasionally some within the Psychobilly community often view more polished studio productions with suspicion, seldom realising that many bands with a number of albums under their belt often want to move forward and mature in the studio. Though for some bands this approach has been spectacularly unsuccessful Nekromantix weathered the storm and, despite some critical nitpickers, the album again opened the band up to a wider audience. Crucially these new fans were gained during the late period in the 1990s when Psychobilly was retreating further underground. However, during the following five years only a concert album 'Undead'n'Live' (2000), on ESP Recordings, would appear to keep diehard fans appeased.

Like The Meteors, Demented Are Go and Mad Sin, Nekromantix' persistent gigging paid dividends in the new millennium. In America particularly a Psychobilly renaissance was gathering pace and many residents in the US of A were looking to early pioneers of the scene in Europe for inspiration. What

HELL'S BENT ON ROCKIN'   PSYCHO ATTACK OVER EUROPE

Nekromantix, Psychobilly's great Danes (Die In Style).

happened next, few could have guessed but Nekromantix' career was about to be thrust forward at an alarming rate. After almost twelve years of keeping the band on track through line-up changes, growing gaps between albums, thinning crowds and scratching a living on the scene, things were about to pay off – big time!

Despite the success of 'Demons Are A Girl's Best Friend', the band were still unsure of when, and on what label, their next studio album would appear. Kim had initially attempted to cast the net a bit further and had sent a demo to Tim Armstrong at Hellcat Records in America. Though primarily purveyors of fine Punk, Hellcat had also dipped their toe into the waters of Psychobilly with Tiger Army. However, after some time no reply was forthcoming and Kim assumed the trail had went cold. When in conversation with Geoff Kresge (Tiger Army, The Daggers) on the internet the subject of the demo, and the band's label-less state, was mentioned. Geoff eventually performed some minor detective work and it was discovered that the demo was lost in a twilight zone and yet to reach the Rancid main man. Armstrong eventually got it and after a listen was on the phone to the Nekroman and, unaware of the transatlantic time difference, roused him from his sleep with an offer of a deal which provided a rude but welcome awakening.

As the boys from Rancid had been following the band for years, it made sense for Nekromantix to join Hellcat's stable, especially in the wake of the growing success of Tiger Army. The band not only gained the support of this sizable label but also the freedom to continue recording their next album the way it suited them. It appears that Armstrong was keen to preserve the classic Nekromantix sound and made no attempt to meddle in their affairs. With their new deal with Hellcat Records freshly signed,

PSYCHO ATTACK OVER EUROPE

Kim and co were back in the studio in 2001 after the longest recording gap in their career. Also back, after an almost ten year break was guitarist Peter Sandorff, this time dragging along his brother Kristian as the band's new drummer.

The result of these sessions was 'Return Of The Loving Dead' which was released in 2002 and was a back-to-basics, low-budget stomper which many saw as a welcome return to the band's unique raw Psychobilly sound. Again, much of the album was created in the studio but some songs had been seeping into the band's repertoire over the previous two years. The only major difference in the recording of the album was the use of a very professional studio and more time to lay down the tracks, resulting in a far more powerful sounding creation.

A second album for Hellcat was recorded in 2003 and the following year Kim relocated to Los Angeles, putting Nekromantix at the heart of the world's fastest growing Psychobilly scene. 'Dead Girls Don't Cry' was released in 2004 and though older fans may whine and groan, this was as much the band's debut album to thousands of Americans as 'Hellbound' had been to masses of early Euro-billies. Backed by the Hellcat/Epitaph promotion machine, alongside the label's street-level reputation for top class Punk and Rock'n'Roll, the album reached a far larger audience than any of their other releases. The following year Hellcat continued to meet the demand for Nekromantix releases by reissuing the band's 1993 album 'Brought Back To Life' in an extended form on CD, catchily titled 'Brought Back To Life (again)'.

Touring also continued to hammer the point home that Nekromantix could really deliver live but alongside all this increased band activity Kim had other business. Unable to control his wanton urges, Nekroman was a member of another band who operated alongside Nekromantix in a beer-soaked parallel universe – Horrorpops.

Kim had hatched a side project with fellow Copenhagen rocker Patricia Day, back in 1996. Both met

Horrorpops (Die In Style).

when Patricia's Indie Punk band Peanut Pump Gun had supported Nekromantix at a music festival in Cologne, Germany. Despite both bands hailing from the same town their paths had never crossed but back in Denmark they got together to work on a band. With no commitment to any particular style and to free themselves from their current band roles, Kim taught Patricia some double-bass technique while she helped him fine tune his guitar skills.

The following year Kim and Patricia recruited a drummer Hendrik Niedermeier, who was a friend of Patricia's and a member of Danish Punkers Strawberry Slaughterhouse, then Horrorpops' story began in earnest. After a few shows as a trio the band once again poached talent from Strawberry Slaughterhouse and added a second guitarist, the wonderfully named 'Caz the Clash', to beef up their sound. Despite Kim's other commitments with Nekromantix, Horrorpops reputation was growing steadily and as the new millennium approached it was time to swell their ranks once again.

As if having an Amazonian beauty slapping a double-bass in front of three rockers was visually not enough to attract audience attention, Horrorpops added a pair of Go-Go dancers to work their magic on the crowd. It certainly had an effect, especially for Psychobilly audiences whose collective jaw dropped at the sight of three sexy she-rockers after years of watching mainly sweaty guys with quiffs. Mille and Kamilla were fellow workers with Patricia at a piercing shop and they became Horrorpops' very own satanic cheerleaders.

With the full band in place, Horrorpops ventured into the studio and recorded seven tracks then focused on building their live reputation. The gigging continued throughout 2001/2002, alongside the Nekromantix' own work recording and releasing 'Return of the Loving Dead', but already tracks from the session had leaked out as some of the recordings had featured on the band's press pack. With some of their songs already bootlegged and gathering a growing following, the band returned to the studio to lay down another six tracks. At this point Caz the Clash left the band and was replaced by Karsten, another member hijacked from Strawberry Slaughterhouse.

In 2003 Hellcat Records signed Horrorpops, after hearing both their recording sessions, and a 1000 copy limited edition twelve-inch single 'Ghouls/Psychobitches Outta Hell' appeared on the Rancid Records label. Things began to proceed rapidly and the band embarked on their 'Aloha From Hell' tour to support the single, a tour which included a major support slot with Rancid and Tiger Army at the Wiltern Theatre in Los Angeles.

The following year saw the release of their debut album 'Hell Yeah!', appearing On Hellcat Records in February 2004. It quickly became apparent that jumping between Denmark and the USA, where the band's following was at its strongest, was unfeasible and the decision was made to relocate to LA. Go-go girl Mille stayed behind but was replaced by another friend of the band Naomi, soon to be known simply as NoNo. The resulting paperwork requirements for the band's move to the states caused a major fuck-up and their first major tour of America, to promote the album, had to be completely scrapped. Lifting them from their despondency came the offer of a European tour supporting The Offspring in some humungous venues (with crowd sizes between 5000 and 15000). This was followed by their own UK dates, two tours of America in the 'Punks Vs Psychos' shows and a main support slot with Lars Friederiksen & The Bastards.

After this mammoth touring schedule Karsten also returned to Denmark leaving the band with a massive fanbase but no guitarist, at a time when they were about to begin work on their second album for Hellcat. As 2004 drew to a close the band drafted in Geoff Kresge, a bass player and vocalist with over fifteen years rockin' experience with the likes of Tiger Army, AFI, Influence 13 and The Daggers.

With Geoff moving from bass to guitar when joining the band, much as Kim had when Horrorpops began, the band were once again back to full strength and as 2005 rolled along the 'Pops returned to the studio with hard rockin' producer Brett Gurewitz (Bad Religion's guitarist and the owner of Epitaph Records). By the spring of that year they were released from the studio having completed their opus 'Bring It On' and almost immediately hit the road with tours in Canada, Australia and Japan. 'Bring It On' was released in September 2005 and, with added input from Geoff Kresge, it saw the band move unapologetically forward to a wider audience with a broader range of influences resulting in what was effectively a classic alternative rock album but one that still hinted at the band's Psychobilly pedigree. This was closely followed by (yep! you guessed it) more touring around the US in their fucked-up tour bus 'Big Joe' which often resulted in a Horrorpops' tour of America's roadside verges.

All this action on the Horrorpops front understandably left Kim with less time for Nekromantix but the band continued to promote 'Dead Girls Don't Cry' and also secured a tour with Lars Friederiksen & The Bastards in Japan. What activity did increase around the band was a particular strain of 21st Century disease – internet sniping. Since Nekromantix, along with Horrorpops, signed to Hellcat Records all manner of negative bullshit regarding both bands had sprung up on Psychobilly-themed notice boards and guest books across the world wide web. It mainly consisted of verbal (and often puerile) sparring between new fans and old often regarding each other as either ageing farts jealously guarding their scene or young upstarts with no understanding of Psychobilly history.

There was also some online debate over whether Horrorpops were some form of Psychobilly-Lite, despite the fact that the band had claimed when they first formed that they would pursue a sound with no boundaries. Though of no real consequence to either band it was relatively unique situation for Nekromantix to find some of their die-hard supporters drift away amongst incoming legions of young fans. Apart from this online bickering something major was to bring another chapter of the Nekromantix story to a close.

In 2005, a decision was made for the Sandorff brothers to quit the band, leaving Kim as the sole, and founding, figure left standing. However, after over fifteen years of hard work there was no question of Nekromantix folding. The band had already survived numerous line-up changes and Kim simply set about recruiting once again. Hooked up with new guitarist Troy Destroy and drummer 'Wasted' James (who was himself replaced by Andrew Pink from Californian billys The Rockets in 2006) The Nekromantix roll on and to this day Nekroman remains one of the hardest working men in (Psychobilly) showbusiness – no mean feat in a genre often rooted in a 'don't-give-a-fuck-can't-be-bothered' attitude.

With Batmobile, Mad Sin and Nekromantix forming a triple-pronged fork which poked the rest of the world in the ass while establishing Europe's importance in the world of Psychobilly it is important to acknowledge this vast continent's many exponents and peddlers of this twisted form of Rock'n'Roll. So, sick-bags at the ready, its time for a whistle-stop tour of Europe starting at the country nearest to London (ground zero of the Psychobilly explosion) – France.

FRANCE

Situated as they are, mere miles from the UK's capital, the French were early devotees of Psychobilly making their pilgrimages to the Klub Foot and a variety of other gatherings. Its no surprise that a home-grown scene was soon to develop. Probably the most complete illustration of French Psychobilly can be found on the excellent 'Kongpilation' collections from the French label Banana Juice. Formed in 1992, the label has consistently tracked down Gallic 'Billy bands and presented many of the country's leading rockers such as Banane Metalik, Washington Dead Cats, Atomic Spuds alongside other more obscure combos. The label has also released a varied collection of Beat, Psychedelia, Soul, Surf and Ska but its four volumes of 'Kongpilation' albums have chronicled the French Psycho scene almost completely along with a variety of other groups related to the genre.

One Banana Juice act in particular have enjoyed a certain worldwide notoriety. Banane Metalik are one of the most gore-fixated French Psycho bands and something of a Psychobilly equivalent to the US metal deviants Gwar. Caked in make-up (open wounds, blood, stitches and grue) their genuinely demented Psychobilly racket demands a 'love' em or loathe 'em' response amongst listeners but they have a loyal following of gorehounds across Europe and Japan. Formed in 1989, it was five years before their debut album, 'Requiem De La Depravation' (1994), on Bananajuice Records. They then mysteriously split a year after their release.

Drunkabilly Records (Christophe @ Drunkabilly Records).

The band were fondly remembered though and after a break of almost a decade they were back in action on their own Killer Bananas label with 'Sex, Blood, Gore'n'Roll' (2005). Though singing mostly in French the band's metallic racket has hooked many admirers of heavy-psycho and onstage shock-rock tactics. Since their reformation the band have played the Tokyo Big Rumble and Calella and have even cracked America with gigs in California late in 2005 to bemused but wildly entertained audiences.

Treading similar ground to Banane Metalik in terms of sheer entertainment are The Washington Dead Cats, a ludicrously colourful combo who squeeze every B-movie cliche available into their own brand of 'Power Punk, Rugged Rockabilly'. Often attired as zombies, mummies and voodoo priests the band have had what amounts to two successful careers on the scene with their debut album 'Go Vegetables Go!' first appearing back in 1986 followed by two albums for Bondage Records, 'Gore A Billy Boogie' (1988) and 'Go Crazy!' (1989). So popular were the band that they already had a 'best of...' album entitled 'The Beast Of...' released by 1990. Often regarded as something of a French equivalent to Trash bands such as The Sting-Rays and The Vibes, the Cats remained on a roll and released two further albums in 1991, 'Golden Age' and 'Whatchamacallit', then split soon after.

It was almost ten years before another Washington Dead Cats release appeared in the form of the five-track concert album 'Live At The Frankenstein Odeon' (2000). From then on the band were back from the dead intent on reclaiming their past glory not by relying on a nostalgia ticket but by unleashing a host of new material drawing on a wider range of rockin' influences. With a revitalised line-up the band have delivered two new albums, 'Treat Me Bad' (2003) and 'El Diablo Is Back' (2006), and now have a more powerful sound which boasts a deadly brass section and pitches them as something close to the devil's own Las Vegas showband.

The early to mid 1990s was a popular time on the French scene and featured a wide variety of homegrown talent including The Celicates, The Screaming Kids and The Gotham Katz, a band who reached the end of the 1990s in a heavier form as Gotham. Around this time the short-lived Atomic Spuds appeared as something of a French Ug & The Cavemen, not afraid to dress in fake fur cavemen suits, but only left behind their debut album 'Garbage Surfers' (1995) on Banana Juice along with a few singles and compilation appearances.

More recently one of France's most successful acts has been The Astro Zombies from Dijon. After a low-budget EP 'Astro Zombies' (1997) the band made their way to P. Paul Fenech's In Heaven Recording Studio to record their debut album for Banana Juice Records 'Astro Zombies Are Coming' (1997). Some years later the band's guitarist Bobby and drummer Gaybeul backed up Mr Fenech as his '10th Key Screamers'.

When the band signed with Crazy Love Records in 2000 they produced their second album 'Control Your Minds' and the label re-pressed their debut which by this time was in short supply but big demand. Never a band to rush into recording, their third album 'Mutilate, Torture and Kill' (2003) appeared on Nova Express Records and proved that the band from the Burgundy region had themselves matured like fine wine and they delivered a monster sounding blend of Psycho, Garage and Rock'n'Roll. A highly collectable picture disc version of this album was released by Drunkabilly the following year.

PSYCHO ATTACK OVER EUROPE

HELL'S BENT ON ROCKIN'

With ex-Kings of Nuthin'/Frantic Flintstones bass man Fantomas on board in 2004, the band's next move was a live album for Raucous Records 'Burgundy Livers', which showcased the band at their peak with a tight set and a quality sound delivering a storming album pretty far from the many slip-shod, cash-in concert recordings which have littered Psychobilly history. With a fourth studio album due in 2007, The Astro Zombies are seriously cementing their status as one of Europe's top Psycho outfits.

The Elektraws were another French band from the mid 1990s who enjoyed success although they had a far shorter career. They released only one album, 'Shock Rock' (1996), for Nervous Records which was recorded in England and produced by Alan Wilson. The band had a strong image and a more Rockabilly-influenced sound. The Elektraws' bassist and vocalist Nick 'Nico' Hervier went on to establish his own label in 1998, Pure & Proud Records, and was also involved in promoting gigs. Nico was also a member of the far heavier Psychobilly outfit Hellbats. Their first single was a split affair with the band Blue Movie which appeared on Pure & Proud in 2002.

Hellbats then released a mini CD, 'Fast'n'Heavy' (2002), on Nova Express Records with a title that hammered the fact home that Hellbats were a far more metal influenced Psychobilly combo. Nico joined the band after these releases and things were looking good for Hellbats with regular gigging and the release of their full-length debut 'Dark'n'Mighty' (2005), which appeared in a European issue and an alternative US version for Hairball 8 Records in 2006.

In 2006, Pure & Proud were releasing some fine albums including reissues of The Hellbillys' back catalogue and CDs from The Mad Mongols, Scary BOOM and Plan 9. However, tragedy struck in June 2006 when Nico was shot and killed in his hometown, the victim of a senseless act of street violence. Though only 32, Nico's contribution to the French scene was huge – playing, recording, promoting – and he remains sadly missed by many Psychobilly communities across the world.

With bands such as Banane Metalik and The Washington Deadcats once again back in action, a new breed of French Psychos have also enjoyed success in the 2000's like sleazy rockers Tight Fittin' Pants & G-String, and more traditional Psychobilly acts The Lucky Devils and Kryptonix. One of the most successful acts of this next generation are Monster Klub who already have four albums out since 1999, all which feature the outstanding artwork of band member, and Psychobilly illustrator extraordinaire, PaSKal Millet. With all this home-grown talent and the huge amount of Psychobilly bands the world over who regularly feature the country on their tour schedules, French billies have enjoyed a solid twenty years of Psycho with more to come. Vive le wreckin'!

GERMANY

Germany has continued to be a stronghold for Psychobilly, storming through the early boom, kicking it in the ass when it started to fade in the 1990s and dragging it back to life in the 21st Century. If any country deserves the accolade of 'keeping the faith' then it has to be Deutschland. The argument that Germany is the true centre of the scene is more than obvious in two main ways. Firstly it is evident in the huge and loyal support which the Germans give to many Psychobilly bands from outside the country, as bands who can barely fill the village hall 'back home' can often expect a large and vocal audience when they cross the border into Deutschland. Bands like The Meteors and Demented Are Go can count Germany amongst their strongholds of support and the German scene also boasts a number of very professional promoters who really know how to deliver the best deals for bands and their audience. Secondly, the country has not been without its own major home-grown talent over the past twenty years or so.

Coming out of Hamburg in 1984 were the impossibly youthful but extremely talented POX (Psychobilly Orchestra X). With barely a pubic hair between them the band were knocking out classic stompers at an early age. They shone briefly with their debut EP '... It's So Dark' (1985) on the Wahnsinn label then after some compilation appearances, including the legendary first volume of 'Psycho Attack Over Europe', they cut six tracks for KIX 4 U which emerged as the mini-album 'Voodoo Power'. Not only are POX fondly remembered as one of Germany's earliest home-grown Psychobilly

1980s Europe. Streets full of Psychobillies (Frank John).

bands but also because 'Voodoo Power' was such a strong offering which proved that German bands could more than compete with the vast wave of foreign bands who were flooding their country. Unfortunately POX were not to remain trailblazers for German Psycho as they faded quickly and a full-length debut never appeared. However, all was not lost as another German group who appeared alongside POX on 'Psycho Attack Over Europe' were fellow Psychobilly pioneers Sunny Domestoz, who formed in 1985.

Sunny Domestoz were a wild live act, and certainly one of the cornerstones of Germany's early Psychobilly scene but they split after only five years together and a handful of record releases. Comprising of 'Mr Domestoz' himself, Ozzi Muenning, on drums and vocals, Manni Feinbein on bass and guitarist Tex Morton (who would later join Mad Sin), they released their debut album 'Barkin' At The Moon' on Drinkin' Lonesome Records in 1985.

Relatively unusually for a Psychobilly band at that time, many of their songs featured the use of the organ. As a staple of 60s garage punk, the instrument fitted the band's sound well even alongside their unashamedly Psychobilly repertoire. Jennilee Lewis eventually joined the band as a full-time keyboard player and the producer of their debut, Jazz buff Goetz Alsmann, also added some ivory-tinkling. Despite their fine quality long-player Sunny Domestozs never released another album. One single appeared the following year 'Get Ready For The Get Ready' (1986) followed by the 'Playing Favourites' EP in 1987. By 1988 Tex Morton had moved on and was replaced by Teddy Conetti but in 1990 the band had split and their sizable legacy to European Psychobilly was posthumously recognised with the CD release 'The Complete Sunny Domestozs' (1991) on Roof Records.

When Tex left Mad Sin in 2006 the reformation of Sunny Domestozs began once more. At the end of 2005 a programme of ltd edition coloured vinyl repressings of their records began and with the resurgence of interest in this seminal German band it was not long before a full reunion gig was booked. In February 2006 the line-up of Tex, Jennilee, Ozzi and Manni took to the stage at the Essen's 6th Wildcat Weekender to a rapturous response. The reissues continued and, with Tex now available more freely, the band began touring and recording again. The first fruits of their new material was the 7" EP 'Playin' More Favourites', a quartet of cover versions and a sequel to their first EP almost two decades later.

While KIX 4 U introduced Sunny Domestoz to a wider audience but never worked any further with

PSYCHO ATTACK OVER EUROPE
HELL'S BENT ON ROCKIN'

the band they did sign another German Psychobilly band, The Bad Dooleys. The band ended their career in a more Rockabilly vein but initially hit the German scene in the mid 1980s with a mini-album for KIX 4 U 'Shark Attack' (1987) followed by a full, self-titled album for the label in 1988. By the early 1990s the band had undergone a lineup change and moved on from their earlier, good-natured, knockabout Psychobilly to a well-produced sound and a harder, Neo-Rockabilly beat on their 1993 LP 'No Escape' for Tombstone Records.

Alongside German Psychobilly bands in the second half of the 1980s there was also an emerging number of Neo Rockabilly bands such as The Hot Rod Gang, Ten Strike, The Rats and Somethin' Else who all crossed over well to Psychobilly audiences. Most notably, one band who came stomping out of West Berlin in the mid 1980s were The Roughnecks, a band probably better described as furious Rockabilly than pure Psychobilly but still a group with a sizable Psycho following. Initially consisting of guitarist/vocalist Tom Reiss, Tex Schmidt

The Bad Dooleys (Patrick Röhrle).

(guitar), Blahmann (bass) and Chicken on drums, Chicken soon made way for drummer Pete Grunn and this line-up released their debut single 'Saddle Soap' in 1986.

The band soon picked up a following, particularly in their homeland, and after drafting in new bass player Martin Buechler they released a follow-up single 'Hard Times' in 1987 followed by their debut album 'Stop, Look & Listen' the following year. Despite their success, which even included appearances on German TV, they imploded before the 1990s and went their separate ways. The Roughnecks story did not end there and after over a decade away they made a brief return to the limelight in 2000 with their long-belated follow up album 'Crash' and their early career was prodded back into the limelight with a collection, largely culled from their 1980s material, 'The Real Deal' which appeared on Crazy Love Records in 2003.

While Germany was undoubtedly shaking throughout the remainder of the 1980s with a huge amount of Psychobilly activity in the form of visiting bands and a throbbing population of Deutchland Psychos the home-grown scene was still to establish itself in a major way. However, the 1990s were about to address that situation. While many simply continued where many 1980s bands had left off, one legacy which many German bands of the 1990s left behind was the growing intensity of Psychobilly as the genre slipped further into Punk, Hardcore, Heavy Rock etc. long before terms like Punkabilly, Speedrock and Punk'n'Roll were ever in common use. Early German trailblazers who turned Psychobilly up "one louder" included Captain Coma, The Punishers and many bands from the German label Tombstone in particular.

What is most notable about German Psychobilly in the 1990s is the number of bands who contributed to a great boom in the country's music scene but who failed to last the decade. While Mad Sin have maintained German Psychobilly across three decades others have lacked the staying power of Koefte and co. The Pilgrims, Captain Coma, The Fears, The Scum Boys, The Brainblasters, The Bogeymen and The Punishers were all bands who delivered debut albums and gigged regularly but never progressed in their recording careers. Others like The Skel'Tons never made it beyond their debut EP and though Rantanplan went straight to UK label Link to produce their debut album 'Two Worlds At Once' (1990) they fared no better than any other acts of the period.

However, some German bands enjoyed more fruitful recording careers. The Rawheads were a heavily

HELL'S BENT ON ROCKIN'   PSYCHO ATTACK OVER EUROPE

Punk inspired Psycho group and began playing in the mid-1980s but released their debut single 'Follow That Demon' in 1993 for Mental Disorder Records. Their first upright bass-player Rob joined prior to the single's release but during his time with the band he took some time out to cover for Mad Sin's Holly and he featured on their album 'A Ticket Into Underworld'. On returning to The Rawheads he used his experience to contribute to the band's debut album 'Inferno' (1993). This was a vinyl only release for Rumble Records but a CD version appeared two years later courtesy of Mental Disorder. Ironically, not long after this release the band's career began to slow down and by 2002 they were no more.

Rob soon picked up his bass again for spicy she-rocker Kathy X who had arrived in Berlin in 2000. Kathy had been a member of The Death Valley Surfers back in London and continued to play with them while establishing her own rockin' three-piece featuring Rob and American drummer Dave Crome. With her band in place Kathy began recording and early tracks were available to download, a stunning stroke of forethought long before MySpace really kicked in. The debut album 'Ready For Anything' appeared in the Summer of 2004 on the Polish label Cosmic Records. Later that year Urban Zombie Records released one of the band's finest early tracks 'I Let The Devil In' on 7".

Eddyhez were another German Psychobilly outfit from the 1990s who made it beyond their debut album, albeit almost a decade later. Their debut album 'Well...' appeared in 1995 on Harybooboana Records and though it was solid enough Psychobilly, bordering on Klub Foot-era Neo, the very plain cover featuring a huge picture of a tramp's face probably did them no favours amongst eager Psychobilly record buyers looking for inspiration (besides, Demented Are Go had already conquered the market for record sleeves featuring hoboes with their 'Holy Hack Jack' 12 inch). Fast forward to 2004 and the band reappeared with a far more rockin' 5-track mini LP on Kamikaze Records, 'Weltschmerz', which included some fantastic covers particularly those of the B52's 'Planet Claire' and Spizz Energi's 'Where's Captain Kirk?'. Altogether not a huge back catalogue but proof that in Psychobilly 'it ain't over till it's over' and the 2000s are rapidly shaping up to be the decade when many rockin' bands resurrect their recording careers.

One 1990s band who have made great leaps forward in the 2000s are Munich ghouls The Grave Stompers. Rehearsing and gigging since 1993 it was four years into their career before they released their debut 'Rising From The Darkside' (1997). Though their first album was classic horror-themed old-school Psychobilly its follow-up 'Funeral Suite' (1999) was far heavier fare and typical of the faster, more metal-influenced sound that crept into the European scene throughout the 1990s. Apart from a split single with garage rockers Pot Belly in 2000 the band reduced their live work and slowly their third album began to take shape... very slowly.

'Bone Sweet Bone' eventually appeared in 2003 on Crazy Love Records and was something of a return to the roots of their debut album but with a stronger production job although still maintaining the morbid subject matter of many of their earlier songs. As The Grave Stompers continued recording new material for their second Crazy Love album in the Autumn of 2006 they found themselves in the enviable position of competing equally with the world's latest Psychobilly talent while still retaining some relatively 'Old School' appeal.

Taking an even longer break than The Grave Stompers are surfin' Berlin Psychos Notorious Deafmen. This band peddled a pretty unique brand of Psychobilly during the early 1990s, releasing a self-titled debut album and an EP for Mental Disorder. The band also appeared on the Wild Youth Records compilation 'Teenage Crime Wave', bizarrely credited as Maggi & His Gaylords. By the mid 1990s their trail was going cold but they sparked back into action in with the album 'Notorious Deafmen Goes White Pussy' (2004) which marked their comeback and permanent name change to (you guessed it) White Pussy. The current guitarist of White Pussy, Maggi, joined The Notorious Deafmen in 1995 and had previously played with Damage Done By Worms.

From the early part of the decade to the end of the 1990s, Damage Done by Worms were a busy band on the German Psychobilly scene and beyond. Formed in 1989 the band's first release was a ten-inch debut album, 'Evil Eyes' (1994), for the (then emerging) label Crazy Love. This was a prime slab of classic Psychobilly featuring a line-up of guitar/vocals, drums/vocals and double-bass and their second album 'Fear Will Freeze You When You Face...' (1996) was more of the same. In 1999 the band had an unexpected burst of activity releasing the CD EP 'Suicide City' and their excellent third album 'Tonight?!' but, though the band are still together in some form, no further albums have appeared for over six years. Nonetheless, the high-quality, unashamedly Psychobilly back catalogue which they have left behind (particularly their last album which adds a few unique twists to the genre) is worthy enough to ensure that the band is still welcome on the scene at any time.

The Pitmen (Crazy Love Records).

One of Germany's finest Psychobilly outfits of last decade were The Pitmen. This quartet from Ruhrpott originally featured Grischa on double bass, Peer Timmer on drums, Christian Waleschkowski on vocals and guitarist Christian Rubbert and they first got together to rehearse in the Spring of 1995. Within their first year together they had supported fellow German Psychobillies Disturbance, played at a festival for the major German promoters Mental Hell and had their debut single 'Misfits' released by Crazy Love. The following year things were moving even faster with the release of their debut album 'Listen To The Engine' (1997) and some major support slots alongside their own headlining gigs. The band were to record a further album but not until 2001 when 'Welcome To The Show' made its belated appearance, yet again on Crazy Love.

A few years later Grischa was busy slapping bass for Punk-fuelled Rock'n'Rollers Heartbreak Engines who have since forming knocked out two solid albums, 'Good Drinks, Good Butts, Good Fellows' (2003) and 'Love Murder Blues' (2005), which blend classic Punk, Pop Punk and Psychobilly in such a way that the band has enjoyed tremendous success across the world. Nonetheless, while The Heartbreak Engines continue to tear up gigs across Europe and beyond while moving on to bigger and better things the boot-stomping beat of The Pitmen is unlikely to be forgotten, particularly in Germany.

Heartbreak Engines (Die In Style).

Its no surprise that Germany, with probably the world's most committed Psychobilly scene, has not been short of specialist record labels either. It has never been simply the bands that have driven Germany's immense rockin' scene but also a variety of crucial record labels and promoters who have influenced the future of Psychobilly not only in Germany but across the world.

The suitably named Tombstone Records from Oberhausen boasts a fine roster of Psychobilly releases including Nekromantix' debut 'Hellbound', The Phantom Rockers' first LP 'Kissed By A Werewolf' and many of The Phantoms' other early albums such as 'Demon Lover', 'Search & Destroy' and 'Shag Squirt'. Tombstone casts its net wide for Psychobilly talent and has snared the likes of Russia's Meantraitors, Scottish rockers The Numbskulls, Holland's Milwaukee Wildmen and Austria's Hounded Prisoner. Like most rockin' labels, Psychobilly is only part of its roster and Tombstone also produces a large number of Rockabilly and Rock'n'Roll albums

Bochum based Rumble Records got their label going in 1991 with The Scum Rats album 'Go Out In A Scum Dream'. The Scum Rats stayed with the label for the length of their career which stretched to two further albums, 'Let Me Be Bad' (1993) and 'Demon Of The Dark' (1995). Rumble continued to sign new talent and was also the home of a number of German Psychobilly bands throughout the 1990s including Splash Bones and The Punishers.

Maybe Crazy Records are a familiar name to many Psychobillies across the world and probably best remembered as the early home of the German trio Mad Sin. The label was established by Peter Patzold and from the late 1980s he signed a number of German rockers such as The Sin, The Scannerz and The Scallywags. The Scannerz were far closer to Neo-Rockabilly and their self-titled debut in 1987 was to be their only release. The Scallywags were another group who spent their short career at Maybe Crazy and knocked out two fine examples of German Psychobilly with their albums 'Speed On 45' (1987) and 'Three Of A Kind' (1988). Mad Sin's debut album 'Chills And Thrills In a Drama Of Mad Sin And Mystery' appeared in 1988 and the band delivered another three albums 'Distorted Dimensions' (1989), 'Break The Rules' (1992) and 'Ticket Into Underworld' (1993) before finally moving on. That was not to be the labels final Mad Sin product as they licensed the band's 1990 album for Fury Records, 'Amphigory', for release on CD.

Another of the genre's main labels, Crazy Love Records, is based in Haan, Germany. Established in 1993, the label's first release was a four-track 7" EP from Finland's The Nightmares. The label's main man is Guido Neumann, a rockin' fan who had previously worked on the German fanzine 'Demon Love' in the early 1990s.

The album which introduced Crazy Love as a label was the release of the Godless Wicked Creeps CD 'Victim of Science' in 1994. This was the Danish trio's full-length debut and they remained with the label for their following three albums. Guido signed other Psychobilly artists to the label, such as Kryptonix, The Ripmen, and Popeye's Dik but Crazy Love was to cover a wider range of genres as its popularity grew. What followed throughout the 1990s and into the new millennium was a mind-bendingly eclectic range of artists appearing on further Crazy Love releases from not only the Psychobilly scene but also bands, peddling Rockabilly, Punk, Country, Rock'n'Roll and any variety of combinations within those styles. On Crazy Love the likes of nine-piece R&B swingers Ray Collins' Hot Club rub shoulders happily with furious Hungarian Psycho from Gorilla.

Crazy Love remain a key player on the current Psychobilly scene with recent major albums from The Dead Kings (2001), Demented Scumcats (2005) and the Klingonz' first album for over a decade, 'Up Uranus' (2003). They have also been responsible for keeping the new blood flowing on the scene with debut albums from The Rock-It Dogs, Tight Fitting Pants and a sizable number of recent German Psychobilly bands such as Cheeky Rascals, The Boozehounds, Godzilla Flip, and The Tony Montanas, whose debut EP, 'Criminal Energy', on Urban Zombie Records showed great promise which transferred easily onto their full-length offering. One of their biggest successes has been with Chibuku. This band from Munster started back in 1992 but their progress had been relatively slow until joining up with Crazy Love. In the mid 1990s they had a couple of full-length demo tapes but from 1997 they were with Gonna Street Records and released two seven-inch EPs, their debut 'Time Of The Devil' (1999) and a mini-CD, 'Voodarian #7' (2000). All these releases captured their increasingly hard-core Psychobilly style but their first album for Crazy Love 'Dans La Rue' (2001) offered a powerfully produced, harder, heavier Psychobilly album which was perfect for the new millennium. The band stuck

Mad Sin in 2006 (www.madsin.de).

with the label for another album, 'Rock'n'Roll Is The Devil's Music' (2003), then seemed to tour a little less for a few years before returning late in 2006 with their third album for Crazy Love 'Novo Mundo'. Though many bands in recent years have stretched the boundaries of Psychobilly to the point where they descend into thrash metal, Chibuku have always remained a solid Psychobilly outfit albeit one with relentlessly pounding double-bass and drums, a grinding guitar and a screaming lunatic with iron-lungs on vocals.

While most modern rockin' labels focus mainly on CD, Crazy Love are often driven personally by Guido's love of vinyl and they regularly release albums on LP. The label has even licensed some classic Psychobilly titles for reissue including long deleted LPs from the likes of Skitzo, The Sharks, The Deltas and Torment which are once again available in mint condition reducing the temptation for many collectors to splash out high prices for original copies. These are also the perfect replacements for any Psychobilly collectors with a stack of well-played, dog-eared albums from the early days which are now covered in lager stains and fag burns. However, as many of these releases are in small pressings of 500 copies, many of Crazy Love's high-quality reissues are destined to be collector's items themselves. The label has also licensed long-deleted albums from other labels such as their CDs from Maybe Crazy's back catalogue featuring The Scallywags, The Scannerz and Mad Sin's 'A Ticket Into Underworld'

Alongside its label business, Crazy Love also operates as a retailer with a well-stocked catalogue of titles available for mail order, selling not only their own releases but also CDs and albums from most of the world's major Psycho and Rockin' labels. With an excellent website and a regular catalogue crammed to breaking point with minute detail, Crazy Love deliver a regular fix to rockers all over Europe and beyond. Like all specialist retailers, Crazy Love are among those providing an increasingly important service in a world where major music retailers have increasingly bland stocking policies regarding the rockin' genre and Independent record shops are disappearing fast.

One other German label in particular has been instrumental in keeping Psychobilly looking, and sounding, in great shape. The charmingly named I Used To Fuck People like You In Prison Records was established back in 2000 by label boss Andre Bahr. Andre is also the owner of Dortmund's rawest record store 'Outcast', serving Punks, Rockers and other misfits with vinyl, CD, clothing and accessories since 1992. The label has never been simply a Psychobilly label but its roster of dark'n'dirty Punks and Rock'n'Rollers is the perfect home for bands of a Psycho persuasion. Assisting Andre in the running of the label is his associate Tobbe.

Occasionally known to uneasy distributors and nervous advertising types as 'People Like You', the label has consistently released albums from a number of hard rockin' heavy hitters from Germany (Heartbreak Engines, Daybreak Boys) and beyond (Deadline, The Bones, US Bombs). People Like You's first release was back in 2000, their four-track 10" 'Cape Canaria' from heavy rockers Zebulon but the label's first truly Psychobilly release would come from Mad Sin. When Mad Sin walked away from Polydor their next release was their debut for People Like You, the excellent 'Survival Of The Sickest' (2002). The Sin then stayed with Andre and Tobbe for a further 2 albums, the reissue of 'Sweet & Innocent...' and their masterpiece 'Dead Moon's Calling' (2005), both released during a period when both the band and the label were enjoying increased exposure.

In 2003, People Like You were firmly anointed as the modern home for demented rockin' when they released The Meteors' long-awaited 'Psychobilly' album. This was a groundbreaking release not only because of the quality of the tracks but also because it marked the return of the band to a slap-bass driven three piece. Featuring the excellent cover artwork of PaSKal from Monster Klub, it seemed to confirm that if The Meteors could sound this good after over twenty years then Psychobilly was far from flatlining. The Meteors continued their collaboration with People Like You in the following year on the their album 'These Evil Things' (2004).

Demented Are Go also found a new home with the label for their first full album for over five years. 'Hellbilly Storm' (2005) was clad in a striking Vince Ray album cover and, although it took a while to get together, it was one of the band's strongest releases for a while. With songs such as Pedigree Scum, Hotrod Vampires, and Destruction Boy, the band were the perfect partner to many of the label's other lewd and crude rowdies.

The album was picked up by Hellcat Records for release in the States with a different cover and an extra track but in 2006, 'Hellbilly Storm' also got a collectable makeover from People Like You and appeared in a limited edition form comprised of four vinyl picture disc singles and an assortment of merchandising all housed in a garish box set. Yet another example of the attention People Like You pay to artwork and design and a far cry from the crude cut'n'paste covers of early Psychobilly albums.

Alongside the importance of providing a steady stream of record and CD releases for hordes of rabid Psychobilly music enthusiasts, is the live music scene. Psychobilly is a genre more ravenous than most for gigs, where each band's goal is to whip up the crowd into a seething, sweating, bone-breaking mess. Promoting gigs in Germany has always been big business and two promoters in particular loom large over the scene. Mental Hell was a Psychobilly/Neo-Rockabilly booking agency led by Lonesome and Lucky, two fellas known by almost every band from, or who have gigged in, Germany. From their first event in 1998, Mental Hell are well known right across Europe and the UK and have achieved a feat few, if any, have matched with their legendary 'Satanic Stomp' Psychobilly festivals which are approaching their 20th gathering in 2007. Over the years the Satanic Stomps have featured nothing less than the cream of Psycho and Neo bands from all over the world and Mental Hell have also produced their own

PSYCHO ATTACK OVER EUROPE — HELL'S BENT ON ROCKIN'

Die In Style, keeping Psychobilly live (Die In Style).

German language fanzine which published six issues.

In 2002, Lucky established Die In Style Concerts, a booking agency which regularly organises gigs across Germany, Austria, Denmark, The Netherlands and the UK along with providing worldwide representation for Nigel Lewis, The Long Tall Texans, Evil Devil and Heartbreak Engines. Other bands such as Reverend Horton Heat, The Damned, Rezurex, Henchmen, The Phantom Rockers, Nekromantix, Calavera, Horrorpops and Mad Marge & The Stonecutters look to Die In Style for sole representation in Germany and often the rest of Europe. Working with labels such as People Like You, Yep Roc and Hellcat/Epitaph, Die In Style are also behind the successful 'Kings Of Psychobilly' all-dayers in Hamburg, an event approaching its seventh boot-stomping hoedown in the Autumn of 2007.

The growing success of German labels and the well promoted live music scene of the 2000s is also mirrored in the wealth of new talent on the rockin' scene. The Neo-Rockabilly movement has continued in good health for nearly a quarter of a century and many bands from the early days are still around but have been joined by newer bands such as Lota Red, Double Cross, The Growlers, Velvetone and Speedswing, a band formed from the ashes of short-lived 1990s Psychobilly outfit Disturbance whose debut album 'We Call It... Disturbance' (1994) appeared on Mental Disorder Records. Speedswing's mission is to deliver a twisted hybrid of Rockabilly, Swing, Ska and Surf and the nine-piece combo have rocked a number of European venues with their unique blend while still managing to knock out a mini-album 'Speedswing' (2005) for Crazy Love.

Germany's modern Psychobilly scene is in even ruder health and arguably as strong now as it was in the 1990s. Bands such as Bad Reputation, Pure Spite, Paddlecell, Shark Soup, The Tazmanian Devils and Up To Vegas have got well established and released a variety of records including their first full-length recordings while newer acts including Go Faster, Rockin' Slickers and Suicidal Lunatics have still to deliver their full debut albums after inflicting their early material on the Psychobilly community. Other groups have have been particularly busy since the millennium and Thee Flanders are probably the most resourceful of the new blood, a band who have launched into all manner of media to promote themselves and the German scene in general. Thee Flanders started back in 1999, initially as Ted Flanders & The Hot Wings, and knocked out a trio of well produced demo CDs before switching to their current title with a further demo 'Die Halbstarken' then making all their early tracks available for free download as a collection titled 'First Blood'.

After all this activity it was no surprise when the band were picked up by veteran German Punk label Halb 7 Records and their debut album 'Punkabilly From Hell' (2003), both in its title and the recordings on it, gave those on the Psycho scene as yet unaware of the band an idea of which direction they were heading in. Their second album 'Monster Party' (2004) leaned a little closer to straight Psychobilly. What sets Thee Flanders apart from many bands on the Psychobilly scene is their professionalism when it comes to maintaining their career. All their releases, from their very first demo, have featured excellent artwork and the band constantly keep themselves in the picture with a variety of other releases such as their mini-album 'Back From Hell' (2005) and their CD-EP 'Erna P' (2006) with added videoclip. Thee Flanders album releases for Halb 7 have also been pressed in limited vinyl quantities and a variety of live tracks, alternative versions of their songs and cover versions have been scattered across a number of compilation albums making much of the band's product very collectable. Far from the lazy, slipshod

Psychobilly bands of 'ye olden days', the band are nothing if not prolific with an album of cover versions, 'Graverobbing', in the pipeline in between vocalist Norman Winter's involvement with the globe's glossiest Psychobilly magazine 'Psychomania'.

Joining Thee Flanders in this vibrant new German scene are German Punkabilly combo Godzilla Flip. The band created such an impression with their debut album 'Kamikaze Attack' (2005) on Crazy Love Records, that they attracted the attention of Tokyo's mighty Toho film studio who immediately ordered the band to cease and desist with the Godzilla moniker and avoid any further use of the cartoon dinosaur artwork on their CD cover. It was all a rather heavy-handed affair, given the band's relatively short stature in the global music biz, but Toho graciously avoided calling for the album to be withdrawn. Collectors take note though as any further pressings or re-releases will feature the group under their new moniker – Rampires. Undeterred by their brush with the might of the Japanese business titans the band have continued their career, pursuing their own brand of Psychobilly, Punk and Heavy Rock, and their first album as Rampires, 'Bat Taste', was released by Crazy Love early in 2007.

With its rich history of home-grown Psychobilly spanning over twenty years, Germany appears to have strolled through any dips in the genre's fortune thanks to its solid network of bands, record labels, promoters and followers of the music. With Psychobilly's recent resurgence and the country's scene growing even stronger it is hard to believe that the Psycho sound will 'ever' fade in Germany.

AUSTRIA

Given the sizable girth of the neighbouring German scene, Austrian Psychobilly is remarkably rare. Although the country is not short of a number of bass-slappin' Rockabilly combos, Psychobilly talent lies relatively thin on the ground. Keeping the genre alive in Austria has mostly been left to Thee Flatliners who have their own unique take on the Psychobilly sound. The band formed in 1995 from the ashes of two popular Austrian Rockabilly groups, Cadillac Rust and The Cryptkickers. By the time of their debut album 'Rhapsody In Black' (1997), they had already shook off any traditionalist sound and were moving in a harder, faster more horror-fixated direction.

Having signed with Crazy Love Records for their first album, Thee Flatliners have stayed with the label for a further two albums, 'Enter The Twilight' (1998) and 'Pandemonium' (2001). Each album gained better production values and incorporated their evolving, heavier sound which began to include further influences from other genres such as Heavy Rock, Gothic and Speed Metal. The band certainly appear unrepentant torch carriers for the darker side of Rock'n'Roll and seem determined not to let any constrictions from the Psychobilly genre hold them back in the quest for a bigger audience.

Thee Flatliners have, however, had some competition from other Austrian bands. Brain Dead were a Psychobilly band who formed in the mid 1990s and though they soldiered on through the rest of the decade securing many sizable support slots with Mad Sin, Demented Are Go etc, regular line-up changes prevented them from progressing much further. In recent years, competition has mainly come from over-the-top horrorpunks Bloodsucking Zombies From Outer Space. Taking the horror element from Psychobilly and steamrolling it through Goth and American Punk, they are direct descendants of every Psychobilly band who have ever slapped on the white facepaint. Signed up to Fiendforce Records, the German label with global appeal for gore-driven rockers, The Bloodsucking Zombies... are labelmates with new Psychobilly titans Resurex and have already produced two strong albums, 'See You At Disneyland' (2004) and 'A Night At Grand Guignol' (2006). Though far from the Psychobilly sound of 'ye olden days', they certainly have bags of what the new kids want and with the backing of their rapidly growing label they look likely to enjoy even more success in the US as they do in Europe.

HOLLAND

Heading something of a second wave of Psychobilly in the late 1980s were a number of Euro bands. Holland again had a lot to offer, in particular Bang Bang Bazooka. The band formed in 1987 but it was over 16 months later before they released their debut album 'Bang Bang Bazooka' on Count

Rockin' in Rotterdam, 1988 (Patrick Röhrle).

Orlok Records. Sharing slightly more in common with Neo-Rockabilly bands of the Klub Foot era such as The Deltas and The Pharaohs they were still a Psychobilly-edged quartet who gigged steadily across Europe. Their debut was followed two years later in 1990 by the album 'True Rebel' also on Count Orlok Records but by the mid 1990s the band was no more. Despite their relatively sparse back catalogue the band were often fondly remembered and in 2004 they were back in action with the original line-up of Marcel Hoitsema on vocals/guitar, Jean-Francois Besson on guitar/vocals, Bart Gevers on bass and drum basher Rene Van Lersal.

Although not as successful as Batmobile, the early stages of Archie's career are remarkably similar. This Dutch band also saw their Rockabilly sound develop into something harder before their success began. Like the Batmobile boys they also were introduced to the wider Psychobilly community by the first 'Psycho Attack Over Europe' album and made their major breakthrough with a mini-LP similar to Batmobile's self-titled effort.

Boasting only eight tracks, 'Listen To What Archie Sez' (1986) on KIX 4 U Records was lean but mean with no filler tracks. Comprising of six self-penned tunes and two covers, including Golden Earring's driving rock classic 'Radar Love', it kicked off with a title track that remains an old school Psychobilly classic. Despite their early promise, strangely nothing more was heard of this rare Eurobilly band. Likewise, early Dutch Psychobillies The Tranquillizers made their mark with an EP on Cat Machine Records, 'Paranoia'(1985), alongside two tracks on 'Psycho Attack Over Europe'. Despite showing great promise, their career was also short but the band's double-bass man Jan Van Hal, has remained active on the Psychobilly scene to this day.

Alongside Bang Bang Bazooka, The Tranquillizers and Archie, the late-1980s Psycho scene in Holland was relatively vibrant and also featured bands such as Scam and The Skrunch. Scam were initially known as The Juvenile Delinquents who released only one album, 'Jumpin' Around' (1987), for Tombstone Records. As Scam, the band released two albums of relatively straight-up Psychobilly in the 1980s, 'Gamblin' Fever' (1988) and 'Infant Years' (1989), before adopting something of a cleaner, Rockabilly sound on their following album for Rockhouse Records, 'A Million Dollar Scam' (1991).

After almost a decade off the scene the core members of Scam made a triumphant return with the Power-Rockabilly combo 69 Beavershot (not to be confused with fellow Dutch rockers Beavershot). With their own brand of musclebound rocking, the band signed with Raucous Records for their powerful debut 'Beavershot' in 2002 then delivered a further album to the label with the follow-up 'Maximum Rockabilly' (2005). Double bassist Mars and the band's earlier drummer Marc Burger have also worked more recently with Batmobile's Jeroen Haamers as Triple Dynamite.

The Skrunch were active on the Dutch scene between 1987-91 and also featured regularly at events

The Tranquillizers (Jan Van Hal).

across Belgium and Germany. They never set the Psychobilly scene alight but they did produce a self-titled debut album (are Psychobilly bands too lazy to think of a name for their albums?) for Tombstone Records in 1988 followed by an album for KIX 4 U with a memorable cover featuring a big-knockered woman squeezed into a Skrunch T-shirt and the excellent title, 'Smelly Sally' (1991). However, after that titillation there was little else from the band.

The late 1980s/early 1990s also kicked up many short-lived Dutch Psycho bands such as Blazin' Saddles, Sons Of The Yompin' Cockroaches, Tiny Minds, The Cavemen, Es-Feiv and The Rockats alongside a huge number of home-grown Dutch Neo-Rockabilly bands.

One of the major factors in maintaining a healthy Rockin' scene in Holland has been the establishment of Count Orlok Records. The label is based in Rotterdam and was created by Batmobile's drummer Johnny Zuidhof along with Eddie, an associate of the band. Appropriately, the label's first release was Batmobile's second album 'Bambooland' in 1987 and the band would go on to release a further eight albums on the label over the ten next years. The label has continued to champion Dutch acts such as Asmodeus, Bang Bang Bazooka, Scam and Sin Alley alongside other bands such as The Rattlers and The Atomics.

Originally signed to Count Orlok Records, Asmodeus have released a sporadic but high-quality trio of albums spanning the early 1990s to the present day. Formed in Holland in 1992 the original line-up featured Dimitri on guitar, Arie Reisinger on double-bass and vocals and drummer Ko. Their first album for Count Orlok was 'Psycho On Hell's Request' (1993), a thirteen track affair which set out their stall as a furious Rock'n'Horror band pushing their Psychobilly sound to the heavier end of the spectrum. Setting a standard for future releases it was to be five years before their next offering 'Diggin' Up The King' (1998) appeared and time had not withered their 'Heavy-Psycho' approach and obvious love of all things demonic.

Despite relatively large periods of time between albums, Asmodeus remained a popular act on the Eurobilly scene and were one of the earlier European acts to draw on elements of heavy rock such as

The Cenobites (Christophe @ Drunkabilly Records).

Thrash, Doom and Black Metal. Unusually, despite many similarities between genres (black T-shirts, extreme music, preoccupations with the dead, the Devil, graveyards etc) many bands have kept the many forms of Metal at arms length, remaining in the seemingly more acceptable worlds of Punk and Rockabilly but Asmodeus have never appeared to hold such convictions.

Be it by accident or design, Asmodeus steadfastly continued to do their own thing. In 2004 they finally made their way to America and played a series of dates in California and Texas including the 2nd West Coast Wreckers Ball and the 'Texass' tour, a package deal featuring Peter Pan Speedrock and Concombre Zombi amongst others. With a sound far closer to many emerging US Psycho bands with a similar heavy edge, their long-awaited third album 'Diabolique Royale' (2004) was released on the Tombstone label then picked up in a transatlantic deal with Hairball 8 records.

With this release their new sound reached its peak with a furious collection of demonic Psychobilly and also completed a trilogy of excellent album sleeves as every Asmodeus cover boasts an excellent full-colour illustration accompanied by lurid artwork in every booklet. Though they have taken their time, Asmodeus could never be accused of rushing their recording career, it has resulted in a trio of well-produced albums all in their own unique style and with their sound running parallel to much of the American scene, perhaps a move stateside like fellow European heroes Nekromantix would take Asmodeus to another level.

While Holland has enjoyed Psychobilly for some time their scene has continued to develop. One Dutch band who have experienced some global success in recent years has been The Cenobites. The band have toured way beyond their own borders with gigs in Germany, Spain, the UK and America. More exotically they have taken their demonic rockin' to Brazil on four separate tours. The Cenobites formed in 1994 but bizarrely none of the current line-up are from this period. However bassist PG Vogeli is the longest serving member as he joined The Cenobites around eighteen months after they first formed. Current vocalist, Dimitri Hauck, has also had a long-standing commitment having joined the band near the end of the 1990s and contributing much to the sound that the band now have.

On their most recent album for Drunkabilly, 'Snakepit Vibrations' (2005), they offer a sound which pushes the Punk influence in Psychobilly to its limits and almost touches on Heavy Metal on a few tracks. This has been a style which has evolved as much as their line-up. Their earlier recordings such as their self-titled, eight-track 10" for Tombstone Records were far closer to traditional Psychobilly, as were their appearances on compilations such as 'Rumble Party Vol. 6' (1998) and 'Best Of Fury Psychobilly' (1999). However, each line-up change appeared to draw the band closer to their Punk and Heavy Rock influences. Citing Demented Are Go, Motorhead and The Exploited as influences, they really began drawing these elements together most potently in their first full-length album 'Demons To Some, Angels To Others' (2002) for Drunkabilly Records. With their sound having grown even heavier with their current album, The Cenobites are in a good position to appeal to fans of heavy-Psycho and many outside the genre but equally those who prefer a little more 'billy in their Psycho may find the band heavy going.

The 2000s have kicked up a number of other Dutch Psychobilly acts who are also pursuing a heavier direction combining far more elements of Punk and dirty, heavy Rock'n'Roll into what has been known as Speedrock, amongst other things. Bands like The Gecko Brothers, Dicemen and Speedcocks are moving in this direction but the godfathers of this sub-genre are the band who gave it their name – Peter Pan Speedrock. Formed in 1997, the band evolved from the Dutch Rock'n'Roll scene but musically they veer far closer to acts such as Zeke, Nashville Pussy and The Supersuckers. Though a long way from the Old School sound this type of high-octane, relentlessly rockin' beat has a huge fanbase amongst followers of Psychobilly, particularly in Europe, and 'Speedrock' in general has undoubtedly had an influence on the Psychobilly genre allowing bands such as Asmodeus and The Cenobites to broaden their style without fear of alienating a large part of their audience.

The Milwaukee Wildmen have also played a major part in stretching the boundaries of Psychobilly in Holland and have stayed true to the spirit of the genre while pushing it to extremes at the same time. Their classic Rockabilly line-up of double-bassist, guitarist/vocalist and drummer bursts at the seams with pounding rhythms and brutal, metal-tinged riffing. The band spent over six years with Tombstone Records and knocked out four increasingly powerful albums, 'Hard Times' (1996), 'Death's Deputy' (1998), 'Scars Remain' (2000) and 'Psychosomatic' (2002) before taking a breather, only to return in 2006 with their stunning 'Strike Back' album for Drunkabilly Records.

Milwaukee Wildmen (Monique Wildenburg).

The Milwaukee Wildmen have toured all over the world and with their own brand of heavy-rockin' Psychobilly they have occasionally raised a few eyebrows amongst many followers of the scene who are unfamiliar with their genre-busting sound. Regardless of this the band have persisted in proving, both live and in the studio, that theirs is the way forward and in the far more open scene of the 2000s it seems that many would agree.

There is no doubt that the Dutch

Psychobilly scene is simply one facet of the country's Underground rock scene and far less ghettoised than it is in other countries. This seems to be one reason why Psychobilly bands in Holland are often more experimental and individual and this attitude, along with excellent support of some fine promoters and record labels (particularly Drunkabilly and Count Orlok), has ensured that Dutch Psycho has been consistently strong for over two decades.

DENMARK

Alongside the barnstorming success of Nekromantix and Horrorpops, Denmark has also produced another top Psychobilly band with their own unique take on the genre. Godless Wicked Creeps did not really make their presence felt on the scene until the early-mid 1990s but throughout their career, along with support from their record label Crazy Love Records, they have continually produced inventive records and gathered a strong following particularly amongst members of other bands and new converts in America.

Originally formed in 1993 as a trio in the Danish town Aarhus, Denmark their line-up featured Thomas Mejer – aka Dax Dragster (vocals/guitar), Kim Kix (bass) and Martin Budde (drums). After gigging round Denmark, the band attracted record label interest and they appeared on a 7" vinyl compilation for Crazy Love Records in 1994 with their song 'Crazy Hormones'. That same year their first album for the label was also Crazy Love's first CD release, 'Victim Of Science'. It was a Punk-fuelled fourteen-track rocker which was a fine example of 1990s Psycho – undeniably 'Billy enough for the purists but with enough to keep other lovers of street music happy. Though their sound developed and improved they could never be accused of taking their foot off the gas and their follow-up album 'Hellcoholic' (1995) was another furiously paced collection but one which never descended into thrash.

What probably attracts many to the Godless Wicked Creeps is how they always manage to move forward musically without distancing themselves from Psychobilly. The first play of each new album always offers something extra rather than simply another helping of the last album. Their third album 'Hystereo' (1997) again moved things on with a collection of well-crafted songs that still shook the speakers with a bit more depth. Up to this point their touring to support album releases had seen them perform regularly across Europe but when supporting 'Hystereo' they made a trip to the States and spent one month in the Spring of 1998 touring the West Coast of America. Although this tour opened the band up to a large emerging audience it also marked the end of the original line-up as Thomas decided to leave the band. Though this was a blow, he did work around a year's 'notice' as the remaining members worked on their plans to continue the band.

With a founder member out, Martin and Kim decided to stretch the line-up to a four-piece and set out to recruit a new singer as well as a guitarist. They did not have to look far for a vocalist as Kim's brother Lars took over on the microphone and Martin brought guitarist Nikolag in from his other band, The Defectors. After a lengthy rehearsal period they took to the road again, which included another trip to the States and Canada.

Though the Creeps had always been Psychobilly with an increasing Punk influence, by 2001 the new line-up was far closer to pure Punk itself mixing post 1977 sounds with 1960s garage. The band produced 'Smile' (2001) for Lucky 7 Records, an album with plenty of appeal to fans of their earlier releases but also one which looked set to propel them to a wider audience. However, it was not to be and 'Smile' was the band's curtain call as they split in 2002. Kim Kix went on to form Powersolo, a group pursuing a crossover sound of rockin' roots music, surf and Punk while also releasing a side project album, 'Vodka and Kalashnikov' on Crazy Love Records with the demented Rockabilly trio Siberian Mad Dogs. Martin Budde is now a full-time drummer with Danish Garage Punk big-shots The Defectors and Thomas Mejer is fronting a hard rockin' trio, Spenzer, after his short-lived cowpunk band Bull'It released only one album, 'The El Vado Hayride', for Crazy Love.

Despite being prime candidates for a Psychobilly reformation, as each member is now enjoying further success with other bands the Godless Wicked Creeps saga appears to be at a dead end. With

Nekromantix, Horrorpops and The Wreckin' Dead moving to America and Godless Wicked Creeps no more, Denmark is not experiencing a Psychobilly rebirth in the manner of other European countries such as Germany and Spain but with its healthy Rockin' and Garage scene, Rock'n'Roll Danish style is as vibrant as ever.

FINLAND

Their cannot be too many countries in the European Union who have escaped the deadly strain of Psychobilly fever and Finland is no exception. By no means a Psychobilly hot spot, the country has played its own part in the history of European Psycho. For most listeners outside of the country the first signs that any rockin' was going on came from two major compilations. Finnish Rockabilly combo The Housewreckers made an appearance on Nervous Records' 'Hell's Bent On Rockin'' in 1985 and the band have continued to play and record to this day.

With a more Psychobilly edge, The Stringbeans first made themselves known on the first 'Psycho Attack Over Europe' (1985) album but did not deliver their debut until 1988 with their mini-album 'Crime And Punishment' for Tombstone Records. Often regarded as a sort of European equivalent to Restless, the band moved away from their Psychobilly influences and showcased a more pop/rock themed Rockabilly sound over their further two albums, 'Robots And Motions' (1993) and 'String Alone' (1997). Never a band to rush into things, their 2001 album '21st Century Timemachine' was a collection of earlier material and rarities (capturing the band at their most experimental) which included in the liner notes the band's own apology for their "laziness". Nonetheless, though their output has been limited The Stringbeans have produced some inventive Rockabilly over the years and went a long way to shake off the Restless-copyists tag.

Generally, Neo-Rockabilly has dominated the Finnish scene from Deathrow in the mid-1980s to 1990s bands such as The Crestlers and The Jokers right up to more recent bands like Nine Lives. While most Neo bands in Finland enjoyed a sizable Psychobilly following one band who genre-hopped in quite a dramatic style were Francine. The band first hit the scene back in the late 1980s and released their solid Rockabilly debut album 'Fire' (1990). This was

Nekromantix, top of the bill… again (Christophe @ Drunkabilly Records).

PSYCHO ATTACK OVER EUROPE — HELL'S BENT ON ROCKIN'

immediately followed by their LP 'Hard Enough', released the same year and produced by famed producer 'Psycho' Pete Gage.

As the decade progressed, the band moved away from their pure Rockabilly sound and took on board a variety of Rock'n'Roll influences which have progressed through six other albums to their current long-player 'King For A Day' (2005), a hard rockin' creation for Poko Rekords (a Finnish subsidiary of EMI) which included enough modern alternative music influences to carry the band onto a wider stage. In Finland they have always been big business with many album chart appearances and major TV and

4th PSYCHO-FESTIVAL
KEIZERSHALLEN AALST BELGIUM
30 JUNE - 1 JULY CAPACITY: 3000 Pers.

FRIDAY 30 JUNE DOORS 7PM PRICE 400 BFr.

- YANCATOES (B)
- GRISWALDS (UK)
- RATMEN (B)
- MAD SIN (D)
- WASHINGTON DEAD CATS (FR)

SAT. 1 JULY DOORS 11 AM PRICE 700

- SPOOK and the GHOULS (UK)
- The CARAVANS (UK)
- HAPPY DRIVERS (FR)
- GUANA BATZ (UK)
- The HIGHLINERS (UK)
- THE BOPPIN' KIDS (S)
- TORMENT (UK)
- BATMOBILE (NL)

PHONE: 052-21.53.93
FOR ALL INFORMATION WRITE: VZW SPINNEKOP St ROCHUSSTRAAT 34, 9330 DENDERMONDE BELGIE

European audiences have always had a thirst for live rockin' (Frank John).

HELL'S BENT ON ROCKIN'   PSYCHO ATTACK OVER EUROPE

press coverage. In the early 1990s they even tasted mainstream success when an incarnation of the band became the Finnish pop sensation PääesiintyJät, but like all major label acts across the globe their fickle audience moved on to the next big thing and the band returned to their rockin' roots.

Throughout the 1990s Finnish Psychobilly really got rolling with acts such as Gazoo Bill, Deep Six, The Flatline Rockers, The Cellar Beasts and The Apple Thieves. All of these bands do have their own version of the Psychobilly blueprint particularly Gazoo Bill, Deep Six and The Cellar Beasts who all have a heavier sound while The Apple Thieves chose a more Indie/Ska crossover direction. Apart from Gazoo Bill, who have two albums on Crazy Love ('Fire On The Line' (2000) and 'Think About It!' (2002), the rest have yet to go beyond recording their debut albums. However, with all these bands releasing material in the 2000s, the Finnish Psychobilly scene is hotter than it has ever been.

BELGIUM

The Belgians were never slow in clasping Psychobilly to their bosom and the first major Psychobilly festival in Belgium took place one weekend in April 1986. Psychos from all over Europe descended on the Koningshof venue in the city of Dendermonde to witness an impressive line-up including Torment, Demented Are Go, Batmobile, Frenzy, The Go-Katz and The Ratmen.

Though only a teenage spectator at that event, Christophe from Drunkabilly has become one of the major Psychobilly promoters in Belgium. Having been involved in the Psychobilly scene since 1986 Christophe new exactly what the punters were after and since 1991 he has organised concerts in his home town of Gent featuring the cream of Psychobilly talent such as The Meteors, The Lost Souls, Batmobile and Restless.

In 1998 Drunkabilly diversified into providing a small mail-order service for Belgian rockers who were finding it hard to get their fix of Rock'n'Roll. Along with the mail order service, Christophe also dipped his toe into record production with a ten-inch slab of vinyl from top Belgian Psychobilly outfit The Yancatooz, who had remained

Homegrown Belgian mayhem (Christophe @ Drunkabilly Records).

131

unrecorded since their 1991 debut album 'Let's Woy'. The single, 'Belly Boxing' was limited to 500 copies, setting an early standard for the label as producers of collectable vinyl. The first Drunkabilly CD followed soon after from another Belgian combo The O'Haras, purveyors of fine 'power-surf-a-billy'. These first two releases established a template for over twenty further releases over the next eight years comprising of limited edition CDs, seven-inch singles and LPs, making Drunkabilly a collector's favourite.

While Psycho-flavoured talent such as The Phantom Rockers, The Cenobites and The Milwaukee Wildmen have featured on Drunkabilly the label draws from a far wider range of genres such as Surf (Fifty Foot Combo, Speedball Jr, The Andrews Surfers), 1960s Garage (The Mighty Gordinis, The Astro Zombies), sleazy Rock'n'Roll (Hetten Des, Gecko Brothers) and all avenues in between. Drunkabilly has also had success with Hot Boogie Chillun, whose '15 Reasons To R'n'R' album for the label highlights the more Garage side of this popular rockin' band who remain notoriously difficult to pigeonhole. The label also became the recent home of Neo-Rockabilly pioneers The Caravans who delivered their hardest, most powerful album in years with their 2006 release 'No Mercy'. Although the label focuses largely on home-grown Belgian talent, Drunkabilly, with its high-quality and often collectable releases, is quickly becoming one of the major labels on the international Psychobilly scene.

Belgium's earliest Psychobilly scene in the 1980s featured a number of bands who burned brightly then disappeared such as The Jekills whose self-produced, self-titled debut album sold out quickly and was picked up by Tombstone Records for a re-pressing. Another short-lived Belgian act were Melody Massacre, a Belgian garage band who left only their self-titled Trashy debut from 1986 to remember them by. The Ratmen made a touch more of an auspicious debut with their LP 'Live Fast, Die Young' for Nervous Records in 1989, which boasted a killer version of Joan Jett's 'I Love Rock'n'Roll' alongside their own Neo/Psycho compositions.

The late 1980s also saw a number of Neo-Rockabilly acts appear on the homegrown Belgian rockin' scene, with The Wild Ones and The Tigermen as probably two of the most popular. However, the country's most unashamedly full-on Psychobilly act were Swampys, a band whose debut album 'Come Back To the Swamp' (1989) was a knuckleheaded classic of frantic slapping Psycho for KIX 4 U. Few of the early Belgian groups ventured far into the next decade but a few members of the bands continued to be involved in the scene such as The Ratmen's guitarist/vocalist Walter Broes who has enjoyed great success with top Belgian Rock'n'Roll combo The Seatsniffers.

The early 1990s were relatively lean times for new talent in Belgium with The Yancatooz and The Tasmanian Devils playing host to a growing number of visiting Psychobilly acts. Probably one of the most fondly remembered, yet relatively least recorded Belgian rockin' acts of the 1990s were Sin Alley. In 1994 they produced their debut EP 'Let's Dance', and their album 'Headin' For Vegas' (1994) for Count Orlok followed by a CD/double-vinyl single 'Detroit 442' in 1996. Passing through the line-up was Batmobile's Johnny Zuidhof but probably of most interest to hordes of slavering Psychobillies and Trash fanatics was the sex-bomb vocalist Martine Van Hoof, who was blessed with a powerfully sexy image and an even more powerful voice. The band peddled a more Garage Punk sound on their final EP and inexplicably drifted apart for some time, focusing on other projects, then reuniting in 2006 for some rare live appearances.

Drunkabilly certainly played their part in dragging Belgian Psycho through the 1990s and the eclectic nature of the label can also be reflected (intentionally or not) in the country's rockin' scene of the 2000s with acts like Hetten Des, The Hellsonics and The Demon Teds all peddling their own unique combinations of Psychobilly, Garage, Surf and Country. For the old-school rockers however, The Mudmen have many treats in store. Formed in 1998, and initially known as The Miami Mudmen, the band's name was inspired by The Sharks' song 'Mudman'. After a number of early demos, they were eventually poached by Tombstone Records and produced their debut CD 'No Fuck No Ride' (2004) with some assistance from Batmobile's Eric Haamers. Famed once for their live use of both double and electric bass players, the band have since trimmed their act to incorporate a single bassist who alternates between both instruments both live and in the studio. Regardless of which bass they are pounding the band remain a shit hot act and probably Belgium's most solid hope for future Psychobilly supremacy.

SWITZERLAND

Switzerland may not be the first place you think of when it comes to Psychobilly, and while it is true that the country is relatively short on straight-ahead Psychobilly bands they have had their share, while also contributing a few fine rockin' acts who have garnered a sizable Psychobilly following.

Switzerland has certainly seen some Neo-Rockabilly action, particularly from early 1980s rockers The Crazy Cats, but in the 1990s and beyond the country's rockin' scene has been overrun with frenzied Garage Trash outfits such as The Monsters (and their front man's solo project Reverend Beat Man) and beat-crazy newcomers The Dead. With Swiss bands it appears to be a question of quality over quantity and among the relatively few bands rocking the Swiss underground scene is a rich vein of unique talent.

One of the most underrated records from the first ten years of Psychobilly is the six-track, self-titled debut mini album from Switzerland's Hillbilly Headhunters. Released on KIX 4 U in 1990, this was a slab of twelve-inch vinyl featuring all killer tracks that would not have been out of place alongside classic early 1980s rockin' from the likes of The Ricochets and The Sharks. With their debut now something of a lost classic it must be remembered that the band continued to pursue a Psychobilly direction through a further two albums, 'Mad' (1992) and 'Girls, Guitars, Jaguars' (1993), but seemed to be gradually losing interest in the singularly Psychobilly tone of their first album and were obviously experimenting with less bludgeoning rocking styles such as 1950s R&B, 1960s pop and Rock'n'Roll. Their final EP 'Rainy Day' (1994) confirmed the band's exit from the scene and two years later double-bassist Olivier Baroni reappeared, with his girlfriend Emmanuella, as The Hillbilly Moon Explosion who continue to peddle their excellent but ultimately less frantic hybrid of 1950s/1960s Rock'n'Roll to this day.

Probably Switzerland's greatest export to the world of modern Rock'n'Roll is a band whose dominance on the global scene is still expanding – The Peacocks. Following the release of their prophetic album 'It's Time For The Peacocks' in 2004, the band seemed to be overnight sensations on the rockin' scene but the road to this release was a long hard

It's always time for... The Peacocks (Olli Rust/The Peacocks).

one. Hailing from Zurich in Switzerland, The Peacocks current line-up features Hasu Langhard on vocals/guitar, his brother Simon Langhard on double-bass and drummer Jurg Luder. From their inception in 1990, Hasu is the only original member but Simon has been on board since 1991. Drummer Jurg joined up in 2002 and has only appeared on 'It's Time...' but has undeniably played his part in the band's current success.

The Peacocks debut 'Come With Us' appeared back in 1995 and it would be another five years before the follow-up 'In Without Knocking'(1997). Both albums showcased the band's style which carries the influence of Psychobilly along with a sturdy portion of Pop, Punk, Ska and Rockabilly. While the band are far closer to similar souls such as The Living End and the multitude of Punkabilly groups who have emerged from the States in the 2000s they remain uniquely The Peacocks.

In concert the band have a far heavier sound and with their fine back catalogue of melodic, hook-filled songs and their sweat-soaked delivery they can match almost any act from 'any' scene and shake the audience to their boots. This expertise has been hard-earned however and The Peacocks have honed their performance after over fifteen years of hard touring, busting their asses from shithouses to stadiums across the globe. Nowhere in Europe has escaped them and the trio have also made trips to the US, Canada and Japan, headlining their own tours, supporting many of the big names in Punk and Psychobilly and bashing the ears of unexpected punters at a variety of festivals.

Aside from their sterling live work, their recording career has continued with a fistful of singles and compilation appearances alongside the album 'Angel' (2000) and two versions of 'It's Time For...', the original on Leech Records in 2004 and a redesigned version with a slightly altered track listing for the American market from Asian Man Records. The band's back catalogue has also been plundered, first by Sprinter Records who released early recordings and rarities on the album 'Dem-O-Lition' (2006) followed by Hairball 8 Records' 'Greatest Hits And Misses' (2006). After a decade and a half in existence The Peacocks are being hailed as the next big thing, touted as an unholy union of The Clash and The Stray Cats and carrying the torch forward from the likes of Reverend Horton Heat and The

Wreckin' Euro-style (Christophe @ Drunkabilly Records).

Living End. However, peeking through all this hyperbole The Peacocks remain what they have been since their earliest days, a blistering live act who have claimed the singalong Punkabilly anthem as their own and are living proof that there is still a lotta rockin' goin' on in Switzerland.

SWEDEN

The early days of Swedish Psychobilly began with the Cramps influenced trio The Voodoo Dolls, a group who trod a similar path to Lux and company, with their stripped-down brand of spooky, minimalist Rockabilly. The group's self-titled debut album from 1984 would prove to mark the end of their career but in 2005 a collection of their earliest recordings appeared on CD.

Around the time of The Voodoo Dolls, Sweden also boasted an authentic Neo-Rockabilly mob called The Moondogs who kept a little distance from the murky Psychobilly scene which was spreading rapidly across Europe at that time. In a similar style, one Swedish band who have made the biggest impression on rockers across the world are The Go-Getters. This power-Rockabilly trio have been tearing up audiences all over the globe since 1988 and have impressed many Psychobilly fans who they have encountered with their raw, petrol-headed rockin' which was showcased perfectly to many new punters during their live performance at the UK's Speedfreaks Ball in 2005.

Whether it is simply a case of mischievous Swedes living up to their stereotypical image as a nation of free-loving spirits, or they really are a randy nation, Swedish Psychobilly has a distinctly sexy feel. Slapping Suspenders started off at the end of the 1980s as a relatively straightforward Psychobilly band and launched themselves on the rest of Europe with their debut album 'Bloodsucking Freaks' (1990) for Count Orlok Records. They stayed with Count Orlok for a further two albums, 'The Good, The Bad And The Keeper Of The 7 Waffles' (1992) and 'Greese' (1995), a concept album of sorts – ripping the piss out of the 'Grease' movie soundtrack. So far, so sleazy, but by the end of the 1990s the band had moved into perv-overload, draped over some posh cars like a trio of porn stars on the cover of their CD EP for Crazy Love 'Zuper Oldies' (1996) and releasing a host of smut-filled tracks in their album for the same label, 'Slice Up Your Wife' (1998). Still peddling their own brand of sleazy rockin', the band are now known as Thee Suspenders and remain a favourite of many Swedish Psychobillies and other Rock'n'Roll lowlifes.

While Slapping Suspenders have a relatively kinky name and gradually grew more smutty as their career developed, Small Town Pimps set out their agenda from day one, promising songs devoted to "zombies, hookers and Rock'n'Roll direct from the red light district of Sweden". They did not disappoint on their debut album 'Pimplyfied' (1997) which boasted a number of zombie themed tracks alongside good old fashioned smut such as 'Blow Job Bonnie', 'Freaky Horny Little Nurses' and 'Dead Girls Don't Feel A Thing'. In 1999 their second album delivered more of the same, red-hot Psychobilly and songs about sex and zombies, along with one track which combined both – 'Suck My Zombie'.

After a new deal with another German label, Knock Out Records, the Pimps released 'B-I-N-G-O!' (2001), an album which was unsurprisingly packed with songs about... you guessed it, sex and zombies! (at least they are consistent). The contents of their fourth album 'Sexparty 4' needs no explanation and the band have consistently delivered the goods for over a decade now, dragging their tales of hookers and the undead across Europe including (bizarrely) a short appearance on Swedish Television's coverage of the 2002 Eurovision Song Contest.

While The Slapping Suspenders and The Small Town Pimps are probably Sweden's greatest Psychobilly exports they are not the country's only contribution to the genre. The Nocturnal Teds were a popular Heavy Psychobilly band in the late 1990s and ex-Small Town Pimp Thomas Palin formed his own Psycho outfit The Spinballs who also showcased a far heavier direction on their debut album for Black Sky Records 'Hell And High Water' (2002). Their individual style continued on the 2005 follow-up album 'Phreak-A-Bility' for Crazy Love Records. The band have also appeared on the compilation albums 'High Voltage: Vol. 2/3' and 'It Came From Hell: Vol. 4', appearing under their original name The Pinballs. Alongside The Spinballs in recent years there has also been even newer talent in the form of Joe Hellraiser & The Graverobbin' Bastards and Wreckers, proving that in between relentless bouts of shagging the Swedes still have the time to Rock'n'Roll.

SPAIN

Over the past fifteen years Spain has also been in the sights of Psychobillies from all over the world for one major reason. Sure everyone loved the Big Rumbles of the early 1990s and they were an undisputed highlight of the global Psychobilly scene that will never be forgotten but if anyone had sobered up at any point, or actually been conscious for any more than a few hours in daylight, surely they would have noticed that it was usually dull, wet and windy (particularly the Autumn gatherings).

Surely many fans making the pilgrimage from sunnier climates must have thought they were entering a prisoner-of-war camp rather than a sun-kissed holiday venue. Who would not have wished for a Psychobilly gathering which allowed you to rock all night then get your oiled-up body baked in the sun by day? Okay, so many Psychobillies are pasty-faced ghouls and the sun, as any tattooist will tell you, is the enemy of body art but surely an opportunity to get pissed-up in Spain without having to listen to brainless tourist-friendly, Euro-pap or moronic dance music would be one not to be missed?

Thankfully the chance to experience an event of this kind arose in 1993 with the first Calella Psychobilly festival. Following a Psychobilly meeting arranged by German rockers in 1992, where a Broncats gig in Barcelona was hastily organised to accommodate them, a group of Spanish psychos took it upon themselves to organise a gig in the holiday resort of Callela, 45 minutes east of the Catalonian capital. Over the years the festival has been host to most of the major Psychobilly groups on the scene and built steadily each year, even through some lean times for the genre, and the event has been particularly popular through the 2000s.

2006 saw Calella enter its 14th meeting with a body-bronzing bonanza of beach parties, barbecues, booze and (of course) bands stretching over eight days. The line-up was particularly strong with a powerful American contingent (Barnyard Ballers, The Quakes, Kings of Nuthin', Calavera) and a classic mix of Psycho and Neo from The Frantic Flintstones, Batmobile, Long Tall Texans and Restless. Quite rightly a new generation of Spanish bands also featured prominently with Nightbreed, Los Twangs, Hellbilly Club and Calamitiez alongside one of the highlights of the event, the appearance of The Dead Kings with special guest Nigel Lewis.

The Spanish Psychobilly scene itself has taken a little longer to get going than most other European countries but in recent years they have made up for this in a big way. In the early 1990s the Spanish Psycho scene revolved around one band – The Broncats. Previous to this other bands, such as Departmento B, had introduced home-grown Psychobilly to Spain but with their mile-high quiffs and furious sound The Broncats quickly established a rampant following in Barcelona before demanding the attention of the rest of the country along with interest across Europe.

Before The Broncats formed in 1992, the band's bass-player Xavier McGavin was plying his trade fruitlessly in a Stray Cats-inspired band called The Pink Cats. Bored performing endless covers, Xavier joined up with another Xavier (J. Roman) who played guitar and drummer Keko. Together they broke away violently from the Spanish Rockabilly scene and moved in the same direction as other 'harder-faster' Psychobilly bands of the time, such as The Klingonz, Mad Sin and Nekromantix, who were beginning to dominate the scene.

Despite their fine songs and strong live reputation, which rapidly gathered them a loyal following, The Broncats split in 1993 but remain one of the most fondly remembered Spanish Psycho bands despite their short time together. Though they never made a debut album, the band's legacy has refused to die and in 2004 the Japanese label Revel Yell collected together all their recordings from the 1992/93 period and released them on the CD 'Psychsoma'.

The Broncats undeniably led the way for Spanish Psychobilly and a number of bands followed in their wake. Inoportunos were a Neo-Rockabilly outfit who found a number of Psychobillies amongst their followers from the mid 1990s onwards. Previous to this the band had been following a stricter

Rockabilly template since 1989 with a myriad of line-up changes. The band released a self-titled mini-album in 1995, followed by their full-length debut 'Twister!!!' the following year. After a considerable period away from the recording studio they returned in 2003 with a harder set of tracks which were far closer to Psychobilly on their album 'In Your Loudspeaker...' for Downer Records. They had never stopped playing live between records but the album was to be their swansong and that same year they decided to call it a day. Their demise saw the release of '1989-2004' on Burning Crew Records which was a collection that gathered together their finest tracks from previous albums along with unreleased material and it proved to be a fitting tribute to a Neo band who attracted a wide range of Spanish 'billies.

Later in the 1990s, the Spanish scene began to expand but some of the acts were short-lived like Iberia Trash who formed in 1998 and featured drummer Alfonso Carlos from Departmento B. They appeared on a number of compilation albums including Revel Yell's 'Revel Without A Cause' and Black Sky Records' 'High Voltage Vol. 2&3' but to date they have only left behind a single album, their full-length debut 'Mondo Psycho' (2000).

The Hellmaniacs are another Spanish outfit with only their debut LP left behind for posterity. 'Somewhere In Our Minds' (1998) appeared on Nightmare Productions and, like The Broncats, it showcased a heavier style of Psychobilly on an album which showed some real potential had the band recorded further.

Joining the likes of The Hellmaniacs and Iberia Trash in late 1990s Spain were Smell Of Kat, an unapologetic Psychobilly quartet who drew their influences from a little earlier in the genre than many others and offered a far less frantic, but no less rockin', sound reminiscent of The Guana Batz and The Ricochets. They signed to Vampirella Music producing an EP 'Raw Beat' (1997) and a debut album 'Beware, The Kats' (1998). The band also toured Spain and other parts of Europe but success for one member of the band was to follow much later.

The Brioles also appeared near the end of the decade but with their borderline Psycho/Neo-Rockabilly they enjoyed a little more recording success bashing out their debut 'Train Of Fools' in 1998 and another eight-track mini-album 'Rocket Men' in 2000. These later recordings saw them approach a more Rockabilly sound in direct contrast to fellow Spanish rockers Inoportunos whose music grew harder and faster as they progressed. Though the band's second album never appeared, Revel Yell released 'Jungle Jamboree' (2006), an album which included a combination of Briole's material from sessions recorded between 2000-2003.

Hellbilly Club are one Spanish combo who stand out a little further from the rest with their stylish mix of Psychobilly, rockin' blues and Neo which bares a closer resemblance to American acts such as The Stray Cats and Reverend Horton Heat. Established in 1995, the band's recording career has been a slow and steady burn with their debut album 'Hypnotic Ultra Bizarre Circus' (1999) and its follow-up 'Hell-O' (2003) appearing reasonably far apart. Both these releases were for Crazy Love but a move to Temps Records saw the release of their most powerful album 'Black Leather Danger' (2006), a CD with high production values and a stack of great tunes which lift the best elements from a variety of rockin' genres without losing their hard edge. While Hellbilly Club keep rockin' their own individual style, guitarist/vocalist Santi Lluch and double-bassist Davide Lluch also have a more head-on Rockabilly side-project called The Atomic Leopards.

Heading a new breed of Spanish Psychobilly talent are Barcelona's The Calamitiez – two guys and two gals who are bringing Spain's Psycho sound to the rest of Europe and America. Though the band, as they are today, began around 2003 their roots were in in a Rockabilly covers group from the early 1990s known as The Calamities. From this combo, guitarist Julio was joined by ex-Smell Of Kat double-bassist David. They gigged as a trio, with drummer Pep, and played some sizable support slots along with appearances at the 12th and 13th Calella Psychobilly meetings. They also recorded a 4-track demo before Pep left to be replaced by the sexy, tub-thumping, hellcat Nadia. Another lady was also brought in, and with rhythm guitarist Angie on board they recorded their self-titled, debut album for Crazy Love which was released in 2006. With their striking image of two ghouls and two spooky gals, The Calamitiez could easily rub shoulders with the likes of Resurex and Horrorpops and their sprightly brand of Horror-Punkabilly has tremendous potential to place Spanish Psychobilly proudly on a global scale.

ITALY

While far from the epicentre of European Psychobilly, Italy has produced some quality bands. 1980s Italian 'Billies The Boppin' Kids had some early success both on the Euro-rockin' scene as well as being big 'back home'. The trio signed to the Italian division of major label Polygram and released their debut 'Go Wild' in 1986. This was followed two years later with 'Just For Fun', again for Polygram. That would spell the end of the band's career but Crazy Love were to resurrect both albums on a single CD in 2002 as the demand for 'old school' bands grew. Both The Boppin' Kids sound, and their major label relationship, share many similarities with The Polecats and the band gave many Italian rockers their earliest fix of home-grown, bass-slapping action.

Cyclone were another Italian band of the 1980s who sounded far closer to many of the UK Psychobilly acts of that time, particularly on their debut album 'First Of The Cyclonemen' (1989) for Klang Records. Sticking to a relatively standard Psychobilly template the band were pretty strong players and made up for what they lacked in originality with quality musicianship. After five years they produced another album for Klang, 'Cyclonic Zone' (1994), and a further two live tracks crept out on the Nervous Records compilation 'Live At The Big Rumble' but despite their relatively short career Cyclone are still fondly remembered as one of Italy's many originators of the Psychobilly scene.

The late 1990s saw Italian Psychobilly take a bit of a turn with the appearance of whacko rockin' trio Spamabilly. Something of a distant relation to The Klingonz, Rochee & The Sarnos and King Kurt, Spamabilly threw a variety of influences into the pot to create a bass-slapping, singalong riot with songs such as 'Muff Divin' Cowboy', Stompy Foot', 'My Daddy Is A Mummy' and 'Spamzilla'. The band released two albums, 'Tales From Zungurugungunz' (1998) and 'We Do Voodoo Beer Songs' (1999), both titles which certainly would give even the thickest of record buyers an idea of their direction.

Throughout the madness of their career the band remained a solid Rock'n'Roll trio and 'We Do Voodoo...' in particular boasted an excellent production. The band featured two Italians, Johnny Electrolux on double-bass with drummer Pixie Foolish, who were teamed up with exiled Scot Andy (Randy) Silver on guitar and vocals. When the band split, Andy moved on to join The Hormonauts who have since eclipsed the success of Spamabilly but these loonabillies remain an essential part of Italian Psychobilly history.

While it is true to say that the Italian Psychobilly has progressed slowly it has consistently moved forward and one group has already dragged the country onto the worldwide stage in the 21st Century. Evil Devil from Novellara evolved from the ashes of an earlier Psychobilly group Bone Rest in 2001 and practised no further than their first demo before securing a deal with Crazy Love Records. Initially a five piece, boasting two guitarists, their debut 'Devil Scream' appeared in 2002 and was a no-nonsense Psychobilly album with an authentic 'old school' sound, hammered home with a choice cover version of The Coffin Nails' 'Let's Wreck'.

As a relatively new band, Evil Devil have a refreshing attitude and seem happy to create unashamedly Psychobilly music without seeking to distance themselves from the genre. Their second album 'Breakfast At The Psycho House' (2003) had a better produced sound but lost none of the raw fury of their debut creation. Hooking up with top German promoter Die In Style, the band blitzed Europe with some rigorous touring and even made it to the USA before cutting down the frequency of their gigging to focus on the production of their third album for Crazy Love. The result was 'Drink To Kill My Pain' (2005), their most powerful album to date but still an album that is resolutely Psychobilly and never descends into thrash. Evil Devil are pretty unique, not just in the history of

Italian Psychobilly, as their sound would not have been out of place in their earliest days of Psycho yet it still manages to be fresh and new for today's audience and hopefully will lead the way for more Psychobilly "all' Italiana".

EASTERN EUROPE

The Psycho-disease spread rapidly across Europe and the Ukraine was not to be outdone. In 1991, Ukrainian trio Mad Heads got together to produce their own unique take on the genre. Initially formed by Vadim Krasnooky (guitar/vocals), Vladimir 'Stalik' Stalinsky (bass) and Roman Sharkevich (drums) their first vinyl appearance was in 1993 with two tracks on the compilation 'The Rage Team' followed by a single, 'Mad Heads Boogie' which was also released before a major line-up shuffle in which Stanislav Lisovsky and Bogdan Ocheretyany took over on bass and drums respectively. This was the band that featured on their debut album 'Psycholula', released by Crazy Love Records in 1996. A concert recording' Chernobilly Attack Live' kept the band rolling through the following year and a second studio album 'Mad(e) In Ukraine' appeared in 1999. The band then caught the attention of a number of UK and European Psychobillies when they played the Callela Festival that year to promote it.

Despite a bit of a dip in their fortunes at the turn of the millennium their 'Naked Flame' (Crazy Love) album in 2002 saw their return to the European Psycho-scene and they continued to progress with a further studio album 'Contact' (2003). In 2004 the band expanded with three new members on trombone, trumpet and sax and the band became known as Mad Heads XL. Pursuing a rocking sound with a hint of swing and some Ukranian folk, Mad Heads XL have enjoyed tremendous success in their country and produced their first album as a six-piece 'Nadiya Yea' (The Hope Is Here)' (2005) which has been a national chart-topper.

Though Psychobilly was enjoying mixed fortunes at the end of the 1990s, few would have expected salvation to appear from Hungary which is not renowned as one of the world's Psychobilly hotspots. However, the debut album from Hungarian trio Gorilla merged the band's solid old school Psychobilly with modern production values and created 'Too Much For Your Heart' (1999) for Crazy Love Records.

Pete Gorilla (vocals/guitar), Tom Alien (double-bass) and Tubus (drums) presented Gorilla as a no nonsense, stripped-down, flat-topped combo who chose musicianship and well crafted songs over any elaborate costumes or haircuts. Their debut album delivered a crystal clear combination of break-neck Psychobilly speed trials combined with more measured Rockabilly tracks that offered a little breathing space but never became boring. With its lively mix of styles and influences 'Too Much For Your Heart' brought some depth to the Psychobilly scene at the time and quickly brought the band to a wider audience.

In 2001, Gorilla were still moving forward and their follow-up album for Crazy Love, 'Genetic Joke', appeared. Yet again the band delivered a hard-slappin' blend of Psychobilly and Rockabilly wrapped in a crystal clear production. The songs were hard and frantic and while they captured the energy of Punk they never strayed as far in that direction as many bands in the 2000's were. Though resolutely original and modern, Gorilla were closer in style to bands like Batmobile and The Krewmen.

While never a band who toured that often, Gorilla's third album 'Flamenco Death' (2002) was an unusual combination of studio tracks and concert recordings (featuring many of the songs from the first two albums). It certainly proved that they could cut it live but the four studio tracks hinted that a classic new album had not been completed. With Pete Gorilla now living in Canada any new recordings or gigs appear to be restricted to his return visits to Hungary but future Gorilla material is distinctly possible.

Though Gorilla remain Hungary's main Psychobilly export, Crazy Love recently signed fellow Hungarians The Silver Shine whose 2006 album 'Nightmare' was an accomplished chunk of Psycho albeit one with a more modern Punkabilly flavour. Formed in 2004, the band have already bashed their way around Europe and supported the likes of Mad Sin and The Klingonz.

PSYCHO ATTACK OVER EUROPE

Poland has also provided a small breeding ground for rockin' acts with Komety and Robotix being two of the most popular. Komety are something of a mixed bag for Psychobilly bands as their debut album 'Komety' (2003) featured a slapping bass and some fine twanging guitar but by the time of their second release 'Via Ardente' (2005) many of their songs were a lot closer to a 1980s Indie sound that may leave fans outside of Poland wondering if they are the same band. Nonetheless, in Poland the band are big news on the national music scene and 'Via Ardente' was re-released in 2006 in an English language version. Their latest platter, 'Komety 2004-2006' gets a bit back to the rockin' and if you fancy an album worth of songs which sound like Hank Marvin playing with The Smiths and singing in Polish, then Komety are the band for you.

Robotix are Poland's most authentic Psychobilly act and a four-piece band based near Warsaw. They formed in 2002 and in a relatively short time they have dominated the East European Psycho scene. The band have a definite old-school Psychobilly sound and both their albums, 'Kosmiczna Odyseja Helvisa' (2003) and 'Wrakobill' (2005) are mostly sung in Polish and appear to cover subjects which are solid Psychobilly favourites such as horror, sci-fi and sex. Their vocalist Sivax also sounds suspiciously like the bastard son of Boris Karloff.

Across the border in the Czech Republic, Prague's The Gangnails (apart from the occasional slip in the singer's accent) sound as if they come from Los Angeles. First surfacing in 2002, the band have a solid, well-produced sound that is not a million miles away from America's top Punkabilly bands. They even have a deal with LA-based label Dr. Acula Records who have recently cherry-picked tracks from the band's previous two albums, 'Taste It' (2004) and 'Can Their Pussies Do The Dog' (2005), and compiled them on the CD 'Gangnails' (2006).

The most complete overview of the whole East European Psychobilly scene can be found on the compilation from Polish label Cosmic, 'Saturday Psychobilly Night' (2004), which captures the cream of talent from Poland, Ukraine, Russia and The Czech Republic alongside other Euro talent from Germany, France and the UK.

So there you have it, a snapshot of the continent where Psychobilly has never died. An unholy union of countries where the genre that dare not speak its name has thrived for a quarter of a century. What is consistently noticeable in Europe is how strong the Psychobilly scene remains to be. While the UK had an early boom from which it has yet to surpass and America arrived a little late but made up for their tardiness with a tremendous explosion of action, Europe has remained nothing less than solid, even through the long, hard ice age of the late 1990s when the Psychobilly beast almost entered extinction. European 'billies have kept the faith with extraordinary determination and all the promoters, bands, labels and fans have each contributed to the survival of Psychobilly without doubt.

CHAPTER SIX

HELL'S BENT ON ROCKIN'

PSYCHO STYLE

Like any branch of street culture, Psychobilly has always had its own distinctive style. In the same way that Psychobilly music is largely a bastardisation of other musical genres, Psychobilly style also borrows heavily from a variety of influences to create its own highly individual look. Most notably the fashion, like the music itself, draws on key elements from the wardrobes of Rockabilly and Punk – but early Psycho-style also lifted heavily from the washing basket of Skinhead culture.

Unsurprisingly, Skinhead standards such as tight denims with small turn-ups, pilot jackets (olive and black), good ole Doc Martens and a variety of other army and steel-toecapped boots stuck to the bodies of a large number of early 1980s Psychobillies like poison ivy. Many early Psychobillies had arrived at the wreckin' lifestyle by way of natural selection, evolving from Punks to Mods, then Skins before finally becoming members of the stomping fraternity. As money was often too tight to mention for many teens in Thatcher's Britain, legions of Skins could be miraculously transformed into Psychobillies with simply a cheap trip to the barbers to remould overgrown suedeheads into short flat-tops. With a few spare pounds to purchase a Meteors or Guana Batz T-shirt, the transformation was complete.

The Skinhead influence could arguably also be credited to Punk as the aforementioned clobber was often considered by many within the Skin community as the uniform of the 'bonehead' or 'baldy punk'. Back when the Skinhead nation was at its peak inner divisions existed and many traditional (or 'Spirit of '69') Skins often looked down on this type of garb, preferring the hard-but-smart option of Crombies, mohair suits, Sta-prest trousers, Levi's red tag 501 jeans and jackets and occasionally brogues and loafers as an alternative to Docs. With few of these suited to an evening's wrecking it is perhaps no surprise that it was the punkier elements of Skinhead fashion which were adopted by many Psychobillies.

Also in the spirit of Punk came the wholesale adoption of the leather biker's jacket by hordes of Psychobillies. Simply paint out that old Vice Squad and Anti-Nowhere League artwork with some of dad's left-over black gloss and you were ready to get started with a King Kurt or Meteors logo. The leather jacket was by no means the sole preserve of Punk as it is essentially an item of clothing linked to Rock'n'Roll; the garb of choice for ton-up boys, rockers and budding Danny Zukos everywhere. Many Rockabillies were also at home in a biker's jacket but often favoured high-quality, sparsely decorated jackets as opposed to the fucked-up, hand-painted items on the backs of Punks, Psychobillies and Heavy Metal fans.

The variation offered by biker's jackets is also tremendous. Studs, chains, patches, badges and paint jobs are all options and often elements initially pilfered from the world of Heavy Metal, a genre which holds the leather jacket sacred. Beyond these forms of decoration more advanced custom jackets even featured butchered (mock) tigerskin seatcovers being used to reupholster collars, lapels and back-panels. However, the crowning glory of all modifications was the removal of both sleeves creating the sleeveless jacket (also available in denim) which will forever remain a Psychobilly style icon.

Another key item in every Psychobilly's dirty laundry basket is the tartan shirt, also referred to across the Atlantic as the 'plaid' shirt. This simple workshirt is a key piece of 1950s Americana, the standard apparel of hoboes, rednecks and rockers in post-war America and the honest garb of hard-working Yanks: rugged, comfortable, warm and dependable. This type of shirt immediately brings to mind

PSYCHO STYLE

HELL'S BENT ON ROCKIN'

White T-shirts were all the rage in the olden days (Patrick Röhrle).

images of sweaty cowhands, large numbers of The Grand Ole Opry's audience and Elvis (both of them) in 'Kissin' Cousins'.

While this romantic imagery may have influenced the adoption of the tartan shirt by Rockabillies it is unlikely to have been behind the wholesale uptake of this classic item of clobber in Psychobilly circles. Quite simply it's a stylish, relatively cheap and hard-wearing item which was often on sale in the same Army & Navy and workwear stores where Psychos shopped for boots and denims. The fact that it also conjures up images of Ed Gein and 'Deliverance' style demented backwoodsmen is perhaps only another small part of its attraction.

The tartan shirt also offers a tremendous variety of styles and colours despite its simple construction. Quality shirts have the pattern on both sides, tartan through and through, while cheaper variants were simply a pattern printed on rough white cotton. Button-down collars, quilted padding and smoother material are also available but generally left on the shelves for dad-types, hill walkers and country bumpkins. Generally colour combinations drawing from a selection of red, blue and green are most popular but occasionally strips of yellow and black are available for the stylistically flamboyant.

The tartan shirt is not the only item liberated from the Rockabilly style arsenal – the biker (or engineer) boot has often had its place in the Psychobilly footlocker, albeit in a slightly more scuffed form. These solid black leather boots with a slight heel and some devilishly stylish straps have transformed even the weediest herbert into a Brando-esque 'Wild One'. Undoubtedly a fine quality pair always look fantastic nestling under a denim turn-up but they are often an expensive option, especially for many Psychobillies who would rather spend a weekend on the piss than a sober session breaking in new boots.

Another key item of footwear which provides maximum opportunity for stomping are creepers, or crepes, a direct filch from the cult of the Ted. Blue (or any other colour) suede shoes are as Rock'n'Roll as quiffs, Cadillacs and thumping someone with a bike chain outside the local hop. When renewed interest was sparked in the common creeper in the late 1970s, many shoe producers unleashed further variations such as all-leather crepes, round or pointed toes, laces or buckle-ups – all available in increasingly bold colours and patterns with faux leopard and tigerskin leading the way.

In what can only be assumed as a nod to the growing Psychobilly customer base of the 1980s, shoe manufactures also offered a variety of crepe sole sizes from the standard one-inch thickness to some approaching Glam Rock proportions which transformed the wearers into flat-footed Frankensteins. Other items liberated from the British Ted catwalk include the bootlace tie, though not always worn with a traditional shirt and collar, and luridly coloured drape coats when they could be secured at bargain basement prices.

In direct contrast to the sturdy stomping capabilities of boots and creepers, slip-on canvas pumps were frequently worn in Psychobilly's early days. Just peek at any early Klub Foot photographs for confirmation. Many still remain puzzled at the popularity of this flimsy footwear as they offered no protection against the spillage of beer and fag ash or the rigours of the wrecking pit. Thankfully, they soon became another cast-off of 1980s culture.

Another unusual item which seemed at odds with much of the resilient, hard-wearing Psychobilly

HELL'S BENT ON ROCKIN'   PSYCHO STYLE

Bleached denims, shorts and bleached denim shorts! Old School Psychobilly essentials (Jane Williams).

clobber was the ski-jumper. This was another early 1980s curio beloved of then youthful bands such as The Sharks and The Guana Batz and possibly a knitted nightmare with some vague Rockabilly connection or perhaps a distant cousin of the 'Y' cardigans of the late 1970s. Each jumper had a whacko, varied design but basically they were crew-neck pullovers with a 'winter' pattern. The more subtle designs had combinations of snowflakes in various sizes but for the advanced ski-jumper-clad rocker options with snowmen, reindeer and Christmas trees were available. Generally, most of these bizarre creations boasted different bands of colour at the waist and neck. Again, changes in fashion have moved on and it now seems that no one can experience any emotion other than shame when they remember how they paraded the high street wearing those knitted monstrosities.

Other short-lived but stylish items from the Psychobilly closet included baseball caps (before they were claimed by the nation's half-wits, townies and chavs), fringed suede jackets (very Wild West, very cool but very expensive) and denim cut-down shorts. Once Psychobilly concerts were awash with scuffed, bare knees above white or fluorescent socks and boots but now prudish Psychos rarely bare their legs. Denim dungarees were also highly popular in the trouser department, yet more clothing liberated from hillbilly heaven and still worn today by many bumpkin Psychobillies. Pyjamas were also briefly fashionable as a concert-going accessory, influenced not by The Boomtown Rats' keyboard player but by the kings of Rockabilly bedwear – Restless.

One item which surprisingly drifted from the everyday Psychobilly collection was the baseball jacket. This American sportswear generally consisted of a button-stud, collarless fabric jerkin with different coloured vinyl sleeves. These were decorated with sporting embroidery and patches of a specific baseball team often along with the original owner's forename sewn onto the left breast. As Yankee as bald eagles, these prime pieces of 'Jock-wear' were reclaimed by the UK's rockin' fraternity and appeared up and down the country in a huge variety of colours and styles. Sussed second-hand and retro clothes shops imported these by the skipload and they enjoyed a massive popularity which bizarrely faded during the 1990s. Still a classic emblem of Psycho-style these jackets are spotted

PSYCHO STYLE

intermittently, particularly up for grabs on internet auction sites, but they have yet to regain their boom of 1980s popularity.

The core items of Psychobilly style have always been unisex, in as much that they looked equally fetching on the huge number of Psychobilly's female followers. Apart from a brief spate of male dress-wearing at early King Kurt gigs, the ladies have always had further fashion options than the gents. Mini-skirts or denim hot-pants worn with tights and boots were probably the most striking early addition, always guaranteed to arouse a pleasant trouser-tingling sensation amongst leery Psycho-fellas – but further kinky offerings were to follow.

As Psychobilly progressed in the 1990s, relatively standard Psychobilly gear began to expand in a number of genre-crossing directions. More leather and rubber items

Old School Psychos stomp the streets (Kenny Mitchell).

appeared and perv-wear in general, undoubtedly under the influence of bands such as Demented Are Go (who had been at it since the mid 1980s) and The Klingonz, began to appear in the guise of bondage gear, gimp masks, studded jock straps and dildoes as a fashion accessory. This was also good news for the ladies (or gents, depending how you look at it) as they had a wider selection of titillating, kinky clobber in their arsenal. The suspenders, saucy tops, skirts, trousers and dresses in rubberwear or figure-hugging leather were light years ahead of the standard jeans'n'T-shirt combos worn by Psycho-ladies in the early to mid 1980s.

What Psychobilly has consistently displayed is a far less puritanical attitude to its dress code than many other youth cults. It draws on a wide range of influences and it allows its followers to express themselves individually while still staying true to the Psychobilly image. The style spectrum can stretch from an 'old school' jeans/T-shirt/boots follower to a devotee with yellow PVC trousers, make-up, a fish-net top and a steel pin through his bell-end. What other street cult offers such variety?

All this gear was secondary to the ultimate mark of Psychobilly. The defining aspect which could brand a Psychobilly follower even at a naturist's convention was the haircut. The flat-top, the pompadour, the buzz-cut... names of very different hairstyles that all boil down to the same thing – the quiff, every Psycho's pride and joy. Many followers would happily leave the house with their toes sticking through worn boots and arses peaking through ripped denim but never without immaculately teased, combed, shaved and sculptured quiffs.

As a hair style which was clearly Rock'n'Roll and Rockabilly's biggest influence on the genre, Psychobilly took the quiff to weird and extreme new realms by colouring it in a variety of lurid shades, increasing the contrast between short and long hairs and

Psychobilly essentials. Cool quiffs, warm Buckfast (Kenny Mitchell).

HELL'S BENT ON ROCKIN'   PSYCHO STYLE

introducing gravity defying spikes and peaks. Early followers generally fell into two camps: ex-Rockabillies who simply shaved more from the back and sides while maintaining their quiffs and ex-Skinheads/Punks who took the remould option. For everyone else a short flat-top was the way in. As media coverage and increased touring schedules gave many Psychobilly bands an increased visual presence in those early days this also pointed the way forward for Psycho-barnets, with King Kurt in particular striking ahead into bizarre new dimensions in personal grooming.

The divisions between hair on top and everything else was the first major difference as barbers across Europe were soon ordered to ditch the 'number one' razor guard and make with the naked blade on the back and sides. The flat-top itself then mutated from a one inch table-top of hair to something increasingly longer. It also began to appear at an exaggerated gradient, moving from an inch long at the back to 4-5 inches at the front. Eventually, many quiffs started from nothing at the back to infinity and beyond at the front.

The icons of Psychobilly: the quiff, tattoos and double-bass. Eddie of The Klingonz in Austria, 1996 (Jane Williams).

Increasingly bizarre variations on the quiff also began to appear. The 'rim' enjoyed some continued success and involved not only shaving the back and sides but also most of the top. This left only the outline of the quiff standing proud and required extreme hair control. When this style was in its relaxed, unsupported, state it often left its owner looking like an escapee from a monk's asylum. The rim could also be curled inwards for those seeking a more rounded, but still distinctly mental, look.

Other variations of more extreme hairstyles included a simple spike of hair at the front of the head, usually a foot long or larger, and occasionally spikes at either side of an otherwise shaved head to accompany a quiff. Short 'devil's horns' spikes were also very popular as far back as King Kurt's original line-up and an example of how far Psychobilly hairstyles moved from their Rock'n'Roll roots (sic) to become a far closer cousin to legions of mowhawked Punks. Probably The Klingonz did more than most to showcase new creativity in hair sculpture and were even showcased in a 1992 article in British 'porno' newspaper 'The Daily Sport'. The rag reported that Klingonz' lead singer Titch was arrested for possession of a 'dangerous haircut' when he knocked a policeman's hat off with his barnet during a struggle in Covent Garden, London, after a busking session.

His 'n' hers haircuts... psycho style! (Jane Williams).

Hair colour has also progressed through the years

145

PSYCHO STYLE　　　　　　　　　　　　　　　　HELL'S BENT ON ROCKIN'

with blonde quiffs being the first examples of follicle dyeing. Why blonde was, for some time, the only option for many is yet another quirk of Psychobilly. Black would seem to be a tone which more closely embraced the horror, menace and 'dead Elvis' chic of Psychobilly but the punkier bombshell barnet colour initially reigned supreme. Other shades were always around on the heads of a few innovators but it took until the late 1980s and onwards for varied colours to take a grip on the cult. After that, single tones gave way to an array of multi-coloured quiffs limited only by a Psychobilly's imagination and the patience of their mate or partner enlisted to slap on the colour-changing potion with deadly precision.

German Psychobilly ladies (and one bloke) in the 1980s (Frank John).

The standard Brylcreem and pomade of the original Rockin' quiffs failed to handle these extreme new versions of this classic hairstyle but luckily, as the Psychobilly boom flourished in the decade of

Psychobilly ladies on the run, Alcoholic Rats SC, 1985 (Jo Jackson).

HELL'S BENT ON ROCKIN'   PSYCHO STYLE

Far left: Joe Psychodame, well-groomed gal (Jo Shalton).

Left Centre: Quiffs move into other dimensions, Titch from The Klingonz (Jo Shalton).

Left: Immaculate quiff control, Christophe from Drunkabilly (Drunkabilly Records).

'big hair' all round (Flock of Seagulls, Kajagoogoo, 'Dallas' et al) as new powerful hairsprays and gels littered the high street. Forget the 'gentle' hold of Granny's tin of Silvikrin, 'firm hold' was the aerosol of choice after slapping on a cement-based pot of gel. Often once it was up 'it was up' – quiffs created on a Friday night had to be chiselled down on Sunday as they refused to yield to their original flaccid state. Unsurprisingly, two decades on, Psychobilly has left behind a generation of thirtysomething slapheads who's follicles never recovered from that increased period of hair dyeing, combing, teasing and spraying. A cruel fate indeed for a cult so defined by its hairstyles.

For Psychobilly ladies the fate of acquiring a baldy pate was less of a worry so they consistently launched into a variety of hairstyles with frightening regularity. Some early Psycho-queens stuck to variations of the flat-top while a good few also maintained more Rockabilly-style quiffs which were often simply long hair, quiffed up and accompanied by pony tails, pleats or pig-tails. Many girls also succumbed to the lure of the razor and hair dye while utilising all the quiff combinations available and including other influences such as beehives, bobs and Bettie Page fringes to create some of the most impressive, striking and sculptured barnets in the realm of underground music followers.

Though hair was the priority a far more permanent branding of the Psychobilly cult was also available. Tattoos are increasingly commonplace today, with Mums and Dads shaming their kids by displaying microscopic designs on attention-seeking parts of their body, however in the 1980s tattoos were often the sole preserve of bikers, rockers, football hooligans, hard-nuts, Skinheads and sailors. It is from this heritage line that Psychobilly played its part in popularising the sting of ink and needle. Nobody ever claimed that tattoos were a mark of inclusion to the Psychobilly brotherhood but it was generally accepted that they were as much a part of the cult as boots and quiffs.

In an anxious bid to get branded, many early Psychos often picked flash designs at random from tattoo shop walls and had them hurriedly carved onto their arms. Others picked designs that at least illustrated some of Psychobilly's lyrical themes such as horror subjects (bats, gravestones, grim reapers etc), musical instruments and band names. Top of the 'band tatts' must surely have been The Meteors with The Guana Batz, Demented Are Go and Frenzy close behind. In the 21st century bands like Tiger Army are surely firm favourites for tattoo designs but The Meteors are still up there when it comes to the inking of today's Psychobilly clans.

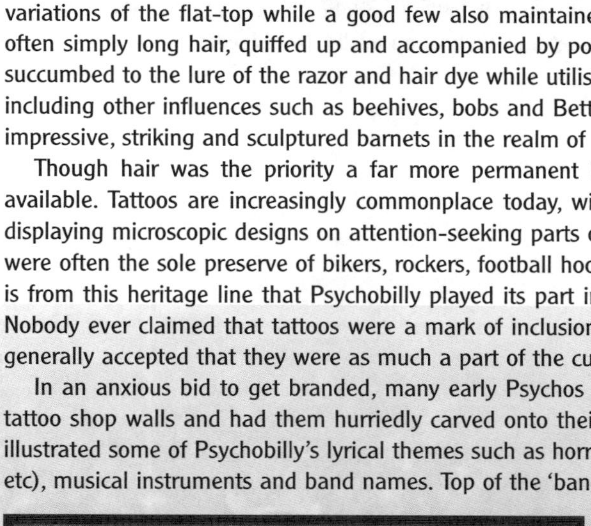

The days before tattooing reached its peak (Patrick Röhrle).

Unlike the majority of today's professional and hygienic studios, many tattoo parlours in the early/mid 1980s still had the unmistakable whiff of back-street sleaze. As many discovered, unlike

PSYCHO STYLE

modern craftsmen, many shady tattooists operated with little eye for detail and occasionally the inability to even spell 'Skitzo' properly. A close peek at the bodies of many ageing Psychos will often reveal a frightening array of cack-handed attempts at band logos, wobbly Psychobilly illustrations and sprawling lettering.

It is, however, unfair to claim that all tattooists from that decade were shaky-handed butchers – good artists have always existed but in the 1990s the artform developed rapidly. High-quality artists really made their presence felt by introducing greater detail and a more elaborate range of designs, such as those with tribal and Celtic influences. With this rapid growth of tattooing as a respectable artform every Tom, Dick and Harry got on board the skin art bandwagon and soon the odd 'tatt' slapped on the upper arm, back or forearm could be overshadowed by elaborate ink on local poseurs, glamourous grannies and trendy vicars.

For this reason, many Psychos chose to increase their bodily artwork to Yakusa-like proportions and introduced the needle to many other parts of the body. Tattooed 'sleeves', back pieces, chests, stomachs and legs were obvious choices with neck, head and face tattoos also entering the mix. Finally, never let us forget the importance, and perennial humour, of the countless arse tattoos lurking beneath the underwear of Psychobillies old and new. Ultimately, tattooing is such a varied artform and one so dependent on individuality and personal taste that it is impossible to clearly identify 'Psychobilly Tattooing' especially as the genre is only one of the many musical styles associated with skin art. Although tattooing has always been a key element of the cult's image it is far harder to recognise specifically than Psychobilly fashion and hair styling.

Despite many accepted standards of clothing, hair and body artwork, Psychobillies often dress in a manner as original and varied as the music itself without ever feeling bound by any unwritten laws of Psycho-fashion. Just turn up at any Psychobilly gig with yellow work boots, green body paint, a leather jockstrap and a leopard-spotted quiff and see if anyone bats an eyelid. Not bleedin' likely!

CHAPTER SEVEN

THE NEXT DEGENERATION
PSYCHOBILLY IN THE NINETIES AND BEYOND

The 1990s were a time of mixed fortunes for many Psychobilly bands and the early part of that decade saw some early Psycho-pioneers take a back seat while a new breed of bands took control. The Meteors and Demented Are Go continued their dominance over the scene but no band made a bigger impact in the UK on turn of the decade Psychobilly followers than The Klingonz.

Supposedly beaming in from 'Mars', The Klingz were a foul-mouthed speed-crazed, four-piece hurricane that hit the Psychobilly establishment with an unapologetic bang. When the band first appeared in front of UK Psycho audiences in the late 1980s it seemed that they already knew they were good and it was simply up to everyone else to realise it. Taking the Punk element of Psychobilly and pushing it to the front, they never left behind their Rockabilly roots but unashamedly pushed their Psychobilly beat louder and faster than any before. Determined to beat the audience over the head with their style they left many other bands who saw them, or were supported by them, thinking twice before trotting out a standard set of their repertoire. With body paint, costumes, nudity, sex aids and sheer onstage abandon The Klingonz were always a hard act to follow.

The Klingonz... early days (The Klingonz).

Before coming to London in 1986 Mark 'Titch' Nolan, Philip 'Doyley' Doyle and Brian 'Mocker' McDonald were all teenage Teds in Dublin. Titch and Doyle had always talked of forming a band since boyhood so when Titch made his move to the UK's capital Doyley followed on shortly. Holed up in London, the pair began writing what would become the earliest Klingonz creations then they were soon reunited when Mocker left Ireland behind and joined them.

The hunt for a fourth Kling was originally a deep-space quest to find a guitarist as although Doyley was an accomplished six-stringer he initially intended to be the band's double-bass player. The guitarists the band put on trial never shaped up so with Doyley back on guitar a vacancy for a double-bass slapper lay empty. Titch's chance meeting with Tony 'Strangy' Gilmore at a Psychobilly festival in Gent, Belgium led to the Scots bass-man returning to London with Titch and practising with the band for a fortnight. Not long after this period, Strangy packed his bags for the trip down south from Aberdeen as he joined the band full-time.

The Klingonz made their debut downstairs at The Clarendon, Hammersmith supporting Skitzo in 1987 though it would not be long before they would make the move upstairs to the hallowed stage of The Klub Foot. Their following built steadily and after six months of gigging they were spotted while playing at the LMS pub in Hendon by Dell Richardson and the band signed a deal with Fury Records to start work on what would become the label's first full-length Psychobilly LP. The band entered the studio and within a day they had produced their debut album 'Uurrrnchk: Psychos From Beyond' (1988).

The Klingonz stayed with Fury and delivered their second album 'Blurb' in 1990. This album really

THE NEXT DEGENERATION

HELL'S BENT ON ROCKIN'

established the band with songs such as 'Destructobotz', 'VD Blues' and 'Psycho Mansion' which would become fan favourites. Their choice of covers was inspired and illustrated the variety of the band's influences: Punk on The Dead Kennedys 'Too Drunk To Fuck', Rockabilly on The Stray Cats ' 'How Long Do You Want To Live' and sheer dementia with their stoner version of the theme from 'Sesame Street', the perfect tune for any bong-toking, Psychobilly party.

This was to be Strangy's last album (for a while) with the official reason for his departure given at the time because he was "leaking liquid nitrogen". The replacement bass-man Darren 'Eddie' Edwards was found lurking around The Klingonz' twenty-four hour party pad, The Gosterwood Palace, and lynched into double-bass duties. The band were never shy of playing live and consistently spread their disease across the UK and Europe. The LP 'Mong' was released by Fury in 1990 and showcased their live performance captured in the Spring of that year at the Hemsby weekender.

The Klings plan world domination (Mason Storm Archive).

The Klingonz were one of the main bands to push Psychobilly in a harder, faster direction but their 1991 album 'Flange' rammed the point home that Rock'n'Roll was just as big a part of The Klingonz sound as Punk. Subtitled 'Martians V Rockers', Side One was eight tracks of the self-penned madness that the band were famous for and Side Two featured all cover versions torn from over forty years of Rock'n'Roll, Rockabilly and Psychobilly history. Though each song got The Klingonz treatment, these songs were far from a speed-crazed piss take which some may have expected. Many Londoners and passing tourists regularly caught the band busking live in Covent Garden with a faithful set of rockin' covers and the tracks on 'Flange' were a solid tribute to the band's Rockabilly roots. Particular stand out tracks included The Klingonz take on Matchbox' classic 'Rockabilly Rebel' and a cover of Frenzy's early Psychobilly milestone 'Cry Or Die'.

The rockin' influence continued the following year with their fifth album for Fury Records 'Jobot' (1992), which not only included their version of Crazy Cavan's 'My Little Sister's Got A Motorbike' but also a version of Rockin' Johnny Austin's 'Rockabilly Stroll', renamed 'Rockabilly Stroll (Klingabilly Stroll)' and featuring guest vocals from the original rocker himself alongside The Klingonz' unique interpretation of his song. This album also hinted at other influences within the band with a keyboard-heavy, 1960s Garage Punk screamer, the delightfully named love song 'Nympho Slag'.

Their next album 'Bollox' (1994) was a milestone in the band's career. It was to be their final studio offering from Fury Records and Doyley left soon after its release. Ironically it also saw The Klingonz sound reach its peak with a powerful production that proved that their many years of writing, recording and gigging had not been wasted.

Though always a popular live act, the late 1990s Psychobilly meltdown had taken its toll on The Klingonz but though the band fractured they continued to spread their influence across the scene. When Doyley moved on, the band drafted in Mick from The Phantom Rockers on guitar but never recorded with this line-up. They then left The Klingonz name behind and changed to Looper, pursuing a more Garage Punk direction and Eddie moved from double-bass to electric. Though short-lived they did record one demo entitled 'The Mad Are Sane'. Looper gigged sporadically for a few years but by 1998 things were slowing down and as Titch puts it simply, "We got bored and split up" and, while the others remained in London, Mocker returned to Dublin.

When Strangy left the band in 1990 he had wasted no time in joining another band, in fact he was working with The Numbskulls prior to his split with The Klingonz. The Aberdeen-based Numbskulls were a fast and furious Psychobilly band with a heavy sound that also included a fair mix of Punk and Metal influences. Though horrifying to many, heavy rock influences were to become a continuing part of Psychobilly's evolving sound and what true fan of the genre would not admit to possessing a touch of Motörhead, AC/DC etc. in their collection?

Things move relatively fast for The Numbskulls as they secured a deal, and were about to record an album for Kix 4 U records when Strangy joined. 'Psychophobia' appeared in 1991 but surprisingly it was another six years before the band released another album, 'Life In Limbo' (1997) on Nightmare Productions. During this period Strangy was also involved in managing the first all-girl Psychobilly band The Dypsomaniaxe. Though only active for around three years this UK quartet of she-devils boozed their way around Europe and released the album 'One Too Many' (1992) for Tombstone Records.

Strangy of The Klingonz, The Numbskulls, The Dead Kings... and the rest! (Simon 'Fatbloke' Ling).

As their career drew to a close, Strangy took up the offer to play with Mad Sin following the release of their 'A Ticket Into Underworld' album and he stayed with the German combo for over a year prior to the release of the second Numbskulls album. Soon after Strangy was on the move again, this time teaming up with Doyley and drummer Skum to form Celtic Bones, prime exponents of 'Punk'n'Roll'. Some of the remaining Numbskulls would later resurface in Aberdeen's rock'n'horror combo Karloff, who feature Strangy's brother Ash 'Ghoulmore' on vocals.

Celtic Bones toured furiously as a super-tight three-piece with a Punk and Psychobilly sound that was especially suited to a period when Psychobilly in the UK and Europe was merging with Punk, Garage and Heavy Rock into one big genre of dirty Rock'n'Roll. In the studio they produced two EPs, 'Time's Up' and 'The Betty Ford EP', alongside a full album, 'Who Dares Gins' (2001). The Celtic Bones story would eventually draw to a close as Strangy and Doyley became involved in other projects.

As two players so well known in the European Psychobilly scene their services were often in demand and Strangy worked with a number of other bands including The Rattlers, The Deltas, The Grit and Texas Shakedown (featuring Martin 'Griswald' Clark). Doyley had already worked with Mad Sin on their album 'Sweet and Innocent...' and both became members of Koefte's side-project band The Dead Kings. When the bass and guitar positions in Demented Are Go fell vacant in 2002 Strangy and Doyley were ideal replacements and they were propelled into the twilight zone of music and madness that is Demented Are Go on the road. This culminated with their appearance on Demented's 2005 album 'Hellbilly Storm' before they both moved on.

Miniskirt Blues (Miniskirt Blues).

Still intent on indulging his enthusiasm for Garage Punk, Titch got straight into a new band teaming up with guitarist Peter from Swedish psycho band Nocturnal Teds and his brother-in-law Mikey to form Miniskirt Blues. Titch then brought in Kieron as lead guitarist, Mikey enlisted bass-player Dean and the five-piece was complete. Lifting their name from the 1960s psyche classic song by The Flowerchildren the song was probably better known to a Psychobilly audience from covers of said tune from The Cramps and, more definitively, The Vibes.

Miniskirt Blues pursued none of the 1960s purist attitude to Garage that is often in vogue and took from it only the dirty, savage beat of primitive Rock'n'Roll. Adding their own heavier sound, Miniskirt Blues were the logical progression to the likes of 1980s Trash boom heroes such as The Sting-Rays and The Vibes.

Despite The Klingonz' individual involvement in other bands, by 2002 the original line-up were back together and released a six track EP 'Lost It In Space' on their own Ring Sting Records label. It featured all new compositions and while the songs were still classic Klingonz their collective studio experience was now evident and their sound was far more powerful, taking off where 'Bollox' had ended. With the band back together and still creating material a new album deal was signed with Crazy Love Records and just before 2003 drew to a close 'Up Uranus' was released. It featured versions of some tracks from 'Lost It In Space' and boasted a similarly well-recorded sound that was far heavier and more powerful than their earlier albums.

HELL'S BENT ON ROCKIN' THE NEXT DEGENERATION

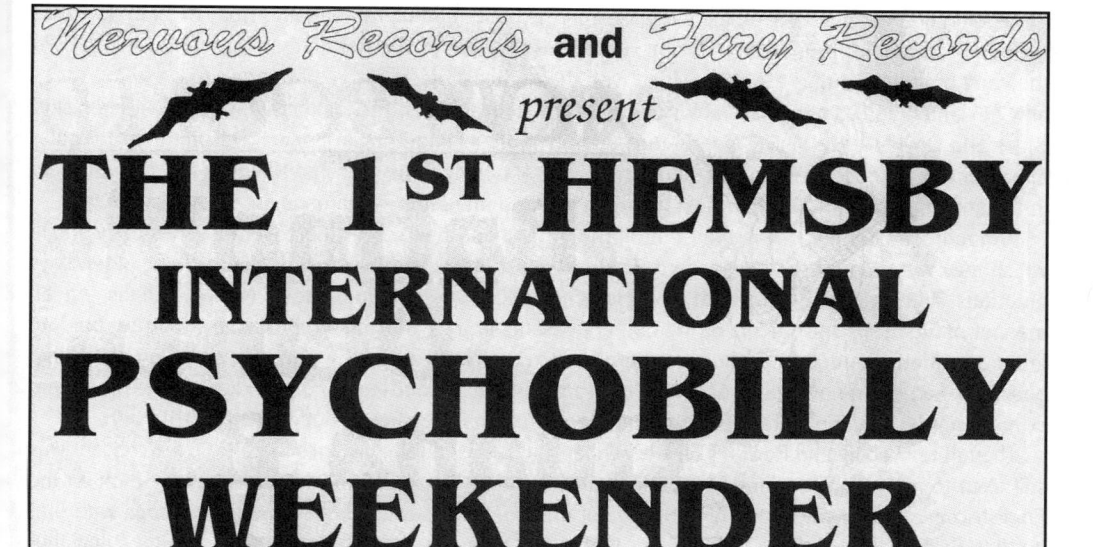

Nervous Records and *Fury Records* present

THE 1ST HEMSBY INTERNATIONAL PSYCHOBILLY WEEKENDER

Friday 27th – Monday 30th April 1990

AT

PONTINS HOLIDAY CENTRE, BEACH ROAD, HEMSBY, NORFOLK (NEAR CAISTER)

STARRING THE BIGGEST AND BEST PSYCHOBILLY BANDS IN THE WORLD!
(See inside)

look at all this!

Music Times: Friday – 6.00pm-3.00am
Saturday – Noon-3.00am
Sunday – Noon-3.00am

Record Stalls �֎ Tee Shirt Stalls �֎ Tattooist ✶ Indoor Heated Swimming Pool
Restaurant ✶ Supermarket ✶ On-site Pub ✶ Snooker ✶ Pool

ALL NIGHT PSYCHOBILLY VIDEOS IN YOUR CHALET

LOADS OF COMPETITIONS AND PRIZES

Hemsby begins, 1990 (Mason Storm Archive).

THE NEXT DEGENERATION   HELL'S BENT ON ROCKIN'

Gigging accompanied the album's release and the band made a triumphant return to Japan followed by their mammoth, 'You Fuckin' Clownz', European tour. While The Klingonz still remain a solid outfit, the band members' duties are still divided with their other projects such as Strangy's role as King Kurt's new bass-man and as a member of Vince Ray & The Boneshakers, Titch's continuing work with Miniskirt Blues and Doyley's role in The Dead Kings and his 'Guitar Slingers' solo project. Despite their irregular appearances, it's good news for earthlings that after almost twenty years The Klingonz are still out there in the stratosphere plotting their next move for world domination — 'Humans are such easy prey!'

Although The Klingonz have toured furiously throughout their career there were a series of events in which they were almost the house band. The East coast of England has a dark history. In ye olden days notorious Witchfinder General Matthew Hopkins rode across plague ridden Norfolk unleashing all manner of hideous punishments on trembling peasants in their filth-ridden hovels. Dark times, but late in the twentieth century a new horror emerged from the Norfolk coast. A grinding, sweating, wrecking, booze-soaked cloud hovered just close to the sea emitting a blood-curdling sound. Not a crash, a bang or a scream but a deep, dark menacing rumble. Not a small rumble… but a BIG RUMBLE.

Though Rockabilly and Rock'n'Roll weekenders have been on the go since the 1970s the concept was still alien to many Psychobillies. The basic theme was to colonise an out-of-season holiday park on the English coast and fill the venue with bands, fill the bars with plastic glasses and fill the bogs with that horrible itchy toilet paper. These holiday camps from a bygone era were self-contained, meaning that attendees could eat, drink, sleep and rock all within the confines of the camp and purely in the good company of other rockin' devotees.

It was only a matter of time before the concept was applied to Psychobilly and Dell Richardson from Fury Records was the man who established the first 'Big Rumble Weekender' in April 1990 at the Pontins Holiday Centre in Hemsby near Gt Yarmouth, Norfolk. Initially working from within his friend Val's event promotions company, Pollytone Weekenders, Dell soon generated sizable interest for this concept from across Europe's Psycho nation while also attracting a number of further travelled enthusiasts from Japan and the USA.

The line-up featured a number of heavy-hitters such as The Guana Batz, Demented Are Go, Long Tall Texans, The Klingonz, Torment, The Deltas, Frenzy, The Frantic Flintstones and some bands including The Griswalds, The Radium Cats, The Termites, The Lost Souls, Nekromantix, Niteshift

Old School flyers. Crude but effective (Mason Storm Archive).

HELL'S BENT ON ROCKIN'   THE NEXT DEGENERATION

Psychobilly by the sea at the first Big Rumble, April 1990 (Jane Williams).

Trio, The Boppin' Kids and The Falcons who were only beginning to really establish themselves.

Generally the events involved three days of live entertainment with punters arriving throughout Friday to a full evenings entertainment followed by a solid weekend of day and night gigs and the whole of Monday used by organisers to prise knackered festival gatherers from their chalets and prod them in a homeward direction.

The 2nd Big Rumble followed soon after in October 1990 and as word had spread about the success of the first event, and the majority of that audience were keen to make a return visit, it also brought another solid contingent of Psychobillies to witness the return of many of the first event's headliners and see Skitzo perform (what was then to be) their final gig. A third gathering was held in the Spring of 1991 and with all the interest generated by the first two events this was the peak of the scene, a Psychobilly Valhalla with great bands, T-shirt and records stalls, an on-site tattooist and yet more of Zorch TV – Psychobilly videos and assorted nonsense from Captain Zorch himself (Roy Williams) alongside Dell and a variety of tanked-up band members and other loons.

In November of the same year the whole shebang made a move a little further down the coast to the Vauxhall Holiday Park, Gt Yarmouth for the 4th Big Rumble. Throughout the first three events Dell had worked with fellow promoter Tom Ingram but when the Rumble moved on he was in sole control. This new venue was a residential caravan park so the accommodation was a little more susceptible to damage caused by on-site rowdiness but the venue offered much the same combination of food outlets, bars, services and a sizable main hall. The change of sites proved to be a success and a fifth event was organised for the following year. From this point, however, The Big Rumble became purely an annual event. While other Spring events were considered the gathering would remain an Autumnal treat.

The 6th Big Rumble in 1993 was another Halloween bash with the annual evening of ghoulish goings-on falling right at the heart of the weekender. Once again the event was at the caravan mecca of Vauxhall Holiday Park but the twenty five band line-up had a distinctly different feel. UK bands were in relatively short supply (particularly if you actually believe that The Klingonz actually were from Mars as they were billed) with The Sharks, Frenzy, The Frantic Flintstones, Demented Are Go, Restless, The

THE NEXT DEGENERATION   HELL'S BENT ON ROCKIN'

The Highliners rock it up on MTV (Russ Ward).

Pharaohs and The Lost Souls keeping the British end up.

The International line-up featured a wide variety of European and American acts. From across the Channel came French gorehounds Banane Metalik, The Broncats from Spain, Swiss rockers Blown Mad, The Stompin' Mad Bats from Italy and a double-barrel of German talent from Mad Sin and The Percolators. The Mad Mongols and The Falcons made it all the way from Japan and the American acts were a combination of Psychos (The Hellbillys, Stompin' Pompadours) and Rockabillies (The Razorbacks, Hi-Fi & The Roadburners and Three Blue Teardrops). As in previous events some further styles of music were featured with demented cowpunk from The Cowpunchers and Thee Waltons and blistering streetpunk from Klingonz' associates Self-Destruct.

By the time of the 7th Big Rumble in Autumn 1994, things were starting to get tight as, despite a fantastic line-up including Demented Are Go, The Sharks, Frenzy, Long Tall Texans, Nekromantix and Skitzo, numbers were dropping. This was not helped by the increasing amount of damage being dished out in the accommodation and surrounding premises. With organisers footing the bill for the destruction it was becoming increasingly harder to make the event financially viable. Even featuring a strong line-up of Rockabilly bands with Dave Phillips, Colbert Hamilton, Red Hot & Blue and Restless, was not enough to attract more punters.

After the 7th Big Rumble's shameful bouts of caravan smashing the event scheduled for the Spring of 1995 was cancelled and it looked as though the wrecking which took place off the dancefloor at previous meetings was putting the gathering in serious jeopardy. However, in late October of that year Dell and his team adopted a different arrangement and the 8th Big Rumble went ahead. Gt Yarmouth was again the venue but the hall this time was in the heart of the town. Tiffany's nightclub hosted what amounted to a Friday night gig followed by alldayers on the Saturday and Sunday.

By choosing a non-residential venue the organisers, although happy to recommend accommodation, were no longer financially responsible for the room-trashing antics of pissed-up festival-goers. This went some way to breaking the mentality of many Big Rumble patrons who believed that the ticket price for the weekender gave them the automatic right to smash windows and set fire to their beds. Bedroom bashers now faced the rough-end of a Norfolk landlady's rolling pin should the desire to wreck the place grip them.

Though the venue had changed, the booking policy for bands was as strong as ever with Batmobile's first UK appearance for over five years and almost a Klub Foot reunion with Restless, Skitzo, The Coffin Nails, Long Tall Texans, Frenzy, The Caravans, The Klingonz and The Sharks. There was also new talent in the form of French newcomers The Elektraws, sexy voodoobilly from The Empress Of Fur, The Blue Devils, local stompers Shakeout and solid Psycho from The Lost Souls.

Despite the quality on offer, the event lost a little something when everyone went their own way at nights and the feeling of living in a Psychobilly community for three days was gone. However, there was a better choice of boozers for daytime supping and a wealth of take-aways nearby after gigs which certainly beat staggering back to a caravan and struggling to open a tin of beans.

The following year it was business as usual and the 9th Big Rumble rolled back into Vauxhall Holiday

HELL'S BENT ON ROCKIN' THE NEXT DEGENERATION

Park as the venue's caravan owners took a deep breath in anticipation. This event was a Psychobilly survivors special featuring The Klingonz, Skitzo, Mad Sin, Demented Are Go, The Coffin Nails, The Highliners, The Lost Souls, The Hangmen and The Frantic Flintstones. There was also a fair sprinkling of new talent such as The Cenobites, Kill Van Helsing and The Atomic Spuds. A fragile truce between the organisers and the caravan demolition specialists lasted across the weekend so a 10th Rumble was organised for November 1997. On a sour note, both past Rumbles had witnessed a drop in attendance so the margin between profit and damage bills had grown tighter. Things looked bleak but few were prepared for the final chapter of the Big Rumble story.

On a cold November morning in 1998 the 11th Big Rumble began but little did anyone know, including Dell, that this was to be the event's swansong. Times had been hard but after eight and a half years the Big Rumble had refused to die. Billed as "The biggest 3 day International weekender for Psychobilly, Surf, Neo-Rockabilly and Punk" things started off well enough with headline action from Batmobile, Nekromantix, The Sharks, The Caravans, The Klingonz and Punk legends, 999. The international theme was supported by Denmark's Godless Wicked Creeps, French rockers Lone Sharks, Sweden's Nocturnal Teds and Smell of Kat from Spain alongside Transatlantic action from yank bands Hayride To Hell, TR6 and even Brazilian Psychos Os Catalepticos. Once again, Dell attempted to broaden the range of acts on offer and lined up a number of rockin' acts with their own unique flavour such as The Blue Devils, Blackfoot & The Voola, Hot Boogie Chillun and Punk'n'Roll exponents Celtic Bones.

Though prospects for the event's success were looking good a recurring bout of increasingly ferocious caravan wrecking would nail the lid firmly on The Big Rumble's coffin. As Dell remembers, "On the 11th Big Rumble there was a lot of damage to the caravans and the camp were not happy that they had rented out these caravans the following week to holidaymakers. The most damage caused was from two of the acts that were playing at the weekend!!" So that was it, the death of The Big Rumble! Despite Dell's best efforts to keep the UK's most prestigious Psychobilly gathering a regular event it was all over. An eerie silence once again hovered over the Norfolk coast... at least until 2005, but that is another story.

Though band's like The Klingonz came to prominence in the 1990s, Psychobilly's 'Old

Klingonz over Europe (Christophe@Drunkabilly Records.

The Meteors...
never giving up!
(Simon 'Fatbloke'
Ling).

Guard' were still on active duty with, unsurprisingly, The Meteors leading from the front. They kicked into the 1990s with the third album of their live series 'Live III – Live Styles Of The Sick And Shameless' on Anagram Records, and it was to be their last on the label for some years. For the next five years all of The Meteors' new recordings were to be issued on the label Sonovabitch Records, a deal which saw the creation of classic Meteors' albums such as 'Madman Roll' (1991), 'Demonopoly' (1992) and 'No Surrender' (1994), along with a number of CD singles and EPs and also the band's fourth (official) live album 'International Wreckers' (1992).

The 1990s was also a strong period for The Meteors in terms of re-releases and compilations on CD. 'Corpse Grinder' (1995) was a 'best of' collection on the US label Cleopatra Records and intended as an introduction to the band for a broader American audience as any switched on Yank 'billies were already aware of the band and their place at the top of the Psychobilly genre. 'In Heaven' finally made it on to CD on Edsel Records in 1995 after years of contractual wranglings which saw this groundbreaking album linger in deletions hell for over fifteen years. This edition was accompanied by some detailed liner notes from the band's first manager Nick Garrard unlike the shady bootleg which appeared just before the official release and rather mysteriously listed the band as The UK Meteors on the front cover.

The battle to keep the album in print was to continue as Edsel's licence eventually drew to a close, leaving it in limbo once again until Anagram Records secured the rights and brought the album back to life again as part of their 'Psychobilly Collectors Series'. This series also features another thirteen Meteors albums, mainly reissues of previous Anagram albums but also new compilations,'From Zorch With Love' (1999) and 'Anagram Singles Collection' (2001), as well as a live album 'Hell In The Pacific' (2003) recorded in Japan and 'The Meteors Vs The World' (1999) an album combining new recordings and live tracks which had previously been available on Raucous Records and Cleopatra over the years.

Raucous Records has been another label dedicated to tracking down deleted and, more importantly, unreleased Meteors material. As well as reissuing the live Meteors albums 'Psychobilly Revolution' and 'Live I'/'Live II', Raucous also presented 'The Final Conflict' an album recorded at what was (then) intended as the final Meteors' concert ever. P. Paul Fenech had announced on the band's website in the Summer of 2000 that the band were to stop performing live after over twenty years of almost constant touring but thankfully their absence from the live scene was short-lived.

Raucous also unearthed two collections of previously unreleased Meteors material from their earliest days together. 'From Beyond' (2003) was a live recording of The Meteors dating from 1982 and featuring the Fenech/Lewis line up while 'The Lost Album' (2004) gathered together tracks recorded prior to 'In Heaven' which really document the band's transition from Rockabilly to their creation of Psychobilly. The label also gathered together all three of P. Paul's spin-off albums, as The Legendary Raw Deal, which had previously been available at a variety of other labels.

Given The Meteors' prodigious recording output it is surprising that P. Paul Fenech would have time to entertain side projects but he has recorded a number of albums in guises other than The Meteors. Though Fenech essentially is The Meteors, his other recordings all have an independent style but still one that is undeniably P. Paul. As a solo artist in the early 1990s, Fenech's first album, 'The Rockin' Dead', appeared on Sonovabitch Records and was followed by 'The Disease', created for Hellrazor Records.

P. Paul Fenech's desire to present The Meteors' recordings in the best possible way began around the release of 'Madman Roll' which he produced himself. Frustrated with penny-pinching record labels and hurried recording sessions he spent over three years studying sound engineering and sound production both in the UK and the US then established his own recording studio in 1996. In Heaven Recording Studio was a converted chapel in Swindon and as well as being a busy working studio, in between recording other acts Paul was able to work freely on Meteors and his other solo material without time or budget constraints.

His following solo album, 'Daddy's Hammer' (1996) was recorded entirely at In Heaven and released by Anagram Records. The deal with Anagram continued with two further albums, 'Screaming In The 10th

THE NEXT DEGENERATION

HELL'S BENT ON ROCKIN'

Key' (2000) and 'Fenechaphobia' (2002), before Paul took his sixth solo outing 'The F Word' to Germany's People Like You Records in 2006.

The solo albums were not P. Paul's only output beyond The Meteors. In 1997 he recorded and album of instrumentals, 'Powertwang', for Mental Disorder Records under the guise of The Surfin' Dead. His other main outlet was a series of more Rockabilly-led albums issued throughout the 1990s under the monicker of The Legendary Raw Deal, a name which harks back to Fenech and Lewis' pre-Meteors career as Raw Deal. The first release was 'Southern Boys' on Raucous Records and it set the standard for future albums with its mix of Rockabilly covers and new songs from Fenech which delivered some intensely hard-edged Rockabilly. Again these tracks had Mr Fenech's signature all over them but still with a style independent of The Meteors' output.

Mental Disorder released the second Legendary Raw Deal album under the record store baiting title 'Flick Knifin', Low Lifin', Bone Chillin', Dinosaur Killin', Kick Arse Fuckabilly Boogie' (try asking for that in HMV without the nitwits behind the counter asking you to repeat yourself). This was yet another mix of Rockabilly originals and Fenech creations featuring some slap bass that Meteors fans remembered fondly from The Meteors' earliest days. The Legendary Raw Deal project then attracted interest from Vinyl Japan Records and in 1997 they released the band's third album, 'Outlaw Man'.

2001 was an important year for The Meteors as it saw the release of 'Psycho Down'. Initially intended to be the band's final album, it would have been a fitting epitaph as it seemed to feature elements of all the qualities that had seen the band survive at the top for so long and it also brought The Meteors full circle with four tracks featuring the return of the double-bass to the band's sound. As ever it was a defiant creation, particularly on tracks such as 'King Of The Mutilators' and 'Fuck Off And Die', and the title track seemed to bring the whole Meteors saga to an explosive end. Combined with Raucous Records' 'Final Conflict' live recording the following year, this really seemed to be the end but in reality it was simply the end of another chapter in the band's history.

All day action in the late 1990s (Pip 'n' Tobe).

HELL'S BENT ON ROCKIN'   THE NEXT DEGENERATION

In 2003, I Used To Fuck People Like You In Prison Records was rapidly becoming 'the' home of high-grade Psychobilly and other malignant forms of Rock'n'Roll and their might was behind the continuing growth of Mad Sin's recording career and the resurrection of Demented Are Go on a global scale. It was fitting then that the label was behind the first new Meteors material since the band's short-lived retirement. With a solid line-up featuring Wolfgang Hordemann on drums/backing vox and Mark Burnette on double bass/backing vox, The Meteors were as tight and as furious as ever and with the slap bass back on board their entire back catalogue was revitalised.

Their first album for People Like You was a powerful collection of new Fenech originals and a cover of the Anti Nowhere League's 'I Hate People'. The title was as bold as the album itself, simply titled 'Psychobilly' (2003). The message was clear, The Meteors were still rolling, more relevant than ever and the album was serving as a reminder to any new conscripts to the scene as to where Psychobilly began.

As well as boasting a discography that few, if any, bands could come close to (apart from perhaps Billy Childish) The Meteors' career has been built on the road, continuing throughout the 1990s with relentless, globe-trotting gigging. The Meteors have cosistently taken Psychobilly to the far-flung corners of the earth where others fear to tread while still maintaining their grip across Europe. The brief spectre of the band retiring from the live arena faded and being back on the road allowed The Meteors to really establish themselves in America on a far larger scale than ever before through the first half of the 2000's. The band's concerts have also remained furious and intense affairs regardless of the size or location of the venue.

As their old merchandise once boasted "I Survived The Meteors Live" and over the years a tremendous amount of spilled blood, loose teeth and broken bones have been the result of audience reaction to the band's unique performances. From the hardened wrecker to the kamikaze Meteors' live virgin, few bands have ever inspired such a physical reaction amongst the followers. Add to this the band's constantly present brotherhood and inner circle The (K)attle, and few Meteors gigs are anything less than electric. This atmosphere has occasionally inspired some colourful bouts of (un)armed conflict but The Meteors play on through it all, delivering the goods from the stage with an unsurpassed record of live performances which could easily reach the 5000 mark between 2007/08.

After yet more rigorous touring The Meteors' deal with PLU continued and 'These Evil Things' was released in October 2004. The line-up was the same for this album and it also boasted more terrific cover artwork from PaSKal Millet from French rockers Monster Klub. The label also issued a very limited edition 25th Anniversary 7" picture disc featuring two tracks, 'When Darkness Falls'/'The Crazed', which were recorded rough and raw in the studio not long after a live performance when the adrenalin was still flowing.

Mark Burnette moved on in 2006, to be replaced on bass by Simon Linden but, twenty five years on, the band are in a stronger position than ever with previously uncharted parts of the globe waking up to their legacy and a back catalogue, live reputation and fiercely loyal following that can not be beat. Never sinking into revivalist hell, P. Paul Fenech's creativity shows no signs of flagging and The Meteors remain as current now as they did over a quarter of a century ago.

Alongside The Meteors' growing dominance in the 1990s, The Guana Batz were another early Psycho band whose career had continued well into the new decade. When Dave Diddle had left the band in the late 1980s, his drumstool was taken by former Get Smart sticksman Johnny Bowler. Get Smart were already a band known to many Guana Batz fans having appeared on compilations such as 'Zorch Factor One' and they were often in the line-up of many Psychobilly/Neo-Rockabilly live gatherings showcasing their good-time, knockaround Rockabilly style. With Johnny on board, this line-up ventured into the studio to record 1990s 'Electra Glide In Blue' album. The title was lifted from a cult 1973 American motorcycle cop movie of the same name and, along with the cover artwork, it reflected the Guana Batz' unashamed love of motorbikes. Despite retaining a loyal following amongst scooterists to this day, many of the Batz (Pip and Stuart in particular) are loyal ton-up boys and Ace Cafe regulars.

THE NEXT DEGENERATION

HELL'S BENT ON ROCKIN'

The Guana Batz, up close and personal (Mark Pennington).

Along with a new decade came a new record deal and 'Electra Glide In Blue' appeared on the World Service label. This album was probably the band's most mature, well-recorded creation which still stands well amongst their other releases but it arrived at a time when Psychobilly was moving into more extreme, Punk-influenced territory and many original Batz fans were moving in that direction or drifting back to the rockin' scene. After the album's release, bass player Sam Sardi also moved on making way for Caravans bassist Mark Pennington to join the group. With this new line-up, The Guana Batz faced up to a different scene and lean times ahead.

The Guana Batz career in the 1990s was far closer to King Kurt's in that the band activity decreased but they remained popular amongst many Psychobilly types who had made it through the previous

Guana Batz in the 1990s (Mark Pennington).

162

decade. 'Powderkeg' (1996) on Vinyl Japan was to be the last Guana Batz LP but the band continued to play live sporadically across Europe and still maintained headline status. With Mark Pennington continuing to work on his career with The Caravans, Johnny Bowler emerged from behind the drum stool to take over on double-bass with John Buck replacing him on tub-thumping duties. Pip then moved to San Diego, California and was shortly followed by Johnny Bowler. This understandably slowed down the Guana Batz touring schedule but occasional visits over the Atlantic and appearances on the booming American Psycho-scene have ensured that the Guana Batz' reputation as one of the rockin' scenes most valued bands has never diminished.

The CD boom also kept the Guana Batz flame burning with all of their first four studio albums represented on two CDs by the reissue specialists Castle alongside a 'greatest hits' package 'Guana Batz 1985-90'. Like all good bands, their back catalogue has continued to be plundered with the CDs 'Best of the Batz', 'Very Best of the Batz', 'Can't Take The Pressure' (a 'best of' with some live tracks) and 'Now That's What I Call Guana Batz: Volume 54' (Note: one of these titles is bogus... honest!). Further illustrating their well-stocked back catalogue, Guana Batz are one of the few Psychobilly bands to warrant a 'Peel Sessions' collection of British radio recordings (a Meteors collection was issued on Raucous but quickly deleted) and also an album bringing together the majority of their cover versions – the appropriately titled 'Undercover' on Anagram Records.

After all this the band cemented their place in Psycho-history with an anniversary gig at London's Klubtastic in April 2005, celebrating their 25 year career. This was followed, seven months later, by a headlining spot at the 2005 Speedfreaks Ball, the major UK Punk/Ska/Psychobilly event held in Hemsby, Gt Yarmouth and a return to that same event in 2006. No doubt their occasional live appearances will continue as The Guana Batz are truly a band that have travelled the rocky road of Psychobilly highway showing no sign of ever completely letting go.

In the early 1990s many of Psychobilly's originators were drifting off or completely disbanding. This vacuum, along with a lengthy series of consistently quality shows and continued appreciation of their albums, placed Demented Are Go up there with The Meteors as one of 'thee' headlining Psychobilly acts. In fact a growing rift between both bands had almost caused many Psycho fans to jump into

Titch and Mocker of The Klingonz in Austria, 1996 (Jane Williams).

THE NEXT DEGENERATION HELL'S BENT ON ROCKIN'

separate camps. Nonetheless, there were many who appreciated both these class acts. In the wake of the Klub Foot and Night of the Long Knives' demise came new gatherings of the Psycho clans at the likes of Billy's in Stoke and the Hemsby/Gt Yarmouth weekenders, two regular venues hosting multi-band line-ups. Demented Are Go were often regulars at many of these events and similar festivals throughout Europe. During this period some prime material was also created by the band and a deal with Fury Records in 1991 provided an outlet for it.

'Orgasmic Nightmare' was a classic return to form after the scattered madness of 'The Day The Earth Spat Blood'. Fury were establishing themselves as a real home for Psychobilly in the 1990s and Demented fitted snugly into their roster. Lex Luther was back in the band and back in the studio, alongside the mysterious Billy 'Munster' Favata on bass. The band were seemingly working together well with shared credits on all new DAG compositions and, as ever, material was not in short supply. Perversion and sleaze were certainly not rationed with songs such as 'Orgasmic Nightmare', 'Anal Wonderland', 'Clitoris Bite Boogie' and 'Love Seeps Like A Festering Sore' maintaining Demented Are Go's supremacy in creating classic Psychobilly tracks detailing many forms of depravity.

Response to the album was good and alongside continued demand for more gigs in the UK and Europe they began touring further afield. They also continued to play at many Punk gatherings, events that would prove far more important later in their career. Though the Punk and Psychobilly movements are now often closely linked, coming out of the 1980s there was enough support on both sides to warrant separate scenes. The few Punk bands who drifted onto early Psychobilly line-ups often got a muted response despite the fact that many Psychobillies had been fledgling Punks before they discovered flat-top fever.

Whether through accident or design, Demented became regulars on the Punk scene while still serving the Psychobilly faithful. This also increased their touring schedules as demand grew for their lengthy sets of Demented classics, made even more entertaining when combined with their often elaborate stage make-up. Phillips especially embraced the 'slap' and unleashed a variety of monstrous transformations involving greasepaint, false foreheads, flapping skin and buckets of blood. One particularly gruesome 'melting face' effect had many pissed-up Psychobillies wondering if their beers were laced with LSD. Demented Are Go of course were not the only band to make with the horror make-up. The Frantic Flintstones had most memorably appeared in a selection of ghoulish guises for the cover of their 1986 LP 'Nightmare On Nervous', while bands like The Klingonz took it to extremes with complete body paint and Spook & The Ghouls rested their career on their demonic imagery.

As Demented Are Go delivered the goods both visually and musically, they were kept busy throughout 1991/92 but during this time Billy Favata set sail for America (later appearing with US Psycho band Wreckin' Ball) leaving the way clear for the return of Graeme Grant. This reunited the classic 'Kicked Out Of Hell' line-up and saw the quartet return to the studio to record their second album for Fury Records. 'Tangenital Madness (On a Pleasant Side of Hell)' was released in 1993. While still classic Demented, the album had a fuller sound thanks to a selection of studio mixes and a stack of guest musicians contributing mouth

The Charlotte kick in to the 21st Century with an excellent line-up (Raucous Records).

HELL'S BENT ON ROCKIN'   THE NEXT DEGENERATION

Demented Are Go (Simon 'Fatbloke' Ling).

organ, saxophone, fiddle, banjo and slide guitar. Into this Psychedelic-Psychobilly hoe-down were some choice covers including Jimi Hendrix's 'Up From The Skies' and Devo's 'Mongoloid', a song which could well have been written for the band.

Yet again, the album was well received and set the band up for more globe-trotting gigs, including their first visit to Japan for a three week tour and another Japanese tour the following year. After five studio albums and nearly a dozen years in existence the Demented story up to that point had been one of steady progress on a rocky road but from the mid 1990s onwards, the whole saga was to become an even more volatile, myth-fuelled parade of bust-ups, bunk-ups and break-downs.

At the very centre of this portion of Demented history is the very centre of the band itself, Mark 'Spark'

THE NEXT DEGENERATION   HELL'S BENT ON ROCKIN'

Phillips. During the past decade the band has often revolved around rumour, gossip and eyewitness accounts which have in turn been filtered through booze-soaked and/or drug-addled memories. Some would characterise Phillips as a wild card – unpredictable, unhinged and (often) undressed but he also has a reputation for regularly delivering a top-class performance and rarely short-changing Demented devotees. This is a man known for getting royally fucked-up before, and after, a gig yet still appearing onstage, often in elaborate make-up, and delivering up to 30 classic Demented Are Go songs.

The band has also remained at the top of their game for another reason – the strength of their back catalogue of songs. The legend would have it that the band shambled into every recording session with hangovers, knocked together a few tunes and simply struck it lucky. In reality it would appear that their stack of quality songs were a result of good writing, plenty of practice and a desire to capture their best sound in the studio. A listen to the snippet of studio banter which appears before 'Don't Go In To The Woods' on their 'Holy Hack Jack' 12" would go some way to backing this up.

Regardless of this fragile balance between twisted genius and total dementia, the 1990s were a period of mixed fortunes for the band. In 1995, whilst touring Germany, tensions within the band ran high and they broke up completely. Thankfully this early retirement scheme was short-lived but what followed was a blur of activity that continued for the rest of the decade. Part of Mark Phillips' twisted genius results in him often being what is diplomatically referred to as being 'interesting' to work with and the late 1990s was a period of steady line-up changes.

Lex Luther left the band (again) after a tour of America and was replaced on guitar by Stan 'The Man' Standen. Shortly after, Graeme Grant left, leaving double bass duties to Choppy Lambourne, a member of UK Neo-Rockabillies The Caravans. No sooner had Choppy slapped some bass for the band than it was time for Darren 'Eddie' Edwards from The Klingonz to take over. During this period Ant Thomas had a serious back injury but, after a short break, reclaimed his position on the drum stool.

As the 20th Century drew to a close and the line-up of Sparky, Ant, Eddie & Stan stabilised, the band inked a deal with top German Psychobilly label Crazy Love Records. The first rancid fruit of this

The Klingonz... still rockin' in the 2000s (The Klingonz).

Bedlam Breakout! All-day Psychobilly action from Northampton (Mason Storm Archive).

collaboration was their 1999 LP 'Hellucifernation. This was their first studio album in six years with only the 10" EP 'I Wanna See You Bleed', released by Pin Up in 1997, to keep record buying fans happy. Understandably it was long awaited and a welcome arrival for stacks of Demented fans across the globe while it also saw the band see out the decade which almost strangled Psychobilly as one of the scene's top bands despite a chaotic eighteen year career.

'Hellucifernation' took the band into the 21st Century and a new dawn of Psychobilly. As the genre spread its disease across America, Demented Are Go found themselves with a rapidly growing number of fans on the other side of the Atlantic. This was no doubt a combination of their continuous progress in releasing quality albums and their near legendary status as one of a select band of Psychobilly survivors from the 'Klub Foot' days. However, in a double-pronged attack of mixed fortunes as demand for live performances grew Mark Phillips' behaviour on the road was causing concern for the rest of the band.

Having cancelled much of a European tour to promote 'Hellucifernation' and returning home without their singer, Ant, Eddie and Stan warily accepted a booking for a major show in New Jersey, USA. Almost on arrival, Sparky caused chaos and after pinching a teenage girl's butt in a local shopping mall he found himself banged-up in jail for molesting a minor. With the rest of the band unable to finance a $60,000 bail request for Phillips' freedom, they returned home and their time with Demented was at an end. Soon after, Ant Thomas and Eddie would re-emerge as Thee Exit Wounds.

After a month of porridge American-style, Mark Phillips was released from jail and he returned home to create a new Demented Are Go. Despite numerous line-up changes, Ant Thomas had always been the backbone of the band and now Sparky was the only remaining original member of the group. Luckily, another stalwart of the Demented Are Go dynasty, Lex Luther, was available and brought his unique guitar style back to the band. Choppy was again drafted in for double-bass duties and Ant's vacant drum stool was soon taken up by a friend of Phillips, Criss Damage. Criss fitted well into the

THE NEXT DEGENERATION

band and as a Punk drummer, he previously played with bands such as External Menace and Zero Tolerance, so was well suited to the growing audience for Demented outside of the Psychobilly scene.

Choppy's stay was slightly more unsteady and shortly after taking on double-bass duties he was off again leaving new boy Kelvin Klump with a little time to learn a lot of Demented's top tunes before embarking on a US tour. This time the band's trip to the States was more successful and with the US scene booming they found themselves on the road with pioneering Yank Psychobilly bands like The Barnyard Ballers and The Slanderin while playing at the first annual 'West Coast Wreckers Ball'. The American tour was so successful that a rapid return booking was soon placed and the band played coast to coast, spreading the Psychobilly gospel and also releasing their first American recorded concert album 'Live At The Galaxy' which was released by Crazy Love Records.

Despite a period of 'near stability' since the beginning of the new millennium, in the Summer of 2003 Kelvin and Lex left the band and Demented were once again plunged into crisis. A new record deal had been secured with another German label 'People Like You Records' and a month-long European tour was rapidly forthcoming. Completing yet another Demented Are Go line-up were two players who had already been a part of the band's chequered history. Doyley and Strangy, on guitar and double-bass, were both members of Psychobilly legends The Klingonz & Punk'n'Rollers Celtic Bones and had both helped out at previous Demented Are Go gigs and recordings when required.

Demented had built up many close links with other bands on the scene throughout the years but none more so than The Klingonz and Mad Sin. For this reason Doyley and Strangy were far more than hired hands and instantly became an integral part of the band. With this revitalised line-up the touring continued but within a few months double-bass player Choppy was back in the band. This time not because of another personnel change but as a temporary replacement for Strangy who broke his leg on tour.

Alongside Demented Are Go in the last few years Mark Phillips has also been behind Demented Scum Cats, a side project featuring Spark, guitarist 'Stan' Standen and drummer Johnny Gizmo alongside a host of Demented friends and associates. The result of this has been a self-titled four track CD single and the 2005 album 'Splatter Baby' on Crazy Love Records, both of which were undeniably Demented but with a far more Garage Punk influence, trashy keyboards and Standen's distinctive driving guitar style. The album also includes a fair touch of Country with the emphasis on Western, distinctly more Spaghetti Western than John Wayne.

Though the Scumcats material was strong, there never appeared to be any doubt that Demented Are Go would remain Phillips' priority and new songs

The Sharks in the 1990s (Alan Wilson).

Halloween hi-jinks at the Big Rumble, 1992 (Jane Williams).

were being created for the next Demented album which was now long overdue. People Like You Records were patient and were rewarded with 'Hellbilly Storm' a thirteen-track album which finally surfaced in 2005 and featured Phillips, Strangy, Doyley, Stan and Criss Damage.

After over 23 years on the Psychobilly scene Demented Are Go are a phenomenon. Despite numerous line-up changes (including Ant Thomas' return to the band) they have remained a headline act at Psychobilly gigs across the world and a well-respected live act at a number of other underground scenes. During this time they have never courted or attempted to impress the mainstream music biz and continued to write and record jaw-dropping songs of sleaze and perversion all wired to their distinctive 'Frenzied Beat'. While Mark Phillips is shrouded in a fog of scandalous truths, half-truths and bullshit lies, he has always (somehow) kept the band on track with fans rarely witnessing a less than 100% performance at every gig. Even now after the success of side project Demented Scum Cats, the Demented Are Go story shows no sign of ending because for Sparky and the rest of the members it is more than a band – its a way of life.

Alongside Frenzy and Restless in the 1990s, Steve Whitehouse had another role and in 1995, after a 12-year gap, he also returned to The Sharks completing the original line-up of himself, guitarist and vocalist Alan Wilson and Paul 'Hodge' Hodges on drums. Wilson, The Sharks mainman, had got the band back in action in 1993 after Rockabilly double-bassist Gary Day (an ex-Frantic Flintstone) suggested that a Sharks revival would be well received. With Day on board the band started recording and their second studio album 'Recreational Killer' was snapped up by Anagram Records and unleashed in 1993.

The Sharks had always been a band way ahead of their time and many agreed that with their pioneering Neo-Rockabilly/Psychobilly sound they had initially split up too soon. Likewise, their reformation after a decade away generated great interest and saw them back on tour across Europe. Gary Day was also a member of Morrissey's band, alongside fellow rocker Boz Boorer, and with increased touring and recording commitments eventually it became too demanding for him to remain a Shark. This then cleared the way for Steve's return. To cement this Sharks' reunion the band recorded another album 'Colour My Flesh', which was again released on Anagram in 1995. This was followed by a seven-inch EP for Fury Records, 'Sir Psycho'. In 1996, Hodge left the band and was replaced on drums by ex-Restless snare-basher Ben Cooper. More confusingly, a few years later Cooper made way for Carl Parry who was previously a guitarist for Frenzy.

As The Sharks story continued, Whitehouse maintained his parallel universe of Frenzy recording and gigging. As the band entered 1990 they consisted of Steve, Hodge and a new guitarist, the youthful Carl Parry. Hodge never saw the year out with the band and after the temporary return of original Frenzy sticksman Merv Pepler, to help the band through a European tour, Adam Seviour was coaxed back into the line-up. With touring to support 'This Is The Fire' reaching across Europe and into Japan, Rage Records were looking to consolidate the band's success and issued 'The Best Of Frenzy' later that same year.

'(It's A) Mad Mad World' (1992) on Rage Records was the band's next album and confusingly contained eight tracks from 'This Is The Fire' which had by then been deleted. The line-up of Whitehouse/Parry/Seviour had continued but a session drummer had been employed on some of the sessions which contributed to the album. Though demand for the band (and many other Psychobilly outfits) across Europe had declined slightly, Frenzy's profile in Japan was huge. As a mark of respect to their Japanese followers, and to celebrate their tenth anniversary, Frenzy released the 'Eastern Sun EP' on CD in 1993 and also their second official concert recording 'Live In Japan' (Raucous Records).

With Steve leaving Restless in 1994 and rejoining The Sharks, creating the next Frenzy album was a long process. Originally planned for Rage Records but eventually released by Count Orlok Records, 'Nine O Nine' appeared in 1997. This was to be the last album featuring Carl Parry and Adam Seviour, who had already been unavailable to drum on some of the tracks on the album.

In 2002 Frenzy celebrated almost twenty years in the business with the release of their tenth album 'Dirty Little Devils' on Crazy Love Records. No mean feat when even mighty behemoths of the early Psychobilly scene such as King Kurt and Guana Batz come nowhere near to a studio album release of double digits. By this time Steve Eaton was on board as guitarist and drummer Rob Chapman was behind the tubs. Yet again the varied musical experiences of all three gave this Frenzy release a solid Rockabilly foundation with elements of Punk, Blues and heavy rock.

Touring to promote the album continued and saw the band (unbelievably, given their past worldwide success) play the US for the first time, striding the stage at the 2nd Wreckers Ball in LA in 2004. Though Steve Whitehouse has a number of other interests, particularly his collection of World War II vehicles (including a tank) which are much in demand for film and TV productions, Frenzy are still moving forward with their new album 'Nitro Boy' which was released in January 2007. The album appeared on the band's own label Crash Records and coincided with Adam Seviour's return to the band in preparation for a more thorough return to live performances.

Not all bands on the Psychobilly scene thrived in the 1990s and for The Coffin Nails times were initially hard. Despite some steady gigging in the early part of the decade, in 1993 the band entered the dead zone which many Psychobilly groups experienced in that decade. While not actually splitting up, their band activity decreased almost completely. Nasser had drifted off and at the Big Rumble in Gt Yarmouth that year the band announced it as their final gig. With Nasser gone, Humungus and Mad Man played one other gig using a drum machine at Stoke's finest Psychobilly hotspot 'Billy's', a bizarre and entertaining appearance but unfortunately too radical for many Psychobilly puritans. After this the band returned to their other interests with Klunky focusing on his career as a tattoo artist and hot rod builder and Scott playing with ex-members of The Loafers in a 60's themed band called Skooby, who later became Big Boss Man.

Though Nasser initially did not return, Klunky and Scott were back in action in 1996 with a new drummer, 'Granpa' Neil Fisher. Scott ditched the double-bass in favour of electric and once again The Coffin Nails' back catalogue was refreshed. The band were still a household name on the Psychobilly scene and, along with the first hints of a big time Psychobilly revival, there was no shortage of gigs on offer. Within a year 'Granpa' Neil took early retirement and Nasser returned for the recording of their 1997 release 'Wrecker's Yard' on the new label 'Greystone Records'. Greystone was started by Klunky and Scott initially to release solely Coffin Nails material beginning with a CD re-issue containing two of the band's earlier albums 'Fistful Of Burgers' and 'Who's He?' but it soon became a growing label with Scott at the helm and an eclectic roster of acts. 'Wrecker's Yard' saw The Coffin Nails move their sound forward yet again. Scott's bass change automatically brought an immediately punkier influence and certain tracks were far heavier than previous Coffin Nails' album tracks. Humungus' guitar and vocals had both matured and undoubtedly Nasser was a super-tight drummer.

The Coffin Nails establish their own label, Greystone (Coffin Nails).

Nasser was not available for live work so new boy 'Pip' plonked his arse on the ever revolving drum stool and the band set about promoting the album. A live album, 'Big Night Out', followed on Greystone then Nasser was persuaded to return to the fold once again as The Coffin Nails continued with the studio album 'Out For The Weekend'. The band's style continued to evolve with Scott playing both electric and double-bass and the band effortlessly borrowing from Psycho, Rockabilly, Country, Punk, Ska and even something approaching Heavy Metal. Throughout this The Coffin Nails never lost the sense of humour that has always been their trademark and tales of drunken debauchery with dirty women remained a key theme.

After the album's recording, Nasser moved on and Clive Cornwall joined up as The Coffin Nails eighth drummer (the band even featured a 'drummers' section on their website to document their high turnover of skin-bashers). Clive settled in throughout 2001/2002 during yet more of The Coffin Nails' regular touring, then made his studio debut with the band in 2003 during the recording of their third studio album on Greystone, 'Hard As Nails'. By now The Coffin Nails were enjoying worldwide success, particularly in America where they toured for the first time and where they are regarded as one of Europe's premier 'Old School' Psychobilly bands. Their latest albums have delivered a harder, heavier more well-produced sound and Klunky has also found the time to open his own tattoo studio, 'TAT2-U' in his home town Reading, while Scott has taken a larger role in Greystone's growing success.

Nearly two decades on, The Coffin Nails like many of the UK's Psychobilly survivors are in a stronger position now than they have ever been. As a testament to their long and varied career, Cherry Red Records brought together 25 of The Coffin Nails' finest moments from seven of their albums with 'Let's Wreck: Gravest Hits Of The Coffin Nails', a 'best of' compilation released in 2004 as part of the label's 'Psychobilly Collectors Series'. As 2005 drew to a close, the band found themselves once again on the main stage at Hemsby, Gt Yarmouth, playing to a packed house at the first 'Speedfreaks Ball' then returning the following year as Nigel Lewis' backing band.

The 1990s were also a healthier period for The Frantic Flintstones. In 1990, still promoting their Link Records release 'A Nightmare Continues', The Frantic Flintstones continued to tour including a spot at the first ever 'Big Rumble' in Gt Yarmouth, before another album hit the shops. 'Schlachtof Boogie Woogie' (Link) had been recorded before Gary Day's return and featured Chuck, Pug, drummer Andy 'Baldrick' and a trio of bass-players, Wayne T, Andy Crowdy and Gasty. Yet again it was an album of varied styles, particularly the gospel sound of 'Drugs In The Valley', which aped the chapel-shaking holy-roller classic 'Peace In The Valley', and 'Pantman' the band's unique take on Neal Hefti's 'Batman' theme. Chuck and Jonny were also working well together, collaborating on five tracks alongside Chuck's own creations.

As the first year of the new decade drew to a close The Frantic Flintstones were consistently busy and other labels had been releasing the band's material such as Raucous Records' 'The Raucous Recordings Vol. 1' (1990) and two releases from the European label Kix 4 U, 'Yahbahdahbahdoo!' (1989) a six track mini LP and the full length LP 'Well Gone In Europe' (1990). Chuck had also started his own label, Chuckadee Records and recorded The Caravans album 'No Excuses'. However, after a drugs bust at his home Chuck was up in court in January 1991.

When the court case was adjourned, The Flintstones did some touring in Europe before returning to the studio to record what would be the album 'Cuttin' A Fine Line' (1991) for the German label Rumble Records. This was followed by some UK gigs, including a return to The Big Rumble that spring, then Chuck received a double blow of very bad luck. In March, Chuck and some friends were seriously injured when their van crashed returning from a gig in London. After recovering from this Mr Harvey found himself behind bars in late June 1991, beginning a seven month stretch. After serving half his sentence, Chuck was back on the streets to find 'Cuttin' A Fine Line' was selling well. Gary Day had again left, this time to join Morrissey with Boz Boorer, and Demented Are Go's Graham Grant stepped in briefly on the slap-bass. Soon after Rich Taylor also left and The Frantic Flintstones entered 1992 as a two-piece with only the hardcore left standing – Chuck and Pug.

As the early 1990s continued The Frantic Flintstones record releases hit the shops with all the subtlety of a carpet bombing. Continued interest in the band boomed in the CD age and combined with their prolific studio work a mind-bending selection of reissues and new material were unleashed. 'Cuttin' A Fine Line' was the crossover point, being a simultaneous release on vinyl and disc. From there on The Frantic Flintstones CD collection bloomed. Kix 4 U released a combination of new and old recordings on 'Take A Hike' (1991) before Link exploited their time with the band on a 19 track 'Best Of The Frantic Flintstones', combining the cream of their four albums for the label, followed by a two-albums-on-one-disc affair of 'The Nightmare Continues'/'Schlachtof Boogie Woogie' on their Streetlink imprint.

Rumble Records continued their relationship with the band releasing the acoustic CD 'Skin Up, Chill Out' (1991) and 'Rock It Boy' (1993) which featured material from a 1992 recording session that also spawned the album 'Speed Kills' which would not see the light until its release by Raucous Records in 1998. As with many of the Flintstones albums each title had their fair share of covers and a liberal dose of hard-slapping Rockabilly. 'Skin Up, Chill Out' was particularly memorable with its laid-back, busking style – an 'unplugged' album for the Psychobilly generation, demonstrating Chuck's ability to experiment with a variety of musical styles while never alienating their hard-core following. Another CD collection 'Flesh'n'Fantasy' (1992) appeared on the Tombstone label before the band moved on to their next album proper and the landmark Flintstones release 'Jamboree' (1993).

Chuck had struck up a relationship over the years with record producer, and former mainman of The Sharks, Alan Wilson. In the early 1990s Wilson was operating his own recording studio, X-Ray, near Bath and after an initial weekend session with The Frantic Flintstones a song-writing partnership between himself and Harvey was forged that lasts to this day. After recording a succession of rough demo tracks, some of which would eventually appear on the Crazy Love Records album 'The X-Ray Sessions' (1993), work began in earnest on what would become 'Jamboree'. After a two week recording session at a studio deep in the woods near Bath, 'Jamboree' emerged with all band members (just) intact and boasting a healthy roster of rockin' talent including Gary Day, Hodge (Sharks) and Rich Taylor (Caravans) alongside Chuck and Alan Wilson. This session was also memorable as it witnessed the reformation of The Sharks with Gary Day agreeing to join the classic line-up of Wilson and Hodge to work on new material.

'Jamboree' was released in the middle of 1993 by Anagram Records as part of their new two album deal with the band. Touring across the UK, Holland, Finland and Germany continued and it was during some time off in Sigen that romance bloomed for Chuck. Having met his future bride Sonja, Chuck began to spend more time in Germany until moving there for good in 1994. It was during one visit back home that the band recorded their second Anagram album 'Enjoy Yourself'. Jonny Pug had organised the session bringing in drummer Clem and stand-in bass man 'Matt the Rat' as Gary Day had moved on once more, closely followed by Rich Taylor. To accompany the new album, Anagram also added two of Link Records' early Flintstones albums onto one disc, 'Rockin' Out'/'Not Christmas Album', as part of their 'Psychobilly Collectors Series'.

The following years saw gigs, not unsurprisingly, increase in Europe but it was not until 1997 before a new Flintstones CD appeared. 'Hits From The Bong' was recorded for Vampirella Records and featured an expanded Flintstones line-up of Chuck, Jonny Pug, Alan Wilson and a combination of two drummers, Hyppo of The Celicates and Ben Turner. This was to be Pug's last album for the band as, despite the band's reputation for high times, his boozing was affecting his performance and his Frantic Flintstones days were over. For the rest of the decade, Alan Wilson would take the role of Flintstones' guitarist when required. Though gigging continued into the new millennium, it was 2001 before new Flintstones' material appeared. Meanwhile The Frantic Flintstones back catalogue on CD was selling consistently and still available across a number of labels, with further collections to appear such as Raucous Records' 'The EP Collection' (2003) and Western Star Recordings' 'Billy Overdose' (2002).

'Too Sweet To Die' (2001) was The Frantic Flintstones' third studio album for Anagram then things went quiet in the studio for a time. In 2003 a revitalised Flintstones were back with a new album 'Champagne For All' on Crazy Love Records. Despite their reputation for putting their own unique spin on a variety of cover versions this album, produced by Alan Wilson at his own Western Star Studio, boasted a dozen Frantic originals with a sharper, more powerful sound. Traditional themes such as sex ('Baby Bent Double'), drugs ('Trips Me Out', 'Baby Bong') and booze ('Champagne For All') were all present and the band sounded tighter than ever. This was a serious Psychobilly album putting the band back on the scene with a vengeance and suitable listening for old diehards and Psychobilly newcomers alike.

However, Chuck Harvey maintained his sense of humour throughout 'Champagne For All' and his following project was a non-stop soundtrack to the perfect, pissed-up rockin' party. Chuck and the Hulas' 'Smells Like A Party' was another collaboration between Harvey and Wilson, recorded and released by Western Star in 2004. A whacked out collection of good-time tunes with a slightly demented edge and a singalong theme, it conjures up images of a rowdy knees-up populated by beer-soaked punters in Hawaiian shirts and grass skirts. Chuck managed again, as he did with the 'unplugged' release 'Skin Up, Chill Out', to deliver a full album in one unique style, something few artists on the rockin' scene would have the nerve to attempt.

Chuck has never been afraid to stretch the confines of the Psychobilly sound mixing Country, Ska, Rockabilly, Blues, Gospel, Rock'n'Roll and many other genres in Frantic Flintstones creations. These themes appear in almost all Flintstone albums and obviously are some of Chuck's main musical influences which have stayed with him throughout his recording career. These elements to the band's sound are also one of their main attractions as other styles are used frequently without self-consciousness or the need to be employed purely as a piss-take. The Frantic Flintstones could never be accused of accepting any restrictions as to what a Psychobilly/Rockabilly band 'should' play and, in a similar way to The Long Tall Texans, they have pursued their sound with a 'take-it-or-leave-it' attitude and their fans have loved them all the more for it.

The Long Tall Texans themselves strode into the 1990s with the release of their fourth album for Razor, this time a 'live' LP 'Five Beans In The Wheel'. This was actually recorded in a studio near Brighton with a few rowdy mates and some studio effects making up the 'audience' as the band delivered a continuous performance straight to tape. Surprisingly, it still demonstrated the beer'n'sweat party atmosphere that the band were famous for and highlighted some of the soulful cover versions the Texans regularly played live. Many of these tracks endeared the band to the booming scootering community and even the most po-faced, rockin' disbeliever could not fail to be moved by the Long Tall Texans' versions of the likes of 'Heatwave' and 'Breakaway'.

The band's following studio album was to be something of a landmark for the Long Tall Texans as it was the last to feature founding member Mark Denman who retired from active duty to focus on his career as a teacher. Too many nights in the back of a van followed by too many days marshalling spotty-faced youths obviously took its toll. The album, 'Singing To The Moon' (1991), was another accomplished release with an increasingly slick production which, again, deserved to be exposed to a wider audience. This album was the band's first release for Rage Records but also their last chunk of 12" vinyl as the CD age began to take hold in the 1990s.

THE NEXT DEGENERATION HELL'S BENT ON ROCKIN'

Above: Long Tall Texans, 2006 (Simon 'Fatbloke' Ling).

Right: The Long Tall Texans in Europe (Christophe @ Drunkabilly Records).

Rage Records were effectively one of the newer labels on the UK scene in the late 1980s. Founded by Nick Sellors, they made up for their later arrival on the scene by immediately signing some of the scene's heavy hitters including the Texans and Frenzy. In 1993 things were looking a little shaky at the label and, fearing that Frenzy's Rage material would fall out of print, Steve Whitehouse engineered a meeting between Nick and Roy Williams which resulted in Nervous acquiring Rage as part of their organisation.

With effectively one third of The Long Tall Texans gone, what followed was a somewhat unsettled period within the band with a trio of guitarists coming and going before the arrival of ex-Ratttlers axeman Doug Shepard. The Texans then became a four-piece for the first time with the addition of saxophonist Paul Mumford.

With Paul and Doug on board, The Long Tall Texans sound entered a new dimension. The Ska and Reggae elements of their songs increased again and their entire set was revamped. Even their classic 'Bloody' got a new sax-blown makeover. Although having a sax player in a Psychobilly band was not unheard of (King Kurt, Highliners...) combined with their increasingly diverse musical style, the Texans were wondering how their new sound and personnel would settle with their hardcore following of motley rockers. However, rather than dick about testing the water at some smaller gigs, they unleashed their four-piece line-up at a major gig supporting The Stray Cats in London. Understandably, they received a warm reception and continued touring to take their evolved sound to the Psycho nation across Europe.

The first album to feature the new line-up, 'Aces & Eights', appeared in 1994 on Anagram. Heavy on the sax, the album continued to stretch the band's range of influences while still remaining strictly Long Tall Texans. This release captured the band at the peak of crossover success with an album stacked with mass appeal but still holding something for the faithful. The touring continued across Europe then onto the Far East but eventually things went very quiet down Brighton way.

Though The Long Tall Texans continued to tour sporadically in the late 1990s, things in the recording studio went quiet for the best part of a decade. The Texans' legacy had continued in the CD age though new material was in short supply. 'In Without Knocking' on Rage Records gathered their first two albums along with the 'Saints & Sinners' EP and some previously unissued live tracks on one shiny disc while 'Ballroom Blitz' (Crazy Love) gathered the band's earliest recordings, produced by former Polecat Boz Boorer, making them available commercially for the first time. Acknowledging their status as one of the key bands of the early rockin' scene, The Texans appeared on 'Texas Beat', their very own greatest hits compilation on Cherry Red Records, followed by 'The Long Tall Texans Story', on the same label, which provided a more comprehensive double CD collection.

However, The Texans' story was far from over and in 2005 the band burst back onto the scene with a new album and a return to more regular gigging. 'Adventures Of The Long Tall Texans' featured twelve new tracks released by the band themselves and showed the Texans continuing to develop their sound with a harder edge. Their sax player had left the fold but the memorable tunes and lyrics which had earned the band their reputation were still present and in the new dawn of Psychobilly it is this album that could serve as a strong introduction to many new fans of the 'Texas Beat'.

The Lost Souls were one of the UK's most popular acts of the 1990s but with the odds often stacked against them and a relatively small recorded output they have yet to get the respect they actually deserve. Throughout their career they have tirelessly toured across the UK and Europe, headlining their own gigs and supporting most of the biggest bands on the scene but as peers of The Klingonz, Mad Sin and Nekromantix it is clear that they have yet to fulfil their true potential.

The band actually formed way back in 1985 in the town of Walsall in the West Midlands of England. The original line-up featured Mark Broome on upright bass and lead vocals, Neil Hattersley on guitar and backing vox and Ian Lydell on drums. The band's live reputation, based on their furiously-paced songs and sense of humour, saw them supporting the likes of King Kurt, Guana Batz and Frenzy relatively early in their career. Grabbing the attention of such large audiences as they did, their debut LP was keenly awaited and Nervous Records put the punters out of their misery in 1990 with the album 'Chasin' A Dream'.

Having played so much in their early career, the band's set was tight and the tracks on the album were all well-crafted compositions with no fillers alongside some inspired covers, such as Billy Idol's 'Dancing With Myself'. After yet more steady touring for over two years to promote 'Chasin' A Dream' the band set to work on a follow-up. After striking a deal with Tombstone Records the band delivered their second album 'Erazerhead'. With a great understanding of the scene The Lost Souls really knew what UK and European audiences wanted and they delivered it – straight-up Psychobilly, catchy tunes, humour and flat-out wreckin' anthems.

Initially things were looking good for the band, with two quality albums behind them and a solid live reputation. Demand for them to tour was great and then tragedy struck when guitarist Neil Hattersley died. After some time, local six-stringer Kieron Lee was enlisted as Neil's replacement. Kieron never settled and Mark Broome soon found himself the only original member as Kieron moved on with Ian Lydell following soon after. Jay Luker took over on guitar and the usual procession of drummers ensued until Paul 'Benk' Benson settled on the stool.

Diminishing audiences in the UK made little difference to The Lost Souls as they simply focused more

THE NEXT DEGENERATION HELL'S BENT ON ROCKIN'

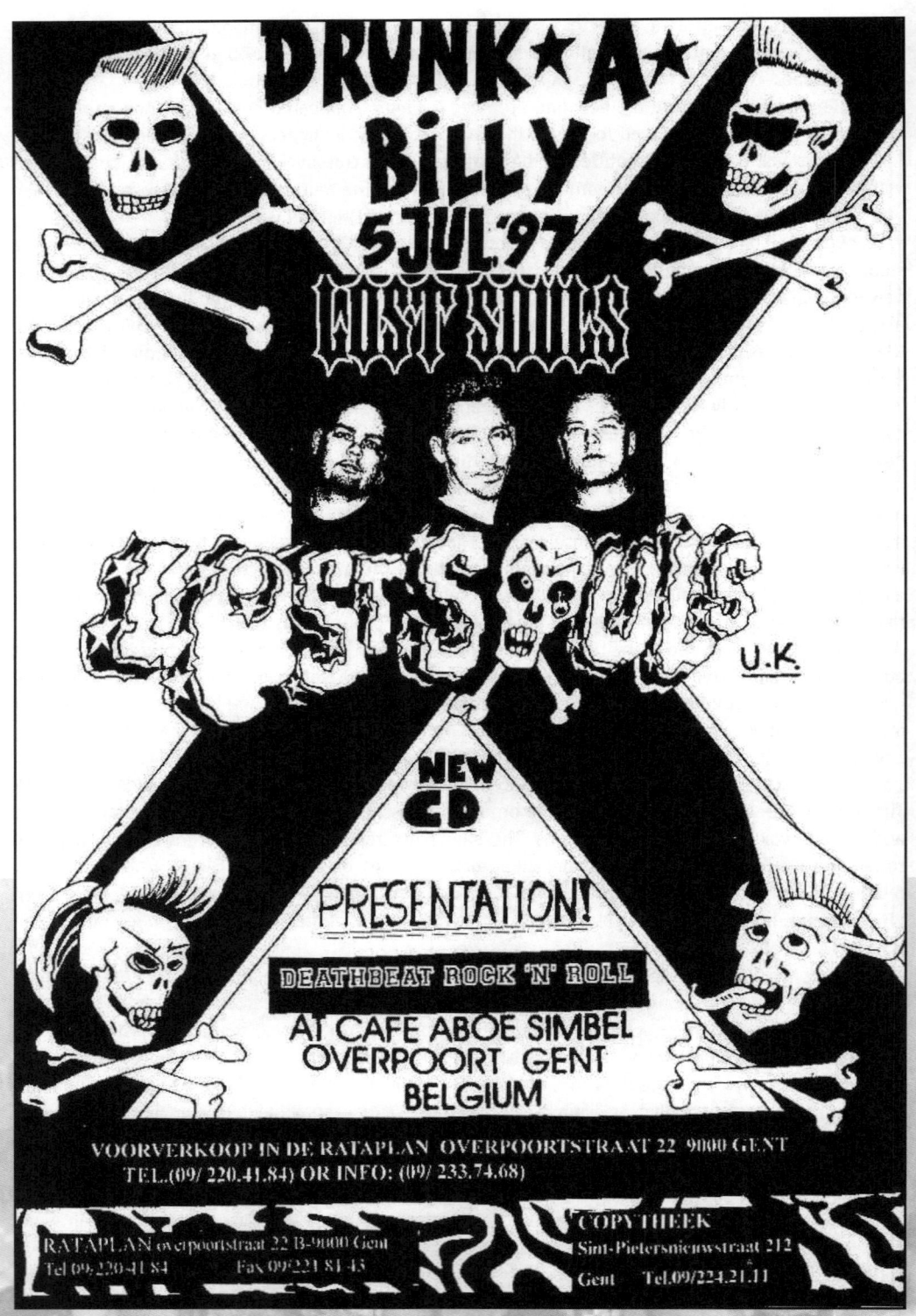

Lost Souls, regularly touring Europe (Christophe @ Drunkabilly Records).

of their time playing in Europe. So much touring that Jay Luker could take no more and left the band. Despite suffering this setback, the band were rolling on and still in demand. A new guitarist, Dainty, joined up and had to get used to the regular touring alongside preparations for a further album. The band had hooked up with Loz Dolan from The Hangmen who released their third album 'Deathbeat Rock'n'Roll' (1997) on his Bone Tone Corporation label. The album was long-awaited by their army of fans and alongside the production input from Loz the whole collection had a darker, heavier feel that was still undoubtedly Psychobilly but showed how much the band's sound was progressing.

The Lost Souls have always deserved to be amongst the top UK and European Psycho acts but things for the band were rarely simple. Despite playing his part in the band's strongest recording to date, Dainty left leaving Mark once again trying to complete the trio to honour outstanding gigs. Thankfully Jay returned to the fold, touring continued and The Lost Souls were back on track until disaster struck and ceased the band's activities immediately. In 2000, Mark Broome's car was involved in a collision with two trucks and he sustained life-threatening injuries. Thankfully he pulled through but for many years The Lost Souls story was over as Broome began a long period of recovery. Mark had always been the heart of the band, lead vocalist and main songwriter, and without him the band did not exist.

In the summer of 2006 a distinct scent of unfinished business was in the air when the band reformed, featuring a fully recovered Broome on bass and vocals, Jay on guitar and new drummer Timmi. Maybe now The Lost Souls can regain their die-hard audience, enlist some of the many new followers of the genre and enjoy the success which many of their peers have experienced.

Whilst decamping to the US has been something of a standard career move for many European bands in recent years, The Phantom Rockers were early pioneers, and after progressing through the European scene in the 1990s they arrived at the heart of the revitalised American scene with a large back catalogue and a strong reputation. The band were formed in Aachen, Germany in 1989 by Mark Burke, formerly a double-bass player with the Krewmen. Striking a blow for European unity, Burke brought on board Dutch drummer Marcus Losen, German guitarist Olaf Schubert and fellow Englishman Mike Carroll on lead guitar.

The band signed to Tombstone Records and released their debut 'Kissed By A Werewolf' (1990) closely followed within a year by their second album for Tombstone, 'Demon Lover'. By this time Olaf had left the band and The Phantom Rockers were to remain a three-piece outfit for some time. Rarely less than fully active as a band they played regularly throughout the early 1990s and a succession of albums followed; 'Search & Destroy', 'Shag Squirt', 'Vampire Love' and even the band's own 'best of' compilation 'Av Some Of This'. The line-ups altered occasionally but Burke remained the core of the band and lead songwriter.

The Phantom Rockers had been one of the first Eurobilly bands to tour the US, first arriving in 1993 then making further visits in the following two years. After one such tour the rest of the band went home for good but Burke remained in the US with nothing more than the band's name and reputation. After some more transatlantic hopping between Germany and America The Phantom Rockers' frontman eventually settled in Dallas, Texas and with the US scene beginning to flourish Mark wasted no time in recruiting a new line-up. A six-track mini-album, 'PSM (Psycho Sick Motherfucker)' appeared on Hello Records and showcased The Phantom Rockers' evolving sound.

Increasingly pursuing the Punkier end of the Psychobilly spectrum it made perfect sense when Mark brought in another ex-pat who had landed in Dallas, ex-Exploited guitarist Karl Morris. The teaming was powerful and their first album together was the band's hardest and heaviest to date. 'Rise Up' was released by Drunkabilly Records in 2002 and saw the band at the heart of America's hottest Psychobilly scene while possessing a fine pedigree and far more live experience than most of the bands around. Burke's dedication appears to have paid off and despite putting in some serious air miles through the years and marshalling an ever-rotating line-up, the band remain where the action is. Their 2005 album 'On The Loose', for Split 7 Records, simply cemented their reputation as hard-working, constantly horny, pissed-up old school psychos – which cannot be a bad thing.

The Phantom Rockers (Christophe @ Drunkabilly Records).

HELL'S BENT ON ROCKIN'   THE NEXT DEGENERATION

When the Klub Foot breathed its last gasp and succumbed to a different kind of wreckin', crowds of wandering Psychobillies were looking for a place to go. Like huge legions of the quiffed-up living dead they stalked the streets, haunted by the demise of the Clarendon Hotel – pining for the strains of demented Rock'n'Roll!!! Well, not really. In reality London had many venues that welcomed Psychobillies and featured live bands including Dingwalls, The Headstone and the similarly doomed Hope & Anchor. However, one boozehole became a regular meeting place for old Klub Foot-ers and it hosted a number of live appearances featuring bands of the Psychobilly persuasion.

The LMS pub in Hendon, North London had a weekly rockin' club presenting live bands. The promoter, Tony Dangerfield, had a rockin' history of his own as a recording artist for legendary producer Joe Meek and despite being of a 'mature' standing had a real interest in the Psychobilly and Neo-Rockabilly scene. Mick Geary was another promoter and DJ who used the LMS as a venue for his promotions.

Another North London venue which embraced a wealth of Psychobilly, Neo-Rockabilly and Trash bands was The Sir George Robey, a crumbling Victorian venue near Finsbury Park which, as legend would have it, boasted hooks on the bar where crustie soap-dodgers could tie their 'dogs-on-a-string'. The Robey promoted a variety of multi-band line-ups right into the 1990s and hosted many a classic evening, often hosted by The Klingonz and friends such as Duncan's Drunks & Self-Destruct, but will probably always be remembered for their delightfully decrepit bogs which may well have been the inspiration for the 'toilet scene' in the movie 'Trainspotting'.

While Psychobilly was surviving in Europe and about to be reborn in the USA, back in the UK Psychobilly was about to reach a period of intensive care in the mid to late 1990s. All over Britain the scene was slowly dying and even major bands such as Restless, The Long Tall Texans and The Klingonz did the unforgivable and almost ceased to exist. Even The Meteors announced on their website in 2000 that they would no longer be performing live. Few bands toured the UK and the infamous Gt Yarmouth Psychobilly Weekenders ended after the 11th event in 1998 pulled in less than 300 punters, a far cry from the earlier Rumbles when audience figures could reach over 1000. However, Psychobilly is a resourceful beast and though in the UK, and even parts of Europe, times were hard the sickness was spreading further abroad.

Though there has always been a certain brotherhood (and sisterhood) within the Psychobilly community it would be a bare-arsed lie to suggest that the entire scene is a major 'love-in' of mutual harmony. Certainly inter-band rivalry has always existed, and particularly bitter feuds have been well documented, but antagonism and apathy have also been shared between bands and Psychobilly followers.

This breakdown of communication often centres on how far a genre mainly based on Punk and Rockabilly can exceed each style at either end. Suspicion and indifference have both been unleashed by Psychobilly puritans on any band deemed 'too Rockabilly' or 'too Punk'. Alternately, this mistrust of any bands stretching the boundaries a bit is often bamboozling for broad-minded Psychobilly fans attracted to the genre in the first place by its huge melting pot of Rock'n'Roll influences.

Certainly in the 1980s things were different as most bands on the scene had a double-bass, a stack of Rockabilly LPs and a pile of Punk 45s in the bedroom. Though many groups carved their own unique style from these key ingredients there was a large enough core audience across the UK and Europe to maintain the status quo. Any band who delivered lightweight Rockabilly or alternately pushed the sound to its extreme limits in concert often faced a thinned out audience who retreated to the bar until the next band appeared. Though possibly foreseeing the Psychobilly future with eerie accuracy, Skitzo's 'hardcore-billy' set at an early Hemsby – delivered with the ferocity of Napalm Death – caused many Psychobillies to raise their eyebrows in disbelief rather than run to the wrecking pit.

Psychobilly bands which formed in the early 1990s often found the existence of an 'old guard' of Psychobilly fans resistant to new approaches to the genre. In retrospect this seems bizarre as a similar attitude from the Rockabilly scene a decade earlier had effectively launched Psychobilly into existence.

THE NEXT DEGENERATION

While a large contingent of bands were keen to move forward, and audience demand existed for a 'second wave' of Psychobilly bands, there were also those unwilling to embrace a change in the scene.

No band persisted to push through this wall of indifference more than North-East of England troubadours The Hangmen. Formed in 1991, the band almost immediately found the Psycho-scene dwindling with many fans paying little attention to support bands, which The Hangmen often were, and reserving their fist-pounding energies for the headline act. Frontman Loz Dolan describes how they felt at the time: "Our band was regarded as 'Johnny-come-latelys' – starry eyed members of the audience imitating or emulating the old status quo rather than contributing to it".

As the cliche goes 'What don't kill you makes you stronger' and instead of imploding through lack of encouragement from the Psychobilly scene the band forged ahead beyond the circuit and into any venue where the words 'rock' and 'roll' were mentioned together. Though still part of the Psychobilly universe, the Hangmen also pummelled audiences of Goths, Punks and Heavy Rockers into submission with their unique brand of 'Rotten to the Bone Punk Rock'n'Roll' and soon gathered a motley band of followers from a variety of musical backgrounds.

The band's first album 'Gutbucket Rock'n'Roll' (1991) on Rockhouse Records is far closer to early Psychobilly and features a collection of early demos which the band generally felt was unrepresentative of their style. Then followed four more years of indifference from the Psychobilly scene in which The Hangmen began to finely tune their unique sound. 'Last Train To Purgatory' (1995) was the first result of this period of transition and it reflected the band's outside influences with its gothic horror subject matter and unashamedly heavier sound. This was the band's first release on their own Bone Tone Corporation label and their growing success, mostly maintained by continuous touring, led to another long-player on the label, 'Tested on Animals' (1998).

If the band had ever felt like outcasts on the Psycho-scene as the 21st Century dawned The Hangmen's brass-necked persistence saw them emerge as Psychobilly headliners with the added bonus of a loyal following of all types of Rock'n'Roll misfits gathered during their years in the musical wilderness. The Hangmen then signed a deal with the legendary Crazy Love Records and unleashed their fourth album 'Original Sins' (2000). By this time the band also had a fistful of releases on singles and on compilation albums and had settled on a line-up of Loz on guitar and vocals, Spoony on drums and Johnny Death on double-bass. However, Johnny would eventually make way for bass-slapping powerhouse Kirky.

In addition to their UK and European dates The Hangmen left the North-East of England far behind for a 1999 tour of the US and a return visit in 2000 which included a spot at New Jersey's infamous 'New York Rumble'. These concerts, and further gigs in the US and Canada, placed the band in an enviable position as support band of choice for visiting acts from the Hellcat stable such as Tiger Army and Nekromantix when they made their visits to the UK.

Despite little support from the mainstream music press, The Hangmen have remained on the road gigging for over a decade and continued to lay their blood-soaked back catalogue of songs down in the studio – 'Twitch of the Death Nerve', 'I Was A Teenage Suicide', 'Whore for the Devil'... just some of the titles employed by a band whose lyrical imagery is darker than a coal miner's trousers. Even after over 15 years their music shows no sign of diminishing as their seventh album approaches behind the long-players 'No Happy Endings' (2002) and 'Play Dead' (2004). During 2005 The Hangmen had a major line-up change when Spoony moved to Texas, Kirky moved on and the band ended up with new drummer Hell Burns and ex-Sugar Puff Demon/Lunkhead Steve 'The Original Sinner' Kincaide on bass.

Another band from the North of England who have trodden a similar path to The Hangmen are The Hyperjax. Their journey began in 1996 with singer/guitarist Sam Woods, double-bass player Bob Corner and short-term drummer Martin Cox. Cox was replaced within a year by Fido Banks and the band began to pay their dues knocking out 50s covers and a few original tunes on the 'rockin' scene' circuit of pubs'n'clubs. This slog around Britain to occasionally unappreciative audiences left the band spinning their wheels until 2000 when the departure of drummer Fido saw the entrance

HELL'S BENT ON ROCKIN' THE NEXT DEGENERATION

The Hangmen (Loz Dolan).

of tub-thumper Wally P. Parkinson and an ideal opportunity for a musical change of direction.

With growing audience indifference to their 'streetwise punkier sound' on the rockin' circuit, the band decided to push ahead with a set featuring a majority of their own compositions and breakout of the confines of the genre. This involved playing to audiences at a variety of venues and, much like The Hangmen, they discovered audiences from a wide background could appreciate the band's Psychobilly-influenced sound which also featured elements of classic Punk and Rock'n'Roll. The gamble paid off and The Hyperjax gained a loyal following both in the re-emerging Psychobilly community and within the wider alternative music scene. The early part of the decade saw the band gig across the UK, Europe and America before finally delivering their debut album 'Generation X-Rated' (2002) on Raucous Records.

After seven years of a slow-burning career the release of the album propelled the band forward and in 2003 highlights on their calendar included a week long blast of gigs across Britain and two nights playing at The Carling Reading Festival, the UK's largest alternative music gathering. They also achieved a feat seldom witnessed by any band with Psychobilly connections, that of gaining mainstream music press attention, when they appeared on a covermount CD freebie for Uncut magazine. This glossy monthly devoted to music and movie musos, compiled a 'Tribute To The Clash' which featured The Hyperjax' version of 'Capital Radio' alongside contributions from Punk legends Stiff Little Fingers and Joe Strummer himself.

The band's appearances in the US in 2004 also paid dividends with support slots alongside Hellcat Record's Tiger Army and Horrorpops, during their UK tours. Yet again the band gained some serious column inches with reviews for these shows in the mainstream headbanging mag 'Metal Hammer' and Punk glossy 'Big Cheese'. In recent years The Hyperjax have also expanded to a four-piece with Wally making way for new drummer Bundie and Matt Cooley joining to add an extra guitar to the band.

From their late 1990s appearance as rowdy upstarts, The Hyperjax are now mainstays of the Psychobilly scene and a band with a growing following within many genres of alternative music. They are also a band with a healthy disrespect for any musical confines and seem to revel in any opportunity to ruffle feathers amongst Psychobilly puritans in the same way that they shook up stern Rockabilly types at their earliest gigs. Certainly the introduction of a rapper called Roskrypz at some of their gigs raised a few eyebrows initially which probably suited the band's sense of mischief as much as it suited their musical adventurousness. Always looking to push their sound beyond any confines, The Hyperjax story appears to be far from over especially with their new album, 'The Bottom Line', released by Raucous Records in early 2007.

Despite being starved of the oxygen of much of the mainstream music press publicity available, which can often elevate new bands to godhead status within months, bands such as The Hangmen and The Hyperjax have built their lasting success the hard way – through endless gigging (often at the blunt end of the touring circuit), local press, specialist magazines, fanzine reviews and sheer bloody-minded persistence which would have most flavour-of-the-month Indie starlets throwing in the towel and pissing off back to Art School. What they have gained is a network of support across the globe from followers who genuinely dig what they do and not a rabble of fickle fashion-followers ready to ditch them when the next big thing rolls into town.

Though The Hangmen and The Hyperjax weathered the 1990s well there were also a number of bands who came and went in the decade. One band whose career progressed erratically throughout the decade were Wales-based perverts Popeye's Dik. They formed in Wrexham on the first day of 1990 after a New Year's Eve party and featured John McVicker on vocals, Mike Allen on slap-bass, Terry Allen on guitar and drummer Diane Wharton. Diane left midway through 1990, not because the band's repertoire was a smut-filled bonanza but to have a baby. Lee Fletcher took over on drums and the band began to demo their first songs.

Popeye's Dik eventually signed their first deal for a single with Kix 4 U. The result was 'Lose Your Load' (1994) but even though the cover featured McVicker, Mike Allen and Fletcher the band had already fractured and John was joined for the recording by drummer Tom O'Carroll and Stuart Jones on bass and guitar. 'Lose Your Load' set the tone for what would become a back catalogue predominantly obsessed with sex and perversion.

The band drifted apart and in 1999 McVicker recruited another trio of musicians to work on a second single which eventually surfaced as 'Country Smokin' Blues' on Spanking Herman Records. Some gigs accompanied its release but

Popeye's Dik. Sleaze overload (John McVicker).

HELL'S BENT ON ROCKIN'   THE NEXT DEGENERATION

Steve Whitehouse, always slappin' (Jan Van Hal).

then the band, once again, disintegrated. That may have been the end of the story but in a bizarre twist, John managed to prise a lump of lottery cash from the hands of the Arts Council to fund studio time. Despite being a one man band, McVicker chose Alan Wilson's Western Star Studio and the studio boss offered to provide a backing band as well. The band turned out to be a set of Frenzy and The Sharks all-stars with Alan Wilson on guitar, Steve Whitehouse on bass and Frenzy's Rob Chapman on drums. This line-up recorded three tracks which McVicker presented to the Arts Council. What they made of 'Searchin' For The King' (a song concerned with digging up dead Elvis), 'King Sperm' and a cover of The Sex Pistol's 'Lonely Boy' is unsure but they coughed up enough cash for John to establish his own label, Puerto Rican Porn Dealer Records, and press the tracks as a CD single in the Summer of 2001.

Guido at Crazy Love then picked up the band for an album deal featuring the same line-up. With Alan Wilson as the main songwriter, collaborating with the others, he managed to maintain the suitably sleazy atmosphere which was present on the band's other releases. Understandably, the musicianship on the album 'A Fix From The Fez' (2003) was far better than that of McVicker's previous cohorts. Despite never having played live in the 21st Century Popeye's Dik have appeared on a number of compilations in recent years and John also gathered together a collection of the band's tracks and released 'The Good, The Bad and The Ugly' in 2006.

The Batfinks from the North East of England were the band that drove The Sugar Puff Demons to their debut album glory. Unfortunately it was not through offering inspiration but because the Demons were horrified that their local rivals had snared a deal with Link Records before them and immediately badgered Chuck Flintstone into gaining their own deal. Though there was no love lost between the bands, and their sound was very different, they both shared elements of metal and hard-core in their sound and far less traditional Rockabilly influences.

The band's debut, 'Wazzed N' Blasted (Day Of The Mushroom)', appeared in 1989 and was a rough'n'ready affair which rapidly shot through its fourteen tracks. To be fair it was probably a little before its time as their style of mental-thrashabilly would no doubt have gained a few more followers in the more broad-minded 1990s scene but in 1989 many folks still expected a more traditional Psychobilly sound. As was often the case with Link artists, a 'Live and Rockin' album followed in 1990 but the band were soon to split.

The Surfin' Wombatz were another part of the second wave of UK Psychobilly. This South London band were another combo weaned on The Meteors, Guana Batz, Demented et al, who decided to do their own thing. Following an appearance on the 'Zorch Factor II' album they arrived on the scene in 1990 with their debut album 'Lager Loutz' on Nervous Records. Although they could be found on the bill of many major Psychobilly gatherings a follow-up album was not initially forthcoming from this beerabilly combo but surfing on the recent Psychobilly boom they were back in the studio in 2006.

The deep South-West of Britain was never a Psychobilly hot spot but it has had its moments with most of them focusing on the efforts of journalist and long-term Psychobilly Simon 'C.S. Simes' Nott to keep Devon rocking with a number of gigs at The White Ball Inn and The Tube in Tiverton. The Frantic Flintstones, The Meteors, The Sharks and many more made their way deep into Devonshire and the support often came from the Cornwall trio Break-Out.

This Rockabilly three-piece were initially a quartet but by 1992 they had settled on a line-up featuring drummer Sean 'Mudman' Lee, guitarist Ant Hill and double-bass player/vocalist Andy Fifield.

Though Cornish locals had seen little like Break-Out before, the elements of Punk, Blues and Garage in their sound was enough to secure them regular local gigs. Their appearance at the Tiverton gigs soon led to many support slots including a tour with The Frantic Flintstones in London and Germany but though their debut album never came to fruition Andy and Mudman still maintain Break-Out to this day as a going concern. Mudman also established a rockin' club at the Waterfront bar in Truro for some time, yet again exposing the good folks of Cornwall and their many visitors to Neo, Psycho and many other forms of 'billy. Sean has remained a steadfast fixture on the Psychobilly scene both as a roadie and rampant gig goer and was also a contributor to 'Deathrow Database' magazine. Recently he has reappeared back behind the kit for Plymouth Horrorbillies The Devilriders.

Russ Surfer of The Death Valley Surfers (Russ Ward).

Even though the late 1990s was often a quieter time for UK Psychobilly there were still new bands on the scene. In the mid 1990s former King Kurt roadie Russ 'Surfer' Ward had left The Highliners and decided upon a new challenge, establishing a new band and moving from behind the drum kit to become lead vocalist and frontman. The Death Valley Surfers were formed late in 1998 with Russ on vocals/guitar, Thomas Lorioux on double bass (now with Kings Of Nuthin'), sexy she-rocker Kathy X on lead guitar, drummer Sprex and saxophonist Ricky. Since that original line-up, DVS have had a bewildering number of personnel changes featuring former members of many other bands including The Blue Devils, The Pharaohs, The Lurkers and The Arousers.

In 1999 the band's first mini-CD 'Goin' Nowhere… Fast' appeared on their own Punkabilly Records and featured five tracks as did their following CD-EP 'Dead Man's Surf' (2001). The tracks from the second EP were recorded by Alan Wilson at his Western Star Studios and the band also appeared on three of the studio's various artists albums as well as appearances on two volumes of Black Sky Records' 'High Voltage' compilations.

Although gigging for the Death Valley Surfers has occasionally been erratic, the band have notched up an impressive collection of air miles hitting a variety of countries including Poland, Germany, Holland and Argentina. DVS have also been something of a house band for some of the events at London's top Psychobilly gatherings, Klubtastic and The Klub, where Russ is one of the organisers. These events have literally kept the London scene alive at times and have been major affairs – a long way from Russ' early days holding illicit Psychobilly parties in after-hours office blocks. Late in 2006 the band finally completed pre-production on their first full album, 'Biffin's Bridge' and after eight years on the scene, and with their most settled line-up to date, The Death Valley Surfers could be ready to move up a gear real soon.

Psychobilly had almost flatlined during the 1990s, though things were definitely looking up towards the end of the decade. With some major rumblings growing across America, the Psycho-scene was tumbling head-first into a new era.

CHAPTER EIGHT

HELL'S BENT ON ROCKIN'

YANKED INTO THE PIT
PSYCHOBILLY HITS AMERICA

Undeniably, when tracing the roots of Psychobilly almost every influence on the genre appears to have its origins Stateside. With the US as the birthplace of Rockabilly, Rock'n'Roll and (arguably) Punk Rock it seems unusual that America was the last place anyone expected Psychobilly to flourish. Leaving aside the perennial argument over The Cramps' position in Psycho-history, and bearing in mind their reticence to stand at the forefront of the movement, Psychobilly in the early 1980s was a uniquely British phenomenon.

As the cult spread, early European bands were eagerly welcomed on the scene but by 1985 the idea of an American Psychobilly band still seemed to many to be an unusual proposition. This was not based in any form of British arrogance relating to the UK as the home of Psychobilly but simply disbelief that any hard-rockin' underground bands could survive in America's corporate rock universe where big-haired, cock-rock bands with platinum album sales were the supreme rulers. White trash Rock'n'Roll fans were always far more likely to be members of the 'Kiss Army' than the 'Wreckin' Crew'.

Although Hardcore Punk in the 1980s had a respectable underground scene in America, for a nation just embracing the joys of the mohican and skinhead there seemed to be little room for the flat-top and little or no chance of hard-up British Psychobilly bands cracking the scene. Only The Misfits pursued a similar form of Rock'n'Horror within the Punk scene and, like The Cramps, they inhabited their own dark genre far from the Psychobilly label. Meanwhile, Rockabilly on the other side of the pond was stuck in revivalist hell, forcing any band with a doghouse bass to stand in The Stray Cats' mighty shadow. If an American band were to crack the UK scene it would take determination, risk and king-size 'cojones'. Luckily, The Quakes were up to the job.

The roots of American Psychobilly, certainly for many of Europe's legions of Psychos, must begin with The Quakes. The story of the band is almost too long and complex to chronicle but it all started in Buffalo, New York back in the Autumn of 1986. Paul Roman, guitarist/vocalist and core member of the group had been back and forth over the Atlantic to London on a series of failed missions to establish a Rockabilly band in the UK.

Without much success, he had settled back in his hometown fronting a 'pompadours & make-up' band very much in the form of The Stray Cats or The Polecats. Known as The Quiffs, the band were boppin' nowhere fast until they realised that although their playing was (at the time) rudimentary some of the kids on the local punk scene liked their faster-paced live songs. Ditching the fancy threads for boots 'n' jeans and pushing their Rockabilly set harder and faster soon gained The Quakes a strong local following and the belief that their new direction was paying off.

Ripping a page from The Stray Cats history book, The Quakes decided to pack up and head for London in 1987, a time when the city was the nucleus for all manner of Rockin' genres. At this time the band line-up had settled on Rob Peltier on bass with Dave 'The Ace' Hoy on drums backing up Roman. With one solitary contact in the UK, Roy Williams of Nervous, the band managed to secure their debut European gig at the massive Weize Psychobilly festival in Belgium on a recently vacated slot. The band played a rough, but well received, set but when returning to the UK they were victims of the first in a long line of deportations back to the US.

The Quakes, 1988. L-R: Rob Peltier, Paul Roman, Dave 'The Ace' Hoy (Stewart Barker).

After making a shamefaced return to Buffalo so soon, relief was at hand when a tour of Belgium and Germany, supporting The Coffin Nails, was offered to the band. As the tour approached Rob Peltier quit and Roman orchestrated a rapid shake-up of the band bringing Dave 'The Ace' out front on the slap-bass and recruiting new drummer Chris Van Cleve, who had previously played in The Quiffs. After the tour, Chris went home leaving Paul and Dave broke and scratching their asses living in a squat in London while waiting for Rob Peltier to return. Around 1988, once again, Roy Williams played a key role in The Quakes story with an offer to record their debut album which would eventually appear simply titled as 'The Quakes'.

With Peltier back in the fold, the band rattled through the recording of the album and started to play live in and around London, including an appearance at the Klub Foot. However, when a proposed European tour to promote the album fell through, broke and pissed-off Peltier and Hoy headed home leaving Roman stuck in a squat (again) sitting on an excellent debut album but with no band to promote it.

What follows is not so much the rest of The Quakes story but a tale of Paul Roman's persistence in the rockin' music biz. Alone in London, Roman then received news that Dave 'The Ace' Hoy had been killed when hit by a car. Many would have seen this as a bad omen and returned home defeated but Paul persisted with his music career and began gigging round the capital with a new band, 'Paul Roman and the Prowlers'. Around this time Paul also began recording for a solo album but, when returning from a gig in Belgium, he was once again deported back to the US.

Back in Buffalo The Quakes were reformed with old bandmates Rob Peltier and Chris Van Cleve, then Roman (once again) flew to the UK to complete his solo album. Unfortunately this record deal quickly evaporated and, yet again, Paul found himself mooching around London with fuck all to do. However, a chance meeting with Demented Are Go's Ant Thomas landed him the role of the band's stand-in guitarist for a short UK tour. After this brief engagement, Paul found himself back in Buffalo with The Quakes in the Autumn of 1989.

The new decade brought new hope to the band and 1990 saw the band release their second LP 'Voice of America' followed by UK gigs at the legendary first two 'Rumbles' in Hemsby, Gt Yarmouth and extensive gigs back in the US. The band were on a roll with further tours in Europe and Japan in 1991.

A live CD from the Japanese tour was released by Planet Records and soon major label Sony was sniffing around the band.

The company courted the band and secured a deal which led to a more extensive touring schedule and the album 'New Generation' in 1992. With major label backing came the opportunity for major production values but the well-polished sound of 'New Generation' was not to everyone's liking particularly when the European release of the album, courtesy of Nervous Records, reached the ears of many fans of the band who preferred the rockin' roughhouse sound which had made The Quakes so popular in the first place.

Despite being as near to mainstream success as seemed possible for any band with Psychobilly connections, the band's ever-changing line-up may have frustrated Paul Roman's vision of a truly great Rockabilly/Psychobilly band. From 1993, Rob Peltier and Chris Van Deve had drifted in and out of the line-up while members of other bands have filled their vacant positions. The Quakes still continued to record and play sporadically, the most notable highlights being their 1995 album 'Quiff Rock' and 2001's 'Last of the Human Beings', released on their own label Orexxx Records. Both albums feature the more boot-stompin', back-to-basics style which initially attracted most folks to the band in the first place. Gigging has continued with major appearances in the past few years at New Jersey's 'American Rumble', the 'American Nightmare' festival in Pomona and three spots at the Callela festival in Spain in 2000, 2003 and 2006.

Roman moved to Finland in 2004 and initially focused on his new group The Paul Roman 3 but by the summer of 2005 Paul was recording again almost entirely on his own, as he had done on 'Last Of The Human Beings', using a few session drummers. The result was a hard rockin' new album, 'Psyops'(2005) on Orrexx Records, released at a time when American Psychobilly has never been so popular.

Paul also began playing live again with drummer Chris Van Cleve and Finnish double-bass man Aki Savolainen. Most recently Paul spends his time between Finland and the States and The Quakes have a new line-up featuring double-bass player Mark Burke (Phantom Rockers) and drummer Mike Minnick and despite their long and turbulent career the band are as important to the scene now as they were back in 1986 when they more or less started the whole damn thing in America.

While The Quakes built their reputation in Europe and the Far East, back home another band created a sound with similar Psychobilly influences within the US Punk scene. While never truly Psychobilly, Elvis Hitler were damn near it and surely played a larger part in the acceptance of Psychobilly in America than they were ever given credit for. Though formed under the guise of the titular character, the band actually consisted of singer/guitarist Jim 'Elvis Hitler' Leedy backed up by two brothers, John and Warren DeFever on guitar and bass respectively, alongside drummer Damian Lang.

Elvis Hitler's debut album 'Disgraceland' appeared on the

The Quakes' 'Psyops' album from 2005 (Jet Electro Productions).

YANKED INTO THE PIT

HELL'S BENT ON ROCKIN'

Wanghead label in 1987, and while it was far closer to their Punk roots it certainly illustrated their developing direction into their own brand of white trash Rock'n'Roll. With tracks such as 'Hot Rod to Hell' and 'Live Fast, Die Young' the band acknowledged their rockin' influences while the cover artwork featuring an Elvis-esque skull with a Hitler moustache backed by a cartoon Hitler dressed in Elvis gear, was pure Punk. This artwork was always going to offend someone (particularly anti-Nazi Elvis fans) but this was probably the band's intention. Motivated more by mischief than any dodgy politics and despite

The Hellbillys hit the UK (Mason Storm Archive).

the scandalous cover, the album was picked up in 1988 by Restless Records, a rapidly expanding Indie label with interests in a variety of alternative and underground acts.

The following year saw Elvis Hitler back on vinyl for Restless with the album that probably was as near to Psychobilly as they would get, 'Hellbilly'. For a band whose sound would evolve from Punk to Rock'n'Roll and almost into Thrash Metal, 'Hellbilly' was their ground zero release, an album which combined a host of white-trash references (hot-rods, horror, violence...) with an ultra-heavy, well-produced sound. These fourteen tracks of hillbilly fury were stadium-rockin' Psychobilly, with the title track as its crowning glory. Other tracks with real ass-kickin' potential include 'Gear Jammin' Hero', a cover of 'The Ballad of the Green Berets' and 'Showdown', an Elvis Hitler penned track which recklessly steals the riff from '(Ghost) Riders in the Sky'.

Though touched by brilliance, 'Hellbilly' got a lukewarm response throughout Europe, perhaps because many perceived the album a little too 'metal' for what was a far more lo-fi Psychobilly scene at the time or because the album came from a company not known for their Psychobilly output. Its subject matter of white trash tales may also have left many folks cold but in an age when trailer park tramps like Eminem, Kid Rock and even Britney Spears are treated like royalty perhaps it may still be an album ripe for reappraisal.

In 1992, Restless released the band's third and final album 'Supersadomasochisticexpialidocious'. By this time, Elvis Hitler appeared to focus on the Punk and Thrash Metal elements of their sound and for 'billy fans only the hilarious 'Shove that Sax (Up Your Ass)' and the sewage-soaked, surf instrumental 'Dickweed' provided much in the way of rockin'.

Alongside their ever genre-defying sound the band's name was always going to be a problem, especially in the hypersensitive 1990s. Elvis Hitler reserved the right to name their band whatever the fuck they wanted to but while they kept the monicker they still made sure that fans understood right-wing politics were not on the agenda. Regardless of this, even in the new millennium, the name still attracted unwanted attention. In August 2001 the webmaster of the Elvis Hitler website announced: "First off let me just say that the shit that is being posted on both the message board and the Guestbook makes me sick! The band has NOTHING to do with Nazis or racism! Because of this I'm taking down the Message Board. I've since deleted all the offensive posts from the Guestbook but if this shit continues it's gone too." Soon after, the site ground to a halt.

Long before this, Elvis Hitler himself was laid to rest and, ditching the controversial name, Leedy and John DeFever teamed up with drummer Tod Glass to form Splatter. This revitalised three-piece continued in the Elvis Hitler vein of hard rockin' trailer-park boogie and produced the 'From Hell to Eternity' album for Sector 2 Records in 1994. Described as Reverend Horton Heat meets Motörhead, their sound was far closer to Elvis Hitler's 'Hellbilly' output in sound and in subject matter with tunes such as 'Hard Rockin' Daddy', 'Hot & Sweaty Already' and 'A Million Redneck Women'. Despite this, their trail soon went cold and Elvis Hitler/Splatter unfortunately may both remain bands who peaked too soon for the American Psychobilly revolution.

Meanwhile, on the West Coast, one band were battling to establish their own brand of fast'n'furious Psychobilly for so long that they practically deserve long-service medals. While The Quakes were probably the first hard rockin' American outfit introduced to European Psychobillies, arguably the first full-on American Psychobilly act were The Hellbillys. Breaking out from San Francisco's Bay Area in 1989 the band unashamedly pledged their allegiance to the Psychobilly flag and have continued to do so with dogged determination until this day.

Lead singer Barrie 'Scary' Evans was previously a member of Punk band Christ on Parade which proved a bonus when securing early gigs in the 'Psychobilly-Free-Zone' that was the States in the early 1990s. Although anyone deemed 'too punk' for the sizable but traditional Rockabilly scene of the time were made to feel about as welcome as a fart in a spacesuit, Punk promoters were often willing to take a chance on The Hellbillys. As the decade progressed the band also found themselves welcome at American scooter events. These punters were obviously far more open to the varied delights of the UK influenced street culture which contributed to the global scooter scene.

The Hellbillys slid onto vinyl through Dionysus Records in 1991 with the three track single 'Rhythm & Ooze'. In the same year the band eventually made it over the ocean to the UK to make their debut European appearance at the 4th Big Rumble in Gt. Yarmouth. Though still 'early days' for US Psychobilly, this weekender also introduced Euro-punters to fellow Yank 'billies Elmer's Shotgun from California, and the sexed-up sound of Wisconsin in the shapely form of The Psycho Bunnies. As if this was not enough to persuade unbelievers that things were really kicking off in America, The Quakes topped the bill reminding everyone that US Psychobilly was brewing up a storm.

The Hellbillys' debut LP 'Land of Demons' appeared on the Japanese label Planet Records in 1992 and the band continued to tour across America and even down Mexico way. Along the way, they released further singles 'Knocked Up and Gun Crazy', 'It's Alive' and 'Evil' for a variety of labels. The band also made their presence felt on a number of compilation albums, particularly on Raucous Records' 'Only Freeways To Skinner Kat' and Hairball 8 Records' 'Hotter Than Hell', both LPs which were groundbreaking in different ways. Raucous' 1994 album was the first ever compilation of American Psychobilly, and it introduced The Bea Pickles, The Barnyard Ballers, Cosmic Voodoo and The Psycho Bunnies alongside more established acts such as The Quakes and The Hellbillys themselves. Hairball 8's 1996 offering, featuring a variety of rockin' outcasts alongside The Hellbillys is also credited as the first home-grown Psychobilly compilation produced by an American label.

In 1995 the all important second album 'Torture Garden' appeared on the US label Ransom Note Recordings and presented further examples of the band's hardcore Psychobilly sound. Hinting at influences from the Euro-scene, Demented Are Go and Mad Sin particularly, it was a raucous, kick-in-the-pants, collection of new tracks that was luridly packaged with some excellent cover artwork from Psychobilly artist Paul Van Horn.

The most notable strength The Hellbillys appear to have had was their determined attitude in pursuing their hardcore Psychobilly sound despite the general antipathy to the genre which existed in the 1990s. Nevertheless, the band recorded little for the rest of the decade and only their CD compilation of singles and unreleased tracks, 'Cavalcade Of Perversions', kept the flame burning.

The new century saw the band embark on their groundbreaking 'Blood Trilogy' albums. 'Blood Trilogy Vol: 1' appeared in 2001 on the FOAD label and was a well-produced affair both in sound quality and cover artwork, courtesy of Pusshead the twisted artistic genius behind (amongst others) many of Metallica's most disturbing record covers. 2004 saw the theme continue with yet more Pusshead artwork and another collection of powerfully dark songs on 'Blood Trilogy Vol. 2' (Split 7 Records). Since then the band have continued to peddle their twisted East Bay Psychobilly to this day.

Though times were hard in early 1990s America, bands like The Quakes and The Hellbillys were not alone and were joined by ex-Demented Are Go bass man Billy Favata who had made the move to Chicago. He formed the Psychobilly band Wreckin' Ball but had a far harder time establishing the group at a time when American Psychobilly was in its infancy. They did produce the album 'Born To Wreck' for Tombstone Records in 1994 but since then nothing more, even though the album was a solid slab of trad Psychobilly with a heavy edge and some powerful slapping.

Though the Psychobilly scene in the US was initially slim pickings it would be very wrong to suggest that there was little in the way of other forms of Rock'n'Roll. The Rockabilly 'Swing' scene was big news and Surf, Trash, Instrumental and horror-themed Rock'n'Roll have always enjoyed a huge Stateside following leading to bands such as Man Or Astroman?, The Mummys, Southern Culture On The Skids, Rocket From The Crypt and Los Straitjackets gathering a huge international following. From a similar background to these groups were one band who have also made huge waves on the American Psychobilly scene, Reverend Horton Heat. Like Elvis Hitler, Reverend Horton Heat take their name from lead singer and guitarist Jim Heath's alter-ego. This holy rolling nickname was suggested to Jim by a Texan bar owner who felt that the band's high-octane live performances regularly whipped the crowd into the same state as 'I have seen the light', bible-thumping congregation.

HELL'S BENT ON ROCKIN' YANKED INTO THE PIT

This trio of Texan rockers came to life in Dallas during the mid-1980s. The original line-up featured Mr Heath alongside 'Swingin' Jack Barton on upright bass and Bobby Baranowski on drums. They released only one record together, 'Big Little Baby' (1988) for Four Dot Records, before they parted company. Jim then recruited the soon-to-be-legendary Jimbo Wallace on double-bass and drummer Patrick 'Taz' Bentley, then the Reverend Horton Heat story began in earnest.

After regular gigging around a variety of roadhouses, sleazy bars and shithole venues The Rev was picked up by Sub Pop Records, a fine, long-standing Indie/Punk label who now (unfortunately) only seem to be remembered as the home of Nirvana before they exploded onto the major label scene and worldwide notoriety. At the time, Reverend Horton Heat did seem to be an unusual signing to the label as they were probably as far away from the sound of Kurt Cobain, and countless other 'Grunge' labelmates, as any band could possibly be. However, the Rev would prove to be a band who would move beyond the Psychobilly genre and even approach almost mainstream success themselves.

The deal with Sup Pop resulted in two albums for Reverend Horton Heat, 'Smoke 'Em If You Got 'Em' in 1992 followed by 'The Full-Custom Gospel Sounds Of The Reverend Horton Heat' (1993). Though far from much of the European Psychobilly of the 1990s, these were hard-rockin', well-produced albums which also benefited from Sub Pop's not inconsiderable promotional power and the label's existing worldwide fanbase. Many Indie rockers in the UK who would rather shit themselves than allow a Psychobilly LP into their homes would happily play the sounds of Reverend Horton Heat, as it came with the famous label's seal of approval. This must also have been the case across the States as the band was introduced to an audience which they themselves referred to as "gutterpunks, skatekids, metalheads, Rockabilly scenesters, guitar geeks and recovering Guns'n'Roses fans".

Benefiting from this increased exposure and building on their shit-hot live reputation, the Rev then signed a deal with major label Interscope Records in 1994. In the same year, Mr Horton Heat himself made his acting debut in the trailer-trash, crime flick 'Love And A .45'. One of the band's tracks also featured in the film which set them up for future appearances on movie soundtracks such

Testify to the Reverend Horton Heat (Die In Style).

as 'Ace Ventura: When Nature Calls', 'Auto Focus' and 'The Flintstones In Viva Rock Vegas'.

In the mid-1990s the Horton Heat sound was evolving, broadening its appeal with not only elements of Psychobilly, Rock'n'Roll and Country but also some of the booming Rockabilly/Swing style that was rapidly gaining popularity, partly due to the hit movie 'Swingers' but also the success of Interscope labelmate The Brian Setzer Orchestra. The first fruits of this deal appeared in 1994 in the smut-soaked form of 'Liquor In The Front – Poker In The Rear', a cross-label release between Interscope and Sub Pop with a rock-hard production job courtesy of Al Jourgensen from noise-terrorists Ministry. The same year, drummer Taz moved on after five years with the band and Scott Churilla became his replacement.

The swing vibe particularly made it's presence felt in the 1996 album 'It's Martini Time' and even resulted in a minor hit single in the form of the title track. In the late 1990s the Rev continued to progress, spreading their frantic live gospel across the globe, garnering countless ecstatic gig reviews and crossing over to anyone who ever held a secret love for bone-crunching Rock'n'Roll. Jim made an appearance on the TV programme 'The Drew Carey Show' and 'It's Martini Time' also crept into America's album chart, The Billboard 200, a feat almost unheard of for any band with a rockin' style.

1998 saw the release of the band's final Interscope album 'Space Heater' before they moved on to pastures new. Seizing the opportunity while the band considered a new label deal, Sub Pop slapped out the album 'Holy Roller' which was a cunningly disguised compilation featuring the cream of their previous releases with the label plus two unreleased tracks. By the spring of 2000, Reverend Horton Heat's sixth studio album was in the stores. Signing up with Time Bomb Recordings, home of Social Distortion and The Amazing Crowns, the result of this union was the Western swing flavoured 'Spend A Night In The Box'.

The deal with Time Bomb was not to be a lengthy affair as the Rev moved on to Artemis Records in 2001 and started work on their following opus, the album 'Lucky 7' (2002). Artemis was a New York based label with a firm stake in American Roots music, courtesy of their roster which included Steve Earle, The Fabulous Thunderbirds and John Hiatt. Impressive surely but they had experienced nothing with the raw power of Horton Heat and despite producing an album with many strong tracks (particularly 'Like A Rocket' which became the unofficial theme of the Daytona 500 car racing event) the band moved on once again.

Though they had been wandering like railroad hoboes between labels for some time, Reverend Horton Heat eventually found some stability in 2003 with Yep Roc Records of North Carolina and delivered 'Revival' (2004), their roughest, rawest, rockin' effort for the best part of a decade. This was closely followed by the completely off-the-wall Christmas album 'We Three Kings' (2005) which guarantees non-stop festive rockin' for your stereo for at least one month of the year.

In 2006 Reverend Horton Heat rolled on relentlessly. Interscope tried to squeeze a bit more life from the band with a 'Best Of…' culled from the band's time with the label and after over a decade with the band Scott Churilla left to join The Supersuckers and was replaced by Paul Simmons from The Legendary Shack Shakers. Beyond this it was business as usual for the Texan trio – more shows, more booze and plenty more rockin' in their unique style. To this day the Reverend remains a fusion of American roots music shot through with a furious intensity and while mostly standing apart from the Psychobilly scene, in much the same way as The Cramps, they undoubtedly appeal to huge numbers of Psychos along with many other Rock'n'Roll degenerates. Amen to that brothers and sisters!

The Amazing Royal Crowns were another American outfit similar to Rev Horton Heat, who had real Rockabilly roots with a touch of swing but enough of a Punk edge to appeal to hordes of Psychobillies alongside something approaching a mainstream audience. Formed in Providence, Rhode Island in the early 1990s, they borrowed from the same influences as many Psychobilly bands (Rockabilly, Country, Surf etc) yet still maintained their own sound. Their four-piece line-up featured frontman Jason 'King' Kendall on vocals alongside Jack 'Swinger' Hanlon on upright bass, Johnny Maguire on guitar and, after an army of failed sticksmen they settled with Judd Williams on drums.

Having built their own following touring across the States the band moved towards their debut

HELL'S BENT ON ROCKIN'   YANKED INTO THE PIT

release and a shit-storm of epic proportions. 'Amazing Royal Crowns' their self-titled first album had three releases, first as a private pressing of 1000 copies followed by a signing to Indie label, Monolyth, which shifted ten times that amount. The band eventually moved to Velvel Records in 1998 and the label agreed to re-release the album and give it the major promotional backing it deserved. However, as the album began to sell well it popped them onto the radar of the Californian Rocking Swing combo Royal Crown Revue. The band members and major label record honchos behind Royal Crown Review felt that the Amazing Royal Crowns' name could lead to confusion in the minds of some punters who may inadvertently cough up some dollars for 'Amazing' albums and concert tickets instead of lining the pockets of the 'Revue'.

A showdown was set for an East/West, Indie/Major battle which, unsurprisingly when backed by the global might of Warner Bros, resulted in Royal Crown Revue winning a court case which neither the Amazing Royal Crowns or their label had the financial muscle to contest. Despite the ruling, The Amazing Royal Crowns shipped out their final release under their original name, the excellent 'Do The Devil' single, before trimming their name to the more legally acceptable Amazing Crowns. However, the name change did little to halt the band's popularity and they continued to increase their following of Psychobillies, Punks and other alternative types.

In 1999, after Velvel went bust and Johnny Maguire walked out, the band signed to Time Bomb Recordings and began work on their second album with Mighty Mighty Bosstones' bass player Joe Gittleman in the producers chair and new guitarist J.D. Burgess. The result was the cheekily titled 'Royal', an album which was a powerful sounding blend of their previous influences but far closer to the alternative Rock'n'Roll of the likes of Rev Horton Heat and The Living End than their debut, which had contained a stronger Psychobilly edge. The band also released a live album 'Payback Live' on their own, a rough, raw recording of one of their gigs at Providence in front of a hometown audience.

Despite their growing fanbase and two fine albums The Amazing Crowns surprisingly called it a day in the Autumn of 2001 with a final 'Fuck You' concert under their original name. The 'Royal' was back for one night only and, far from outstaying their welcome, they bowed out at the very peak of their career. Too much touring for too little gain and the usual record company woes resulted in the band simply burning out. Not long after the final gig, vocalist Jason Kendall set to work on his new band The Deterrents, enlisting the help of one-time Amazing Crowns' guitarist Dennis Kelly and veteran Cro-Mags drummer Mark 'Evvo' Evans. With The Deterrents pushing a far Punkier sound the Rockabilly beat of The Amazing (Royal) Crowns is just a memory but with better luck and less record label meddling the band would surely have been perched atop America's recent new wave of Psychobilly.

While Psychobilly in the US was sparse in the early 1990s there were some Rockabilly acts with enough cohones to attract a Psycho following and one such act was a trio of Chicago roughnecks – Three Blue Teardrops. Once described as 'hard core Rockabilly' they had a rugged sound with enough hard slapping and brutality to attract Psychobilly audiences on both sides of the Atlantic.

Formed in 1991, the band featured guitarist/vocalist Dave Sisson, bassist Rick Uppling and drummer Randy Sabo. Performing mostly their own material from the very start, the band recorded a dozen tracks and put them on the streets as a cassette album 'Heads Up For '53'. A copy of this eventually made its way to Roy Williams and their debut album 'One Part Fist' on Nervous Records was recorded in Bath, with Alan Wilson at the controls, while the band were in the UK for an appearance at the 6th Big Rumble in 1993. While far from home, the band was captured during a week of recording and the album has continued to win fans among Psychos old and new with fourteen portions of leather-gloved knuckle sandwich.

The album was released in the spring of 1994 but by the autumn of that year Randy Sabo, suffering from a debilitating condition and a general disillusionment with the music biz, left the band to be replaced by Rick's workmate Kevin Lee Myers. This line-up recorded the band's second album '(Stiletto) Poised In Hate' (1995) for Teen Rebel Records, a CD that included some re-recorded versions of tracks from 'One Part Fist' alongside tracks from their earliest tape-only release from 1992.

1997 saw the band's third album released, 'Greetings From Milemarker', but life was never easy for the band, especially in the early days when they were too rough for the Rockabillies and too rockin' for the Psychos, and even gigging around the US was a hard slog often leaving the band out of pocket. Along with other record label and family issues the band ground to a halt in 1999. Nevertheless, by 2004 the band were back in action, re-united with original drummer Randy Sabo and back in the studio to produce their fourth album 'Rustbelt Trio' (2006) which they released themselves. Now back on the road, the band are part of a much more open-minded rockin' movement and no doubt their status as veterans of the early American scene will attract a new generation of fans.

Another band who faced lean times on the early American Psychobilly scene were San Diego perverts The Barnyard Ballers. The Ballers began in 1992 when vocalist Spike and guitarist Rob got together with a shared interest in European Psychobilly, a form of music deeply underground in the States at the time. Sharing similar experiences to The Hellbillys, The Barnyard Ballers often found a more appreciative following amongst American Punk audiences as opposed to those on the Rockabilly scene. No surprise with a set mostly preoccupied with bestiality, murder, sex, drugs and booze – their own brand of 'Calipornication'.

Within the first eighteen months of their time together, Spike and Rob made drummer Ricky and double-bass player Max full-time Ballers. Their debut album 'Rock Out With Yer Cock Out' followed soon after and was a low-budget production on San Diego based label Insane Records. The band were also captured early in their career on the 1994 Raucous Records compilation of fledgling American acts 'Only Freeways To Skinner Kat'. Along the way Max vacated his place on the bass and was replaced by Vic.

After hooking up with Ryan Davis at Hairball 8 Records, and appearing on the label's 'Hotter Than Hell' compilation they signed up for an album deal and delivered their second long-player 'Punkabilly Invasion' (1997), which featured a guest appearance from Guana Batz bass-man Johnny Bowler. Gradually the Ballers, through sheer persistence, became one of America's biggest Psychobilly exports through word of mouth and their sleazy reputation. Their second album, alongside appearances on compilations such as Hairball 8's second Psychobilly feast 'Kicked Outta Purgatory' reached far beyond the audience of their rudimentary 'Rock Out...' album and gave the band the opportunity to finally tour Europe – their spiritual home.

Their connection with European Psychobilly became even stronger when they inked a deal with German label Crazy Love Records and released their third album 'Nudie Bar Blues' in 2001. The album boasted a fine production and included appearances from Godless Wicked Creeps and Kim Nekroman. The band kept touring both sides of the Atlantic, almost as ambassadors of old school Psychobilly – American style, but by 2006 the pace was beginning to show and in the Summer of that year The Barnyard Ballers took a break from life on the road. Though the break was cited as a result of Spike's 'family problems' it may be a while before farm animals can rest easily again as the Ballers' story seems far from over. The Barnyard Ballers persistence (through a period when The Hellbillys, Cavalera and them 'were' the American Psychobilly scene) has seen them become one of the USA's major underground Psychobilly bands with a set of smut-filled recordings too crude for any crossover.

From a similar dimension to The Barnyard Ballers, Boston's Photon Torpedoes are another US band who chose to plunder from the lyrical corpse of classic European Psycho bands such as Demented Are Go, Nekromantix and Mad Sin. Focusing mainly on a songbook drenched in sex and horror, The Photon Torpedoes probably hide their motivations less than others. Their debut album 'It Came From Outer Space' was released in the UK in 1999 by Raucous Records, and with song titles such as 'The Woman With Two Vaginas', 'Zombie Riot' and 'The Wizard of Gore' it is not difficult to find out where their interests lie.

After gigging steadily, in the US and European festivals circuit, their second album 'Creature Double Feature' appeared on Spindrift Records in 2002. Yet again, their songs smash the point home with 'I Fuck On The First Date', 'Midget Porn Boogie' and 'Alien Vagina' as only a selection of their smut and

HELL'S BENT ON ROCKIN' YANKED INTO THE PIT

FRIDAY NOVEMBER 5th
STOMPIN' in BELGIUM & LINTFABRIEK

PLACE: LINTFABRIEK-MECHELSESTEENWEG 199-KONTICH (NEAR ANTWERP) BELGIUM

BARNYARD BALLERS (USA)
http://www.barnyardballers.com
San Diego's chaotic hillbilly ranging from psychobilly, Tex-Mex, and punk to country

DICEMEN (NL)
http://www.dicemen.net
hardstompin' forward psycho-punkabilly-laced rock'n'roll

MINI SKIRT BLUES (UK)
sideproject from Klingonz frontman
rockabilly-psychosis w/ untemped garage-punk
influences and a passing nod to The Vibes

DOORS: 19.00hr
FIRST BAND: 20.30hr

ROCKIN' DJ'S DURING THE BREAKS AND AFTERPARTY

HUGE RECORD & MERCHANDISE STALL
Drunkabilly Records

YOUNGER THAN 18 = 2 euro less on entrance !!
(bring your ID!!)

DESIGN: MIGHTY SAM

INFO: lintfabriek@skynet.be or drunkabilly@pi.be
RESERVATIONS+ ROUTE: www.heartbreaktunes.com

WWW.DRUNKABILLY.COM
tel/fax: ++32 (0) 9 233 74 68

The Barnyard Ballers invade Europe (Christophe @ Drunkabilly Records).

195

sci-fi songs with a sledgehammer subtlety. It's a well-trodden path but few revel so gleefully in the deviant lyrical depths of Psychobilly songwriting.

Los Gatos Locos are another combo who braved the lean years of American Psychobilly and reaped the dividends when the scene progressed. Hailing from Seattle, Los Gatos Locos are a band whose influences are a lot closer to UK and European Psycho than many American bands and for many years throughout the 1990s they more or less 'were' the Seattle Psychobilly scene and as the genre has progressed in America they remained well respected.

The band feature Charlie 'Chuck' Slpatterhead on vocals, Yasua Saito on double-bass, John Moony on drums and Dusty Dunkel on guitar. Dusty was once an honorary member of Demented Are Go when he stood in for Lex Luthor during one of Demented's jaunts to America. Given the band's length of service on the American scene their recording career is relatively small. Their only full studio album, 'Psychobillyun Baptism' was recorded in the Summer of 1997 and eventually released by Tombstone Records. A further CD, 'Demos, Out-takes & Rarities', on Spindrift Records followed which contains the band's earliest (and long-deleted) EP 'Juvenile Delinquent'.

Los Gatos Locos career has been patchy at times but they fought their way through some hard times and though never a huge touring act they have popped up at gigs across the globe, including an appearance at the 10th Big Rumble in the UK and a short European tour in 2006. Though many other band's have outdone Los Gatos Locos in terms of touring and recording they are one of the American bands closest to the roots of Psychobilly and their contribution to the US scene should not be underestimated.

While the American Psychobilly scene continues to grow, one band in particular are pushing ahead at the greatest rate. With four albums and an 'early tracks' collection behind them, Tiger Army are a full-blown American-Psycho success. Though the trio's line-up has fluctuated wildly the band have always remained the vision of frontman, guitarist and songwriter Nick 13.

From a young age Nick was a fan of Punk and Hardcore but also a connoisseur of 1950s Rock'n'Roll. In the same way that many others discovered the perfect hybrid of both genres, Nick caught The Meteors live in 1993 during a US tour and everything changed from then on. His old band, Influence 13, bit the dust and in 1994 he had no band but a clearer idea of the Psychobilly direction that he wanted to follow.

After attending a German Psychobilly festival in the Summer of 1995, Nick was further driven to create his own brand of American Psychobilly. After recruiting double-bass player Joel the first incarnation of Tiger Army began gigging early in 1996. Although the band was effectively without a drummer, skin-rattlers were 'borrowed' from other bands, firstly from AFI and then The Swingin' Utters. Tiger Army then began to manoeuvre, supporting The Meteors at Berkeley, gigging occasionally when drummers were available and releasing their first three-track single, the 'Temptation' EP, on the underground Chapter Eleven Records label.

Early in 1997 bass-slapper Joel quit and Nick 13 was a one-man band yet again – no group, no gigs, no record deal. The Tiger Army story may have ended there but, out of the blue, Nick got a message that Tim Armstrong from US Punk superstars Rancid had heard an old Tiger Army demo and was keen to get in touch. Armstrong had recently became supremo of Epitaph Records off-shoot label 'Hellcat' and he was keen to get Nick into the studio and begin recording an album. While ecstatic at the offer, 13 had to confess that he was all that was left of the band at that time. Armstrong was unfazed and encouraged Nick, as the creative force of Tiger Army, to go ahead and create a studio line-up to lay down the tracks. The result was the self-titled debut album in 1999, an appropriately numbered 13 track affair featuring mostly Nick 13 penned originals alongside a solitary cover of Eddie Cochran's 'Twenty Flight Rock'. Lining up alongside the Tiger Army frontman were ex-Quakes bass-slapper Rob Peltier, AFI drummer Adam Carson and a host of backing vocalists including other members of AFI and Tim Armstrong himself.

For many Americans this major label release, and the solid distribution network behind it, was a first taste of Psychobilly. Though many bands had established a cult following for the genre previously, the sheer marketing might of Epitaph/Hellcat alongside the label's solid reputation as purveyors of high-octane Punk Rock'n'Roll thrust Tiger Army into the spotlight attracting curious listeners from a variety of underground genres. With its strong production and 13's own unique take on the Psycho-sound the album also attracted a number of established Psychobillies across the world and perhaps even restored a bit of faith at a time when the genre was almost in decline. Despite the album's popularity, Nick 13 was still effectively a one-man band so in 2000 he relocated to Los Angeles and set up a recruitment drive for fellow 'Army' members. His quest resulted in securing the talents of Geoff Kresge, an experienced double-bassist equally at home on an electric four-stringer and drummer Fred Hell.

The time to prove themselves on the road had come and in the summer of 2001 the band set out to promote Tiger Army's second full-length release 'Tiger Army II: Power of Moonlite'. This album, also released on Hellcat, appeared in stores in July 2001. Similar in theme to their self-titled debut but showing a little more of the many influences on 13's songwriting beyond Psychobilly it was also structured similarly to the debut with its opening 'Prelude' track and total of 13 songs.

With the album on the streets an eighteen-month tour of duty began as the band began spreading the Tiger Army gospel across the states, the Far East then back to the source... in Europe. This mammoth set of live dates saw the band perform in a variety of venues, from tiny clubs to full-blown music festivals. It included several support slots, including dates with The Damned, Reverend Horton Heat and The Dropkick Murphys, alongside their own headlining gigs.

The hard work paid dividends and, despite the relatively low press and TV publicity which naturally follows any band with Psychobilly connections, Tiger Army gained an even more fanatical following across the world. Certainly for any young Punks searching for something new following the band became almost a way of life with 'Tiger Army never die' their battle cry and all manner of band-themed tattoos being etched on the faithful. At the start of 2003 the third album was already beginning to take shape in rehearsal and their reputation was building further when tragedy struck a cruel blow – drummer Fred Hell was shot four times during a home invasion robbery. Thankfully he survived and understandably the Tiger Army story was put on hold. After a period of months it became clear that the severity of the attack on Hell would prevent him from returning to the studio to commence work on what would become 'Tiger Army III: Ghost Tigers Rise'. Instead, Nick 13 and Geoff Kresge began recording with the band's longtime drum tech Mike Fasano. Despite this, when the album was released Fred Hell remained on the credits as the band's drummer, while Fasano received thanks and acknowledgement for his studio contribution.

Fred did indeed return to the band in the run-up to the release of 'Ghost Tigers Rise' in June 2004. The band supported Rancid on tour then completed some headline dates of their own in the US. However, Hell's injuries would prove to have a lasting effect and after two major shows at Sunset Strip's House of Blues to promote the album's release he left the band, unable to continue in the punishing role as Tiger Army's drummer.

The band were already booked to play on the massive 2004 Vans Warped Tour which would place them on the main stage at 28 major shows across America alongside bands such as NOFX and Bad Religion. Mike Fasano was drafted in for dates but after the tour he, and more surprisingly, Geoff Kresge made their departure from Tiger Army. Once again, Nick was a one-man band. Nonetheless, his single-minded quest to keep Tiger Army rolling continued.

There was never any question of Tiger Army drawing to a close their career, especially with 13 as the creative core of the band. As 2004 ended, two new members were recruited. On bass was Jeff Roffredo, an old friend of Nick's and veteran of the small but hard-core Psychobilly scene in California. Roffredo had previously slapped his doghouse bass with Cosmic Voodoo and Calavera. Appearing on drums was James Meza, once a stand-in drummer for some of Nekromantix' US dates in the past.

With the new band in place, Tiger Army embarked on an epic 46 date tour across America supporting Social Distortion. The gigs put the band to the test but the line-up appeared to work well and by then

YANKED INTO THE PIT   HELL'S BENT ON ROCKIN'

Tiger Army had an impressive back catalogue to work from. The live work continued and in 2005 the band made a flamboyant return to the UK with a full tour taking in Scottish, Welsh and Irish venues as opposed to the strictly English dates haunted by most visiting bands. A whole new following was awaiting the band pushing them beyond a strictly Psychobilly following and saw them making an appearance on Britain's biggest radio station, Radio 1 — a feat rarely accomplished since the early 1980s when the likes of The Meteors and Guana Batz infiltrated the nation's airwaves.

There was to be no rest throughout 2005 as the band toured Australia then embarked on their own major headlining jaunt around America on their 'Dark Romance' tour. Sporadic gigging continued but the latter part of the year saw 13 focus on new material for Tiger Army's fourth album 'Music From Regions Beyond' which was released in June 2007.

Though many Psychobilly bands have been hard pushed in the past to flog the entire first pressings of their records, the rapid ascension of Tiger Army has created a number of special edition releases which are now frantically sought after by collectors. While online trading and auction sites, particularly Ebay, have opened up the collector's market they have also raised prices — sometimes ridiculous in the face of the free-bus-fares and beer budgets of many early Psychobilly recordings.

With Hellcat Records behind them, Tiger Army's releases have uniformly been of high-quality both in recording and packaging and for the faithful, kicking on the record store's doors on release day, there has been a selection of stylish limited editions available. All three Tiger Army albums have had a simultaneous release on CD and vinyl. 'Tiger Army' also boasted 1000 copies pressed in glorious orange vinyl. For 'Power of Moonlite' the run was increased and 1300 copies of the album on 'moon-yellow' vinyl eerily slid from the record pressing plant. 'Ghost Tigers Rise' met the increased demand for these special editions with 2000 white vinyl copies and an equal amount in grey.

The 'Ghost Tigers EP', featuring three tracks from 'Ghost Tigers Rise' and the otherwise unavailable track 'The Loop' is much sought after as it was a vinyl-only release on a ten inch picture disc and only 3000 copies were pressed. Of even greater value are 200 copies of the EP which were signed. Hellcat also released a very collectable clear vinyl 10" (2000 copies) of the band's mini-album collection of early tracks and demos, 'Early Years EP'. Though the vinyl release of this EP is long gone, a CD version was also created.

Finally, the holy grail of all Tiger Army collectables remains their 1997 self-titled 7" EP released by the Indie label Chapter Eleven Records. Also referred to as the 'Temptation EP', this plain black vinyl disc is long out of print and the 500 copies in existence gather value by the day. It is a small consolation for vinyl-sniffing bloodhounds but all three tracks appear on the 'Early Years' CD. With their new album in the stores and their fanbase growing rapidly its undeniable that Tiger Army collectables will remain a healthy investment for years to come.

Though they often leave the impression of hailing from the deep south, Hayride To Hell are actually a Californian Psychobilly quartet. Formed in 1995 from the ashes of a band called Wrecking Ball (not to be confused with Billy Favata's Wreckin' Ball) this Santa Cruz based band have taken the horror influence from Psychobilly and ground it to the bone, with the majority of tracks from their 1997 self-titled debut album on Nervous being preoccupied with horror, murder, monsters and other subjects of a ghoulish nature.

The original line-up featured Craig Hart on double-bass and John Long on guitar with Joey Myers on drums. John and Craig initially shared vocal duties but when extra guitarist Mark Canepa was drafted in to beef up their sound, Craig became lead vocalist. As probably one of the most horror-obsessed Psycho bands on the West Coast scene, Hayride To Hell have perhaps isolated many folks who believe Psychobilly has a bit more to offer than tales of gore and grue but at least the band wear their (still pumping, blood-squirting) hearts on their sleeves and make no attempt to disguise their eerie influences.

In a sterling example of poor timing Hayride To Hell drifted apart around 2000, following Mark and Craig's moves to other states, and this pioneering US Psycho act left a scene which was growing rapidly after the lean years of the band's earliest days. No doubt realising that the audience for Hayride To Hell could be bigger than ever, John and Joey got together around 2002 to plan their comeback. John returned to vocals and guitar and with Joey back behind the kit they enlisted new bass-slapper Rob Mellberg. As a power trio the band were reanimated but to many of the audience at the first gig of their new line-up, The LA Wrecker's Ball, they were making their 'debut' once again. Second time around they were playing to larger, more responsive, audiences and in the whirlwind that followed Rob Mellberg was replaced by Mal Wrecker, bass man with The Slanderin' and one time stand-in for The Meteors.

After striking a deal with Hairball 8 subsidiary label US Psychobilly, the band's eventual follow-up album '... and Back' was released in 2005. The band had already been featured on Hairball 8's first two Psychobilly compilations, 'Hotter than Hell' and 'Kicked Outta Purgatory'. With tracks on the new album such as 'Death Dealer', 'The Thirst' and 'Graveyard Romp' the band have lost none of their earlier taste for horror but after travelling a rocky road for over a decade they remain a solid Psychobilly trio with plenty of gas in the tank to go further.

Hayride's influence on the US scene does not end there as absent guitarist Mark Canepa resurfaced in Texas psycho band Concombre Zombi as a new decade crept onto the horizon. Having met up with Texas Psychobilly pioneer (and drumskin tormentor) Destin Pledger, the duo brought on board a flamboyant double-bass man known enigmatically simply as 'Ralphy' and after the usual early compilation appearances they delivered their debut 'Daylight Comes' (2005) on Hairball 8 Records. Certainly unashamed by a variety of rock and metal influences in their sound the band are resolutely Psychobilly and Mark has undoubtedly found kindred spirits willing to indulge in all manner of horror-themed songs such as 'Honeymoon In Hell', 'Purgatory Souls' and 'Hellhounds'.

Two of the biggest bands representing the Mexican side of Psychobilly in California are Calavera and The Dragstrip Demons both who are based in Los Angeles. Calavera were established in 1995 by Cejas Vasquez, a guitarist and songwriter who had been playing and recording with Punk bands since the late 1980s, both in Tijuana and latterly in LA. The first line-up featured vocalist Daniel DeLeon (later to form Resurex) and double-bassist Jeff Roffredo (Tiger Army/Resurex/Cosmic Voodoo). Their first self-titled 7" EP appeared the following year but it was not until 1998 that their debut album 'The Day Of The Dead' saw the light on La Piedra Del Rock Records. Both releases delivered Calavera's unique brand of hard drivin' Psychobilly which alternates between English and Spanish lyrics.

From this point on the band continued to gig regularly on the West Coast and also made the trip coast to coast to play at New York's Psychobilly Rumble in 2000. During this period the band's line-up altered fairly regularly leaving Cejas as sole original member but it did not affect their creativity and five years on their follow-up CD-EP 'Tequilamatic' was released. Their second full-length album 'Plaga De Rock' (2005) followed soon after on Dr. Acula Records. The band also made their first trip to tour Europe in 2005 taking in Germany, Austria, Holland and The Czech Republic. Most recently the band released the album 'Resurrect The Dead, Celebrate The Living' a "best of..." collection featuring the pick of their ten year recording career.

The Dragstrip Demons also have a huge Mexican influence pounding through their LA based Psychobilly sound. They even named their second album 'Mexican Psychobilly' just to hammer the point home. The Demons first got together in 1999, all influenced by original Rockabilly and early European Psycho rather than the home-grown more Punk influenced scene which had already developed in So-Cal. Manuel 'Evil' Lepe was a large and commanding force on vocals and his cousin Cesar Lepe was the drummer. Beside these two Hispanic horror-fiends were guitarist Phil and double-bassist Ralph De La Rosa. In a startling display of musical dexterity Ralph later became lead guitarist with Cesar joining him on rhythm guitar during a line-up reshuffle. Together they stewed up their own evil brew of old-school Psychobilly with an increasingly frantic edge.

Taking their influence from the likes of Demented Are Go, Mad Sin, Batmobile and Nekromantix they developed their Mexican Psychobilly sound which they inflicted on the world both in their debut 'Rise

Cavalera, Psycho Rock'n'Roll - Mexican style (Die In Style).

Of The Panther' (2002) and the aforementioned 'Mexican Psychobilly' (2004), both for Crazy Love Records. Though popular both in their own right and also a support act, to the likes of Tiger Army and Nekromantix, The Demons folded in 2005 – a great pity given that the band had more loyalty than most to the true roots of Psychobilly. Manuel has continued to work within the scene as a promoter and is behind the hugely successful 'West Coast Wrecker's Ball' shows which began in 2002.

The scene in America does not simply feature purely home-grown talent as many bands have gravitated to the States and seen their popularity grow. While The Quakes had to come to Europe to establish themselves, these days the US is the place to be. Like Nekromantix, The Wrecking Dead made the move to America from Denmark and saw their career opportunities increase. When they made the Atlantic crossing from Copenhagen to New Jersey in 2002. They brought with them their self-titled debut album, on Crazy Love Records, then the band settled into the US Psycho scene which eventually led to their five-track mini-album for Hairball 8 records, 'The New Breed'. With their heavily Oi-influenced Psychobilly sound, alongside a debt to The Misfits, The Wrecking Dead have found themselves at home in America's Punk underground amongst the many other Punkier 'billy bands on the scene.

While Europe has continued to be the home of a variety of Psychobilly-friendly labels, the kingpin of the more recent American Psychobilly scene has to be Hairball 8 Records. Formed in San Antonio, Texas by single-minded lover of all things rockin', Ryan Davis, the label was initially started in 1996 with the release of a Pop-Punk compilation 'Keep The Beat'. Though generally unrelated to Psychobilly, the album did contain tracks from The Barnyard Ballers and Frankenstein.

Although Ryan was initially planning no further than Hairball 8's first release, the success of the album led him to progress with the label and he created 'Hotter Than Hell' (1996) the first American Psychobilly compilation from an American label. Featuring a heavy-duty roster of talent from across the globe, including Mad Sin, The Phantom Rockers, Los Gatos Locos, Cosmic Voodoo and Calavera, 'Hotter Than Hell' was a well produced and handsomely packaged CD which easily equalled, and often surpassed, other compilations of the time from many more established labels. It also reinstated the rapid growth of the American scene and was a revelation to many in the UK and Europe that the US could now fill a compilation to bursting point with current acts.

Hairball 8 still continued to keep their options open, signing American Punk acts such as The Scotch Greens and Hate Fuck Trio, but Psychobilly was still on the agenda with a full-length album from The Barnyard Ballers, 'Punkabilly Invasion' (1997), and a second Psychobilly compilation 'Kicked Outta Purgatory' (1998). This collection was an epic 27 track affair boasting the cream of European talent (Nekromantix, Frantic Flintstones, Demented Are Go, The Sharks, The Peacocks...) alongside top Yank acts such as Deadbolt, Kings Of Nuthin', Los Creepers and Ghoultown.

With a real desire to push Psychobilly in the US, Ryan expanded Hairball 8 into a variety of other areas including merchandising, concert promotion and, eventually, DVD production. As business expanded, a sub label 'Psychobilly US' was created as a self-explanatory home for all aspects of the scene. It even boldly announced its own 'mission statement' (or set of beliefs) which roughly philosophised that The Meteors were 'the' band who started the genre, the double-bass is an essential part of any Psychobilly band and other genres such as Goth and metal are acceptable in the scene. While many, or all, of these statements may have ruffled a few feathers amongst those who share a different point of view there can be no doubting Ryan and company's commitment to the scene aside from these broad statements.

With bands like The Barnyard Ballers, Zombie Ghost Train, The Peacocks, Demon City Wreckers, Hayride To Hell, The Rocketz, G-String and The Koffin Kats on their books, Hairball 8 really is the heart of the American scene. The Koffin Kats in particular have become something of a 'house band' for the label with their first three albums appearing under the Hairball 8/Psychobilly US umbrella. This Detroit trio, formed in 2003 by Vic Victor (double bass/vocals), Tommy Koffin (guitar) and Damien Detroit (drums), have knocked out a trio of ass-kickin' Psycho albums with unflinching regularity. Their debut self-titled mini-album appeared in 2004 and was closely followed in 2005 with the long-player 'Inhumane'. Mr Detroit was replaced on drums by Katch along the way and their second eight-track mini album offering 'Straying From The Pack' (2006) cemented their place, much like their label, amongst the front-runners of the American scene.

In 2005 Ryan launched the hour-long DVD documentary 'The Psychobilly Sickness: Episode 1'. The first of a proposed series of DVDs, the film features live footage and interviews from a number of American bands and visiting Eurobillies alongside The Meteors. It attempts to introduce the Psychobilly genre at entry level as well as indulging in a bit of history courtesy of interviews with Pip Hancox, P. Paul Fenech and Kim Nekroman.

YANKED INTO THE PIT

HELL'S BENT ON ROCKIN'

As if soaking the world in Psychobilly sickness from stereos and TV sets was not enough, Hairball 8 (often alongside Destin Pledger's 'Texas Psychobilly' organisation) have also tirelessly promoted Rock'n'Roll gatherings of a deviant nature since their earliest days. Most events have been in California and Texas but nowhere in the US is safe and the label has also organised full tours for Demented Are Go, The Peacocks, Nekromantix and many more as well as a number of major American Psychobilly events such as The West Coast Wreckers Ball, The Psychobilly Masquerade Ball and The Texas Psychobilly Blood Feast! With a more expansive distribution deal signed in 2006 and the recent appearance of Hairball 8's artists on iTunes for the download generation, their triple-pronged attack of production, promotion and retail shows little sign of abating.

Hairball 8 are not the only label promoting audio aggro with a Psychobilly flavour in the US. LA based Split 7 Records have a smaller but no less rowdy roster featuring a variety of dirty Rock'n'Rollers. For Psycho fans the label's compilations such as 'Psycho Ward', 'Attack Of The Hot Rod Zombies' and 'Return Of The Hot Rod Zombies' are bustin' at the seams with tracks from Mad Sin, The Coffin Draggers, Big John Bates, Demon City Wreckers and many others. The label has also released full-length albums from The Phantom Rockers, The Slanderin, The Hellbillys and Los Creepers alongside its wider range of country punkers, surf punks and Hot Rod DVDs.

The American scene has many similarities to the original Psychobilly boom, particularly in the way it joins Rockabilly and Punk together while still containing bands who pull a little further in each direction. The Slanderin' are one of the many bands still with one boot planted firmly in the Punk scene. From their first limited edition 'Zombie Gang' EP, through their 2002 debut LP on Destroy All Records 'Psychobilly Lives' to their 2003 album 'Rhumba Of Rattlesnakes, Murder Of Crows' (Split 7 Records), they are a band who have slapped their double-bass with a fury alongside a rockin' beat heavily dipped in American Hardcore and British Oi.

Generally, many American bands have strayed slightly closer to either the Punk or Rockabilly end of the Psychobilly spectrum but one new outfit has blasted onto the scene with a Psychobilly offering that has the same quality production and crossover potential as Tiger Army but with a sound far closer to the roots of this bastard genre. Californian combo Resurex were formed in 2001, originally under the name Lobo Negro. Vocalist Daniel DeLeon and double-bassist Jeff Roffredo had both been in the original line-up of Mexican-flavoured Psychobilly band Calavera. Daniel had left the band at the end of the 1990s but kept in touch with Jeff (who also recorded with Cosmic Voodoo) then they both began to create a new monster. The Lobo Negro line-up was completed with two other members of the LA rockin' scene, James Meza on drums and Troy 'Destroy' Russell.

Given that all the band members other activities (James and Jeff are in Tiger Army, Troy is in Nekromantix and Daniel works in film and TV) consume so much time it is no wonder that their debut album took almost five years to come together. Before the album, however, came the issue of their unusual name. Lobo Negro was found to already be in use by another band and Troy's suggestion of Hounds of the Resurrection was shot down by the other members. His idea was reduced to the more direct name Resurrects but on finding that this name was also in use Resurex was born.

The band drew the attention of Hellcat Records and made an appearance on the label's 'Give Em The Boot IV' compilation but their album deal came from much further afield. The band had toured briefly in Europe, between all the members other commitments, and German label Fiendforce Records signed them for what was to become their debut 'Beyond The Grave' (2006). Given the band's pedigree, the album was unsurprisingly a tour de force with real potential to take the band forward. Most notably, as well as been a slick, well-written production the album still has a true, undiluted Psychobilly heart which sets the band far from the 'Punk band with a double-bass' label often lazily slapped on American bands.

Though all of the band have heavy schedules outside Resurex (Jeff and James are particularly busy with the 2007 release of Tiger Army's fourth album and its accompanying touring schedule) the band still found time to play around the US and Europe in 2006, this time with the album's strong reputation

Resurex, America's Psychobilly super group (Die In Style).

behind them. Whether each of the band member's outside commitments will have a lasting effect on the group remains to be scene but the potential of Resurex may yet eclipse all their day jobs.

One more unusual American band who have certainly had major appeal on the Psychobilly scene over the past few years have been Boston's The Kings of Nuthin'. Originally known as The Boston Blackouts, this eight-piece Punk collective became The Kings of Nuthin' in 1999 and attempted to create their own version of a Rock'n'Roll big band featuring vocals, guitar, bass, tenor and baritone sax and washboard. With their Punk background being far from the smoothness of swing, they created a fearsome racket that was pure Rock'n'Roll but still wildly original.

Their first album, 'Get Busy Livin' Or Get Busy Dyin'', appeared in 2000 on the Reckloose Records label. The Massachusetts-based company went bust the following year leaving the album out of print for over three years until the band re-pressed it themselves then secured a distribution deal. Though recorded in just two days, it captured the band's unique sound but is now regarded by the band as little more than a mini-album which provided a taster for their first album proper.

The band moved on to the Californian label Disaster Records and entered into a fruitful relationship with producer Jim Siegel. Jim managed to get the best from this rowdy mob and brought them together into a solid wall of sound, making the big band sound even bigger. 'Fight Songs For Fuck-Ups' was released in 2002 and gave the band a full-length debut to be proud of. It also gave them even more reason to tour.

Touring for a band like Kings Of Nuthin' is rarely simple and with so many members and crew they often hit towns like a marauding gang rather than a merry group of travelling minstrels. Instruments, tempers and even band members have all been lost en-route. The band have also alternated between the luxury of support slots with major acts to shivering like hoboes in a fucked-up van between some real shithouse venues. Unsurprisingly, given the rigours of touring and the band's volatile nature (on and off stage) the line-up has seen its share of changes.

As The Kings of Nuthin's sound is a genre-busting combination of many styles, they have obviously found a large Psychobilly following amongst their audience and have enjoyed as much success in Europe as they have in the US. Crazy Love records released a vinyl version of 'Get Busy...' and their second long-player had a separate US and European release. After another successful collaboration with Jim Siegal the band had an album in the bag which was a 50/50 combination of original compositions and covers of 1950s R&B and classic Punk tracks. In Europe the album was picked up by People Like You Records and released in 2005 as 'Punk Rock Rhythm & Blues'.

The American release, on Sailor's Grave Records, followed in 2006 but under the alternate title of 'Over The Counter Culture'. While the name of the American release is taken from one of the album's tracks the title of the European album certainly captures far more of the band's spirit. Despite the line-up changes The Kings of Nuthin''s live horrorshow continues and the band have kept rockin' and rollin' with the punches, while proving that having Psychobilly connections need not be the kiss of death for band's with grander expectations.

Though America is a huge chunk of land, it seems nothing can contain the Psychobilly fever and despite armed mounties on their borders the sickness has also spread to Canada. Big John Bates, The Farrell Bros, The Creepshow and The Deadcats are just some of the Canadian rockers who have made their mark on both sides of the border. For geographically-challenged 'billies, Vancouver on Canada's West Coast is none too far from Seattle and Portland (both Psychobilly strongholds) and on the East Coast, Montreal and Toronto are but a kick in the ass (relatively) from the lively scenes in Boston, Providence and New York.

One of Canada's most recent Psychobilly successes has been youthful gore fiends The Gutter Demons who formed in Montreal in 2002 from the ashes of Rockabilly outfit Rosekill. Featuring vocalist/guitarist Johnny Toxik, double-bassist Flipper and drummer 'Custom' Pat, The Gutter Demons got their act together pretty quickly and released their own self-titled EP in the same year. Though rough and ready, and with only 300 copies pressed, the six-track offering generated some real interest in the band not only across Canada and the US but also Europe.

The following year saw the band release their debut album, 'Enter The Demons', on Halloween 2003. Independently produced, the album was licensed to Pirate Records and was a full-on Punk/Horror/Psychobilly fusion with a heavy sound and some fierce musicianship. It made such an impression that The Gutter Demons were soon as in demand for gigs as many of the established US acts and they made an appearance at the West Coast Wrecker's Ball while also featuring on Hairball 8's 'Kicked Outta Purgatory'. Their standing in Europe also grew, helped along by a 7" release taken from the album, of the track 'Human Remains', which appeared on the Dutch label Fantoom Records.

With their heavier sound, The Gutter Demons attracted a lot of interest from the Punk scene and between 2004-2005 they found themselves supporting Nashville Pussy, The Misfits, UK Subs and Reverend Horton Heat. They also made the trip over the border for several more US dates while still maintaining a heavy presence on Montreal's own Psycho scene alongside other homegrown talent such as The Brains, Flesh and Bloodshot Bill (a Hazil Adkins for the new millennium).

As further proof both of The Gutter Demons' popularity and the growing Canadian scene in general, the band also appeared on the second volume of the compilation series 'Zombie Night In Canada'. These albums boast stacks of Canadian Rockabilly and Psychobilly talent (alongside a few North American interlopers) including the excellent Farrell Brothers and Big John Bates.

As 'Enter The Demons' continued to establish the band well into 2005, Psychos around the world gradually picked up the word on this hot new act and the album's title track even featured on TV and Radio as the background to ads for an LA based hair products company. With such success generated by their debut, there is little doubt that their follow-up album 'Room 209' (2006) should propel them even further, especially with Pirate Records now behind the band full-time.

The Gutter Demons represent Canada's new breed of rockers along with another of the country's biggest exports, Big John Bates – and I mean big! Live, the band are a rattling, rolling three-piece who absolutely filled the stage with Big John out front (roaring and thrusting his Gretsch at the audience) accompanied by sex-bomb, she-rocker sCare-oline slapping her upright-bass while avoiding rivers of drool dripping from the mouths of horned-up male audience members. Add to this whatever drummer

HELL'S BENT ON ROCKIN'   YANKED INTO THE PIT

The Deadneks (Joey Fangface).

is there on the night (from their readily-rotating percussionists) and the band's bumping, grinding dancers The Voodoo Dollz and you have a helluva show. The Big John Bates experience has attracted interest from all over the rockin' scene and far more besides including product endorsements from Gretsch guitars and legendary 'firewater' Jägermeister, features in books and magazines focusing on their 'Voodoo Burlesque' stage show and even an appearance in Season 3 of the revamped US sci-fi show 'Battlestar Galactica'.

Bates himself is pretty unique as he came into the rockin' scene from a major Thrash Metal band. John was co-founder of Annihilator, a band which shared similar early album success to that of Metallica, Anthrax and Slayer. Having initially moved on to the more experimental rock act Bates Motel, John eventually released his first album in his own name, 'Super Chrome Deluxe' (2000), on Spinner Records which was a wild mix of Punk, Psycho, Blues, Garage and Surf that he would continue to refine as his recording career progressed. For his second album John enlisted teen-goth Caroline Helmeczi, a recent convert to the double-bass, and released 'Flamethrower' (2001) the album that brought them to international attention.

This release was a closer representation of their wild stage shows – an ass-kicking concoction of wild songs with a pounding rhythm section and (unsurprisingly, given John's Metal past) a huge guitar sound. Although the band are attracting an even wider ranging audience helped along by two more albums, 'Mystiki' (2003) and 'Take Your Medicine' (2005), and their increasingly wild'n'horny live shows, they still maintain a solid Psychobilly element to much of their material and seem committed to the scene.

Along with The Gutter Demons and Big John Bates many other rockin' bands have formed in Canada this decade including The Creepshow, The Astrobillys, The Alley Dukes, The Deadneks and Zombie Riot but one outfit have been spearheading the Canadian Psycho-scene for far longer, Vancouver's The Deadcats. After their debut album 'Bucket Of Love' (1995) for Flying Saucer Records the band were a bit of a voice in the wilderness for some time, relentlessly plugging their own brand of twisted

YANKED INTO THE PIT

Rock'n'Roll to bemused audiences. However, their persistence paid off and as the US scene got rolling The Deadcats' influence grew.

Four years after their debut The Deadcats bounced back with another album for Flying Saucer Records, 'Millions Of Dead Cats' (1999), followed by a mini-album for Japanese label Revel Yell called 'Cathouse Blues' (2000). At last The Deadcats began to get the attention they deserved for their pioneering brand of Canadian Psycho which, much like Big John Bates, also features heavy elements of Surf, Trash and Punk. The band also switched readily between electric and upright-bass, giving each song the rhythm that suits best.

Despite the slow start to their recording career, The Deadcats' albums began stacking up in the 2000's with a particular highlight being their sleazy garage opus 'Bad Pussy' in 2002. This album showcased a confident band, unafraid to take the pace down a little and experimenting with varied styles from the Rock'n'Roll genre. Continuing their relationship with Flying Saucer Records The Deadcats, after over a decade together, are still rockin' Canada and beyond with their latest album 'Feline 500' (2006) and helping to confirm that Canadian Psychobilly is kicking ass and far from a poor relation to the US scene.

With the American and Canadian Psychobilly scene evolving so quickly it's impossible to predict how deeply the genre will penetrate the United States. Could it cross over to the mainstream in the same manner as Punk has and produce a Psychobilly act which can enjoy as much commercial gain as the likes of Green Day or The Offspring? Or will there be some groups who drop the Psychobilly label quicker than a hot tamale in pursuit of wider fame? There is a certain school of thought, particularly seeping through a number of internet forums, that the American scene in general is a huge fad that could be dropped any moment and follow cock rock, grunge and nu metal into obscurity but this theory is wildly insulting to the huge number of bands, labels, promoters and fans who contribute to the Psychobilly boom in America.

In Psychobilly, even to this day, the monetary gain remains relatively feeble and there are few who get involved with Psychobilly who do not really dig the music in a major way. As a genre to milk for huge stacks of cash then move on, Psychobilly is a pretty poor bet. Most American fans are ravenous for the Psychobilly beat and just because they joined the scene a little later does not mean that they will not still be around in twenty years' time. A hardcore group of Psychobilly bands and fans have already been on the scene as long as many of Europe's leading lights.

What has also been crucially underestimated about the US scene is that American promoters have also coughed-up the cash regularly to bring Psychobilly bands from the UK, Europe, Japan, South America and Australia and, along with some key record distributors, they have opened up the huge American market to many groups who have been desperate to get a foothold in the US for many years, so 'God Bless America' for opening its borders to a flood of Psychobilly sickness.

CHAPTER NINE

HELL'S BENT ON ROCKIN'

WRECKIN' ALL OVER THE WORLD
THE GLOBAL PSYCHOBILLY SCENE

Although Psychobilly has flourished in the UK, Europe and more recently the USA that is not to say that the disease has not spread further across the globe. Since the world wide web has flourished in the past decade it has certainly been easier to unite the global Psychobilly community but it was not always that simple. Communication between bands, promoters and fans was often slow and laboured and Psychobilly record buyers across the world often found imported albums from the UK and Europe were a rarity. However, no single country tried harder to spread the Psychobilly gospel, even in the leanest years of the genre, than the land of the rising sun – Japan.

It should have been no surprise, with Japan a country built on technological advances and supporting a booming media empire of many disciplines, but many British bands who made early pilgrimages to the country were left dumbfounded by the professionalism of promoters and the intensity of Japanese fans. The Meteors, Guana Batz, Long Tall Texans, Demented Are Go and Frenzy were some of the first UK bands to venture to the Far East and were often amazed at the treatment they received. Limo service, high-quality hotels and fan devotion were often the norm while gigs were very well attended with excellent lighting and sound facilities.

Frenzy in particular were big favourites in Japan, returning to tour many times. Steve Whitehouse even managed a unique double-header in 1990 when Frenzy and Restless toured Japan together with Steve as bass-player for both bands. The band also recorded their 1993 album 'Live In Japan' during a further Frenzy/Restless double-bill.

An appetite for all forms of Rock'n'Roll has always existed in Japan and taking Psychobilly on board in a big way was simply a natural progression. As demand grew for Psycho and Neo acts, Britain's main purveyor of rockin' delights, Nervous Records, even licensed a large part of their extensive back catalogue to Japanese label Jimco to keep up with demand in the early 1990s. However, it was not long before Japanese labels specialising in Psychobilly and modern Rockabilly began to establish their own rosters.

Japanese Psychobillies at The Big Rumble, 1998 (Jane Williams).

WRECKIN' ALL OVER THE WORLD

HELL'S BENT ON ROCKIN'

The Falcons join Nervous Records (Roy Williams).

Japan also boasted an early crop of home-grown talent featuring the likes of Seven Steps To Hell, Hellbent, The Strutters, Dog Eat Dog, The Low Heads and the bizarrely-named Acid Connection. From this seminal group of bands came some of Japan's most influential pioneers – The Falcons, The Mad Mongols, Battle of Ninjamanz and The Starlite Wranglers.

Way back in 1989 The Falcons made their intentions clear by naming their debut EP, on the Japanese label Planet Records, 'Psycho War'. This was a storming full-on Psychobilly debut but it was to be another four years before their debut LP for Planet appeared and the self-titled release featured some re-recordings from the single. Again, this recording proved that The Falcons were a more than capable trio who, unlike many Japanese Psychobilly bands to follow, held firmly onto the genre's Rockabilly roots. With both their releases (and a further live album) appearing on Planet Records, a European deal was essential to bring the band to the attention of the worldwide Psychobilly community.

Their first UK release was a six-track mini CD for Nervous Records and perhaps the unfortunate title (taken from a track on the album), 'Balls Balls', was the result of some kind of breakdown in translation. Nonetheless, this mini album (produced in the UK by Psychobilly favourite Pete Gage) was a solid-stomping classic which featured 'Psychos From The Far East', something of an unofficial theme tune for the band. The band were introduced to UK and European audiences at the 7th Big Rumble in Hemsby in 1994 and proved that Japanese Psychobilly was far from the novelty which many suspected it would be. Unfortunately, The Falcons were not to be torch-bearers for Far Eastern Psychobilly as they split soon after their UK appearance but they are still remembered as one of the pioneering Japanese acts to make a sizable impression across the UK and Europe.

The Mad Mongols were another Japanese outfit who outstripped the expectations of listeners in the UK and Europe and have continued to represent Psychobilly in Japan, in a variety of guises, to the present day. They burst onto the scene in 1992, less than a year into their formation, with their 'Mongolian Chop' 12" single on the Vinyl Japan label. Vinyl Japan were an unusual organisation, boasting offices in Tokyo and Camden Town, London. They have always maintained an eclectic roster of Indie, Punk and Trash acts, including The Flaming Stars, The Milkshakes and many of Billy Childish' offshoot bands such as Mickey and Ludella, The Buff Medways, The Delmonas and The Headcoatees.

The label used 'Mongolian Chop' to launch their imprint 'Jappin' & Rockin'' which would feature further Mad Mongols releases alongside records from The Sharks, The Gazmen, The Guana Batz and a number of Neo-Rockabilly acts. The label also released two volumes of the 'Jappin' Psycho Bomb' compilations which were a 'who's who' of Japanese Psychobilly featuring authentic far Eastern dementia from bands such as Tokyo Skunx, Jap Kat, Crazy Billy Rats, The Wankers and Floozy Drippys.

The Mad Mongols stayed with Vinyl Japan, in a deal which made their records readily available all over the Western hemisphere, and continued to peddle their own extreme Psychobilly with the excellent 'Bruce Fuckin' Lee' 12" in 1994 followed by their debut album 'Cripple Satan Scream' on the major Japanese label Teichiku Records. Vinyl Japan released one further album 'Just For The Hell Of It' (1994) which gathered many of the band's early tracks and, in keeping with the band's audio brutality, featured decidedly un-PC cover art from Antoine Bernhart of a skull-faced woman stripped, bound and with a flame containing the band's logo shooting from her bare arse.

The original line-up of the band was Kiyoaki (vocals/guitar), Masato (double bass/guitar) and Takashi on drums but they soon became a four-piece with Masato as the sole-surviving original member when new Mongols Toshi (vocals), Seri (drums) and Hiroki (guitar) were enlisted. Kiyoaki continued to be involved in the Japanese Psychobilly scene with his next band The Eightmen. The Mad Mongols' deal with Teichiku produced a mini-album 'Blood Of Dracula's Castle' (1995) and two compilations of their earlier recordings. Their second studio album 'Frenzied Black Demons' followed in 1996 on the Cyber label then things went quiet when the band initially split for almost eight years then reappeared on the French label Pure & Proud Records with the long-player 'Revenge Of The Mongoloid' (2004).

In 2002, the band's founder and bass-man ditched his instrument to become frontman in his own combo Mad Masato. With his unique rasping scream, Masato continued to pursue a hard-core Psychobilly sound with his album 'My Splendid Psychobilly Life' and the mini-albums 'Sakura' (2003) on Pure & Proud Records and 'Just Movin' On' for Raucous. Before this Masato had also pushed the genre to its limits with another band SxTxH (Seven Steps To Hell) who brought extreme hardcore, bordering on Industrial, to the Psychobilly sound. For those aware of The Mad Mongols' thrash-heavy sound this was just a logical step forward but for unwitting listeners SxTxH were as far away from the scene's roots as they could get.

With their own truly unique sound The Mad Mongols, and Mad Masato's other side projects, have established Japanese Psychobilly as yet another original facet of the scene and far from a simple rehash of European 'billy. They also went some way to popularising the ultra-heavy style of Psychobilly which is now represented by many bands across the world but rarely heard in the band's earliest days. Like few other bands, The Mad Mongols are either loved or loathed – fans either revel in their brand of Psychobilly which is pushed to its extremes or find their tracks ear-bending torture. Regardless of this The Mad Mongols have remained thoroughly modern Psychobilly and have never acknowledged any limits placed on the genre (and probably never will).

With The Falcons and The Mad Mongols remaining two of the earlier established Japanese Psychobilly acts there are also a crop of newer bands who are representing the country both at home and abroad. The Starlite Wranglers are currently enjoying great success across the globe with their hard-edged sound reminiscent of many of the Neo Rockabilly acts from the Klub Foot days.

The trio, currently feature Tatsuya on vocals and guitar, double-bassist Futoshi and drummer Shinji, are deadly serious rockers who have embraced the earliest elements of old-school Psychobilly style with a vengeance. Tatsuya was previously a member of Rockabilly trio The Storm Riders in the early 1990s but by 1993 the band had become The Starlite Wranglers in what was an attempt to break away from what they felt was a stifling Rockabilly scene.

The band saw the rest of the decade out playing around Japan but their first recording appeared on the US compilation 'Friday Nite Rumble! Vol. 3' from Run Wild Records in 1999. Their debut album followed in 2001 with 'Whisper Of The Devil' becoming Crazy Love Records' first Japanese signing. Apart from a solitary single release, 'Rumble', for Japanese label Bluestone the band have stayed with Crazy Love and released their CD-EP 'Europe Tour 2003' and their follow-up album 'Devils' Wheel' (2005).

The Starlite Wranglers (Noko).

With their unapologetic Psycho/Neo style, The Starlite Wranglers are one of Japan's strongest rockin' exports having appeared in Europe to support 'Whisper Of The Devil' they then hit the US twice in less than seven months between 2004/2005. They were also The

Battle Of Ninjamanz (Die In Style).

Quakes' choice of support when the US. Psychobilly pioneers returned once again to Japan in the Autumn of 2005. In 2006 the band were all across Europe once again with a spot at Calella's 14th Psychobilly meeting followed by gigs in France, Germany and the Netherlands. Still less than a decade into their recording career, The Starlite Wranglers are Japan's 21st Century Psychobilly success story.

From a similar demented dimension to The Mad Mongols are Battle Of Ninjamanz, a Tokyo based band who pursue their own unique brand of hard-core Psychobilly. Formed in 1994 with vocalist Mutsumi, Kubo (guitar), Hige (drums) and Shun (bass) the band also have their own 'MC' called Mar.

After a 12" EP, 'Psycore Distortion', for Vinyl Japan in 1997 the band mainly featured on compilations through the rest of the decade while they concentrated their efforts on organising Japan's Big Rumble festival which has been showcasing home-grown talent and visiting UK, European and US acts since 1996. This promotion eventually led to the formation of the band's own record label, Big Rumble Productions, which then released Battle Of Ninjamanz' debut album 'Fuck The World' in 2001. A more genteel version of the album also appeared, with no difference in tracklisting and with new cover artwork bearing the title 'FTW.' for record retailers of a nervous disposition.

'Fuck The World' was a furious debut, with the Punk elements of their 'billy sound being far closer to hardcore. Following this release the band ventured into a split EP deal with one of Europe's finest. Having supported Mad Sin during one of their Japanese tours, both bands appeared on 'The Kamikaze Experience: Mad Sin Vs Battle Of Ninjamanz' which was released in 2003 by Vinyl Japan. As a label, Big Rumble has continued to produce further Psychobilly releases including albums from Gigolo 13, The Cracks and a handful of compilations. Battle Of Ninjamanz have also found time to record their follow-up album for the label, the subtly titled 'Bastards' (2005), which was a fine collection of yet more over-the-top Psychobilly.

Both Battle Of Ninjamanz and The Mad Mongols share similar themes, the lesser being their early connections with Vinyl Japan Records which brought their sound to a far more global audience. More importantly, both bands share a sense of the extreme which appears to be present in many other forms of Japanese culture such as films, comics and tattooing. Both their brands of Psychobilly push the genre to its limits and although for many it is a push too far their contribution is vitally important as they stretch the boundaries of Psychobilly just that little bit more and challenge others to take it a little further.

While America and Australia are currently leading the way with acts approaching something of an alternative mainstream audience, Japan has not been left behind and Punkabilly trio Robin have snared Punks, Psychos, Rockabillies and many more of Japan's underground rockers with their broadly appealing racket. Formed in 2001 by ex- Monster-A-Go-Go vocalist/guitarist Hiroshi, Robin were gigging alongside Battle Of Ninjamanz after only a few months together. Their debut album 'My Way' appeared on Big Rumble Productions and their popularity grew rapidly.

Vinyl Japan signed the band up in 2003 and brought Robin to a more global audience with their second album 'Shout It Out Loud' and a single of the band's very own anthem to Margaret Thatcher (ex-UK Prime Minister and arch-enemy of all 1980s Punks) 'Maggie, Maggie, Maggie (Out, Out, Out)'. With their highly-polished image and well-produced sound, Robin look set to easily enjoy a level of success equal to Green Day or The Living End in Japan but global acceptance may be a little longer in coming.

While North America is currently enjoying a huge boom in its Psychobilly scene, South America has a smaller but longer established scene which exists almost entirely in Brazil. Back in the earliest days of Brazilian Psychobilly, long before the world wide web made the planet a global village, Kaes Vadius were knocking out their own brand of the genre in the mid-1980s. Their debut album 'Psychodema' appeared in 1987, followed by the long-player 'Delirium Tremens' the following year. Taking their influences from The Cramps, The Meteors and Garage Punk and blending it with uniquely Brazilian roots music, they blazed a trail for many bands in their homeland to follow.

They were not alone for long and over the years Kaes Vadius have featured on Brazilian compilation albums such as 'Devil Party' (1989), 'Psychorrendo' (1995) and 'O Monstro' (2000) alongside other rockin' Brazilians such as The Krents, The Mongolords, K-Billys, The Krappulas and Ovos Presley. While many of these acts have enjoyed success at home, a more global crossover has eluded them but in the 1990s Os Catalepticos took Brazilian Psychobilly around the world.

Formed in 1996, Os Catalepticos managed to secure a spot at the UK's 10th Big Rumble in 1997 which then led to a debut album for Fury Records, 'A Little Bit Of Insanity' (1998). Their next release was a four-track EP for Revel Yell Records, 'From Beyond The Grave' (2000). This single showcased a heavier sound along with more of the same speed-fuelled Psychobilly which had appeared on their first album.

In the late 1990s the band were often away from home touring Europe, including a return to the Big Rumble for the 11th gathering, and at home their hardcore 'billy was also welcomed by the Brazilian Punk scene. Their work continued into the 2000s with their classic second album 'Zombification' (2001) for Crazy Love Records which boasted a heavier production to suit the band's harder brand of Psycho.

In the new decade the band also made their debut appearances in America throughout 2002 and played at Calella's Psychobilly Festival 2003. Things were getting established for the band in America, through a new deal with U.S. label Loveless Beat Records which resulted in an EP 'Psychopath Fever' (2003), and work was beginning on a new album throughout 2004. However, new songs were not forthcoming and the band appeared to slip into a cycle of constant touring leaving no time for new compositions.

By 2005 they were no further on and decided to quit at the end of that year with a final gig at the Brazil's Psycho Carnival. Like a prizefighter, the band packed it in at their peak but Vlad in particular wasted no time in devoting more time to his other band The Sick Sick Sinners. With the Sinners quickly gaining a strong reputation on the Brazilian Psychobilly scene, the future of Os Catalepticos looks to remain a proud legacy but one with no further hint of redemption.

In the world of Heavy Metal, Brazilian Thrash from the likes of Sepultura and others has a reputation as often sounding harder, faster and more brutal than that of the same genre in other countries so it was no surprise when Brazilian rockers Frenetic Trio appeared on the scene with a more extreme form of Psychobilly. The trio's brand of death metal Psychobilly has ripped the genre as far from its Rockabilly roots as possible and the band have taken the speed and fury found in many Psychobilly records and turned it up to eleven.

The band gleefully polarised all those who have slapped ears on them, leaving those who want it harder and faster well satisfied while others have cast them aside as an abomination. With Frenetic Trio it is real 'love-em-or-loathe-em' stuff as their brand of Psychobilly leaves no room for fence sitting.

The group first punished earholes in Brazil with their 'Bad Vibrations' EP in 2004 but it was their self-titled debut for Crazy Love in 2005 which delivered their mind-bending sound to the masses. Still touring worldwide to promote their first long-player, Frenetic Trio have cornered the market in nosebleed-inducing Psychobilly and have gathered a loyal following of headbanging, quiff-twitching rockers.

Brazilian Psychobilly merchants, Os Catalepticos, make their debut for Fury Records (Dell Richardson).

As well as producing some pretty unique bands, the Brazilian scene has also boasted an annual 'Psycho Carnival' which has been in operation since 1994 and is organised by Ovos Presley's guitarist Wallace Barreto along with Vlad Urban from Os Catalepticos/Sick Sick Sinners. In the Autumn of 2006 the two-day event boasted the pioneers of Brazilian Psycho, Kaes Vadius, along with new talent such as Rising Scum, Big Nitrons, Freak Phantoms and The Brown Vampire Katz.

Also present were Brazil's hottest new Psychobilly act Voodoo Stompers, a Sao Paulo based trio who look set to replace Os Catalepticos on the global stage. Formed in 2004, they have already supported Os Catalepticos, Batmobile and Demented Are Go but beyond their demo, 'Mad Rock', they have yet to secure a deal. However, with Sick Sick Sinners and other new acts such as Bad Luck Gamblers playing regularly, Brazilian Psychobilly is currently as healthy as ever.

While historically a country which has supported a strong network of Rock'n'Roll and Rockabilly bands, Australia has not been without its moments on the Psychobilly scene but surely one of the Aussie bands to make the greatest impact on the Psychobilly scene have been The Living End. Formed in 1994 from the ashes of a pop and rock covers band they featured double-bass player Scott Owen, drummer Travis Dempsey and singer/guitarist Chris Cheney. Despite their huge Psychobilly following the band are relatively far from the Psychobilly template as is possible for a rockin' trio with a double-bass. Though weaned on the same combination of The Stray Cats and The Clash that has often served as the backbone of a variety of early Psycho acts, The Living End have chosen to pursue a far more American Punk sound similar to Green Day, a band they first supported in the early stages of their career and have continued to work with since.

Their first three singles; 'Hellbound' (1995), 'Its For Your Own Good' (1996) and 'Second Solution'/'Prisoner Of Society' (1997) had a far stronger Rockabilly influence, and their self-titled debut album from 1998 had some real Punkabilly moments, but these elements gradually faded as their sound developed. The band adopted a more pop-punk direction through their following albums, 'Roll On' (2000), 'Modern Artillery' (2003) and 'State Of Emergency' (2006), and it paid off big time especially with the promotional weight of a major label behind them.

The band have never claimed any great allegiance to the genre that dare not speak its name but have garnered many Psychobilly fans, encouraged both by their solid Punk'n'Roll live performances and their high-profile bass slapping. The band have enjoyed tremendous success in their homeland, with

HELL'S BENT ON ROCKIN'   WRECKIN' ALL OVER THE WORLD

Top 40 positions for all their albums and the majority of their singles in the Australian pop charts, as well as establishing a seriously large fanbase in the UK, Europe and many other parts of the globe.

It would be ludicrous to suggest that every band featuring some hard-slapping double-bass automatically fall into the Psychobilly genre, and The Living End have resolutely trodden their own path, but the band undoubtedly offered a new range of possibilities to the burgeoning US scene of the late 1990s. In parts of the UK and Europe where Psychobilly was all but extinct near the end of the 20th Century The Living End also offered a glint of hope that once again rowdy, bass-slapping rockers were still around and gathering major label attention.

The Living End are not the begining and the end of Psychobilly in Australia, however, and acts such as The Fireballs, The Howlin' Moondoggies and Zombie Ghost Train are far more representative of genuine Psychobilly. The Fireballs, like many American acts of the mid-1990s, walked a lonely road with their perfectly manicured mile-high quiffs and bold stage wear. Formed in Melbourne in 1990, the band featured drummer/lead vocalist Eddie Fury, double-bass man Joe Phantom and guitarist Matt Black. It was a long road to their debut, 'Life Takes Too Long' (1995), but their follow-up albums followed at a greater pace with 'So Bad Its Good' (1996) and 'Terminal Haircut' (1997), all on the MDS label.

Being relatively isolated from the rest of the Psychobilly world The Fireballs have perfected their own sound which takes the Rockabilly and Punk roots of the genre and pushes them roughly into the heavy rock scene. Regularly touring not only cities but also dusty backwaters town, the band helped fund their travels with a healthy line in merchandise which included, alongside the usual T-shirts and badges, three volumes of comic books dedicated to the group.

It was not all pit stops and fleapits for the band though as they also played many major festivals and supported Kiss, Dick Dale, Primus and Porno For Pyros. Though the band split in 1997, the opportunity to support Mötorhead and Mötley Crüe in December of 2005 was too good to miss and the experience of playing together again set them back on the road throughout 2006, no doubt helped by a now greater appetite amongst punters for their brand of Psycho/Metal crossover. With all three Fireballs albums now available once again, new material looks likely.

Another Australian band with a similar career to The Fireballs has been The Howlin' Moondoggies. Beginning back in 1991, The Howlin' Moondoggies had the usual line-up reshuffles before producing their own, mostly cover-version led, album 'Doggie Style' in 1999 as the result of a single all-night session in their own home-recording studio. Their second creation was for Crazy Love Records in 2003, 'Chasin' Pussy', and it boasted a host of influences similar to The Living End (American Punk, Ska, Rock'n'Roll) but with a sound far closer to Psychobilly. 'Chasin' Pussy' was a strong album but by 2004 the band had called it a day, with their main man Shakir Pichler moving on to concentrate on his heavy rock band Brutal Pancho and forming his own label, Sex Beat Records.

More recently Psychobilly's global growth has encouraged further rumbles down under and produced Psycho acts with a worldwide following. Creeping out of Sydney in full horrorshow make-up in recent years has been Zombie Ghost Train. Bearing more than a passing resemblance to 1980s UK gorehounds Spook & The Ghouls, the band formed in 2002 with a line-up of singer/guitarist Stu Arkoff, drummer Azza T and double-bass man Aaron Mol. Unsurprisingly the band focus largely on the horror elements of Rock'n'Roll history and have also attracted a large Gothic following who have been weaned on The Cramps and other B-movie fixated rockin' ghouls.

The band's first release was a mini-album, 'Monster Formal Wear' (2004), for Crazy Love Records which boasted five of their own horror-tinged compositions backed by covers of 'Twenty Flight Rock' and 'Blue Moon Of Kentucky'. Despite their ghoulish demeanour, the band have a solid Rockabilly background and often strip off the make-up and play, fresh-faced, as a furious Rockabilly covers band, The Bone Daddies.

Throughout their short career the band have enjoyed a relatively punishing tour schedule and live they are something of a harder, stripped-down outfit away from the spine-tingling delights of eerie

Zombie Ghost Train, ghoulish goings-on down under (Die In Style).

studio trickery. The band bashed their way around Oz solidly for three years, including a support slot with Horrorpops during two of their Australian dates, before making their first trip to America in the Summer of 2005 for a sizable US tour kicking of at The Hollywood Rockabilly Showdown. They stayed in the States for two months, hitting both coasts, and building a major US fanbase as well as securing a distribution deal with Hairball 8 Records. Within a week of touching back on Australian soil the band were gigging once again… it was Halloween after all!

Aside from all this live work, Zombie Ghost Train were wrestling with the production of their full-length debut album. It proved to be a herculean task taking over nine months and featuring a host of obstacles including duff producers, blown budgets and studio bust-ups which required a complete re-mixing to bring out the best sound. The struggle was worth it and 'Glad Rags and Body Bags' finally appeared in 2005. Issued on Shrunken Head Records, the album (despite its difficult birth) was a quality production which expanded on their hard-edged live performances and drenched their tracks in horrorshow theatrics while maintaining a powerful Psychobilly sound.

The subject matter of their songs slipped a little further from the 1950s horror flick feel of their mini-album, delving into more sinister realms on songs such as 'Graveyard Queen' and 'Dark Times' but anyone dismissing the band purely as made-up comic horrorbillies will miss out on one of the most authentic Psychobilly bands of the 2000s with real crossover potential. With further tours of Europe and the U.S. in 2006, Zombie Ghost Train are currently approaching the status of Australia's greatest Psychobilly export so far and will no doubt lead the way for other fledgling Aussie Psycho acts.

Despite huge political and social change in Russia over the past twenty-five years, the universal language of Rock'n'Roll has survived and where there is music there are always those who wish to push their sound to extremes so it seems unsurprising that even the Iron Curtain of old could not hold back Psychobilly.

The Meantraitors are undoubtedly the backbone of Russian Psychobilly. With six albums to their name, they have remained Russia's Psychobilly pioneers to this day. They first got together in 1989 in St Petersburg with Stanislav 'Stas' Bogorad on vocals/guitar, Lesha on double-bass and Zhenia on drums. This trio of 'Psychobilly Outlaws' waited sometime to get on record but made up for it in 1994 with two albums, 'Welcome To Psychobilly Land' and 'Titanic Music', and the CD-EP 'Grim Rock' which saw the band switch to electric bass on the arrival of new member Micha.

In Russia, The Meantraitors do not seem to be treated as outcasts in the same way that many other countries ignore Psychobilly bands and they have been relatively warmly accepted by their nation's music biz with appearances on TV/Radio and at major alternative music festivals. They have also seized the opportunity to break over the border on many occasions in the past decade to tour Europe and the UK.

Their live work rarely impeded their songwriting skills and throughout the 1990s they continued to release hard-edged Psychobilly albums and each one, 'Angry Heart' (1995), 'Welcome To Palerno' (1997) and 'Guts For Sale' (1999), contained a number of brutal, angry songs which have distanced the band from the happy-go-luck side of the genre – these guys are pissed-off and mean business!

Apart from a live album, 'Live & Kicking', things went quiet for a while with the band dropping off the radar for five years before returning in 2005 with a DVD called 'Psychobilly Outlaws' and some dates in Germany, Poland and Russia in the Spring of that year. Gigging has continued during 2006 and a new album looks likely for 2007, cementing The Meantraitors' position as the godfathers of Russian Psychobilly.

Scary BOOM were found lurking around Leningrad (now St Petersburg) in the early 1990s and no doubt the hardships and economic depression of the post-Soviet era informed the pure escapism of their speed-crazed Psychobilly sound. Their earliest recordings appeared on the Pure & Proud Records' release '1992' but their true debut album 'Food Of The Gods' was released in 2000 by Revel Yell Records. Though their sound is a particularly demented brand of Psychobilly the band themselves are no knuckleheads and have a variety of interests outside the group, particularly guitarist/vocalist Kirill Ermichev who is an award winning music video director and also responsible for the 'Psychoburg' series of compilation CDs, which draw together bands of various rockin' styles from across Russia and the Ukraine.

Scary BOOM incorporate far more than guitar, bass and drums in their recordings and live performances and have featured accompaniment from a variety of horn and strings performers during their career. Their second studio album, 'Danke, Auf Wiedersehen' (2004) also appeared on Pure & Proud Records but with the tragic murder of label boss Nico, their next release has yet to appear. Nonetheless, with their high-brow vision of Psychobilly they hopefully have a long way still to go.

Russian promoter, Viktor Kopytin (Viktor Kopytin).

It is fair to say that Psychobilly has yet to overrun Russia but the country has always boasted a strong Rockabilly scene and bands from other genres, such as garage-monsters Jancee Pornick Casino, have always been around to keep things rolling. The Meantraitors and Scary BOOM have also been joined more recently by acts such as The Swindlers, The Poachers, Stressor and The Wanted who all have their own individual brands of rockin'. While not having the luxury of a variety of strong scenes, Russian rockers seem far more open to all avenues of Rock'n'Roll and spend less time analysing the borderline between Psycho and Neo or worrying over the importance of different brands of jeans. The fluctuating economic state of Russia has not helped to keep things going so it has taken real determination for those involved to maintain a rockin' scene.

One such determined individual is Viktor Kopytin of Hepcat Promotions in Moscow. Viktor began DJ'ing in 1994, spinning Psychobilly, Rockabilly, Neo and Ted discs before starting to organise his own magazine 'Hepcat'. However, after eight issues times were too tight to continue but Viktor then moved on to create his own website (www.rockoldies.ru) and began promoting events featuring home-grown talent alongside imported rockers such as The Space Cadets and Helen Shadow. With his own record label, Rock-Tick-Tock Records, in the pipeline Viktor has a remarkably 'old school' attitude to Psychobilly and rockin' in general: "I never earn big money on my deals but I don't really care because the main thing for me is to improve the music and lifestyle I dig the most for Russian people."

As the whole world is at last waking up to Psychobilly, and the Iron Curtain is now firmly dismantled, Russian bands are in a better position than ever to spread their Psychobilly terror worldwide. Combined with Japan, South America and Australia there are few countries yet to indulge in the global Psychobilly revolution. Countries of Earth! Give up! Resistance is futile… the Psychobilly beat is unstoppable!!!

CHAPTER TEN

HELL'S BENT ON ROCKIN'

PSYCHOBILLY NOW

As we stomp past over half of the first decade of the twenty-first century, Psychobilly appears to be in rude health. America is certainly the heart of the scene now or at least where new bands, labels and promoters are driving it forward the most. However, it is best not to forget how many record labels and promoters have done their damnedest to keep the scene afloat in the UK and Europe. Undeniably though, Hellcat Records work with Nekromantix, Tiger Army and Horrorpops has seen Psychobilly brought into what can loosely be called the 'mainstream alternative' scene across the globe.

Hellcat, and its big brother Epitaph, both have a fine pedigree in Punk influenced bands which has no doubt led many curious listeners to sniff around the rockin' end of their roster and many appear to have liked what they heard. It remains to be seen if any major labels will ever really focus on pushing a Psychobilly, or Psychobilly influenced act, into the mainstream.

Very few have attempted and the results have been sluggish such as Polydor's brief period with King Kurt and Mad Sin and Island's relatively poor support of The Meteors' classic debut. Only Warner Bros. really made a go of it managing The Living End's career. Hellcat have succeeded because despite their growing popularity, the label remains a street-level organisation who really know the bands and the fans and are able to cut through the bullshit that often bogs down any major label's attempts to exploit a genre such as Psychobilly. Which is probably just as well as any major label who attempted to ride Psychobilly as some kind of latest musical fad would probably be doomed.

Without a firm understanding of the scene they would always run the risk of falling on their arse or tainting forever the poor band which they chose to pursue. Mad Sin's 'Sweet & Innocent...' album for Polydor did hint that the clash between major label and Psychobilly act could work as it produced a well-polished final item but never blunted the band's powerful Psycho sound or hardline lyrics. However, with neither the band or label seeing eye-to-eye the relationship appeared brief but productive.

But perhaps the monetary and marketing might of the majors is not such a concern any more, if it ever was, as most Psychobilly bands today make use of the mightiest marketing tool of all – the internet. The world wide web alone could almost be credited with keeping Psychobilly alive in those desperate days of the late 1990s. There cannot be too many music genres beyond Psychobilly that have such a far flung following on a global scale and the internet has helped immensely in tying them all together.

Psychobilly fans have always been determined in seeking out information and relaying news of bands, gigs and gossip. With the bands being mostly Psychobillies themselves the band/fans barrier is notoriously weak and any titbits of info are usually passed on straight from the source, unfiltered by press agents and other music biz spin doctors. In the dark, distant days before the internet a sprawling network of newsletters, flyers and demo tapes already existed but it was a slow and time consuming business maintained only by the faithful.

For many Roy Williams' 'Zorch News' and Raucous Records' catalogue updates were amongst the only information on how the scene was progressing, alongside sporadic bursts of news from publications such as SGB Entertainment's 'Billy's Bugle', Mark 'Chip' Waite's 'Short Cuts' fanzine and for German readers the glossy magazine 'Mental Hell'. Alan Wilson's legendary 'Deathrow Database' magazine was originally just that, a database of contacts, names, addresses and phone numbers of bands, fans, movers and shakers which gradually grew into thirty eight issues of the finest Psychobilly news and reviews.

However, little can complete with the speed and sheer volume of information which the internet can handle. An early adopter of website hosting was Dutch Psycho fan Roy Ter Maat whose www.wreckingpit.com undoubtedly provided one of the few links with the Psychobilly scene throughout the late 1990s and beyond. Roy started the site in the Spring of 1995 and it would be no exaggeration to emphasise how important Wrecking Pit was in playing its part in keeping the scene alive through some lean times.

The site has always been about what is happening in Psychobilly currently rather than simply an appreciation of more established bands. Though many of the original groups feature in the 'bands' section, along with a brief synopsis of their career, new bands with record releases and tour dates are given major coverage. Indeed many of the 'new' acts that have appeared in wrecking pit over the years, such as Tiger Army and The Barnyard Ballers, are now major bands.

The site was also the home of the official Meteors website for many years and has also offered some more radical ideas such as 'tabs' allowing budding young Psychos to ape classic tracks on guitar along with published lyrics and the opportunity for everyone to 'comment' on most news items and record reviews. Wrecking Pit also boasts a huge selection of links to other Psycho-related sites and is really the first stop for anyone unaware of its existence or new to the genre but still almost essential daily reading for even the most ancient wrecker.

The 'forum' option of many rockin' websites is that essential part of the Psychobilly universe where fans can slag off bands, each other and those outside the scene. It gives a universal opportunity to bitch, whine and offer a cowardly 'fuck you' to some other poor sod who is probably 800 miles away at the end of a telephone line. While this curse is no different to any other musical style this is only one negative element of the forum which is otherwise essential. More positively, this facility has far greater possibilities in uniting like-minded music fans across the globe and encouraging the sharing of news, gossip and opinion.

Old School Psychobilly keeps going (Kenny Mitchell).

Alongside Wrecking Pit, PORK (www.psychobilly-online.de) is a site dedicated to Psychobilly which boasts a tremendous and mind boggling well stacked forum with a host of fun-loving, piss-taking and good-natured banter. News travels fast on this Berlin-based site and anyone looking for an up-to-date bulletin on what's happening when and where, should make this site a favourite. Christian Mautz is the webmaster of this online Psychobilly community which boasts the usual news, reviews and gig guide info but it is the site's forum (Psychobilly Online Retard Board) that excels. Here you can discuss a huge variety of Psycho related (and non-related subjects) or simply virtually eavesdrop on the many other members conversations.

Somewhat newer on the scene is Patrick Röhrle's website www.oldschoolpsychobilly.de. It delivers a solid database of reviews on bands of a certain vintage and their releases. The site has gone some way to popularise this relatively new term to describe that particular 'authentic' Psychobilly sound that emerged in the 1980s and has existed in every band who get that equal blend of Punk and Rockabilly. Never elitist, Patrick has created a home not for stubborn old billies locked in the past but one for a huge number of Psychobillies (of all ages) who simply love that 'classic' sound. Old School Psychobilly serves both as an archive where new devotees to the genre can find out more about the scene's roots or simply as a place for ageing wreckers to reminisce.

The site is not all about the past as it post regular updates of old-school related news and has interviews with many of the big names of Psycho (Batmobile, Alan Wilson, Roy Williams, The Quakes). Patrick also has an uncanny knack for tracking down band members who have gone to ground over the years such as The Krewmen's vocalist Mark 'Mad Dog' Cole, Rochee & The Sarnos' Perry Bartlett and the original Coffin Nails' singer Tony Szajer.

Completing this quartet of top quality European Psychobilly sites is www.gopsycho.com, which is maintained by French rocker Charly Watzap. This guy's house must be busting with vinyl, CDs and DVDs as his 'Encyclobilly' lists the often complete releases (and re-releases) of over 480 Psychobilly and related bands, most of which include pictures of the cover artwork. The text is almost entirely in French but it is not too hard to decipher the general theme of the reviews which accompany every entry. The site covers all the major artists from Psychobilly worldwide as well as many obscure acts who only released a debut single and/or album then disappeared forever.

You can search for acts from 28 countries and eight different sub-genres (Psychobilly, Neo Rockabilly, Garage, Surf etc.) and a number of major Psycho/Neo compilations are also included. Go Psycho also boasts a stunning photo gallery (www.psycho-pixhell.com) with hundreds of concert photos, mostly from European gatherings, which you can search for by artist or event. With regular news features and an extensive archive of interviews (with English translations available), Go Psycho is the backbone of Psychobilly history on the web and with a full English translation it could be global dynamite.

One of the latest advances on the Psychobilly scene yet again stems from the web – internet radio. Fuck waiting for the bigwigs of National radio stations to deem Psychobilly current enough to broadcast and why scan the airwaves for occasional plays of Psycho tracks when web broadcasting delivers undiluted content right to your home computer. Sites such as 'Psychobilly Fury' and 'Baltimore Psychobilly' offer a steady stream of Psychobilly and its many related genres direct to the listener.

Probably the most dramatic recent development on the web, certainly for Psychobilly bands and fans, has to be the rapid growth of the internet community 'MySpace'. Initially this was a geeky website enabling spotty teens to 'network' with each other and air pointless blogs about their various goings-on but it has exploded into a fantastic way of joining 'communities' together and promoting bands. After years of media indifference, Psychobilly is of course one of the strongest underground communities of all and MySpace's relatively simple concept of 'friends' and 'extended networks' allows Psycho fans across the globe to find out a bit more about each other and communicate freely.

For bands especially, mostly using the sister site 'MySpace Music', it is relatively easy to set up their own web pages with gig guides, biographies, discographies, photos, videos and up to four tracks of their music. Even the most computer illiterate rockers can give themselves a lively presence on the web quickly and for free. Many new bands post their demos online and MySpace Music is such a valuable promotional tool that many bands are ditching their personal websites or redirecting punters from their own web pages back to MySpace for their most up-to-date information.

Though the internet has been the saviour of the modern Psychobilly scene, the good old printed word has continued to be popular (thankfully, or you would be staring blankly at your computer screen not sitting on the bog reading this). Though sadly the Psychobilly/Neo-Rockabilly focused magazine 'Deathrow Database' ceased production in 2000, one other UK publication which has regularly featured Psychobilly and has survived from the early 1990s is 'Southern And Rocking Music'.

First published in 1994, S&R is edited by Marc Fenech (cousin of The Meteors' frontman) and features a bewildering amount of info in every issue. Designed to cover "all forms and roots of rocking music" each edition is literally crammed with articles, some which include the history of rockin' but most place the emphasis on the current scene. The magazine regularly features Psychobilly music but its remit also extends to Rockabilly, Rock'n'Roll, Western Swing, Ted Revival, Surf, Doo Wop, Trash, Bluegrass, Hillbilly and much more.

'Southern and Rocking' magazine has always acknowledged Psychobilly's presence on the rockin' scene, especially at a time when many other mags preferred to ignore it, and throughout their first eighteen issues there was plenty to please the Psycho-nation. However in 1997 the magazine ceased publication and yet another avenue closed down for spreading the word on gigs, albums and more for the rockin' scene in general. S&R continued in the form of an entertainment agency, something Marc had established back in 1987, and the organisation still played a huge part in booking bands and organising gigs, events and festivals across Europe.

In the Spring of 2006, Issue 19 appeared (almost ten years later) and the magazine literally exploded back on the scene with a slicker mag than ever before. This time round 'Southern And Rocking' had an updated look but remained crammed with info on an even broader range of rockin' styles and featured over fifty contributors alongside Marc's own mountain of copy. The magazine also made the unprecedented move of simultaneously publishing in English, Spanish and Finnish.

This global vision is also evident in the magazine's content which not only covers rockin' hotspots such as the UK, US, Europe and Japan but also delves into the South American and Eastern Bloc scenes as well as anywhere else where Rock'n'Roll can be found. If you express a desire to find out what is shakin' in Uruguay, Poland, Estonia and Chile then S&R is the place to find out. With the rockin' scene in general in good health the need for a magazine like 'Southern and Rocking' has never been greater and for a regular fix of info on Psychobilly, Garage and Trash, Punkabilly, Neo Rockabilly and any other related genre it is a worthy publication.

The fate of specialist record labels has had mixed fortunes in the new millennium. Market leaders such as Nervous, Fury, Raucous, Count Orlok and Crazy Love are still going strong and have been joined by a new breed of companies with a strong identity and solid rockin' reputation such as Hairball 8/Psychobilly US, People Like You, Drunkabilly and (arguably) Hellcat. However, many could not survive the swinging fortunes of Psychobilly and went the way of the dinosaur along with others who no longer wanted to continue in that direction. Labels such as Link, ABC/ID, Kix 4 U and Media Burn are now only memories waiting for their back catalogues to be plundered for a new generation. That is not to say that newer labels have been shy in making their presence felt but many, including Halb 7, Pure & Proud, Vampirella and Fiend Force, stretch their net a bit further and feature a number of Psychobilly groups alongside other bands with similar rockin' connections.

Alan Wilson's Western Star label (Alan Wilson).

One company which has developed a particularly strong identity is the UK label Western Star. Since The Sharks first disbanded back in 1983, singer/guitarist Alan Wilson has played a continuous part in the European rockin' scene. Alongside his musical experience, Wilson also began focusing his attention on studio engineering and record production. From the mid 1980s to 1993 Alan had his own home studio set-up, X-Ray Studios, where he performed his earliest productions. Alan also worked freelance as a producer, particularly at Walnut Bank Studios in Bristol where he took to the controls for The Frantic Flintstones, The Sharks, The Psycho Bunnies, Three Blue Teardrops and The Taggy Tones amongst others. He also produced The Flintstones and The Sharks once again alongside a number of other rockin' acts such as Frenzy, The Gazmen, The Elektraws and The Heartbeats at the Koh-San Studios in Bath. The international bands were mostly recorded while these acts were in the country for appearances at the Big Rumbles.

Around the time of establishing his first studio the Sharks' frontman also took his first steps as a record guru – launching the X-Ray label along with Jaz Wiseman, one time member of cult Punk band Virus. X-Ray was relatively short-lived releasing only one three-track seven-inch single, from Wilson's occasional Goth Rock combo Shriek Theatre, and a compilation LP featuring Shriek Theatre, Lux and

HELL'S BENT ON ROCKIN'   PSYCHOBILLY NOW

a number of other Bristol based bands. Alan also became involved with another facet of the music business and in 1991 he established Department X, a publishing company specialising in Rockabilly and Psychobilly and a sub-division of the mighty Nervous Records empire.

As if that was not enough Alan, noticing the general lack of organisation amongst many bands on the scene, established 'Terrorwear' a merchandising company licensing, designing and selling T-shirts and patches featuring Psychobilly and Neo bands. Between 1993 and 1999 Alan's stall was regularly to be seen at many major Psychobilly gigs and gatherings, including the Big Rumbles while he continued his part as singer, guitarist and songwriter with a variety of acts including the reformed Sharks, The Woodies, The Gazmen and more.

Klubtastic, keeping Psychobilly live over London (Russ Ward).

At the end of the decade, Wilson began building his own purpose built studios in Bristol and in the Winter of 2000, Western Star Recording Studios opened their doors for the first time. Offering a state-of-the-art recording system, Wilson could also provide equipment that delivered suitably 'retro' recordings to meet the requirements of any bands who wanted that authentic rockin' sound. In the first six years Western Star proved to be a popular haunt for many rockers including The Rock-It Dogs, Frantic Flintstones, Popeye's Dik and also some memorable faces from British rock and pop history such as The Wurzels, John Leyton, Graham Fenton and Mike Berry. Alongside recording, Western Star also does a lot of work for labels, such as Anagram and RPM, when they require remastering for many of their reissued titles. So great was the volume of work that in 2006 Alan moved to larger premises for Western Star Recording Studios, Mark II.

The success of Western Star eventually led to start of the Western Star Recording Company label. Two full albums of Western Star recorded rockin' were initially released on Crazy Love Records. 'The Best Of Western Star Vol. 1' featured Frenzy, Frantic Flintstones, Hyperjax, Death Valley Surfers, Popeye's Dik, The Woodies and more which was followed by Volume 2 of the series with more of the same bands who passed through the studios. However, the third album in the series 'Depravity In Zero Gravity: The Western Star Compilation Volume 3' was released as Western Star's debut album in 2003.

Full albums from artists such as The Bad Detectives, Kill Van Helsing, Bill Fadden & The Silvertone Flyers and The Frantic Flintstones followed, as did further compilations including 'Western Star Rockabillies Vol. 1 & 2' and 'Western Star Psychobillies Vol. 1'. Where Western Star is very unique is that everything appearing on the label has passed through Western Star Studios and after 26 years in the business, Alan Wilson now also finds himself in the enviable position of being totally self-sufficient and able to write, produce, publish and release his own music.

Although The Klub Foot and Big Rumbles are but dim and distant memories their has been some glimmer of hope in the promotion of live bands of a Psychobilly and Neo persuasion. When times were tight within the UK Psycho scene at the start of the new millennium, two members of the London Psychobilly scene decided to actually do something to keep the music alive and established a new home for fans and bands alike – Klubtastic. Rather than the nation's remaining Psychobillies emerging like zombies from the darkness and drifting from occasional gig to gig, Klubtastic offered a place where punters could congregate on a regular basis and a venue for bands which guaranteed them their target audience.

The first gig was at The Garage in London's Highbury in January 2001 and featured The Pharaohs, The Death Valley Surfers and The Hyperjax. The DVS would play a regular part at the club as the organisers behind Klubtastic were Agent Pisshead and ex-Highliners' drummer and Death Valley Surfers' frontman Russ Surfer. Originally the first gig was to be headlined by King Kurt but with most of the band living in Canada it only took one missed flight to leave the organisers in need of an available Old School band of similar quality to Kurt – luckily The Pharaohs fitted the bill. From that evening on Klubtastic grew in stature with another seven events in the same year bringing Frenzy, Hot Boogie Chillun, Celtic Bones, Nekromantix, The Hangmen, Demented Are Go, The Coffin Nails, The Space Cadets and more to the capital's revitalised audience.

The success of Klubtastic also resulted in the creation of a smaller more intimate Psycho-centric gathering at The Klub, a monthly gig initially held upstairs at The Garage. These events were organised and hosted by Russ and with a much smaller capacity of 200 on a good night The Klub could be a real sweatbox. The Klub has occasional changed venues since it began but could last be found at Bar Monsta in London's Camden Town.

With Klubtastic, The Klub and The Charlotte in Leicester keeping live Psychobilly going throughout the 2000s, the best was yet to come when long-time rockin' promoter and DJ Mick Geary took a huge personal gamble to restore Psychobilly to its spiritual home in the UK – Hemsby.

Mick began his career DJ'ing at the legendary Klub Foot and gained his early concert promotion experience when working with the club's founder John Curd (of Camouflage Promotions and ABC/ID Records). Curd's music events were right across the UK music scene and Mick found himself working with the likes of The Specials, Madness, The Ramones, Dr Feelgood, The Jesus & Mary Chain and even the late soul legend James Brown.

In the wake of The Klub Foot's demise, Mick DJ'ed at London's next rockin' hot spot the LMS as well as other major venues across the capital such as The Mean Fiddler, The Powerhaus and The Venue. It was at The Venue where Mick also began promoting his own events. When the Big Rumble began in Hemsby in the early 1990s, Mick was there from the first event. Initially booked as a DJ, Geary became more involved in the running of events backstage as the weekenders progressed. Eventually Dell handed the stage manager role completely over to Mick which was not an easy position with equipment fuck-ups, bands going astray before their performances and other groups (with no understanding of running times) almost having to be dragged offstage.

Russ Ward of The Klub with some Scotsmen (Kenny Mitchell).

Rockin' at The Speedfreaks Ball, 2006 (Jane Williams).

All this was excellent experience when Mick once again revived Hemsby to its former glory in the minds of underground music fans everywhere. In the Autumn of 2004, Mick began work on organising a three-day festival of street music that would gather legions of Psychobillies, Rockers, Punks and Skins together once more. Assisted by his partner Caroline and Jo 'Psychodame' Shalton, The Speedfreaks Ball 2005 began to take shape.

Given the fact that The Big Rumble had sadly ended with low turnouts and hefty damage bills, an event of this size was a massive personal gamble for Mick. Regardless of attendance, neither the venue, their employees, the security, the soundmen or the bands would be in a charitable mood so the potential outlay before even a bass was slapped was huge. Thankfully, Mick's faith was rewarded as although he confidently expected seven hundred punters, the final roll call was almost double that.

The line-up of the first Speedfreaks reflected the fact that many of the scene's remaining from genres rooted in late 1970s/early 1980s streetmusic now mixed far more freely than they ever had. In the lean periods of the 1990s Psychobillies, Punks, Skins, Scooter Boys and greasers bonded closer together under the triple threat of apathy, grunge and Brit Pop. Scooter Runs had successfully achieved this for years and the Speedfreaks continued to take this to another level with a lethal combination of Psycho, Punk, Ska, Oi and Rockabilly which broadened the appeal of the event while offering punters some real variety.

The choice of bands for the line-up was bold, establishing The Speedfreaks Ball immediately with some real heavy hitters including The Meteors, The Damned, Guana Batz, Bad Manners and The Business. For old school Psychos there were also appearances from The Coffin Nails and The Long Tall Texans. The venue itself had improved greatly since the time of the earliest Big Rumbles with improved facilities and chalets which no longer felt like post-war jail cells. Thankfully, though the event carried much of the atmosphere of those early gatherings, the accommodation wrecking was minimal (apart from one set of soon-to-be-evicted jokers who thought it a good wheeze to drive their scooter around inside their chalet) and along with the healthy attendance, planning for the second Speedfreaks Ball began even before the first one finished.

Though the Psychobilly renaissance has enjoyed a boost in its fortunes throughout Europe and America the amount of new talent coming through in Britain has been sparse. Roy Williams noted in 2005 that on the UK rockin' scene there were little or no bands with members "under 35", a fact which would suggest that most bands still active were from the original Psychobilly boom or closely thereabouts. Considering the fact that even established bands such as The Hyperjax and The Hangmen had faced grumbling from the old guard when they formed, what chance would the wild youths of the 'noughties' have from the aging Psychobilly establishment?

Thankfully, two bands in their teens and twenties don't give a fuck and have thrust UK Psychobilly's next generation into the limelight regardless. Blue Demon and The Rock-It Dogs have burst onto the scene with their own fresh but undeniably rockin' sounds that owe far more of a debt to classic Psychobilly than the watered-down, Americanised Pop-Punk that many would have expected.

Liverpool trio Blue Demon first got together around 2001 and rehearsed for almost a year and a half before they began gigging. Tiring of the huge crop of make-up caked 'horrorpunk' bands around

Blue Demon (Simon 'Fatbloke' Ling).

at the time they took their references from early Psychobilly acts such as The Meteors and Torment and favoured songwriting that steered clear of any 'ghosts and ghoulies' connections. Instead they focused their attentions on "minesweepin' pints of bitter, psychotic ex-girlfriends, Mexican wrestlin' movies, cheap exploitation films and the general indignities of daily life."

Blue Demon's line-up has so far remained solid and features Paul Gonzalez on guitar and vocals, Chris 'Huffy' Hough on double-bass and backing vox and Day 'Demon Dave' Searson on drums. Paul first experienced Psychobilly in the early 1990s at a Liverpool club called The Pink Parrot where he first witnessed what he refers to as "drunken lunatics with haircuts like speedboats, knocking shit out of each other to Demented Are Go." With little happening in the Liverpool area he the spent the next decade travelling on National Express coaches around the country seeking suitable live entertainment. Chris and Day were both Punks who Paul press-ganged into believing that a form of 'Rockabilly For Bastards' was the way forward and they respectively carved their dreadlocks and mohawks into quiffs.

Having antagonised most of Liverpool's Indie bands and promoters, many of which they shamelessly berated in the local press, they finally began to reach a more sympathetic audience with gigs at The Charlotte, The Ace Cafe & The Klub. Their first available recording was 'The Undisputed Kings' on Liverpool Indie label Mimashima Records. This four-track CD established Blue Demon as venomous lyricists with a powerful sound that maintained a strong Rockabilly connection. Along with the added attraction of the band's two sex-bomb cheerleaders Louise and Chantelle (The Demonettes), their furious live show and onstage swagger have gathered them a growing and enthusiastic following.

This determination to avoid their music from descending into Punk or Thrash is reflected in their influences of Country, Bluegrass, Hillbilly and original Rockabilly but the band also draw inspiration from artists such as Reverend Horton Heat and Sin Alley.

In 2006, the band's true debut album was released, again by Mimashima. 'Shot To Ruin' was stacked with hard-slappin', furious guitar riffs and snare-splitting drumming accompanied on occasion by piano, keyboards, trumpet, sax and a variety of screams and yelps from The Demonettes and other sore-throated associates of the band. All the tracks were Blue Demon compositions and most contain the bile-soaked, razor-sharp barbs of venom which the band are now noted for. Successfully avoiding both the 'Rock Pretty Baby' and 'Zombies In The Graveyard' schools of writing, Blue Demon somehow manage to deliver lyrics of cynicism, hate and disregard in a light-hearted manner.

Had the band been from LA, no doubt they would be huge by now but with levels of new blood still trickling notoriously low on the UK scene they have a long, hard struggle. Hopefully this

Blue Demon play fully loaded with the fabulous Demonettes (Simon 'Fatbloke' Ling).

'Rockabilly Hurricane Of Hate' can reach the level of success which they truly deserve.

Another youthful UK Psychobilly combo are The Rock-It Dogs. The band formed in Worcester in 2003 with a line-up of Broughton Hackett (guitar/vocals), Big Danny O (double-bass) and Bob Kat on drums. Broughton and Danny had played together before in a Punk/Ska band called Puffin' but both wanted to start a more rockin' group. Determined to draw their influences beyond the unholy trinity of Psychobilly, Rockabilly and Punk, they also included elements of Jazz, Surf and Ska in their sound. Their earliest gigs involved blagging their way into many local shows and playing with a host of Punk bands, often to a very mixed reception.

After bashing out an eight-track demo in Broughton's basement, Bob Kat moved on to be replaced by Vincent Blackshadow. Vincent got used to the existing set of songs and further compositions were

The Rock-It Dogs, Spring 2007 (Rock-It Dogs).

created. A second demo reached the ears of Crazy Love Records' mainman Guido and the band were promptly shipped off to Alan Wilson's Western Star Studios in 2004 to record their debut album.

Very little of the early demo made it to the album recording but the majority of their second demo was re-recorded and included, apart from their bluegrass version of Kiss' 'Crazy Crazy Nights'. 'Chills, Thrills And Blood Spills' (2005) was generally well received and as the demand for touring grew, Big Danny O left and Broughton assumed the traditional role which many have before him as that of the band's sole original member (What is it about Psychobilly that breeds so many determined front men?).

The addition of new slapper Franklyn Stein completed the band's tightest line-up to date and soon they were headlining in their own right, making moves towards Europe, playing their debut gig at The 2006 Speedfreaks Ball and supporting Psychobilly legends such as Nigel Lewis, The Meteors, Nekromantix, King Kurt, The Long Tall Texans and The Peacocks. The band also began to build their profile on the compilation album circuit with an appearance on Western Star's 'Western Star Psychobillies: Vol. 1'.

Like Blue Demon, The Rock-it Dogs 'doggedly' keep the Rockabilly emphasis in their sound which keeps them at arm's length from many of the world's newer bands who draw their influences from American Punk and Horrorbilly. Like many pioneers of the 21st Century they occasionally face the whines of old school Psychobillies but they have mostly received a warm reception from the rockin' fraternity and with a growing audience, including some words of encouragement from former Sex Pistol Glen Matlock, they must be doing something right.

As Psychobilly has undoubtedly entered a new dawn the continued success of The Meteors appears to rest on the band's ever growing and devoted following of what P. Paul has referred to as 'Meteors People'. The spur which drives this following appears to be centred around two main forces – The Meteors' relentless touring schedule and a prolific number of record releases. There cannot be too many places left on the planet where The Meteors have not ventured, with the UK and Germany as particular strongholds, and accompanying the band wherever they go are the band's inner circle – The Kattle.

The Meteors' network is worldwide and few, if any, bands can boast such a loyal and dedicated following. For every Psychobilly who is a fan of The Meteors there is another for whom 'nothing' but The Meteors will do. While this division has not been without its conflicts across the years it would be impossible to deny the strength of feeling and belonging that The Meteors have instilled among their hard-core following. After all these years the band can still be found recruiting new fans and a recent appearance on the big screen and TV in America may increase their following still.

The Meteors' list of movie influences is too long to catalogue with the obvious lifting of movie titles for many of their songs including 'The Hills Have Eyes' and 'Maniac'. Other tunes boasting implicit movie references such as 'Michael Myers' (from 'Halloween'), 'Eat the Baby' and 'Jupiter Stroll' ('Hills Have Eyes' again). The Meteors themselves also appeared on celluloid in the 1999 British romantic comedy 'Don't Go Breaking My Heart', playing the part of 'the nastiest band in the world' The Bitch Boys and finding themselves on the film's soundtrack album with their version of The Beach Boy's 'I Get Around' alongside artists such as Elton John, Kiki Dee and Leo Sayer. Not forgetting their 1980 film debut 'Meteor Madness' and its accompanying EP.

However, probably Psychobilly's most memorable contribution to mainstream entertainment to date has been not a movie but an American advert. In 2005, Cadillac used The Meteors' track 'The Crazed' as the music behind their mammoth budget sci-fi themed advert for their new model the 345 HP Escalade. Featuring their hulking black SUV being pursued by rocket propelled road cones and a monstrous dinosaur constructed from road safety signs, it pushed CGI effects to the extreme along with relentless pyrotechnics. Despite using a song from an album over twenty five years old The Meteors track fits perfectly with the ads cinematic action fest and sounds as fresh as it did when 'In Heaven' first appeared in 1982. What further proof is needed that Psychobilly now is as relevant and exciting as it has ever been?

CONCLUSION

I started to work on this book around three years ago. Had I started it two years earlier it would probably have taken much less time. Had I started it at the end of the 1990s it would probably have taken the form of an obituary with the future of the scene looking relatively bleak, particularly in the UK.

Thankfully, the Psychobilly beast is a hard bastard to finish off and in the past five years the popularity of the genre has escalated tremendously. The huge growth of the scene in America has undeniably breathed new life into Psychobilly but in Europe, the UK and other parts of the globe it never truly faded away and simply went deeper underground.

Throughout this book I have used the word Psychobilly to cover all manner of musical styles and types of bands. Though only The Meteors hold the crown as 'pure Psychobilly', I feel the term is simple shorthand for all manner of demented Rock 'n' Roll along with the lifestyle that goes with it. To try and tie Psychobilly down to specifics is impossible anyway. Most of the bands mentioned in this book each take their own 'Psycho sound' in a different direction drawing different levels of influence from the huge range of styles which have contributed to the genre over the past quarter of a century.

Some bands have been wary of aligning themselves too closely to this brand of music, perhaps believing they would have to restrict their sound to match the Psychobilly audience's expectations. However, I feel that followers of Psychobilly are probably among the most open-minded music fans amongst any genre of underground music. They are also some of the most active and committed punters in the music world. Being a Psychobilly is not simply a matter of buying records and sitting back down on your arse. Most of the promoters, fanzine writers, merchandisers, DJs and webmasters on the scene are all rockers that want to do their bit to keep the genre alive.

As most of the bands are also Psychobilly fans themselves the dividing line between acts and their audiences is almost non-existent and long before myspace was created, Psychobilly has always had its own 'extended network' across the world. Getting out and socialising with other Psychobillies is a major part of the lifestyle and globetrotting visits to gigs and festivals are often an essential part of the Psychobilly universe.

For all these reasons and more I am proud to have been a Psychobilly for just over 23 years now. It is true that I drifted dangerously close to losing touch with the scene (as I am sure many did) but it drew me back in. Pretty much every element of my life has been influenced by Psychobilly in some way and I wanted to write this book to chronicle this phenomenon, a genre which has literally been cast as a footnote in the history of music by the mainstream music press.

Psychobilly has thrived in the shadows for over a quarter of a century and it is too strong now to be disregarded as simply the briefly fashionable Rock 'n Roll by-product from 1982 which it is often portrayed as from those outside the scene.

We know that it is far more than that.

PSYCHOBILLY... NEVER LOSE IT!

The Bands: check out this motley bunch of Rockers, Rollers and Out-Of-Controllers!
www.kingsofpsychobilly.com
www.coffin-nails.com
www.purevolume.com/thecaravans
www.miniskirtblues.co.uk
www.madsin.com
www.hangmen.co.uk
www.alcoholic-rats.com
www.the-sharks.co.uk
www.popeyesdik.co.uk

The Labels and Promoters: the movers, shakers and record deal makers!
www.cherryred.co.uk
www.nervous.co.uk
www.fury-records.com
www.raucousrecords.com
www.crazyloverecords.com
www.drunkabilly.com
www.western-star.co.uk
www.thespeedfreaksball.com
www.greystone-records.com
www.spindriftrecords.com
www.dieinstyle.de
www.myspace.com/bedlambreakout
www.stormscreenproductions.co.uk

Psycho Style: great gear, great tattoos…and the rest.
www.tartantribe.co.uk
www.landahoytattoos.co.uk
www.monsterclothing.be
www.myspace.com/hepcattattoos
www.myspace.com/retrorebels

HELL'S BENT ON ROCKIN'   RECOMMENDED WEBSITES

MySpace Pages: many bands place their MySpace page on a higher priority than their official websites... and don't forget the stacks of great music it offers.

www.myspace.com/madsin
www.myspace.com/thehangmen
www.myspace.com/thestarlitewranglers
www.myspace.com/termitesthe
www.myspace.com/klingonz
www.myspace.com/thecaravans
www.myspace.com/theeexitwounds
www.myspace.com/thequakes
www.myspace.com/theminiskirtblues
www.myspace.com/bluedemon13
www.myspace.com/thedeadneks
www.myspace.com/nekromantix
www.myspace.com/alcoholicrat (King Kurt)
www.myspace.com/48071027 (The Sharks)
www.myspace.com/therockitdogs
www.myspace.com/itstimeforthepeacocks

STOP PRESS

HELL'S BENT ON ROCKIN'

- New Albums released early in 2007 from:
  The Meteors 'Hymns For The Hellbound' (People Like You Records).
  Necromantix 'Life Is A Grave And I Dig It' (Hellcat Records).
  The Caravans 'Smashed And Stripped Bare'(Drunkabilly Records).
  The Hangmen 'Cackle Fest' (Abattoir Records).
  The Hyperjax 'The Bottom Line' (Raucous Records).

- New 'anniversary' albums announced from Mad Sin and The Klingonz.

- More old school re-releases from Anagram as part of their Psychobilly Collector Series include: The Highliners 'Bound For Glory'/'Spank-O-Matic', The Escalators 'Live At Le Havre 1983', The Frantic Flintstones '20th Anniversary Album' and the compilation 'Rockin At The Take Two: Vol. 1&2'.

HELL'S BENT ON ROCKIN' STOP PRESS

- The Speedfreaks Ball reaches its third gathering in November 2007.

- UK Psychobilly alldayer, 'Bedlam Breakout', returned in April 2007.

- Nigel Lewis announced his retirement in the Spring of 2007 after a number of 'Nigel Lewis and the Zorchmen' gigs in the UK and Europe.

- In the Summer of 2007, Cherry Red Records launched their new label Cherry Bomb Recordings which is their new home for up and coming Psychobilly bands. First offering is the debut album from Norwich rockers Judder And The Jack Rabbits, 'All In'.

OTHER PUBLICATIONS BY CRAIG BRACKENRIDGE:

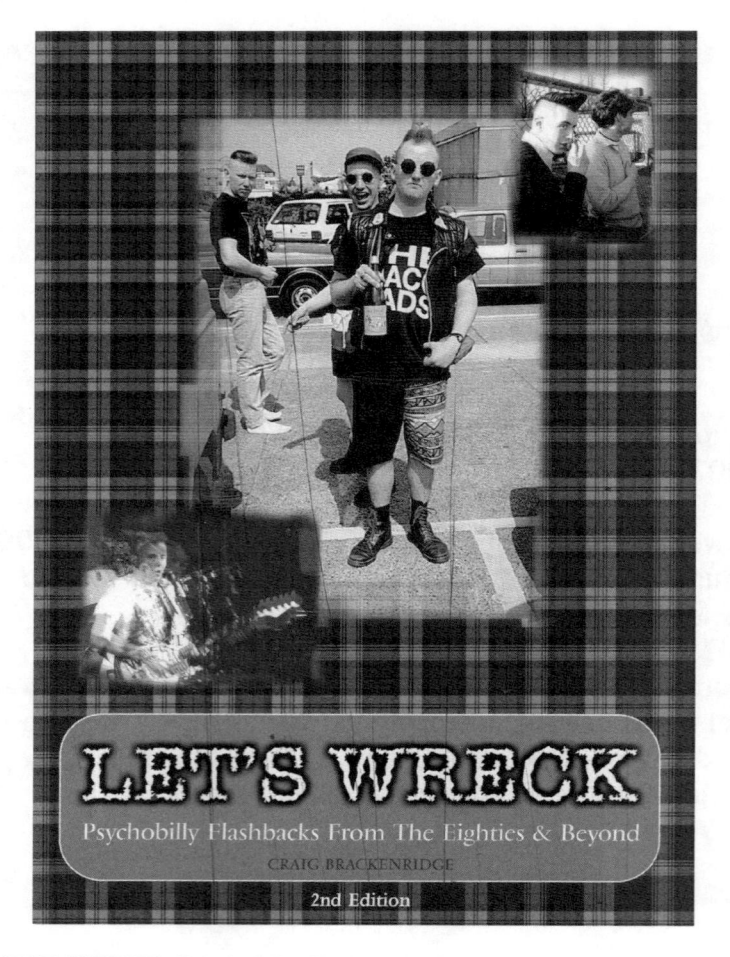

LET'S WRECK: Psychobilly Flashbacks From The Eighties & Beyond
Published by Stormscreen Productions ISBN 0954624904

The wrecking-est, rockin-est bastard offspring of rockabilly & punk, PSYCHOBILLY is the music genre that refuses to die despite being ignored by the mainstream music business and press for over two decades.

Kicked into action in the early 1980s by UK psycho-pioneers such as The Meteors, King Kurt, The Guana Batz and The Sharks, the psychobilly sound has evolved and mutated into a global phenomenon as its sickness spreads across continents and takes its grip on the 21st Century. 'LET'S WRECK' is the story of one man's trip through British Psychobilly, from a spotty teen sporting his first flat-top in the early 1980s to a balding rocker of today.

This is a journey, ignited by the first psychobilly boom in Glasgow, that rolled onwards through The Klub Foot, The Night of the Long Knives, Trash, scootering, Billy's, The Big Rumbles and life on the road with bottom-rung psycho band The Rednecks.

Offering a unique perspective on the Psychobilly phenomenon, 'LET'S WRECK' is a punter's-eye view of the bands, venues, clothing, haircuts, lifestyle and people that are all an essential part of this most underground genre of British street music.

96 pages of Rockin' goodness, containing photographs & images from almost two decades of Psychobilly.

OTHER PUBLICATIONS BY CRAIG BRACKENRIDGE:

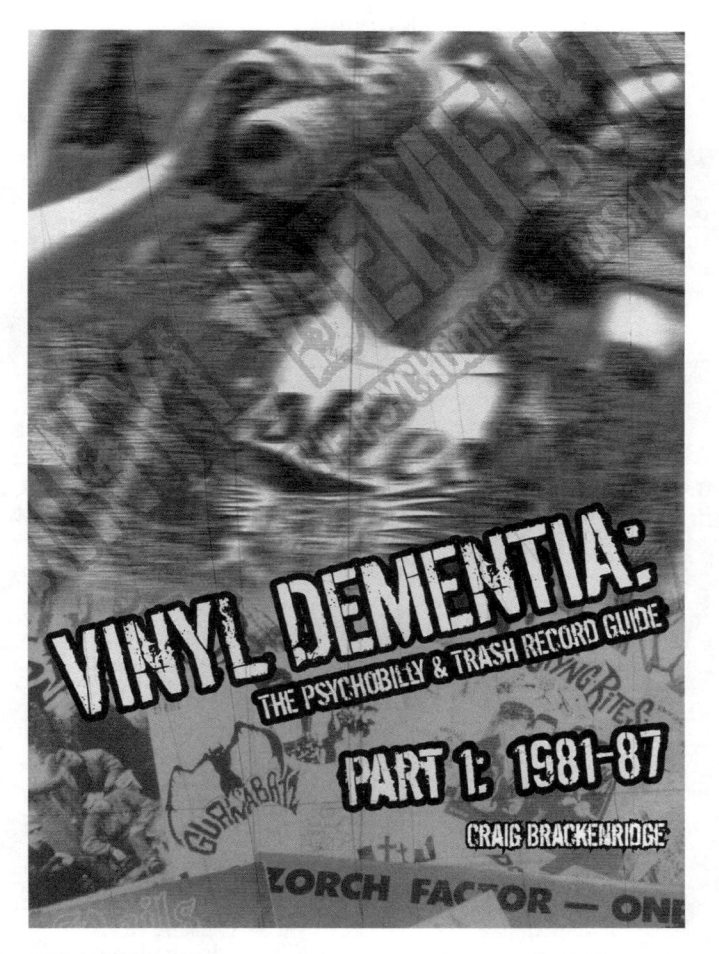

VINYL DEMENTIA: The Psychobilly & Trash Record Guide Part 1: 1981-87
Published by Stormscreen Productions ISBN 0954624912

This 28 page A5 magazine offers full-page reviews of 20 of the most influential releases of the early 1980s, including groundbreaking slabs of infected vinyl from The Meteors, The Sharks, Guana Batz, Frenzy, The Ricochets, The Sting-Rays, The Vibes, Demented Are Go, Ug & The Cavemen, The Coffin Nails, Skitzo, The Krewmen & King Kurt and key compilations such as 'Stomping At The Klub Foot', 'Zorch Factor One', 'These Cats Ain't Nuthin But Trash', 'Trash On The Tube' & 'Hell's Bent On Rockin'. Each review features details of the original release and current availability on CD. All wrapped in a full-colour cover.

For further details check out: www.myspace.com/stormscreenproductions

CHERRY RED BOOKS

ALSO AVAILABLE FROM CHERRY RED

Indie Hits 1980-1989

The Complete UK Independent Chart (Singles And Albums)

Compiled By Barry Lazell

Paper covers, 314 pages, £14.99 in UK

Cor Baby, That's Really Me!

(The New Millennium Hardback Edition)

John Otway

Hardback, 192 pages and 16 pages of photographs £11.99 in UK

All The Young Dudes, Mott the Hoople and Ian Hunter The Biography

Campbell Devine

Paper covers, 448 pages and 16 pages of photographs £14.99 in UK

Embryo - A Pink Floyd Chronology 1966-1971

Nick Hodges and Ian Priston

Paper covers, 302 pages and photographs throughout £14.99 in UK

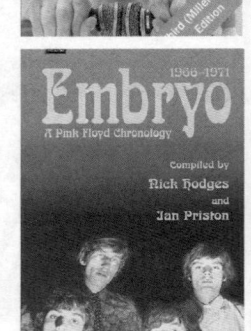

Johnny Thunders In Cold Blood

Nina Antonia

Paper covers, 270 pages and photographs throughout £14.99 in UK

Songs In The Key Of Z

The Curious Universe of Outsider music Irwin Chusid

Paper covers, 311 pages, fully illustrated £11.99 in UK

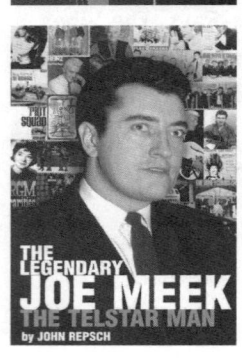

The Legendary Joe Meek The Telstar Man

John Repsch

Paper covers, 350 pages plus photographs, £14.99 in UK

Random Precision Recording the Music of Syd Barrett 1965-1974

David Parker

Paper covers, 320 pages and photographs throughout £14.99 in UK

www.cherryred.co.uk

CHERRY RED BOOKS

ALSO AVAILABLE FROM CHERRY RED

Those Were The Days

Stefan Granados

An Unofficial History of the Beatles' Apple Organization 1967-2002

Paper covers, 300 pages including photographs
£14.99 in UK

The Rolling Stones: Complete Recording Sessions 1962-2002

Martin Elliott

Paper covers, 576 pages plus 16 pages of photographs
£14.99 in UK

Goodnight Jim Bob – On The Road With Carter The Unstoppable Sex Machine

Jim Bob

Paper covers, 228 pages plus 16 pages of photographs
£12.99 in UK

Our Music Is Red - With Purple Flashes: The Story Of The Creation

Sean Egan

Paper covers, 378 pages plus 8 pages of photographs
£14.99 in UK

Bittersweet: The Clifford T Ward Story

David Cartwright

Paper covers, 352 pages plus 8 pages of photographs
£14.99 in UK

The Secret Life of a Teenage Punk Rocker: The Andy Blade Chronicles

Andy Blade

Paper covers, 224 pages and photographs throughout.
£12.99 in UK

Burning Britain

Ian Glasper

Paper covers, 410 pages and photographs throughout
£14.99 in UK

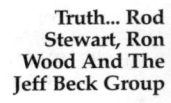

Truth... Rod Stewart, Ron Wood And The Jeff Beck Group

Dave Thompson

Paper covers, 208 pages plus four pages of photographs.
£14.99 in UK

www.cherryred.co.uk

CHERRY RED BOOKS

ALSO AVAILABLE FROM CHERRY RED

**Rockdetector
A-Z of THRASH METAL**

Garry Sharpe-Young

Paper covers, 460 pages
£14.99 in UK

ISBN 1-901447-09-X

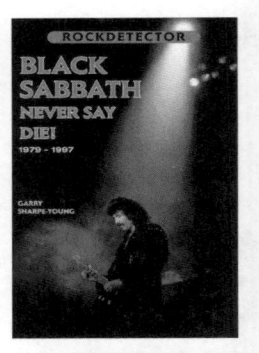

**Rockdetector
BLACK SABBATH NEVER SAY DIE 1979-1997**

Garry Sharpe-Young

Paper covers 448 pages
£14.99 in UK

ISBN 1-901447-16-2

**Rockdetector
A-Z of DOOM, GOTHIC & STONER METAL**

Garry Sharpe-Young

Paper covers, 455 pages
£14.99 in UK

ISBN 1-901447-14-6

**Rockdetector
A-Z of BLACK METAL**

Garry Sharpe-Young

Paper covers 416 pages
£14.99 in UK

ISBN 1-901447-30-8

**Rockdetector
A-Z of '80s ROCK**

Garry Sharpe Young & Dave Reynolds

Paper covers, 752 pages,
£17.99 in UK

ISBN 1-901447-21-9

**Rockdetector
A-Z of DEATH METAL**

Garry Sharpe-Young

Paper covers 416 pages
£14.99 in UK

ISBN 1-901447-35-9

**Rockdetector
OZZY OSBOURNE
THE STORY OF THE OZZY OSBOURNE BAND
(AN UNOFFICIAL PUBLICATION)**

Garry Sharpe-Young

Paper covers 368 pages
£14.99 in UK

ISBN 1-901447-08-1

**Rockdetector
A-Z of POWER METAL**

Garry Sharpe-Young

Paper covers 512 pages
£14.99 in UK

ISBN 1-901447-13-8

www.cherryred.co.uk

ALSO AVAILABLE FROM CHERRY RED

**No More Heroes
A Complete History of UK Punk from 1976-1980**

Alex Ogg

Paper covers, 700 pages with photographs throughout.
£17.99 in UK

The Day the Country Died

Ian Glasper

Paper covers, 471 pages with photographs throughout.
£14.99 in UK

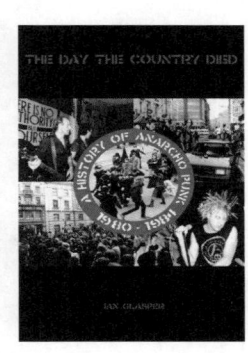

**Hell's Bent On Rockin'
The History Of Psychobilly**

Craig Brackenridge

Paper covers, 240 pages with photographs throughout.
£14.99 in UK

www.cherryred.co.uk

AVAILABLE FROM CHERRY RED RECORDS

PSYCHOBILLY on DVD

CRDVD129
DEMENTED ARE GO
Holy Hack Jack!

CRDVD23
DEMENTED ARE GO
Sick Sick Sick /
Call Of The Wired

CRDVD31
THE LONG TALL TEXANS
Blood, Sweat &
Beers / Wanted

CRDVD18
THE METEORS
Video Nasty &
Live At The Hellfire Club

CRDVD48
THE METEORS
Attack of the Chainsaw
Mutants / Hell in the
Pacific

CRDVD34
GUANA BATZ
Live Over London /
Still Sweatin' After
All These Years

CRDVD64
RESTLESS/FRENZY
Baby Please Don't Go/
Just Passing Thru

CRDVD124
FRANTIC FLINTSTONES
The story of

CRDVD109
KING KURT
Destination Zululand

CRDVD113
THE KREWMEN
Legend of The Krewmen

CRDVD42
VARIOUS
Stomping At The
Klub Foot

CRDVD58
PSYCHO ATTACK
Various

CRDVD128
PSYCHOMANIA
Quakes-Klingonz-Skitzo

CRDVD32
PSYCHO CATS
Various

CRDVD143
PSYCHOBILLY
Behind The Music

DEATHROW
The Chronicles of Psychobilly

This book gives a tantalizing insight into the underbelly of Rock'n' Roll.... a dangerous, exciting world where Rockabilly mutated with Punk to form.... PSYCHOBILLY!

Deathrow was the world's only long running psychobilly fanzine and this book is a collection of all the rare and collectable original issues.

The zine soon became a properly printed magazine with a circulation in excess of 5000 copies per issue. Packed with articles on bands such as; The Meteors, The Frantic Flintstones, The Sharks, Frenzy, Batmobile, Demented Are Go and many more, all harvested from the highly collectable cult music fanzine 'Deathrow'.

A valuable reference of events, bands, and stories for those too young to have experienced the European Psychobilly scene in it's heyday and a nostalgic reminder for those who were a part of it.... and survived!

If you were or still are a psychobilly,
this book is essential reading.

PSYCHOBILLY on CD

- CDMPSYCHO 2 **THE METEORS:** Undead, Unfriendly & Unstoppable
- CDMPSYCHO 4 **VARIOUS: Abc / Id** The Psychobilly Singles Collection
- CDMPSYCHO 5 **VARIOUS: Nervous Records** The Psychobilly Singles
- CDMPSYCHO 6 **FRANTIC FLINTSTONES:** Rockin' Out / Not Christmas
- CDMPSYCHO 7 **GUANA BATZ:** Undercover
- CDMPSYCHO 8 **RAUCOUS RECORDS:** The Psychobilly Collection
- CDMPSYCHO 9 **THE METEORS:** Stampede / Monkey's Breath
- CDMPSYCHO 10 **THE LONG TALL TEXANS:** Texas Beat - The Best Of
- CDMPSYCHO 11 **VARIOUS:** Revenge Of The Killer Pussies
- CDMPSYCHO 12 **THE METEORS:** Mutant Monkey And The Surfers ...
- CDMPSYCHO 13 **THE SHARKS:** Recreational Killer
- CDMPSYCHO 14 **THE SHARKS:** Colour My Flesh
- CDMPSYCHO 15 **FRANTIC FLINTSTONES:** Jamboree
- CDMPSYCHO 16 **LONG TALL TEXANS:** Aces & Eights
- CDMPSYCHO 17 **THE METEORS:** From Zorch With Love
- CDMPSYCHO 19 **DEMENTED ARE GO!:** Satans Rejects: The Very Best Of
- CDMPSYCHO 20 **THE METEORS:** Anagram Singles Collection
- CDMPSYCHO 21 **TORMENT:** Best Of Torment
- CDMPSYCHO 22 **FRANTIC FLINTSTONES:** Enjoy Yourself
- CDMPSYCHO 23 **THE METEORS:** Live Styles The Sick & Shameless
- CDMPSYCHO 24 **GUANA BATZ:** The Very Best Of
- CDMPSYCHO 25 **FRANTIC FLINTSTONES:** The Ultimate Collection (Vol 1)
- CDMPSYCHO 26 **FRENZY: COOL BANANAS:** The Best Of…
- CDMPSYCHO 27 **LONG TALL TEXANS:** Anthology
- CDMPSYCHO 28 **P. PAUL FENECH:** Daddy's Hammer
- CDMPSYCHO 29 **THE SHARKS:** The Very Best Of
- CDMPSYCHO 30 **THE METEORS:** Hell In The Pacific
- CDMPSYCHO 31 **THE METEORS:** Meteors Vs The World
- CDMPSYCHO 32 **COFFIN NAILS:** Let's Wreck, The Greatest Hits
- CDMPSYCHO 33 **THE CARAVANS:** Living With Dinosaurs, The Best Of
- CDMPSYCHO 34 **DEMENTED ARE GO:** Call Of The Wired (Live)
- CDMPSYCHO 35 **THE METEORS:** Psycho Down
- CDMPSYCHO 36 **THE METEORS:** In Heaven
- CDMPSYCHO 37 **THE METEORS:** Sewertime Blues
- CDMPSYCHO 38 **THE METEORS:** Don't Touch The Bang Bang Fruit
- CDMPSYCHO 39 **FRANTIC FLINTSTONES:** Legendary Mushroom Sessions
- CDMPSYCHO 40 **THE TERMITES:** Overload
- CDMPSYCHO 41 **MAD SIN:** Teachin' The Goodies
- CDMPSYCHO 42 **VARIOUS:** Deathrow - The Chronicles Of Psychobilly
- CDMPSYCHO 43 **THE METEORS:** Stampede
- CDMPSYCHO 44 **RADIACS:** Hellraiser
- CDMPSYCHO 46 **VARIOUS:** long lost psychobilly vol 1
- CDMPSYCHO 47 **SUGAR PUFF DEMONS:** Falling From Grace
- CDMPSYCHO 48 **STAGE FRITE:** Island Of Lost Souls
- CDMPSYCHO 49 **RANTANPLAN:** Two Worlds At Once
- CDMPSYCHO 50 **THE METEORS:** Monkey's Breath
- CDMPSYCHO 51 **THE TAILGATORS:** The Tailgators
- CDMPSYCHO 52 **FRANTIC FLINTSTONES:** 20th Anniversary Album
- CDMPSYCHO 53 **THE ESCALATORS:** Live At Le Havre 1983
- CDMPSYCHO 54 **BATFINKS:** Wazzed And Blasted
- CDMPSYCHO 55 **THE HIGHLINERS:** Bound For Glory / Spank-o-Matic
- CDMPSYCHO 56 **GUANA BATZ:** Get Around
- CDMPSYCHO 57 **VARIOUS:** Rockin' At The Take 2 Volumes 1 & 2
- CDMPSYCHO 58 **VARIOUS:** Psychokillers
- CDMPSYCHO 59 **P PAUL FENECH:** Screaming In The 10th Key
- CDMPSYCHO 60 **COFFIN NAILS:** Live And Rockin'
- CDMPSYCHO 61 **DEMENTED ARE GO:** In Sickness & In Health
- CDMPSYCHO 62 **DEMENTED ARE GO:** Kicked Out Of Hell

Also Available
- CDMGRAM 175 **POLECATS:** Polecats Are Go!

Forthcoming CD Releases....
THE NITROS
"Nightshades"

All items available in all good record stores, distributed by Pinnacle.
Alternatively, they can be ordered directly from Cherry Red Records
mail order on 0208 740 4110 or via the website **www.cherryred.co.uk**

Get your favourite psychobilly tunes
from our new download shop at
www.cherryred.co.uk/downloads

downloads

The Cherry Red Records download shop has arrived. We have thousands of tracks available from many of your favourite Cherry Red Records associated labels and artists, including some extremely rare material previously unreleased on CD. The tracks are available in MP3 format, so are compatible with the majority of digital players (including the ipod). Visit *www.cherryred.co.uk/downloads* to discover material from artists such as *Dead Kennedys, Felt, Alien Sex Fiend, Marc Almond, Momus, Everything But The Girl, Sid Vicious, Cabaret Voltaire, Clifford T. Ward, Cockney Rejects, Graham Parker, Marc Bolan, Nico, Spencer Davis Group, The Runaways* and many others.

www.cherryred.co.uk/downloads

CHERRY RED BOOKS

CHERRY RED BOOKS

We are always looking for interesting books to publish.
They can be either new manuscripts or re-issues of deleted books.
If you have any good ideas then please
get in touch with us.

CHERRY RED BOOKS
A division of Cherry Red Records Ltd.
Unit 3a,
Long Island House,
Warple Way,
London W3 0RG.

E-mail: iain@cherryred.co.uk
Web: www.cherryred.co.uk